Methodological
Dimension of
ISLAMIC
ECONOMICS

Methodological Dimension of ISLAMIC ECONOMICS

Masudul Alam Choudhury
Trisakti University, Indonesia

World Scientific

NEW JERSEY · LONDON · SINGAPORE · BEIJING · SHANGHAI · HONG KONG · TAIPEI · CHENNAI · TOKYO

Published by

World Scientific Publishing Co. Pte. Ltd.
5 Toh Tuck Link, Singapore 596224
USA office: 27 Warren Street, Suite 401-402, Hackensack, NJ 07601
UK office: 57 Shelton Street, Covent Garden, London WC2H 9HE

Library of Congress Cataloging-in-Publication Data
Names: Choudhury, Masudul Alam, 1948–   author.
Title: Methodological dimension of Islamic economics / Masudul Alam Choudhury
    (Trisakti University, Indonesia).
Description: New Jersey : World Scientific, [2019] | Includes bibliographical references and index.
Identifiers: LCCN 2018044018 | ISBN 9789813275782 (hc : alk. paper)
Subjects: LCSH: Economics--Religious aspects--Islam. | Islam--Economic aspects.
Classification: LCC BP173.75 .C4865 2019 | DDC 330.917/67--dc23
LC record available at https://lccn.loc.gov/2018044018

British Library Cataloguing-in-Publication Data
A catalogue record for this book is available from the British Library.

For any available supplementary material, please visit
https://www.worldscientific.com/worldscibooks/10.1142/11143#t=suppl

Desk Editors: Herbert Moses/Lum Pui Yee

Typeset by Stallion Press
Email: enquiries@stallionpress.com

Printed in Singapore

Prologue
Oneness of *Allah* and the World System — *Tawhid as Monotheistic Law*

Abu Saeed al-Khudri reported that the Prophet of Allah — peace be upon him — said: *"When Musa [Moses] asked Allah to teach him a prayer to recite whenever he remembered or called upon Him, Allah answered: 'Say, O Musa, There is no god worthy of worship, except Allah.' Musa said: 'O Lord, all your servants say these words.'*
Allah said: "O Musa, if the seven heavens and all they hold, and the seven earths as well, if all these were weighed against this word of 'There is no god worthy of worship, except Allah" the latter would outweigh the former.' "

Preface

As an exceptional expert in the field of methodological groundwork of Islamic economics and its applications, I thank many colleagues and forums of teaching and invited lecture forums that established the currency of the methodological socio-scientific worldview in general and Islamic economics in particular. The analytical and methodological worldview emergent in this work is of a unique and universal nature. It is a conceptual and applied perspective of the methodological worldview that is applicable to all of socio-scientific studies in the world of learning with in-depth critical outlook and avoiding a religious confinement.

This book is thereby a serious and rigorous work in the methodology of unity of knowledge with its conceptual formalism and applications. The study is thereby not of a theological nature. Rather, Tawhid as the primal ontology of unity of knowledge is studied and applied in its socio-scientific methodological worldview of oneness. This attenuates to pervasive organic complementarities and participative nature of "everything" in the learning world system with its generality and details. Even the humanly concocted theological idea of *Tawhid* as of: (1) *Tawhid al-Rububiyah* (Creatorship), (2) *Tawhid al-Uluhiyyah* (sustainership), and (3) *Asmah* and *Sifat* (attributes) — as if these are separable parts of the *Tawhidi* worldview. Contrarily, these are comprised in relational unity by the inter-systemic organic causality of oneness between them. Thereby, *Tawhid* as (1) and *Tawhid* as (2) are unified by the organic relational function of (3) in respect of unity of Being and its Becoming as the law of the world system of "everything". Likewise, the parts (1)–(3) are interdependent by way of circular causation. Only this ultimate functional attribute of such circular causation of unity of knowledge abides in Tawhid.

The approach is comparative in nature with the critical examination of modern mainstream economic theory. The centerpiece of the book is the *Tawhidi* methodology as the universal and unique foundation of all socio-scientific qua Islamic scholarly projects contrasted with all other incomplete systems of perceptions rather than of reality that are contrarily immersed in the belief of rationalism as a contrary methodological outlook.[1] Within the uniquely contrasting field of *Tawhid* against the field of rationalism is launched the study of *Tawhidi* Islamic economics (TIE). *Tawhid* means oneness of *Allah* (God). This precept also comprises the episteme of unity of knowledge of the divine law. While being a rigorous piece of accomplishment, the book also invokes the coverage of the course in epistemology at the level of International Baccalaureate program, though being in Islamic perspective of the *Tawhidi* methodological worldview.

Islam presents the encompassing worldview that centers the study and organization of the details of the world system in the episteme of the divine law. This is a fact of academic understanding of the *Tawhidi* worldview that lends itself to deep erudition in the world of learning. This is a fact that is deeply scholarly, despite the ambivalence of many Muslims today, which as a result, has caused stalemate in Islamic scholarship. Yet, this sorry state of Muslim scholarship in the learning world is destined to change. The potentiality looms

---

[1]In regard to the worldview of the *Qur'an*, that is of *Tawhid*, Nasr, S. H. *et al.* ((Eds.) (2015). *The Study Qur'an*, New York: Harper Collins) writes: "No sacred scripture of which we have knowledge speaks more about the cosmos and the world of nature than does the *Qur'an*, where one finds extensive teachings about cosmogenesis, cosmic history, eschatological events marking the end of the cosmic order as it now exists, and the phenomena of nature as revealing Divine Wisdom. In fact, the *Qur'an* refers to these phenomena as *ayat*" (signs of *Allah*).

bright, as the world of learning today is perpetually in quest of new socio-scientific epistemologies. Heterodoxy in the trans-disciplinary area is in the air.

This book is for the scholarly and analytically prepared researcher. It can be befitting a course of Islamic economics after the students have gone through a thorough analytical training in the mainstream economic theory. This legitimates a critical and methodological study. It is preferred that such students and readers have completed well up to intermediate microeconomics and intermediate macroeconomics. At this level of economics preparation, the students would have gone through an adequately good grounding in mathematics. Besides these areas of preparation, the readership should use the *Qur'an* and *hadith* for exegeses of topics in Islamic socio-scientific methodology, analytics, and examples. Indeed, a thorough course in TIE by its claim to be a distinctive original field of erudition and learning makes TIE to be substantive and rigorously epistemological in nature based on the true foundation of Islamic methodology of *Tawhid*. *Tawhid* means oneness of *Allah* and unity (consilience) of the divine *law* combining conception, formalism, and applications in the order and scheme of "everything".

There are special features distinctly belonging to TIE that characterize this heterodox discipline of knowledge. These aspects of TIE are understood at the outset of this rigorous study as the pertinent direction to the study of all socio-scientific phenomena. Most notably among these studies is that of economics in respect of its wide field of valuation incorporating ethics with the transaction of exchange as embedded endogenous value. Such a moral–material unison causes the meaning of exchange to be understood in its vast extant, including in it material exchange as well as exchange of services that include caring and wellbeing, morality and ethics, social and behavioral norms, and the overview of institutions, programs, and policies.

The following are particular characteristics of TIE to keep in mind:

1. The central episteme of unity of knowledge is the core concept leading to concepts, formalism, and applications regarding

economic relations as a system and cybernetic approach in the study of organically interconnected reality. Such an episteme arises from the primal ontology of *Tawhid* as *the law* of the *Qur'an*. This is also the domain of the divine law of *Allah* (*sunnat Allah*) whose signs are of unity of being and becoming (*ayath Allah*). These essential ontological facts are further explicated by the teaching of the Prophet Muhammad, called *sunnah*.

2. Further to the above characteristic, there is the important essence of continuous participation (complementarity) as discourse (*shura*) is carried out between self, other and society, mind and matter at large, concerning the implications and choices emanating from the fundamental episteme of *Tawhidi* unity of knowledge and the generality and specifics of the particulars under inquiry (*tasbih*). The *Qur'an* refers to such total phenomena as *shura* with *tasbih*.

3. The ethics of exchange and transactions in its widest conception and applications are induced in the defining variables as conscious interrelations between the variables. Such intervariable relations are mathematically evaluated by inter-system and intervariable organic equations.

4. The domains of intervariable relations encompass choices of the good things of life as mandated by the *Qur'an* and explicated by the purpose and meaning of the *shari'ah* termed as *maqasid as-shari'ah*. Their discovery is obtained by continuously visiting renewed discourse with consciousness (*shura-tasbih*) by the method of Islamic jurisprudence (*fiqh al-Qur'an*) based on the *Tawhidi law* (*sunnat Allah*).

5. The ontological, epistemological, and applied parts of the comprehensive model of the *Tawhidi* methodological worldview, called the *Tawhidi* String Model (TSR), altogether form the *Tawhidi* phenomenology. Phenomenology means the scientific way of explaining and revealing the degree of consciousness in mind and matter interrelations (Husserl, 1964).[2]

---

[2]Husserl, E. (1964). *The Idea of Phenomenology*, Translated by Alston, W. P., Nakhnikian, G. and Martin, N. Netherlands: The Hague.

6. The theory of TIE arising from the *Tawhidi* methodological worldview forms a continuously evolutionary learning system in unity of knowledge across the knowledge, space, and time dimensions.

7. The *Tawhidi* epistemology of unity of knowledge and its methodological formalism makes TIE everywhere and in everything contrary to the mainstream and neoclassical economic theory and applications.

8. TIE is also methodologically distinct from the conventional mainstream form of Islamic economics. The formalism and applications are different from the mainstream ones used abundantly in mainstream Islamic economics.

9. The formal model of TIE is vastly applicable to the entire genre of socio-scientific issues and problems. This embodies extensive empirical depth giving rise to inferences on the morality and ethics of the episteme of unity of knowledge and its reformative consequences.

10. The universality and uniqueness of the *Tawhidi* methodology in TIE is proved by its application to the mainstream economic phenomena and the Islamic one, with opposite conceptions, meanings, applications, inferences, and implications. On the other hand, mainstream economics cannot explain the breadth of the *Tawhidi* methodological worldview explained in generality and particular in TIE.

Throughout this book, the logical development of ideas in reference to the exegesis of the *Qur'an* establishes the fact that, indeed the description of all of creation between the heavens and the earth, from these worldly transactions to those of the Hereafter, and the organic interrelations explained to exist between these, are of the nature of perpetual exchange. Such exchange can be financial, in terms of goods and services, and in terms of endogenously embedded morality and ethicality. Such a universal meaning of transaction exists for both the good choices and otherwise. Hence, the idea of exchange and equivalently transactions premised in the concept of total valuation, is of a continuous and extensively systemic nature encompassing the endless domain of knowledge, space, and time dimensions and prevailing from the beginning to the end; and in "everything" between the heavens and the earth in the form of seven heavens of dimensions.[3]

Basic explanations

Some basic definitions are to be understood in studying this book. Firstly, the definition of ethics means the organic unification between the good things of life according to the *Qur'an* and the *sunnah* whose reflections are contained in the purpose and objective of the *shari'ah* referred to as *maqasid as-shari'ah al-Tawhid,* to the avoidance of the catchword and deceptive terminology of "*shari'ah* compliance". *Maqsid as-shari'ah* is treated not as primal ontological law. Rather, it is a premise of choice that must continuously and pervasively refer to the Tawhidi primal ontology of unity of knowledge in making all such choices by reference to the *Qur'an* and *sunnah*. All human discourses in such choices are treated as relative knowledge subject to critical revision, change, and extension. The invoking of the unity of knowledge and its induced systems of relations arises from the nature of the law of *Tawhid* in the *Qur'an* and the *sunnah*.

From the *Qur'anic* explanation of the organic unity of relational unity, arise the many attributes of the good things of life regarding which the *Qur'an* (Chapter 55: *Ar-Rahman*) declares. There is no end to these. Hence, this book addresses the derivation and formalism of the universal theory of truth versus falsehood. From the general theory, particular issues and problems are addressed by TIE. The *Qur'an* (31:28) declares regarding this endless generality of goodness. Within this generalized universality, all meanings of goodness and truth and even falsehood are endowed: "And if all the trees on earth were pens and the ocean (were ink), with seven oceans behind it to add to its (supply), yet would not the words of God be exhausted

---

[3] *Qur'an* (65:12): "It is *Allah* Who has created seven heavens and of the earth the like thereof. His Command descends between them (heavens and earth), that you may know that *Allah* has power over all things, and that *Allah* surrounds (comprehends) all things in (His) Knowledge."

(in the writing): for God is Exalted in Power, full of Wisdom." This book thus makes the argument that there is no need to pick out especial attributes, such as justice, fairness, charity, etc. to explain *Qur'anic* total valuation. These are simply incomplete examples, not the worldview. For instance, above justice, prayer, zakah (mandatory spending for alleviation of hardship), riba (financial interest), and the like is the general *Qur'anic* worldview of submission to *Allah* as the pinnacle of the divine truth and purpose against falsehood and evil. Within the general theory, the issues of justice as balance (*mizan*), fairness as distributive justice (*iqhlas*), prayer as divine communication (*tasbih*), etc. are especial cases of surrendering to the *Tawhidi* law. Thus, the episteme of unity of knowledge in *Tawhid* is primal while all specifics are particulars. Everything ensues from *Tawhid.* Nothing ensues from these other ones to *Tawhid,* if *Tawhid* was not invoked as the quiddity in the first instance. The *Qur'an* (13:39) declares in this regard: "*Allah* effaces and confirms what He wishes. By Him is the mother of the book."

It is because of the above kind of reference to particulars as picked-out attributes, rather than starting from the generality of the *Tawhidi* worldview and then addressing particulars, that has caused missing gaps of profound insight in Islamic thought. Among these kinds of intellectual gaps is the quest for the theory of justice according to the *Qur'an.* There has not been any profound work in Islamic thought that has addressed the principle of justice from the basis of a *general theory of justice* according to the *Tawhidi* worldview. There has simply been laudable treatment of attributes that partly explain while arising from the principle of justice (Kamali, 1991).[4]

This manuscript has shown that consequent to the above type of intellectual gap, there has remained limitation in the way of understanding the wider, generalized meaning of *maqasid as-shari'ah.* The *Qur'anic* cosmic understanding of balance (*mizan*) could not be interrelated with the wellbeing of the physical combined with the

---

[4]Kamali, M. H. (1991). *Principles of Islamic Jurisprudence,* Cambridge, England: Islamic Texts Society.

social world systems to convey the comprehensive meaning of the principle and choices according to *maqasid as-shari'ah* (Choudhury, 2015).[5]

Whitehead (1979) has succinctly explained the wide understanding of the particular in unity of relationship with the total reality, the general. Whitehead wrote on this theme in respect of the learning and unifying nature of the universe (p. 57)[6]: "The creative action is the universe always becoming one in a particular unity of self-experience, and thereby adding to the multiplicity which is the universe as many. This insistent concrescence into unity is the outcome of the ultimate self-identity of each entity. No entity — be it 'universal' or 'particular' — can play disjoined roles. Self-identity requires that every entity has one conjoined, self-consistent function, whatever be the complexity of that function."[7]

The primacy of *Tawhid* over everything of creation in mind, matter, and the hidden (*ghayb*) implies the cardinal function of jurisprudential interpretation (*fiqh*) to be pertinent only by its continuous revisiting the *Qur'an* leading thereby through the *sunnah* to learned discourse as *usul al-fiqh al-Qur'an*. Contrarily, *fiqh* and *shari'ah*, in the absence of the ontological and epistemological references today, have become a sorrowfully exclusive human preference rendered to sects (*madhabs*). This book has avoided this concoction of belief and has turned to the continuity of discourse based on the *Qur'an* and the *sunnah*, these being then brought back to human understanding to develop continuity of *usul al-fiqh al-Qur'an*. A clear distinction here regarding the evolutionary learning universe must be noted between the idea of evolution of species (Darwin, 1936)[8] and evolution as the dynamics of increasing (or decreasing) learning in

---

[5]Choudhury, M. A. (2015). *"Res extensa et res cogitans de maqasid as-shari'ah"*, *International Journal of Law and Management*, 57(6), 662–693.
[6]Whitehead, A. N., Griffin, D. R. and Sherburne, D. W. (Eds.) (1979). "Fact and form", in *Process and Reality*, New York: The Free Press, pp. 39–60.
[7]The term "concresence" means unity between the entities of learning processes.
[8]Darwin, C. (1936). *Descent of Man (or Origin of Species)*, New York: Modern Library.

regard to the principle of consilience, the *Tawhidi* episteme of unity of knowledge.

The *Qur'an* and *sunnah* abhor the species context of physical evolution. In this regard, the *Qur'an* (95:4) declares: "We have indeed created humankind in the best of moulds." The breed of humanity comprises those who treat *Tawhid* as the primal source of knowledge. The *Qur'an* (95:5) further declares on the contrary category of humankind: "Then We return him to the lowest of the low." They are the ones who deny *Tawhid* and instead invoke their own failed experiences of rationalism. The verse (*Qur'an*, 95:6) then continues on to strengthen its promise of knowledge to the believers. These are those who uphold *Tawhid* as the ultimate source of knowledge[9]: "Except for those who believe and do righteous deeds, for they will have a reward uninterrupted."

This book invokes this latter definition throughout. It is also referred to as the *Qur'anic* dialectics of rising towards (or falling from) the heightened understanding of *Tawhidi* episteme of unity of knowledge in continuous phases of evolutionary learning. Knowledge throughout this book means knowledge of *Tawhid*. The other kinds of knowing that do not invoke *Tawhid* as law of unity of knowledge are equated with the belief in rationalism of human genre.

The expression that knowledge is endowed in nature is a static idea. To discover knowledge in its meaning, quiddity, and application in the framework of *Tawhidi* unity as law brings out the dynamics of a functioning world system in such a framework of total reality encompassing truth and falsehood, right and wrong. In this regard, the *Qur'an* (25:1) writes: "Blessed is He who sent down the Criterion upon His Servant that he may be to the worlds a warner." Furthermore, in respect of the final origin of true knowledge, it rests

---

[9]Chittick, W. C. (1989). *Sufi Path of Knowledge*, Albany, NY: State University of New York. Translates Ibn Arabi who wrote: "Two ways lead to the knowledge of God... The first way is the way of unveiling... The second way is the way of reflection and reasoning (*istidlal*) through rational demonstration (*burhan aqli*). This way is lower than the first way, since he who bases his consideration upon proof can be visited by obfuscations which detract from his proof, and only with difficulty can he remove them" [slightly edited by author].

on the *Qur'an*, that is *Tawhid* as law that explains "everything". In this regard, the *Qur'an* (13:31) declares: "If there were a *Qur'an* with which mountains were moved, or the earth were cloven asunder, or the dead were made to speak, (this would be the one!). But, truly, the command is with *Allah* in all things! Do not the Believers know that, had *Allah* (so) willed, He could have guided all mankind (to the right)? But the Unbelievers, — never will disaster cease to seize them for their (ill) deeds, or to settle close to their homes, until the promise of *Allah* come to pass, for, verily, *Allah* will not fail in His promise."

For the above reason of the ultimate and only source of knowledge in *Tawhid* (*Qur'an*), this book also inquires about the nature of universality and uniqueness in the *Tawhidi* methodological worldview and its particularization in the theme of exchange transaction that is studied in terms of its total socio-scientific valuation in TIE.

Summary

This book, while emphasizing the origin of every epistemological methodology in the birth of revolutionary meta-scientific worldview, has made a distinct difference in meaning and application between the terms "*methodology*" and "*method*". An example is that, although all of mathematics is a method, methodology impacts upon the choice of such methods by their selection according to the appropriate approaches used in response to the logical implications of the *Tawhidi* methodological worldview. Thus, while optimization is a mathematical method, such a method is untenable in studying the method of evolutionary learning properties of *Tawhidi* formalism and applications, except for purposes of erecting a study of critical realism (Whitehead and Russell, 1910–1913).[10]

This is a rigorous book for all levels of researchers, students, and scholars and across multi-disciplines that interactively combine the study of ontology, epistemology, and phenomenology of conceptual

---

[10]Whitehead, A. N. and Russell, B. (1910–1913). *Principia Mathematica*, New York: Cambridge University Press.

systems and their applications. The particular emphasis is on Islamic methodological worldview in respect of *Tawhid as law* arising from the exegeses of the *Qur'an*, the *sunnah*, and human discourse exciting consciousness (*shura-tasbih*). Yet, its broadest methodological worldview is of unity of knowledge in a highly realist context. Indeed, such has been the quest of all the sciences always.[11]

Some may have the impression that this book is overly philosophical and in that case an epistemological treatise. The ontological, epistemological, and phenomenological contents of the building blocks of TIE and the generalized theory of *Tawhidi* methodological worldview cannot be denied in the development of the rigorous foundations of what is truly Islamic in terms of the *Qur'an* and the *sunnah*. Yet, this book does not have a speculative containment in philosophy. Its objective in fact is to use philosophical terms and explanations because of the analytical thoughts that emanate from the *Qur'an* and the *sunnah*. Such emergent intellection is encapsulated in the building blocks of every revolutionary theory of meta science.[12] In the particular case out of the general analytical case is the theory of TIE.

The teaching of the book first requires its good understanding by the teacher. The teacher may then like to tailor the content of this book in the way that is appropriate for teaching the students with good critical reasoning and with both a conceptual and an applied perspective. In this regard, the teacher may extract sections of this book according to the need of the students at various levels. The best

---

[11]Whitehead, A. N. (1938). "Nature Alive", in *Modes of Thought*, New York: Macmillan, Lecture Eight, pp. 205: "The doctrine that I am maintaining is that neither physical nature nor life can be understood unless we fuse them together as essential factors in the composition of 'really real' things whose interconnections and individual characters constitute the universe."

[12]The meaning of a revolutionary methodological worldview is borrowed from Kuhn, T. S. (1970). *The Structure of Scientific Revolution*, Chicago, IL: University of Chicago Press. Kuhn (1970, p. 154) remarked regarding the emergence of scientific revolution beyond normal science and paradigm shift: "...scientific revolutions are here taken to be those non-cumulative developmental episodes in which an older paradigm is replaced in whole or in part by an incompatible new one."

dispensation of this book would require students to go through an earlier pre-requisite of the introductory, and more preferred is a course in the intermediate economic theory. The student would also have reached a sound level of mathematical orientation to economic theory. The student would be well off if he/she is further prepared in the introductory field of epistemology of the level of International Baccalaureate (IB).[13]

One suggested way of utilizing this book for the emergent theory and application of TIE in a three credits course is to follow the following structure of lectures:

(1) One month of lectures would be devoted to the study of *Tawhidi* methodology in respect of divulging the essential features of TIE in critical contrast to mainstream economic theory and its different methodology. Exegeses of the *Qur'an* and the *sunnah* would be used to bring out the critical foundation of TIE. Examples and worked exercises are examined to build up the appertaining area of methodology.

(2) A subsequent one month of lectures will be devoted to the contrasting study of microeconomics between TIE and mainstream economics. The methodological reference will be maintained. Examples and exercises are examined to bring out the methodological treatment of microeconomic problems in TIE in contradistinction with mainstream and neoclassical economics.

(3) The last month of lectures will be devoted to the study of macroeconomics in TIE contrasted with the study in mainstream macroeconomics. Once again, the methodological lineage in the critical study is continued. Examples and exercises are examined and solved. The teacher should encourage diagrammatic approach to explain concepts in TIE as being logically different from mainstream economic theory.

(4) The instructor may write note books out of this major book for the benefit of students and scholars at different levels of

---

[13]IB. Theory of Knowledge Program, http://ibo.org/en/programmes.

learning. The example then would be of handbooks and problem-solving notebooks that are associated with major textbooks of microeconomics and macroeconomics.

It was mentioned earlier that this book has three interrelated parts in it. Firstly, there is a substantive part on the distinctive methodology of *Tawhid* as *Qur'anic* law on the derivation of the worldview of meta-science from the *Qur'an* and the *sunnah* (*usul al-Qur'an*). Secondly, there is the part on the emergent theory of TIE distinctly different from mainstream economics and present days' orientation of so-called Islamic economics and finance. Thirdly, there are applications by way of examples and exercises. More items can be formulated. The conscious and erudite scholar can further develop and innovate in these specific areas and beyond. The instructor, scholars, and well-informed practitioners and researchers can formulate their local issues and problems in the light of the total valuation concept of TIE.

It is hoped that this rare work in authentic Islamic method-ological worldview of *Tawhid* as law and its applications will be a substantive learning input in wide erudition to the world of learning. This ought not to be simply a constrained use by Muslims students and scholars alone. Through its publication and dissemination, we hope that the book will enter the realm of the important, revolutionary, and distinctive books of learning and erudition for all, globally. The book is uncompromising to the superficial Islamic meaning being attached today to the field referred to as Islamic economics in the garb of mainstream and neoclassical economics. Islamic thought and writings in the mainstream and neoclassical orientation today are found to have blindly imitated the epistemic methodology and methods in these approaches that remain contrary to the *Tawhidi* methodological worldview.

Teaching philosophy

By the very nature of TIE and its explication in this book, the instructor ought to uphold a system view of explaining concepts, formalism, examples, and applications. This is due to the very

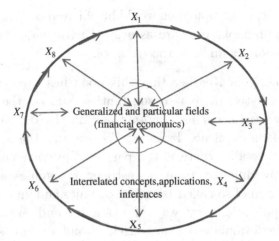

Figure 1. The circularly integrated and interactive dynamic relations in system embedding.

episteme of *Tawhidi* unity of knowledge that underlies the methodological worldview of *Tawhid* as law. Figure 1 presents such a teaching worldview in brief.

$\{\mathbf{X}(\theta)\}$ are multivariates of the multi-systems characterized by organic learning processes between the particulars that are all governed by the generalized episteme of *Tawhidi* unity of knowledge.

About the Author

Professor Choudhury is one of the original initiators of the organized way of pursuing academic activity in Islamic economics. In North America, he was a Founding Member of the Association of Muslim Social Scientists (AMSS) of the United States and Canada. Distinctly, along with his colleagues, he established the Post-Graduate Program in Islamic Economics and Finance (IEF) in the Faculty of Economics, Trisakti University, Jakarta, Indonesia. He is the International Chair in IEF since the last 19 years. Professor Choudhury is an annual summer Visiting Professor in the Social Economy Center of Ontario Institute for Studies in Education in the University of Toronto. Until his academic retirement, he served for 23 years as Full-Professor of Economics in Cape Breton University, Sydney, Nova Scotia, Canada. He also held professorial positions in various universities around the world. Professor Choudhury invented the methodology of Tawhid as the monotheistic ontological law of unity of knowledge as the epistemological foundation of the Theory of Islamic Economics. He is the founder of the Tawhidi Epistemological Methodology in its analytical form as meta-science. In this capacity, he derived the application of the Tawhidi Epistemological Methodology in Islamic Economics and Finance: He is the developer of the Model of Wellbeing (Maslaha); Circular Causation Relational Model for empirical simulation of the objective criterion of well-being in Islamic Economics and Finance. Professor Choudhury discovered the paradigm of endogenous ethics and evolutionary learning social processes in the light of the Qur'an. This scholarly idea is projected in his initiated SCOPUS, ESCI, ABDC (Australian) journal entitled *International Journal of Ethics and Systems (IJOES)*. *IJOES* is published quarterly by the reputed Emerald Publications. Professor Choudhury is the Editor-in-Chief of *IJOES*. He is now writing his great works in the above-mentioned field with focus on Tawhid contra shari'ah according to the Qur'an and the world-system. He teaches and supervises doctoral students in IEF — Trisakti University, Jakarta, Indonesia of which he is a founder.

Acknowledgment

Intellectual work in this book started with the publication of a version of its Chapter 1 in the *ISRA International Journal*. This unfolded in the completion of the work at a time when the *Tawhidi* methodological worldview in the socio-scientific "everything" in its most erudite level has never been approached by those who mistakenly profess the so-called field of Islamic economics and finance. The so-called gurus of this field encumbered this field instead in the garb of the human-concocted experiment of *shari'ah*-compliance. This took out the grand socio-scientific methodological foundation of the be-all and end-all of Islamic worldview of Tawhid as the primal ontological foundation of "everything". The particularity of this grand field of "everything" is the field of *Tawhidi* Islamic Economics, which is the deeply rigorous field of this work.

Much of the work in this original and distinctive field of phenomenological search and discovery of the true Islamic methodology of "everything" was completed when I was Visiting Professor in the Department of *Shari'ah* and Economics, Academy of Islamic Studies, University of Malaya. Within the general theory of *Tawhidi* unity of knowledge was taken up the study of Islamic Economics and Finance as particulars in reference to the worldview of Tawhid as unity of knowledge and unification of the world system studied in generality and particulars.

I also benefited much from my library research in the rich Robarts and OISE Libraries of the University of Toronto during my annual summer visiting professorship in the Social Economy Center of OISE.

The scholarly work pursued in this book is distinctly different from the crass understanding of Islamic economics being done currently. The experience has been waning in methodological credibility and the resulting analytical depth in the global intellectual forum. As a result, both the scholarly depth and the empirical applications of the so-called Islamic economics and finance have failed and continue to exist with borrowed remnants of mainstream economics. *Tawhidi* Islamic economics displaces and replaces the failed scholarship by its own deeply methodological worldview and the imminent quantitative applications that ensue. Logical formalism that the *Qur'an* and *sunnah* permits is at the roots of the inquiry.

It is hoped that this original and distinctive scholarly contribution will fill the gap in pursuit of scholarship in Islamic socio-scientific methodological worldview arising from the *Qur'an* and *sunnah* foundation of primal ontology and epistemology leading to the phenomenology of unity of knowledge and the economic world system.

The book is rendered to students, faculties, researchers, and practitioners in the open global context of evolutionary learning and critical thought. Indeed, this scholarly contribution comes at a time of heterodox methodological investigation in the field of economics. Within this heterodoxy is buried a silent wimp of Islamic economics and finance. But it is not so for the revolutionary field of *Tawhidi* Islamic economics and finance.

Contents

List of Figures

List of Tables

Chapter 1

How to Study Islamic Economics as a Science in Reference to the *Qur'an* and the *Sunnah*

Islamic economics began around 70 years ago with the works of some Indian scholars in the field. The King Abdulaziz University Center for Islamic Economics records the origin of the contemporary approach to the study of Islamic economics to be 30 years ago. The works of the great Islamic scholars, the *mujtahids*, such as Imam Ghazali, Ibn Taimiyya, Imam Shatibi, Ibn Qayyim, and Ibn Khaldun, recorded the study of Islamic economic and social problems either in reference to the *Qur'an* and prophetic teaching, the *sunnah*, or independent of these as intellection borrowed from Greek social and economic thoughts. The latter examples are of Ibn Khaldun (Rozenthal, 1958) and the Muslim philosopher of Greek vintage, Al-Farabi (Waltzer, 1985). The use of the terminology "Islamic economics" is an imitation of contemporary times. It reflects the classification of educational disciplines left to us by the Occidental world. Such classification was devoid of the holistic beginnings of intellectual thought in which all Muslim scholars had drowned themselves in the search of knowledge, not of this or that discipline, but of all disciplines as a holistic methodological worldview.

Thus, while the classification of the disciplines carried with it the specialization and independence of the areas of learning as separable activities, while the spirit of holism disappeared, Islamic economics, by its contemporary term, also became one of the emergent ways of such thinking. Yet, such an emergence of the Islamic economic discipline gradually caused a methodical dissociation of the nature of Islamic moral and ethical issues that are inherent in the framework of the theory of knowledge (TOK) arising from the ontological and epistemological foundations of the *Qur'an* and the *sunnah*. As the spirit of western erudition entered lock, stock, and barrels in Muslim acceptance, the originality of Islamic science and society including economics never took any foundational origin, shape, form, and critical learning pursued via Islamic epistemology, meaning the TOK. This marked the departure of the Islamic methodological worldview and its potentiality to contribute and sustain the Islamic originality, erudition, epistemology, and consequential analytics to the world of learning. Islamic economics entered the scene of the classified disciplines in such a subservient state. Consequently, almost all of its argumentation, modeling, formalism, applications and inferences took the path of the western interpretations. See Mahomedy (2013) for an incisive and insightful critique of the existing field of Islamic economics. Nonetheless, high potentiality remains for Islamic economics as a discipline of metascience that is grounded on the Islamic epistemological foundations. These are the exegesis of the *Qur'an* and the *sunnah* in respect of the *Tawhidi* methodological worldview.

Present days' Islamic economics as a terminology is in such a dire state. It is not original, failing to be derived from the teachings of the *Qur'an*, the *sunnah*, and many of the Islamic scholastic leaders. This is not to mean that the *Qur'an* is the divine book of science. Rather, the *Qur'an* is the revealed book of guidance for those who seek guidance.[1] Yet, the *Qur'an* is the book complete and final in knowledge. It thereby provides guidance for all issues of mind and matter, and thus of science, economics in its metaperspective of morality and ethics embedded in materiality.

---

[1] *Qur'an* (2:2): "This is the Book about which there is no doubt, a guidance for those conscious of Allah."

Islamic economics in its present state does not have a theory and foundation that can be called truly "Islamic" in terms of its systematizing the world of economic and social learning in a holistic way. The methods and models of Islamic economics today ignore the need for modeling the Islamic morals and ethics. The implications are thereby a borrowing and an interpretation that is either crassly Islamic in name, yet without the spirit, rigor, and foundations. Or it is stereotyping the western methodological worldview. Only an outer semblance of Islamic values is attached to the economic reasoning of present days' notion of Islamic economics.[2]

Present state of the study of economics

The Royal Economic Society points out that smaller universities in the United Kingdom have abandoned exclusive focus on economics after the year 1999. Yet, the larger universities in the United Kingdom by virtue of their advanced ideas in economic reasoning and by integrating related disciplines have flourished. One such area that has arisen in the larger universities is heterodox economic theory.

Subsequent to the period of Islamic economics in its heydays in the Muslim world, Islamic economics has by and large been supplanted by the now-stylized caption of Islamic finance. This is an equally problematic field with its western imitation having only a palliative of Islamic instrumentation. This garb of Islamic finance is not epistemologically different and revolutionary in nature in the annals of erudition and originality.

The problem of Islamic learning started when it got increasingly dissociated away from its epistemological origin in the *Qur'an*, the *sunnah*, and intellectual discourse around these to raise what is called *"ijtihad"*, authentic research based on epistemological foundations. This being the case, the axioms, assumptions, nature, methodology, and applications of the core of Islamic economic reasoning, namely morality and ethics, are marginalized by their substitutes in commercialism and materiality. The example is the present failing of Islamic

---

[2] *Qur'an* (30:7): "They know but the outer (things) in the life of this world; but of the End of things they are heedless."

banks. They raise large equity values from the shares market. Yet, they remain oblivious of the cognition and practice of the Islamic methodological worldview applied to the commercial arena.

According to orthodox economic theory to which neoclassical economics belongs, the principal attribute of rational choice-making in goods and services is "marginal rate of substitution" between competing goods and services for the command over scarce resource allocation between such competing ends. We will also refer to this neoclassical premise as "marginalism". Likewise, Islamic economics immersed in mainstream orthodox economics could not belong to the holistic sociological economic school. This was caused by it being immersed in the traditional microeconomic and macroeconomic branches of mainstream reasoning. There was blind acceptance to the underlying postulates of orthodox and mainstream economics with their traditional orientation. Although such orientations are being seriously questioned in mainstream economics by the works in rational expectation theory. The fields of microeconomic foundations of macroeconomics were the results of such theorizing. In Islamic economics of today, such original ideas of formalizing the ethical place of microeconomics in the development of the macroeconomic consequences did not arise. Islamic economics thus blindly followed the traditional theories of microeconomics and macroeconomics. Yet, in none of these following, there is any robust theory of ethical integration in economic theory, formalism and application.

The major problem of Islamic economics like Islamic finance, Islamic banking, and other Islamic socio-scientific ventures is that it has no articulated epistemological foundation. On the other hand, any science, social or natural in category, ought to be based in solid epistemological foundation. Such an orientation subsequently gives shape, form, axioms, assumptions, and methodological formalism to the entire body of theory and application. Einstein (Bohr, 1985) said that science without epistemology remains muddle-headed.

The rise of heterodox economics in the recent times is of a deeply ontological and epistemological type. Even neoclassical economics is epistemological in nature according to its own axiom of economic rationality. Classical economics is thoroughly epistemological in reference to the *Theory of Moral Sentiments* as Adam Smith's first great epistemological contribution to economic reasoning. All of the science as we have inherited rests on the epistemology of heteronomy. Heteronomy conveys the nature of dualism between *a priori* and *a posteriori* domains of reasoning. We will discuss such issues in the subsequent chapters to bring out the distinctive difference between rationalism of the occidental theory of science and the episteme of unity of knowledge of the *Tawhidi* methodological worldview.

Tawhid as the Islamic methodological worldview: the advent of *Tawhidi* Islamic Economics (TIE)

Contrary to all such epistemological moorings, today's Islamic economics, and likewise, all other Islamic socio-scientific fields in the recent times have not been able to formalize and contribute to the internal dynamics and functioning of the primal axiom of the entire Islamic methodological worldview upon which a metascience can be erected. This is the ineluctable axiom of *Tawhid* as the monotheistic law of unity of knowledge. It exists not simply in utterance. Rather, as Imam Ghazali said (Karim, n.d), the understanding of *Tawhid* as methodological worldview has 60 stages with increasing depth. Islamic economic casually adopted an utterance around the outer husk of declaring *Tawhid* (belief) without knowing its world-system dynamics and axiomatic character in the building of socio-scientific thought, metascience, and applications (Naqvi, 2003).

The *Tawhidi* methodological worldview is the universal and unique foundation of all Islamic intellection. It is formal in nature if properly utilized for the construction of the cognitive and material world system and its specifics. Such a formal intellection with its methodology, methods, and application is equally applicable to the building of metascience in the entire world of learning. On the indispensability of the *Tawhidi* methodological worldview in the mundane world system, Ibn Arabi wrote in his Futuhat (Chittick, 1989): "The first way is by way of unveiling. It is an incontrovertible knowledge, which is actualized through unveiling and which man finds in him. He receives no obfuscation along with it and is not able to repel it. The second way is the way of reflection and reasoning *(istidlal)* through rational demonstration *(burhan 'aqli)*. This way is lower than the first way, since he who bases his consideration upon proof can be visited by obfuscations which detract from his proof, and only with difficulty can he remove them."

The Islamic economic approach, which only utters *Tawhid* at the beginning and at the roots, is unable to formalize the monotheistic meaning as a methodology, formalism, and application. Contrary to this narrow attitude is the induction of the progressive knowledge of unraveling the *Tawhidi* methodological worldview into science and economics. We will thereby refer to the *Tawhidi* epistemological foundation of Islamic economic science by the term "*Tawhidi* Islamic Economics" (TIE).

In TIE consequently, the Kantian *problematique* of heteronomy between the moral imperative of the *a priori* domain and the practical reasoning of the *a posteriori* domain has entered Islamic socio-scientific thought in general and Islamic economics and finance, in particular, in the most surreptitious way. Heteronomy is of the nature of rationalism in causing dichotomy between the moral law (*Tawhid* = *a priori*) and the world system (*a posteriori*). Contrarily, the *Qur'an* presents the moral and cognitive world systems as being unified and indivisible holism. It bears its endogenous dynamics of organic unity of being and becoming concerning mind and matter. The *Tawhidi* methodological worldview is thus indispensably required to give the universally and uniquely original, revolutionary, essential Islamic foundation to what may be referred to as TIE and finance, science, and society (Choudhury, 2014).

As was mentioned above, Islamic socio-scientific intellection in general and Islamic economics and finance, in particular, have not been able to blaze the emergence of a field of heterodox economics. Heterodox economics by itself is a deeply ontological and epistemological inquiry (Lawson, 2003). If the ontological and epistemological foundations of the *Qur'an* and the *sunnah* are missed out, then the constructive dynamics of the *Tawhidi* foundation cannot be understood. This is equivalent to uttering but not knowing how to cognize and apply the methodology of *Tawhid* in the building of metascience for rendering to the world of learning. Will it stay this way? Have not the *Qur'an* and the *sunnah* given the challenge to raise the world system to the pinnacle of knowledge for the global wellbeing? The possibility is not to be found in the present state of Islamic thought by missing out the episteme of *Tawhid*. Yet, substantive efforts and contributions in this direction have been made.

The nature of Islamic economics according to the *Tawhidi* episteme

This book elaborates on the epistemological methodology of *Tawhid* in the groundwork of a heterodox Islamic economics and finance. The resultant *Tawhidi* methodology is found both to be rigorously analytical, invoking science, formalism, and analytical depth as well as universal application to particular issues and problems. It is a gross mistake and complete denial of scholarly knowledge to say that *Tawhid* is sheer philosophical, and that deep erudition of it in Islamic economics is not understood. On the other hand, Choudhury's scholarly works in the area of *Tawhidi* methodology have been well published in the West, addressing directly problems and issues of Islamic economics and other ones globally.

The fundamental attributes of Islamic economics in the light of *Tawhidi* methodology (TIE) is to start from the exegesis of the principle of "pairing" in the *Qur'an*.[3] Pairing conveys the meaning of organic unity between the good things of life and contrarily also conveying association of the bad things of life in accordance to the *Qur'an*. The good things are to be accepted, the bad things shunned. Pairing as organic unity of knowledge conveys the universal meaning of God's creation and purpose. It is a reflection of the unity of being and becoming along the dynamics of forming complementarities between the good and recommended things of life. The good things of life participate and complement in unity of inter-causal relationship. The bad things compete and marginalize each other. There is no

---

[3] *Qur'an* (36:36): "Glory to Allah, who created in pairs all things that the earth produces, as well as their own (human) kind and other things of which they have no knowledge."

scope of unifying for purposive unity, except to marginalize each other by association and differentiation. In Islamic economics, borrowing from mainstream and orthodox economics, the postulates of competition and marginalism are accepted.

This book will explain how the nature of *Tawhidi* methodology is related by circular cause and effect with knowledge par excellence. According to the *Qur'an*, *Tawhid* is the bedrock of complete and absolute knowledge. God is the fullness of knowledge that is embodied in the monotheistic law as the primal ontology, meaning theory of being and existence. The world system *(a'lameen)* is described and is spanned by the signs of monotheistic unity of knowledge in the good things of life and its opposite in the bad things of life by association and differentiation. These are both the Signs of God *(ayath Allah)*. They together explain the nature of the paired and the differentiated universe oppositely. They provide the ways of moral construction by consciousness of unity of knowledge in the details of the conscious universe.

Thus, the nature of Islamic economics is axiomatically premised in *Tawhidi* methodology of unity of knowledge functioning as organic relations of being and becoming. The result is the continuous nature of evolutionary learning emerging from inter-causality between the participatory and complementary good things of life. This presents the sure sign of paired unity of knowledge acting upon diversity of things. The world system that is constructed by the *Tawhidi* episteme is a continuously simulated universe of unity of knowledge. The process of participatory and complementary organic relations never ceases. It simply closes in the Hereafter.

According to the *Tawhidi* episteme of unity of knowledge and the imminent methodology applied to Islamic economics, this book will prove that almost all orthodox and mainstream economic thoughts in its critical components are untenable in TIE. Continuous evolutionary learning in unity of knowledge results in the annulment of steady-state equilibriums, optimization models, formal functionals of maximization, and almost all of the economic postulates of rationality. Only evolutionary learning models are to be accepted. This emergent theory is substantively explained throughout this book.

Critique of axioms and assumptions of Islamic economics borrowed from mainstream economics

The use of *Tawhidi* methodology of unity of knowledge and the world system causes almost all of the postulates of mainstream and orthodox economic theory to be null and avoid. They are replaced by the holistic, knowledge-induced, evolutionary learning economic reasoning. Yet, Islamic economics as we have inherited it adheres to such postulates. Following are some of the rejections of mainstream economic theory.

Scarcity: The core mainstream orthodox economic axiom is the scarcity of resources. This assumption is unacceptable in the *Qur'anic* worldview of abundance. This is true both in the absolute and relative meanings of resource scarcity. Scarcity does not exist in absolute terms by virtue of the principle of abundance in the *Qur'an*, except when resources are spoiled by human acts. Yet, such states of scarcity are recoverable ones towards reviving abundance. That is, moral reconstruction is always the goal and possibility of the *Tawhidi* evolutionary learning worldview that increases resources continuously. Scarcity of resources does not exist relatively because in the state of mutual learning and endogenous role of ethics and technology in resources, learning as by complementarities in the pairing universe of the *Qur'an continuously* increases resources. Resources are thus endogenized continuously by knowledge.

Opportunity cost and marginal rate of substitution (marginalism): Because of the continuously endogenous effect of interaction, integration, and evolutionary learning as properties of the pairing, i.e. complementing or participatory universe, there is no steady-state equilibrium point, and no optimal resource surface exists. In this way, the entire consumer indifference curve and the production possibility curve do not take shape and form.

Objective functions of mainstream and orthodox economics: The non-existence of smoothly concave to the origin indifference curves and production isoquants, and smooth convex production possibility curve imply that the well-behaved types of utility function and production function in substitutes do not exist. Besides, sub-stitutes cannot exist in the continuously evolutionary learning by pairing the complementarities of goods, services, and productive inputs. Ethically speaking too, in the first order condition of relation-ship between goods and productive inputs, the economic expansion path remains positively sloped. In the second order condition of allocation of resources, it is possible that one of the goods and services receive differentially less than the other. But both gain along the positive economic expansion path.

Relative prices of goods, services, and productive factors: The non-existence of smooth indifference curves, production isoquants, and production possibility surfaces cannot allow for well-determined relative prices.

Market prices: In the absence of well-determined relative prices, consumer demand curves and market demand curves cannot exist. This also happens due to the absence of simple price–quantity relationship for a specific good in demand and supply. Rather, other critical factors militate. Examples of such systemic interferences are dynamic preferences of choice, and endogenously related variations on other characteristics, e.g. continuously variable relative prices, incomes, and resources in the demand and supply functions (not curves).

Marginal cost pricing: Marginal cost of variable factors cannot exist because of knowledge-induced learning cost curves and produc-tion functions. Besides, under the effect of increasing returns to scale the total cost curve, average cost curve, and the productivity curve of output remain continuously evolutionary and downward shifting with endogenous learning.

Marginal productivities of productive factors: The absence of substitution and its replacement by pervasive complementarities between goods, services, and productive inputs cannot allow for marginal productivities of inputs, goods, and services. All other characteristics of non-existing steady-state equilibrium and optimal points cannot allow for marginal productivities to exist.

Dynamic preferences and technological change: The evolutionary learning properties of utility curve (therefore consumer indifference curve) and production function (therefore production isoquants) are causally related with dynamic preferences and tastes. Consequently, all the properties of rational choice theory are annulled in the presence of evolutionary learning and pervasive organic complementarities caused by the *Tawhidi* axiom of unity of knowledge and its effect on the evolutionary learning (pairing) universe.

The same kind of result is true of technology: Unlike the exogenous nature of technology in mainstream orthodox economic theory, technology is endogenously determined by continuous evolutionary learning. Such learning phenomenon in unity of knowledge affects resources, preferences, and choices by their mutual interaction and integration followed by continuous evolution. These are substantively characteristic of evolutionary learning TIE that will be explained in detail throughout this book.

Economic rationality: This is a mainstream and orthodox axiom based on full-information and pre-ordering of given preferences as datum, so as to establish internal consistency of the neoclassical theory in problem solving. Yet, in Islamic economic theory according to the *Tawhidi* methodological worldview, the postulate of full-information is untenable. The *Tawhidi* universe to which we are exposed by cognition and experience under evolutionary learning in unity of knowledge can never allow for discontinuity of knowledge (and thereby differentiation oppositely in the states of non-learning). Besides, dynamic preferences and endogenous technological change under the impact of evolutionary learning in unity of knowledge cannot be pre-ordered. Problem solving is done not by any consistency assumption. Rather, the formal results and experiences of emergent economic and social models cause the need for addressing the problems at hand in pertinent ways. McCloskey (1985) promoted such an idea of addressing the nature of the state "as is", rather than by theoretical prediction of economic theory.

Optimization and equilibrium consequences of absence of economic rationality

The absence of economic rationality in the *Tawhidi* methodological worldview of continuous evolutionary learning in unity of knowledge and unity of the knowledge-induced world system results in the complete absence of optimal states and steady-state equilibrium. While mainstream economics allow for exogenously induced changes in Pareto-optimal stead-state equilibriums, the *Tawhidi* methodological worldview has only endogenous resource augmentation and changes of organization under the impact of unity of knowledge. The result then is a continuously endogenous change in resource allocations, technological change, preferences, and every other participatory variable. Consequently, all points on the economic surfaces are continuously perturbed by continuous change along non-optimal directions. Likewise, steady-state equilibrium points are changes into evolutionary learning points without convergence into attained states.

Economic systems: The concepts of perfectly competitive markets (economy), imperfect competition, and monopolistic competition, are shown to be untenable in the midst of the continuously evolutionary learning methodology of *Tawhidi* unity of knowledge. The reason for this is that the existence of optimality and steady-state equilibrium makes all genres of economic systems untenable. The attenuating cost and production functions do not preserve their smooth structures to all for calculus of differentiation. Only learning curves in cost and output exist, causing non-existence of the marginal cost curve and marginal productivity measures. This was pointed out above. In the *Tawhidi* perspective of continuous evolutionary learning with inter-causal participation and complementarities, the competition and methodological individualism concepts of self-interest cannot exist, as otherwise found in mainstream and orthodox economics.

Behavioral perspectives: Morality and ethics remain exogenous to mainstream and orthodox economic theory. Knowledge borne out of the monotheistic law of unity of knowledge is centrally poised in morality and ethics. Thus, for example, social justice and materiality, likewise, social capital and private capital ownership, are oppositely competed for substitutes in mainstream economic theory of opportunity cost and scarcity of resources, except as exogenous ethical impacts change behavior though not continuously. Such resource injection occurs exogenously by external imposition. On the other hand, in the case of endogenous nature of knowledge, learning, and thereby of the continuity of moral and ethical consciousness, social and economic choices are treated to be complementary, participatory, and continuously evolutionary by learning in unity of knowledge. Islamic behavioral attribute is firstly based on the consciousness of *Tawhid* as oneness of God and unity of the monotheistic law. This in turn needs the extraction of the ontological knowledge (theory of existence of being) from the *Qur'an* through the medium of the *sunnah* (teachings of the Prophet Muhammad) and discourse among the learned ones in the Islamic nature of a purposive world system.

God, Morality, Ethics, and the World System: The oneness of God as belief, which is projected in the episteme of unity of knowledge in the *Tawhidi* law, is the sole exogenous ontology of the *Tawhidi* world system. All other variables in the *Tawhidi* world system *(a'lameen)* are paired by endogenous interrelations and circular causality of complementary relations (organic "pairing" as in the *Qur'an*). Thus, unlike the exogenous nature of morality and ethics in mainstream and orthodox economic theory, and then too the notion of ethics emerging from the *a posteriori* world of mind-matter, *Tawhidi* methodology sets the emergence of ethics and morality in the monotheistic law of unity of knowledge, and points out the opposite of differentiation. The extraction of such morality and ethics proceeds from the *Qur'an* via the *sunnah* for inducing the paired causality of the world system. The ontology of the *Tawhidi* law is then rendered to human discourse *vis-à-vis* the generality and details of diverse world systems. These comprise the mind-matter dynamics, formalism, application, and context.

The study of moral and ethical induction of Islamic behavior and its representative inter-causal variables in the light of the

Tawhidi methodology of unity of knowledge invokes mathematical methods mostly of the topological type. Topology is the only branch of advanced mathematics that studies relations between non-dimensional categories. Differential calculus is sparingly used in relation to knowledge variable. Time in the tuple comprising knowledge, space, and time dimensions of *Tawhidi* functional categories, remains simply a recorder, not creator of anything. Knowledge remains the sole creator of events and change over the knowledge, space, and time dimensions.

TIE and its applications studied in this work has the following definition: TIE is a scientific study of issues of economics in concert with all possible related fields that together interact to form organic influence on economic issues and events and *vice-a-versa*. Such encompassing scientific worldview of TIE is particularized in the metascience of the principal and sole axiom of all Islamic socio-scientific studies. It is the axiom of the monotheistic law of unity of knowledge in the good choices of life, which are choices derived from the purpose and objective of the *Qurânic* law — *maqasid as-shari'ah*. The same law rejects the bad choices of life. The two categories of goods and services are deciphered out of evolutionary learning according to the monotheistic (*Tawhidi*) law of unity of knowledge and the induced economic world system with its moral, ethical, and systemic congeries.

The above-mentioned contrariety exists between the nature of mainstream economics, its offspring in existing Islamic economics as presently understood on the one hand, and the *Tawhidi* methodology applied to the generality and particular of human cognition and experience on the other hand. An example of the particular is the emergence of the *Qur'anic* study of the economic issues of man and the universe. This book will formalize the *Tawhid* methodological worldview in the rise of the corresponding economic and socio-scientific reasoning. Examples will be provided to bring out the contrariety between the two opposing worldviews of science, society, and the economic world system, and of morality, ethics, and the world system with its particularity in economics.

An example here is of the problem of Islamic economics copying from orthodox and mainstream economic leaning. The example is that of acceptance of marginal rate of substitution or the opportunity cost idea in existing idea of Islamic economics. Such marginalist idea leads into the substitution between social justice and economic efficiency as substitutes. Both of these are dear to Islamic epistemological reasoning. They are internalized in endogenous choice behavior in social preferences and their technological implications. In *Tawhidi* methodological worldview morality and ethics are endogenously embedded in human inclinations by consciousness. They are not determined exogenously by costly external imposition, as by government and policing by the state. Humankind for the common good of wellbeing *(maslaha)* and purpose (*maqasid as-shari'ah*) naturally accepts the *shari'ah* (Islamic law). The *maqasid as-shari'ah* is not coerced law, as the *Qur'an* declares (10:32–33): "Such is God your real Cherisher and Sustainer: Apart from Truth, what (remains) but error? Thus, is the Word of thy Lord proved true against those who rebel: Verily they will not believe."

For whom is this book appropriate?

This book is recommended for students who have acquired a rigorous course of economics as science and with critical thinking. Indeed, TIE studied in the light of its epistemological foundations and as a scientific discipline should only be taken up after the student has obtained introductory economics courses or better has done economics at the intermediate level. Indeed, the study of economics in the light of its epistemological issues is taught to International Baccalaureate (IB) students as a general mandatory course.

The internet version of IB TOK course states the significance of the TOK: "Theory of knowledge (TOK) is assessed through an oral presentation and a 1,600-word essay. It asks students to reflect on the nature of knowledge, and on how we know what we claim to know. TOK is part of the International Baccalaureate (IB) Diploma Programme (DP) core, and is mandatory for all students." For introduction to the theme of epistemology as scientific methodology, see Martin (2010).

"TOK aims to make students aware of the interpretative nature of knowledge, including personal ideological biases — whether these biases are retained, revised or rejected. It offers students and their teachers the opportunity to:

- *reflect critically on diverse ways of knowing and on areas of knowledge*
- *consider the role and nature of knowledge in their own culture, in the cultures of others and in the wider world.*

In addition, TOK prompts students to:

- *be aware of themselves as thinkers, encouraging them to become more acquainted with the complexity of knowledge*
- *recognize the need to act responsibly in an increasingly interconnected but uncertain world.*

TOK also provides coherence for the student, by linking academic subject areas as well as transcending them.
It therefore demonstrates the ways in which the student can apply their knowledge with greater awareness and credibility."

Conclusion: How this book ought to be studied?

In the wide scope, this book on TIE covers five distinctive areas under the *Tawhidi* methodology of unity of knowledge. These are as follows: (i) methodology; (ii) analytical formalism of the imminent theory of TIE; (iii) application to the important field of Islamic financial instruments in the light of TIE; (iv) analytical applications arising from the theory of TIE; and (v) supporting exercises and working examples encompassing all these areas.

The first three chapters are devoted to the study of *Tawhidi* methodology of unity of knowledge used for the nature of TIE in view of the *Qur'an*, the *sunnah*, and comparative intellectual discourse. The rest of the chapters are a combination of theoretical and applied contents in the light of a comparative study of the earlier chapter contents. Given below is the distribution of contents in this book in reference to the *Tawhidi* methodological worldview of this book in comparison and contrast to the mainstream and orthodox economic theory and its influence in the presently received idea of Islamic economics. These are not chapters of the book. The topics listed below comprise those that are contained in this book and which the students must learn. At the same time, the teachers of this book must learn TIE along with the students.

It should be noted that, because this book carries some rigorous and advanced treatment of the subject matter of TIE, it uses terms that are at an advanced level as well. These terminologies and concepts may arise from mainstream economics, which is studied at the introductory and intermediate-level economics courses. They may also arise from epistemological terminologies in establishing the *Tawhidi* analytical methodology, derived methods, formalism, and applications. It would therefore be necessary for the teacher to explain such terms at places where they are used in the text. Besides, the teacher ought to select out specific list of topics of his pertinent choice in TIE for introducing to students and for self-learning. Similar to the book, the lectures should of course use powerpoint presentations, diagrams, simple mathematical formalism, exercises, and examples towards delivering a comprehensive course of TIE.

Topics to be covered

Introduction

The foundational issues

1. *Tawhidi* Islamic economic methodology.
2. The scope of *Tawhidi* Islamic economics.
3. The formulation of *Tawhidi* Islamic economic model.
4. Islamic participatory instruments and the ethical dimensions.

Contrasting Islamic and mainstream theoretical issues: microeconomics

1. TIE contra mainstream consumer theory.
2. TIE contra mainstream theory of the firm.
3. TIE contra mainstream imperfect competition.
4. TIE contra mainstream general equilibrium theory.

Contrasting Islamic and mainstream theoretical issues: macroeconomics

1. TIE contra mainstream generation of outputs and macroeconomic variables.
2. Policy and institutional issues: money, finance and real economy, and general ethico-economic equilibrium.
3. *Maqasid as-shari'ah*, Islamicization, and *Tawhidi* Islamic economic science.
4. Conclusion: more examples and exercises.

Students' preparation

1. Undergraduate courses in microeconomics, macroeconomics.
2. Undergraduate mathematics: set theory, calculus, statistics.
3. Exegesis of the *Qur'an* and the *sunnah*.

A good number of exercises are given in the concluding chapter. Some examples of pertinent issues studied are presented within the respective chapters.

The teacher of this course using this book should keep in view a selective number of topics in mind while leaving out the more detailed and rigorous ones for later treatment growing out of maturity of the students. There is no need to overwhelm the students with difficult areas all at once in the beginning, though this book is a substantively rigorous work of TIE as the explication and application of the *Tawhidi* epistemic core of the truly Islamic methodological worldview contra mainstream economics and Islamic economics in the mainstream garb.

TIE represents a rigorous course of a scientific and analytical treatment of economic issues in general and their Islamic perspective in particular. Its best slot for teaching is after the student has taken up introductory and intermediate courses in microeconomics and macroeconomics. By this level of maturity, the student would have also acquired mathematical preparation to understand the analytics and the terminology of TIE and the concepts of mainstream economic terms and theories. This will help the teacher and students to have a critical approach to the study of mainstream and neoclassical economics. There is no good reason for teaching any good course in Islamic economics at sub-standard levels below the levels comprising TIE. Any such course cannot ignore the inclusion of a sound content of methodology, therefore, epistemology and ontology, and the corresponding analytical understanding of what the true Islamic orientation in economics and socio-scientific project is as a metascientific worldview. Such is the holistic content of TIE. A version of this chapter by this author that deals with Islamic economic pedagogy is to appear in the journal, *ISRA: International Journal of Islamic Finance*, 10:2, 2018.

References

Bohr, N. (1985). "Discussions with Einstein on Epistemological Issues", in *The Philosophy of Niels Bohr: The Framework of Complementarity*, H. Folse (Ed.), Amsterdam, Netherlands: North Holland Physics Publishing.

Karim, F. (n.d). *Imam Ghazzali's Ihya Ulum-Id-Din*, Lahore, Pakistan: Shah Muhammad Ashraf.

Lawson, T. (2003). "An Evolutionary Economics?", in *Reorienting Economics*, London, England: Routledge, pp. 110–140.

Mahomedy, A. C. (2013). "Islamic economics: still in search of an identity", *International Journal of Social Economics*, 40(6), pp. 556–578.

Martin, R. M. (2010). *Epistemology: A Beginner's Guide*, London, England: Oneworld Publication.

McCloskey, D. N. (1985). *The Rhetoric of Economics*, Wisconsin, Minnesota: The University of Wisconsin Press, pp. 36–61.

Naqvi, S. N. H. (2003). *Perpectives on Morality and Human Wellbeing*, Leicester, Leicestershire: The Islamic Foundation.

Rozenthal, F. (1958). *Muqaddimah, an Introduction to History*, Vols. 1–3, London, England: Routledge & Kegan Paul.

Waltzer, R. (1985). *Al-Farabi on the Perfect state*, Translated by Walzer, R., Oxford, England: Clarendon Press.

Chapter 2

Tawhidi Islamic Economic Methodology

What is the meaning of socio-scientific methodology in its wide conception? How is the economic analysis derived from such a broad socio-scientific methodology? What is the relevance of Islamic epistemology in this broad concept of methodology?

These are the fundamental questions that must be first inquired into before a meaningful foundation of the Islamic methodological worldview can be erected, and through this, a generalized foundational worldview of any Islamic socio-scientific field can be explained. It is through such foundational inquiry that the substantive difference between *Tawhidi* Islamic economic (TIE) and mainstream economic ideas, conception, formalism, and applications can be established.

Methodology in occidental thought

Methodology is fundamentally an epistemological matter (Pheby, 1988). The term "epistemology" means theory of knowledge (Bartley *et al.*, 1988). It also explains the most reduced premise of knowledge as a generalized way of studying our real conceptions of the nature of the world and its problems under study. Epistemology also includes the area of formulation of knowledge towards investigating the problems under study. It also gives the expectations that can be derived from the particular form of theory of knowledge used for the study of problems under investigation.

All theories of knowledge assume that reason and rationality and its substantive overarching domain of rationalism are the foundations of the theory of knowledge (Descartes, 1954). Yet, epistemology as the core of methodology remains substantively divergent in its understanding between different cultures, theories, worldviews, and religions. The critically debated issue is based on how the meanings of reason, rationality, and rationalism are derived (Smart, 2000). These are substantive terms in the construction of the worldview of socio-scientific conceptual and applied dimensions. Thereby, we ask the question by the epistemic core of methodology: How can the broadest theory of scientific inquiry be defined for all areas of inquiry? Popper (2004) referred to this selection criterion for the truly scientific nature of inquiry as the problem of demarcation. It means the separation of science from pseudo-science.[1]

The broader question that emerges is this: does science as we have inherited by its characterization in the realm of analytics and applications present a complete theory of science? Or are such theories simply a temporary and incomplete vision for studying reality, which is formally conceptualized and examined experimentally, merely in the light of how the world is observed and interpreted by the inquirer? In other words, such a pursuit of the scientific enterprise in every area of knowledge is defined by the rationalist worldview leading to a reasoned space of concept and action as understood by the inquirer, his model, and the instruments of investigation? These approaches then lead to further abstraction that generate more of the same in diversity *ad infinitum* (Popper, 1998).

---

[1] The Qur'an rejects the field of rationalism because of its vagaries in understanding truth as a holistic unity. The Qur'an (28:50) declares: "But if they hearken not to thee, know that they only follow their own lusts: and who is more astray than one who follows his own lusts, devoid of guidance from Allah? For Allah guides not people given to wrong-doing."

Some examples to bring out the meaning
of methodology in occidental thought

Examples are legion in the above-mentioned areas of questioning on methodology in relation to the concepts of rationalism, reason, and rationality: Water is chemically H_2O — two atoms of hydrogen and one atom of oxygen. Yet, if we are to conceive of the humanly useful meaning of water with all its minerals, the chemical definition does not complete the human wellbeing function of water. Instead of the H_2O definition of water for human wellbeing, the example of *Zamzam* is in point. *Zamzam* is believed by Muslims to continue offering spiritual and health benefits to human kind until the end of time.

Take another example. Rational choices by human will are not necessarily tied to moral conscience. In occidental epistemological sense, rational choices are determined simply by free will as decreed by individual and collective social affirmation. Thus, an open field of choices to accept, to reject, and re-choices appear in the global markets carrying human preferences linked with such rational choices. No moral conscience is necessarily needed.

Such are the ethically defeating markets, choices, and preferences that the *Qur'an* and the *sunnah* overrule out of good choices. In Occidentalism, there are no consciously governing market choices in rational choice theory other than the individual and collective free will. In this sense of individualism, the human claim on free will becomes contrary to the injunctions and the purpose and objective of the *shari'ah* — the *maqasid as-shari'ah* relating to individual, collective, and social choices for the common good.

In this respect, the recent business clamor regarding good corporate governance and corporate social responsibility are merely carried through within the so-called industrial democratic institutional environment. The institutional collective preference on choice is once again governed by the collectivity of individual preferences based on methodological individualism. This in turn is subsumed by the free will of rational choice maker. The free will of rational choice in turn arises from the totality of socio-scientific rationalism.

In the above examples, we note that the overarching presence of rationalism in free will determines rational choices. Such choices reflect the perceptions and decisions of individually determined categories. The underlying notion of abstraction based on methodological individualism does not establish a set worldview. Consequently, socio-scientific inquiry ends up in random conceptions of reality. A plethora of rationalist thoughts concerning free will is called in the literature of political economy as the problem of overdetermination (Resnick and Wolff, 1987). Popper (1998) refers to such a situation of preferences, choice, and abstraction of thought in the venue of methodological individualism as undecidability in epistemologies. Undecidability is the permanent feature of the theory of knowledge in occidental socio-scientific worldview.

Analytical definition of methodology in occidental thought and the Islamic rebuttal

The idea of rationalism that underlies occidental understanding of reason, rationality, and rational choice needs to be explained. In the Western model of epistemology, such randomness of free will arises from the rendering like that of Kant (1949) and Hume (1988).

Kant divided his theory of knowledge in reasoning that is differentiated between *a priori* domain comprising the moral imperative, and the worldly reasoned *a posteriori* domain of sensate forms and schemes. There is independence between these pure and practical ways of reasoning, respectively. The dichotomy referred to as antinomy is shown in Figure 2.1.

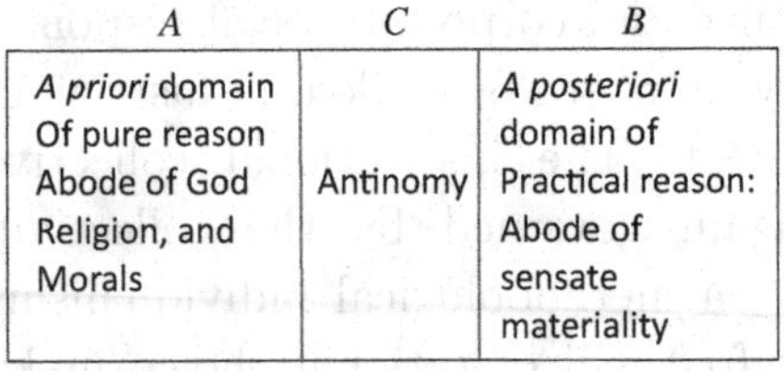

A	C	B
A priori domain Of pure reason Abode of God Religion, and Morals	Antinomy	A posteriori domain of Practical reason: Abode of sensate materiality

Figure 2.1. Rationalism as free will: Independence of the formal law of moral determination from the worldly law.

Islamic rebuttal of Kantian idea of rationalism

Figure 2.1 points out that the divine law as the law of monotheism is not subsumed in free will. It resides in the *a priori* domain independently of the free will, which resides in choices of the *a posteriori* domain independently by itself. Thus, in Kantian socio-scientific methodology (Choudhury, 2016) of independence between *a priori* and *a posteriori* domains of pure and practical reasoning, respectively, the rational process commences in the *B*-domain independently of the *A*-domain. Thus, all worldly rational matter has its emergence in the *a posteriori* domain.

On such a delineation of the origin of knowledge of two independent kinds, Kant (1949, p. 25) wrote: "This, then, is a question which at least calls for closer examination, and does not permit any off-hand answer: whether there is any knowledge that is thus independent of experience and even of all impressions of the senses. Such knowledge is entitled *a priori*, and is distinguished from the empirical, which has its sources *a posteriori*, that is, in experience." Kant (1977, p. 25) continues on: "In what follows, therefore, we shall understand by *a priori* knowledge, no knowledge independent of this or that experience, but knowledge absolutely independent of all experience. Opposed to it is empirical knowledge, which is knowledge possible only *a posteriori*, that is through experience."

These explanations regarding the nature of occidental socio-scientific thought thus point out the subjective nature of a disconnected methodology that separates God from the experimental domain. This is the meaning of antinomy. Contrarily, in Islamic socio-scientific thought, God by His law of monotheism is integral with the experimental domain of reality. This law unifies *A*-domain with *B*-domain and renders the *C*-domain null and void. Islamic knowledge ingrained in the monotheistic law and functioning in the socio-scientific order is thus the law of unity of knowledge. Such a functional unity between *A*-domain and *B*-domain is made possible pervasively in "everything" by the Islamic epistemic methodology of the *Qur'anic* law of unity of being and becoming, and by the *sunnah* that carries the *Qur'an* into our practical domain of human action.

An important reflection arising from the framework of unity of knowledge in Islamic socio-scientific methodology is the fact that, by the annulment of antinomy in the *C*-domain, Islamic methodology premised on monotheism and completeness absorbs "everything" within it. This is possible in Islam by making the *A*-domain and the *B*-domain analytically continuous within its methodological framework of monotheistic unity of knowledge. Such an analytical continuity of interrelationships between *a priori* and *a posteriori* domains of reasoning also explains the organic relational unity between the divine law and the world system. Occidental socio-scientific methodology is unable to realize such a socio-scientific continuity and completeness. That is because of the independence of *A*-domain and *B*-domain by the intervening gap of antinomy (*C*-domain).

The impossibility to obtain unity of knowledge as the methodological core of scientific holism

Hume (1988) gave the opposite understanding of scientific thinking as methodology in Kant. In Kant's methodology that predominantly governs all of occidental theory and reasoning in science, the moral imperative is primal. But it is separated from the experimental and sensate world system. Hence, the inability of integrating the *a priori* and the *a posteriori* domains in Kant's methodology led to surrendering to the free will in the *a posteriori* domain. The moral law was indeed primal above all. This law ought to be invoked in the elucidating thought and actions concerning the world system. Yet, there is no analytical function to integrate the two domains by any permanent law. The idea of rationalism in Kant is thus the idea of integrating the moral imperative of the *a priori* domain with the *a posteriori* domain of experimental and sensate actions. But there is no original law in place, and no command by law and guidance that would cause the two domains to become integrated and blended in the continuous sense. Such integration is referred to as endogenous functional relationship between interrelating domains, that is, between *a priori* and *a posteriori* domains, each reinforcing the other by cause and effect circularly. In Kant, this kind of unification of knowledge of the two domains in a continuous interactive and integrated way is not possible. So, the Kantian (occidental) methodology of rationalism made the moral law rest on the free will of the individual and collectivity in the *a priori* sense. But, the *a posteriori* domain does not establish an analytic and endogenous interrelationship with the *a priori* moral imperative.

The endogenous (interactively combined into integrated system) and continuous nature of inter-system cause–effect feedback relationship (circularity) is otherwise essential in understanding the role of the theory of unity of knowledge and its induction of the generality and details of world system in which sciences are erected. Indeed, for a long time now, the methodologists of the history of economic thought have argued on opposite sides whether economics is a science or not in the sense of whether economics has an extensive experimental possibility over human affairs and rational behavior (Schumpeter, 1968; Blaug, 1968). The matter is disputed at the methodological level of questioning regarding interconvertibility of reversible relations between multiple domains, or systems, or between variables representing these systems. Examples are emergent *a priori* and *a posteriori* domains across sequences of abstractions. Each of these abstractions stands for a perception under rationalist scientific theory.

The gap between *a priori* and *a posteriori* domains means that any law cannot explain certain domains, e.g. the Kantian antinomy. The result then is rendering the continuity and the inter-system endogenous relations to be null and void. Friedrich, in his translation (Kant, 1977), writes on such a characteristic of Kantian and thereby about the occidental nature of scientific methodology in the following words by translating Kant. Kant wrote in regard to the dualism in rationalist reasoning: "In what follows, therefore, we shall understand by *a priori* knowledge, no knowledge independent of this or that experience, but knowledge absolutely independent of all experience. Opposed to it is empirical knowledge, which is knowledge possible only *a posteriori*, that is, through experience. *a priori* modes of knowledge are entitled pure when there is no admixture of anything empirical." We note thereby that Kant's epistemology fails to provide a unity of knowledge at the origin of thought pertaining to science, its entities or variables, forms, their mathematical relations, abstractions, applications, and explanations.

The properties of continuity and interconvertible analytic functional relationship are essential to understand the methodology of unity of knowledge and its opposite, the property of antinomy, as shown in Figure 2.1. This point of the difference between endogenous interrelations and its opposite as exogenous mono-causal relationship is essential in understanding the substantive differences between occidental methodology of rationalism, rationality, and reason and the Islamic methodological worldview of unity of knowledge. The *Qur'an* refers to this grand design of the universe in terms of the law of *Tawhid*. The overarching field of the term stands for the strictest monotheism, of the divine law, just as also of the teleological precept of *Allah* as the Absolute One.

Endogeneity, multi-causality, and unity of knowledge in scientific methodology

At an early point in this book, Figure 2.2 explains this substantive difference between occidental and Islamic epistemic methodology in regards to multi-causality, organic interrelations of unity of knowledge, endogenous circular causation relations, continuity, and reversibility. These properties are not universal in occidental socio-scientific thought. Thereby, the methodological implications of the occidental socio-scientific thought and Islamic methodological worldview in science are not identical. Despite this, there are details of phenomena that can be equivalent, as far as reason and logical formalism of unity of knowledge establishes or rejects acceptance of facts.

An example in occidental and Islamic methodological contrasts of socio-scientific meaning

A salient example of acceptance of scientific domain is coplanar mathematics in mono-causal reasoning and rejection of Cartesian formulations in multi-dimensional ethically induced formal analytical complexes. The opposite scientific views are by monotheism in

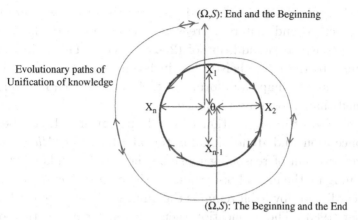

Figure 2.2. The *Tawhidi* methodology of unity of knowledge: From the Beginning to the End.

Islamic epistemology and free will in Occidentalism. Consider the issue of pre-determinism of the divine law in Islamic creation methodology. Contrarily, there is the anthropological belief of creation in terms of free will of the occidental genre.

Definitions: rationalism, mono-causality, multi-causality, organic relations, unity of knowledge, circular causation relations, continuity, reversibility

The term rationalism was explained in reference to Figure 2.1. From the concept of rationalism *vis-à-vis* free will, inter-system differentiation, and antinomy, there arises the derivation of the concept of reason and rationality. We explain the latter attributes now, as derived from the overarching concept of rationalism in the occidental methodology of science.

Reason via rationalism

By the nature of rationalism according to occidental methodology of scientific belief as was explained in terms of Figure 2.1 and by Kantianism, reason by free will is the intrinsic quality of humankind and the consciousness nature of the conscious world. For example, consider $(2+2)$ do not equal anything else than 4 in whatever ways

the system of addition is defined. Yet, this is an *a posteriori* truth
as so observed and materially reasoned. On the side of the *a priori*
domain, consider the addition of (2+2) for God. This is impossible
according to the monotheistic law in Islam, for God (*Allah*) is not
incarnate in any shape and form.[2] Yet, *Allah* has given laws and has
ordained shape, form, and balance.

Therefore, the implication of the Supercardinal Being bearing
no conception and dimension for the attributes of *Allah*[3] in the
a priori domain of reasoning must be the unique explanatory root
of defining mathematical operations in the *a posteriori* domain. Yet,
supercardinality by itself remains the immeasurable large cardinality
(Rucker, 1983). The implication then is reversible authentication by
the material world system to confirm and advance the original epistemology of Supercardinal Being.[4] (2+2) is then imminently contained
in the supercardinality of the divine law. Yet, the supercardinal

---

[2] *Qur'an(Iqlas,* 112, 1–4).

[3] *Qur'an* (87:1).

[4]Supercardinality (Ω) is the abstract mathematical topology (non-dimensional
mathematical function) that establishes the following continuous functionals: (i)
$S \subset \Omega$ by way of the reversible relational functional, $\Omega \leftrightarrow S$. (ii) Likewise the
functionals, $S \leftrightarrow X$; and thus, $\Omega \leftrightarrow S \leftrightarrow X$. (iii) Therefore, the example of the
organically unified domains of *a priori* and *a posteriori* multi-causal reversible
relations are defined by knowledge flows according to unity of knowledge and
denoted by $\{\theta\} \subset \{X\} \in (\Omega, S)$ by the relationship $(\Omega, S) \leftrightarrow \{X\} \leftrightarrow \{\theta\}$.
In the example of mathematical operation, $\{X\} \leftrightarrow \{\theta\} \Leftrightarrow \{\mathbf{X}(\theta)\}; (\Omega, S)$ as
the epistemology; thereby, say, $(2+2) \leftrightarrow 2^\theta.2^\theta = 2^{2\theta}$ and higher analytic forms
of 2^θ. In the end, since $\{\theta\} \in (\Omega, S)$; therefore, the functional, $\{2^\theta, 2^{2\theta}, \ldots\} \equiv$
divine law in one case (*sunnat Allah*) $\in (\Omega, S)$, the totality mapped by the
advancing understanding and application of the *sunnah* as ontological mapping
of the supercardinal domain of *sunnat Allah*, denoted by S. Hence, a numerical
equivalence is established between the supercardinal domain of *sunnat Allah*
through the *sunnah* and the experimental world system. All functions are
interrelations $(\leftrightarrow)$. Such interrelations are interconvertible by reversibility of
knowledge production and continuity, involving simply the corporeal function
and extension of the reading, understanding, and applying of the monotheistic
law (unity of knowledge) in the order of world system in all shapes and
forms (extendability across systems and their organically relations, meaning
complementary multi-causal reversible relations. The property of multi-causal
reversibility by the organic interrelations is that of continuity in knowledge, space,
and time.

attribute of the divine law defines "reason" (2+2) as logical formalism in the *a posteriori domain*. We write:

$$\text{Supercardinality } (a \ priori) \rightarrow (2+2) \ (a \ posteriori)$$

$$\rightarrow \text{Supercardinality } (a \ priori).$$

Completion of reasoning

The positioning of the Supercardinal Being through the monotheistic law has now become extendable in the multi-dimensions of knowledge ($\{\theta\} \in (\Omega, S)$), space $\{X(\theta)\}$, time $(t(\theta)) \equiv Z(\theta)$. The methodology of and by reasoning in socio-scientific details take place by the continuity of evolutionary learning in the event domain $(E(.))$ across (knowledge, space, time). Thus, reasoning in Islam pervades the continuity of the *a priori* and the *a posteriori* domains by the logical annulment of "antinomy" in Figure 2.1 and its replacement by the continuous (Figure 2.2) multi-causal circular organic relations between entities, variables, and systems. Each point of the path of events, $E(Z(\theta))$, is a co-ordinate point interrelating God, man, and universe in unified consciousness that is determined and continued across history by the emergent events.

In Kantian domain and thereby the occidental socio-scientific thought, $E(Z(\theta))$ is dichotomous between *a priori* reasoning $\equiv$ $E_1(Z_1(\theta_1))$, all symbols belonging to the *a priori* domain and *a priori* reasoning. $E_2(Z_2(\theta_2))$ denotes the presence of antinomy. $E_3(Z_3(\theta_3))$ denotes the *a posteriori* domain. In Islamic epistemological reasoning (methodology), $E(Z(\theta))$ is unified, continuous, and organically interrelated by circular causation across systems from the beginning to the end.[5]

Rationality via reasoning and rationalism

Rationality in scientific terms comprises the reasoned attitude governed by rationalism to make choices of everything that underlies such *maqasid*-choices, be they of individual preferences or

---

[5] *Qur'an* (57:3; 92:13).

institutional, national, and collective preferences. Being based on choices governed by reason via rationalism, the scientific meaning of rationality becomes a convenience attained by assigning convenient attributes to solve problems. The implication then is this: Individual, institutional, national, and global preference arrangements are formed such that they can solve impending problems facing such choices for the interest of the decision-making groups.

Rationality derived from rationalism

How is rationality in the methodological sense derived from reason via rationalism? An example is used here to explain such derivation. We consider here three kinds of rationality as attributes of individual and collective preferences on decision-making. These are moral rationality, procedural rationality, and consequentialist rationality (Etzioni, 1988).

Moral rationality in terms of Kantian *a priori* reasoning is a differentiated ethical concept of humanism as opposed to the existence and application of the moral law. The example is the moral imperative of the competing concept of freedom in choices that substitute between social justice and economic efficiency (economic growth). In the *a priori* sense of the Kantian moral imperative, social justice substitutes for economic efficiency and economic growth. This is also the approach of Rawls (1971). The predominance of the moral imperative is an altruistic view of moral rationality. This claim was once voiced in the Soviet Union. Yet, it proved to be at the utter disadvantage of economic goals. The possibility of integrating social justice and economic growth (efficiency) remains unexplained as a methodological fact.

On the other hand, the neoclassical approach to rational choices causes substitution of social justice by economic choices based on self-interest and personal gains under given amount of resources and the freely competing will of the decision-maker. This is Nozick's (2001) approach on the topics of taxation, property rights, and what he refers to as the moral abhorrence of government intervention in economic resource allocation.

The integration between the goals of social justice and economic growth cannot be possible in the case of an endogenous and continuously complementary interrelationship. Exogenously, governments may opt for external injection of funds and technological advancement coming out of taxation. Endogenous nature of production relations and resource distribution is abandoned. Consequentially, social participation and continuity of resource development and resource mobilization are lost.

Procedural rationality

This is the form of rationality arising from convenience and social pressure to accomplish tasks. Such an attitude towards problem solving is driven by the postulate of self-interest to optimize certain so-called objective goals. Procedural rationality is also a form of mismatch between *a priori* and *a posteriori* reasoning based on the optimal use of limited resources of opportunity to otherwise make more discursively oriented mutual benefit available to all parties in discourse and in the context of continuous opportunities to share knowledge-induced resources at all levels. An example in this case is to confront a common enemy by befriending old enemies, which is the case of procedural rationality caused by the absence of a discursive social behavior overall. Much of the global wars and conflicts continue on because of belligerent character in the absence of participatory behavior that can generate understanding (Choudhury, 1996).

Consequentialist rationality

This concept carries an empirical meaning. That is, rational behavior relating to either material acquisitions or political acquisitions, which turn out into self-interest material considerations, are weighed in terms of quantitative benefits and costs (net benefits) to determine the decision to act or not to act on a specific course of decision-making. Game-theory method is used to determine the optimal payoff for strategies. In every one of such approaches to evaluate the effects of the consequentialist rational decision-maker, there is no methodological explanation to endogenously interrelate *a priori* reason of the transcendental ego and the *a posteriori* reason of empiricism. Walsh (1985) forcefully writes: "He saw no possible intermediary form of intellectual activity between that of an intuitive intelligence, creating its objective, and that of an informing intelligence, imposing intelligible forms on sensed objects. He (Kant) completely overlooked and ignored the possibility of abstracting intelligence. Thus, in the Kantian 'reconstruction' of knowledge, the value and function attributed to the objective datum is so reduced that the weight of reconstruction must be borne almost exclusively by the activity of the knowing subject."

An example of consequentialist rationality is the quantitative cost-benefit evaluation of an investment project upon which an acceptance or rejection of the project is decided. Yet, not simply by the question of non-acceptability of this method based on consequentialist rationality, but also by the absence of endogenous ethical quantification of cash flows and exogenously felt moral appropriateness of the projects, the methodology of the moral imperative remains uncertain, undetermined, and thus void.

By taking the above three kinds of rationality concepts, we can premise the rationality concept on the rationalist and consequential reason according to the Kantian calculus of dichotomy and moral differentiation, his antinomy. This problem of differentiation between *a priori* and *a posteriori* components of reasoning, rather than establishing their organic unity of being at the level of the ontological truth (oneness of God) is referred to as heteronomy.

The following conditions for rational economic behavior are categorized in respect of mainstream economic arguments:

(1) Economic resources remain fixed and given for preferred decision-making unless these are exogenously changed by injection of resources and technological change.
(2) The objective criterion is optimized by means of scarce resources that are allocated between competing ends.
(3) Steady-state equilibrium is the result of allocating scarce resources between competing ends.
(4) Self-interest rather than sharing prevails. Consequently, preferences remain datum.

(5) Freedom of property rights prevails.

(6) The combination of the above-mentioned properties of allocation of scare resource among competing ends leads to marginal substitution of one choice by another.[6]

(7) All agents are predicted to abide by the above-mentioned rules as internally consistent behavior in optimal decision-making.

(8) The combination of the above-mentioned properties of economic rationality establishes transitivity of choices and preferences for economically rational agents, e.g. consumers, producers, and other agents.[7]

The postulates of mainstream economic rationality contra knowledge-induced theory

The entire mainstream economics, especially that explained by neo-classical microeconomics and neoclassical macroeconomics, upholds the above generalization of the postulates of economic rationality. In turn, as explained above, such postulates are derived from the concept of rationalism and reason and different concepts of rationality in the framework of the Kantian-type methodology of the *a priori* contra *a posteriori* reasoning.

Consequently, in the event-plane of learning denoted by $\{\theta\}$, ethical choices denoted by $\{X(\theta)\}$, which includes technological change, innovation, and policies and strategies, the preferences of all kinds by agents, denoted by $\{\wp(\theta)\}$ over time $t(\theta)$ must necessarily generate endogenous interrelations. Such an event domain is not possible in the case of economic rationality of the mainstream genre. Consequently, the induction by the endogenous learning effect of $\{\theta\}$ causes continuous changes across all the elements of the rationalist-based reason and economic rationality. Only the presence of exogenously enforced new forms of change can cause shifts.

---

[6]Marginal rates of substitution between goods, inputs of production, and social choices are the logical derivation from the condition of optimal allocation of resources between competing ends.

[7]Preferences thus remain datum and are devoid of the endogenous learning behavior and technological induction.

But such shifts are not endogenously automated in the system of analysis that is driven by continuous learning interrelationships between diverse entities, variables, and systems. Consequently, the role of endogenous induction of knowledge arises from the unity of relations of *a priori* and *a posteriori* domains.

David Hume's *a posteriori* materialism in socio-scientific methodology

Contrary to the moral imperative foundation of Kantian thought, though disabled by the problem of antinomy persisting all through, there is the epistemological thought of Hume. Hume's epistemological thought has also profoundly influenced occidental socio-scientific methodology in the domain of empiricism and experimental foundation of scientific knowledge. Hume, contrary to Kant, argued that the epistemological origin of science lies in the sensate world of forms and relations and their interactions.

To Hume, the origin of knowledge is derived from the cognition of memory, impression, imagination, relations, modes, and substances. Thus, through these elements of human possibility to attain reason and to construct a methodological order, Hume took the mind and matter relationship purely at the level of human free will. This was reason determined at the sensate origin of meanings by interrelations. Human imagination, memory, and the continuity of forms and relations in space–time domains were the building blocks of Hume's characterization of scientific methodology. The divine law, which is the *a priori* domain, was thus divorced from Hume's *a posteriori* reasoning. The latter accounted solely in Hume's methodological development of scientific thought.

Thus, while Kantian approach to methodology was of the deductive type, Hume's methodology is premised on logical positivism and induction.

Hume (1992, p. 1) wrote:

> "All the perceptions of the human mind resolve themselves into two distinct kinds, which I shall call Impressions and Ideas .....
> Those perceptions, which enter with most force and violence, we may name impressions; and under this name I comprehend all

our sensations, passions and emotions, as they make their first appearance in the soul. By ideas I mean the faint images of these in thinking and reasoning."

On his extended methodological premise Hume wrote (*op cit.* p. xvi):

"And as the science of man is the only solid foundation for the other sciences, so the only solid foundation we can give to this science itself must be laid on experience and observation."

Furthermore, he wrote, (*op cit.* p. xvii):

"For me it seems evident, that the essence of the mind being equally unknown to us with that of external bodies, it must be equally impossible to form any notion of its powers and qualities otherwise than from careful and exact experiments, and the observation of those particular effects, which result from its different circumstances and situations. And tho' we must endeavor to render all our principles as universal as possible, by tracing up our experiments to the utmost, and explaining all effects from the simplest and fewest causes, [i]t is still certain we cannot go beyond experience; and any hypothesis, that pretends to discover the ultimate original qualities of human nature, ought at first to be rejected as presumptuous and chimerical."

The above narration clearly establishes the ultimate source of scientific phenomena to which Hume assigned the roots of knowledge. It is also clear that the source of the divine unity of knowledge remained beyond the realm of Hume's idea of rationalism. The divine law could not be incorporated in Hume's extension of the relational order of impressions, forms, imagination, and memory to the deductive and the inductive knowledge-induced domains organically unified with each other by intercausality. This is the essence of the episteme of unity of knowledge integrating the *a priori* with the *a posteriori*, the deductive with the inductive, and divine knowledge with the knowledge-induced world system taken in generality and detail.

Hume's relational order is categorized from simple to complex. His complex form is simply a causal assemblage of simple forms. Hence, in the language of linearly separable forms and the meaning of causality between interacting forms, these are not substantively integrated in forming complex forms. There is only a lateral aggregation of simple forms to cause complex forms to arise.

Hume wrote in regard to his concept of causally determined complex forms in relation to simple forms (*op cit.* p. 13):

> "Amongst the effects of this union or association of ideas, there are none more remarkable, than those complex ideas, which are the common subjects of our thoughts and reasoning, and generally arise from some principle of union among our simple ideas. These complex ideas may be divided into Relations, Modes, and Substances."

Hume's concepts of modes and substances in themselves are also a collection of simple ideas. He wrote (*op cit.* p. 16):

> "The idea of a substance as well as that of a mode, is nothing but a collection of simple ideas, that are united by the imagination, and have a particular name assigned them, by which we are able to recall, either to ourselves or others, that collection."

Hume's concept of "relation" exists in association with the infinite divisibility of space and time. His universe reflects unity within which every part is infinitely reducible. A relation in such an infinitely divisible order is a linear concept of interconnectedness by means of contiguity and continuity purely in the *a posteriori* domain.

Summary of the occidental methodology in reference to Kant and Hume

Thereby, the dichotomous nature of epistemological reasoning is firmly established in occidental scientific methodology. The consequentialist nature of the world is devoid of the unity of knowledge in the framework signified by unification between deductive reasoning and inductive reasoning. This is the same as the differentiation between *a priori* reasoning and *a posteriori* reasoning, and between Kant and Hume. Yet, each and every one of these perspectives of reasoning is barred from the analytic nature of endogenous continuity and logical formalism of the law of monotheism (unity of knowledge).

Summarizing Kant and Hume's rationalist thought

1. Kantian impossibility of deriving complex forms for the quantitative forms of the world system was discussed earlier and carried over into a footnote.

2. Consider a numerical example: Hume's *a posteriori* reasoning assigns the numerical value to the sequence, $\{n^\theta, (n+1)^\theta, \ldots\} \rightarrow \infty^\infty$, with $n = 1, 2, \ldots, \infty$; $\theta = 1, 2, \ldots, \infty$. This is an undefined result in the *a posteriori* domain of empirical relations. Hence, such a sequence cannot explain the *a priori* result in terms of the precept of Supercardinal Being (Ω), which cannot be taken as infinity because of the non-numerical nature of supercardinality. Rather, Ω denotes the topological entirety of the divine law (*sunnat Allah*), immeasurable, but generating causal relations ($\leftrightarrow$) between the divine law and the experiential world system through the mapping by the *sunnah*, S. These dynamics were explained earlier.

Another example is this: Hume's inductive reasoning independently of the divine law implies that the postulate of economic rationality cannot have a time measure explained by $t(\theta)$. This would otherwise mean the determination of events recorded in time but under induction of unity of knowledge. Contrarily, in the explanation of the postulate of economic rationality, time, preference, and technology are datum. Knowledge as learning is terminally benign at the optimal and steady-state points of fixed resource allocation. Economics is non-processual science. If knowledge flows are endogenously continuous, then resources are continuously reproduced and distributed in society at large under the impact of intervariable causality and continuity of knowledge flows recorded over time.[8]

---

[8]Let $R(\theta)$ denote resources as a function of inputs, $\mathbf{X}(\theta) = \{X_1, X_2, \ldots, X_n\}[\theta]$. Thus, $R(\theta) = R(\mathbf{X}(\theta))$. Thereby, by continuous knowledge induction, $dR(\mathbf{X}(\theta))/d\theta = \Sigma_{i=1}^n (\partial R/\partial X_i).(dX_i/d\theta) \geq 0$ because of each $(\partial R/\partial X_i) \geq 0, (dX_i/d\theta) \geq 0$. But contrarily, $dR(\mathbf{X}(t))/dt = \Sigma_{i=1}^n (\partial R/\partial X_i).(dX_i/dt) = 0$, where the optimum and steady-state equilibrium points are attained as on the production possibility curve, the indifference curve, and production isoquants. In such a situation, $t(\theta) = t$, is independent of knowledge induction. If exogenous shocks $(\varepsilon(t), t = T_0, T_1, \ldots)$ are introduced, then, $R(t) = R(X(t)) + \varepsilon(T_i), I = 1, 2, \ldots$. At the resource optimal point, $R(T_i) = R(X(T_i)) + \varepsilon(T_i)$; $dR(\mathbf{X}(t))/dt = \Sigma_{i=1}^n (\partial R/\partial X_i).(dX_i/dt) + \Sigma_{i=1}^m \partial \varepsilon(T_i)/\partial t = 0$. Hence, the exogenous effect of resource injection dies away at a subsequent optimal and steady-state point. The nature of the theory of resource allocation in mainstream economics thus remains intact even following resource injunction. In endogenous resource allocation, the addition $\varepsilon(T_i)$ is unnecessary.

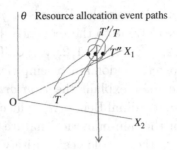

Figure 2.3. Historical paths with spheres of evolutionary neighborhoods of events $E(\theta, \mathbf{X}(\theta), t(\theta))$.[9]

Let us consider: If it is the case that a household budget, production function, and social choice individually or together sets up their resource allocation by way of economic and social participation, then such participation generates intercausal knowledge continued by knowledge induction of the interrelating variables. At any given point of time by continuous regeneration of knowledge via participation, the knowledge flows induce the continuous and endogenous participatory relationships between the variables. Thereby, the following intercausality occurs: $t(\theta) \leftrightarrow \{\theta\} \leftrightarrow R(\mathbf{X}(\theta))$. In such a case, the postulates of economic rationality are altered towards a knowledge-induced study of reason and rationality that annuls every trace of neoclassicism and its full mainstream methodological effect. Figure 2.3 depicts the knowledge-induced resource allocation path with some details.

In the end on rationalism, reason, and economic rationality

On the methodological scale of socio-scientific characterization, the attributes of reason and economic rationality are derived from the domain of rationalism. According to the nature of deductive and inductive thought and the postulates and models built on them,

---

[9]By characterizing the event path as a functional transform, we note the following result: $dE/d\theta = \Sigma_{i=1}^{n}(\partial E/\partial X_i)^*(dX_i/d\theta) \geq 0$, with plim $\{\theta_i\}_{t(\theta i)} = \theta_t$, hence, a convergent path TT is derived from multiple paths T', T'' etc. as shown.

contesting methodological worldviews arise. Scientific doctrines and methodologies are thereby demarcated between such contesting epistemologies.

The postulates of economic rationality as were noted have no endogenous ethics in them. There is therefore no *a priori* context in the postulates. Ethical endogeneity belongs to the *a posteriori* domain of humanism in every case. Endogenous ethics means inter-system causality of relations determined by the episteme of unity of knowledge. In occidental socio-scientific methodology, ethics acquires the role of the human free will in choices, decision-making, and individual, institutional, and social behavior even though sub-optimal and non-steady state conditions are conveyed by the simulation idea of satisficing. Satisficing conveys the postulate of bounded rationality (Simon, 1957).

The postulates of economic rationality in particular and in socio-scientific domain in general have remained benign of ethics as consciousness defining the endogenous interrelations. Morality and ethics everywhere and in "everything" of scientific investigation has remained an exogenous practice. It is precisely in the area of developing a sound and applicable theory of endogenous ethics and moral consciousness along with the experiential world system, as of economics and the natural sciences, the possibility lies (Wilson, 1998). This challenge of methodology belongs most profoundly and clearly to the Islamic methodological worldview of monotheistic unity of knowledge derived from the *Qur'an* combined with the *sunnah* and a discursive learned society.

Other definitions

Unity of knowledge

The foundational epistemological precept of unity of knowledge conveys the meaning of unity by multi-intercausal relations between all components of the *a priori* and the *a posteriori* domains. This invokes the nature of the law that drives reason and rationality as an endogenously integrated reality in human preferences constructed individually and collectively. Islamic understanding of reason and rationality also means the integration between the deductive reasoning and the inductive reasoning to reveal the reality of unity of knowledge and the consequential relational unity of the knowledge-induced world system.

The episteme of unity of knowledge as the epistemological origin of intellectual thought also conveys the meaning of organic pairing by relationship between entities, variables, and diverse systems. Organic pairing conveys the idea of participative shared relations. This involves learning gained by participation and complementarity, which present a form of systemic unity of knowledge between unifying knowledge-induced verities. The organic relationship of intercausal unity by pairing all around is caused by interaction leading to integration. This dynamic is thereby followed by the further potential for evolutionary learning arising by the confirmation of mutual wellbeing of the participants gained from the total learning processes.

Circular causation

Figure 2.2 explains that every selected variable, whether it is an ethical choice or otherwise, has reverse multi-causal relationships with the rest of the vector of variables to display the degree of positive complementarities or negative relations signifying substitutions that exist intervariable. This kind of a multi-regression equation model conveys several properties of learning systems:

(1) Unity of knowledge between the selected variables is conveyed by their endogenous intercausality.

(2) Such a meaning of unity of knowledge conveys organic relational unity by pairing.

(3) The evaluation of the multi-equations system is done at two stages. Firstly, the use of actual observations in the variables leads to "estimation" of the system. The results represent the positivistic state of circular causation intercausal relations.

The normative picture is conveyed by improvement of positive complementarities between the ethically chosen variables. This is the normative case study. It follows in the light of possible allocation of resources between the selected variables and their entities. The change from the positive (estimated) to the normative (simulated) change is done by selecting the coefficients of the intervariable relations to make them more complementary by a positive-signed change or less negative-signed coefficients as plausible. These technical methods will be explained further in this book.

Negative coefficients imply marginal rates of substitution, and thereby, an end to learning between the variables (or a "de-learning" state). Positive coefficients imply complementarities intervariable and thereby promote enhancement of learning.

(4) From such results, the total wellbeing conveyed by the interaction, integration, and participatory learning between the selected variables can be quantitatively evaluated.

(5) Policies and strategies can be generated by means of the "estimation" and "simulation" of the circular causation equations and the quantitative form of the wellbeing function also as endogenously related variables work with the rest.

(6) The "estimation" and "simulation" equations are further used to generate predictors of the circular causation variables.

(7) Interprocess evolution by means of the simulated results can be developed (Figure 2.3).

Continuity and reversibility

In what has preceded by way of explaining the endogenous inter-causal circular causation interrelationship between the diverse *a priori* and *a posteriori* domains, reversibility and continuity was implied by the interrelationship as of the circular causation equations (Figure 2.2). Such interrelations are symbolized by ($\leftrightarrow$). The interrelationships lead to the annulment of antinomy in Figure 2.1.[10]

---

[10] $dE(\theta, \mathbf{X}(\theta), t(\theta))/d\theta = \Sigma_{\mathbf{X}}(\partial E/\partial \mathbf{X}).(d\mathbf{X}/d\theta) + (\partial E/\partial t).(dt(\theta))/d\theta) > 0$ for every $\{\theta\} \in (\Omega, S)$ in the sense of multi-causal relations denoted by ($\leftrightarrow$). This means that the knowledge of the monotheistic law Ω and its transmission via S increases from the proofs of the experienced world system. On the other hand, if change is not functionally based on $\{\theta\}$, then t is independent of θ. Consequently,

The idea underlying the ultimate dependence of everything in Figure 2.3 on knowledge flows to describe a continuously changing system is that knowledge is instrumental in change whereby no consequences ever remains still in the midst of a participatory, complementary, and discursive medium. On the contrary, events in time in the absence of a methodology of knowledge embedding imperceptibly may not create change. Thus, the revolutionary change that had occurred in the modern world system is due to the endogenous nature of technological change (Romer, 1986).

Exercise 1

Try the following revisionary exercise in the extract given below:

(1) Identify the following properties: unity of differentiation of knowledge; organic relationship; mono-causality; multi-causality; endogenous interrelations; *a priori* domain; *a posteriori* domain; institutional discourse via preference formation.
(2) Construct a system-wise diagram like the one given in Figure 2.4 with answers to (1).

Palan (2002, p. 215) writes in regard to the axiomatic nature of neoclassicism and its prototypes vis-à-vis prescribed preferences and their enforcement by corporate and political governance versus the discursive worldview:

> "Modern institutionalist thought in particular is united in rejecting rationalist, progressivist, and crude-materialist explanations of social processes and practices. Rather than adopt simple ideas versus practice type of theory, they view 'the materiality of social institutions and their dynamics (as product) of evolving interrelated systems of institutions and discourse rather than as grounded in externalised and objective social realities'" (Cameron and Palan, 1999).

To economic neoclassicism, the externally imposed and institutionally enforced "objective external realities" are its axioms of

---

$dE(\mathbf{X(t)})/dt = \Sigma_{\mathbf{X}}(\partial E/\partial \mathbf{X}).(d\mathbf{X}/dt) = 0$, when optimum in $\mathbf{X}(t)$ values are attained.

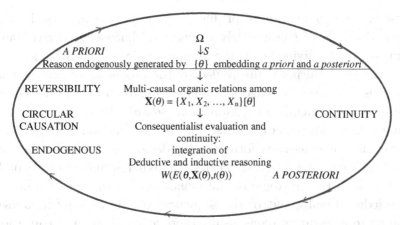

Figure 2.4. Interconnection between various properties of the learning relations: Unity of knowledge.

choices premised on the assumption of economic rationality. To other paradigms, the premise is one of assumed conflict and engagement between opposing sides in development paradigms. Such conflicts are construed as a form of marginal substitution appearing on the social versus economic planes with the intervening medium of institutions and polity. Even when discourse is promoted, it centers on one or the other form of such contending epistemologies of the development debate.

The Islamic monotheistic law as the methodological worldview contra Occidentalism

The central keynote and the substantively contrary methodology of Islamic world system in "everything" and thus in Islamic economics as a specifically methodology-driven scientific enterprise is its principal epistemology of monotheism (*Tawhid*). Thus, the caption we use in this book is *Tawhidi* Islamic Economics (TIE). In terms of the methodology of unity of knowledge, the representation of monotheism (*Tawhid*) is cast in the following way.

The domain of monotheism overarches the Supercardinal Being of the divine law (*sunnat Allah*). From the divine law is derived the precept of unity of knowledge as the phenomenon of multi-causality between the good things of life.[11] Such multi-causality in the embedded field of continuously regenerated knowledge derived and returned to the divine law is the manifest universal law of pairing in the *Qur'an*.[12] Pairing is unravelled by the properties of interaction, which is discourse by reflection and participation as established by the *Qur'anic* principles of consultation (*shura*) with conscious reflection of the issues under discourse (*tasbih*). Interaction is followed by integration as consensus formation in decision-making. Interaction together with integration describes the dynamic induction of preferences with the episteme of the monotheistic principle of unity of knowledge. Finally, out of the sequences of interaction (discourse) leading to integration (consensus), there arise the circular causation relations between the knowledge-induced variables by way of evaluation followed by continuity of learning as shown in Figure 2.4. This stage of the methodology of the monotheistic law is referred to as re-origination, and thus continuity of the new stages of knowledge reproduction and re-discovery regarding the generality and details of the world system taken up in diversity. Such evolutionary learning processes progress on continuously over the dimensions of knowledge, space, and time.[13] The monotheistic law thus transcends the sheer space–time structure on epistemological grounds (Bohr, 1985) to the widest limit of human intellection, responses from creation as inherent consciousness (*fitra*), and cognition, application, and empirical work all through.

The monotheistic law as the completion of the divine law (*sunnat Allah*) being in "everything" as the law of organic unifying interrelationship arising from the divine unity of knowledge, it performs two important tasks to establish its uniqueness and universality. The monotheistic overarching worldview brings out the nature, search, and discovery of the intercausal holism of the world systems (*a'lameen*) in terms of the monotheistic, i.e. *Tawhidi* meaning of

---

[11] *Qur'an* on the good things of life, *hallal at-tayyabah*. See also *Qur'an* (14:24, 25).

[12] *Qur'an* (36:36).

[13] *Qur'an* re-origination (27:64).

unity of knowledge and unification of the world system by organic pairing in and of "everything" (Barrow, 1991).

The uniqueness and universality of the monotheistic epistemological methodology is also manifest in the parallel formalism and application of the method and methodology of all disciplines of thoughts and distinctively by their organic combinations. All such studies are derived from the monotheistic law (*Tawhid* as law) (Choudhury, 2003, 2006). The methodology followed by the conformable method and modeling applies to the case of differentiation of the forbidden and non-recommended things of life, as also to the unification of the good things of life. Thus, the methodology of unity of knowledge corresponding to the monotheistic law explains both — the phenomenon of unity of knowledge and the phenomenon of heteronomous differentiation of knowledge and reasoning between the *a priori* and the *a posteriori* domains. The latter reflects the consequences of the rationalist free will that is devoid of God and the divine law reflected by monotheism at its analytics.

The analytics of the monotheistic methodology in the development of circular causation model and its implications concerning continuity, organic pairing of relations, and institutional policy and strategy development by focusing on participation and complementarities as endogenously interrelated dynamics of being and becoming, altogether embrace the good and recommended choices. The methodologies of unity of knowledge and its opposite differentiated behavior, as of the mainstream postulates of economic rationality *a la* neoclassical economics, are both contained in and explained by the monotheistic methodological worldview in its analytical form.

The monotheistic methodology also points out the legal framework of the good choices made individually and socially, and the rejection and impermissibility of certain choices according to the legal framework of the *shari'ah*. This comprises the domain of the purpose and objective of the *shari'ah*. It is referred to as *maqasid as-shari'ah*. In such a meshing of multi-system embedding of interaction, integration, and evolutionary learning, the TIE system engages deeply in inseparable issues. The prominent example of such an embedded factor is the Great Event of the Hereafter (*Akhira*).

This precept builds into the organic interrelations bringing out important analytical theorems and properties of the inter-systemic evolutionary learning systems (Choudhury, 2012) and their implications in the nature and structure of the social, economic, and scientific world systems (Choudhury, 2014a).

The holistic feature of the *a priori* domain of the monotheistic law and its endogenous relationship with the *a posteriori* world-system in the field of Islamic economics is generalized in Figure 2.4. The same explanation is repeated here in terms of two important features and consequences. These will be referred to throughout this book as the unique methodology according to which we feature Islamic economics and its applications — theory and practice.

Methodological formulation of socio-scientific relations by *Tawhidi* analytics

These methodological formulations of monotheism analytics are explained as follows:

1. The induction of knowledge into socio-scientific variables in the form, $\{X_1, X_2, \ldots, X_n\}[\theta]$, with $\theta \in (\Omega, S)$, subject to circular causation in continuity and reversibility of intervariable and multi-causal relations like $X_i(\theta) = f_i(\mathbf{X}_j(\theta))^{14}$, $i, j = 1, 2, \ldots, n$. Because of the trace of unity of knowledge $\{\theta\} \in (\Omega, S)$ in the knowledge flows and their induction of the $\mathbf{X}(\theta)$-vector of variables, the nature of moral reconstruction of the interacting composition of the world system also reflects the unity of knowledge. This marks the all-comprehending unity of multi-causal circular causal interrelationships between the *a priori* and the *a posteriori* domains of reasoning that emanates from the *Tawhidi* understanding of unity of knowledge.

2. All the postulates of the concept of economic rationality mentioned earlier for the case of mainstream economics are rejected

---

[14]More extensively this expression is written as, $X_i(\theta) = f_i(\theta, \mathbf{X}_j(\theta))$, where $\mathbf{X}_j(\theta)$ denotes the vector of variables without the variable $X_i(\theta)$, thus $i, j = 1, 2, \ldots; i \neq j$.

and changed for those that are induced by $\{\theta\}$ in TIE along with the complete change in the concept of reason and rationality. The underlying explanations were presented earlier. The consequences are utterly damaging for the postulates leading to the permanent *problematique* of the entire mainstream economic theory.

For instance, consider the interrelated event co-ordinate, $E(\theta, X(\theta), t(\theta); \wp(\theta))$, on any economic surface or in the bundle of social choices, be these of the microeconomic nature (Walras, 1954) or macroeconomics (Solow, 1980). Because each of the entries in $E(.)$ is interactive with the rest by way of continuity, reversibility, organic unity of knowledge, and circular causation, therefore, the learning neighborhood around $\{\theta\}$ will sensitize all the other entries.

The result as shown in Figure 2.3 will be perturbation of the geometrical co-ordinates on the economic surfaces, and thereby perturbations of the historical path of evolutionary learning events. The economic optimal surfaces with steady-state equilibriums explained by marginal rates of substitutions create perturbations all around in neighborhoods. As well as the economic expansion path as shown in Figure 2.3 by the effect of continuously endogenous increase in resources, compound together to create perturbations everywhere. Now the only way to regulate such perturbations is to study the intercausal relations between the variables "nearest" to their point of occurrence (Choudhury, 2014b). Such points are denoted by $(\cdot)$ in Figure 2.3. Such extensive intervariable complementarities by means of participation and discourse describe the entire socio-scientific analytical surface.

With the above kind of analytical consequences, the underlying neoclassical method of marginal rate of substitution to measure relative prices between substitutes and choices of inputs and goods, fail to exist. The end result is a completely corrugated destruction of the smooth type of surfaces yielding choices of goods and productive inputs, and relative prices of goods and inputs. Such perturbations leading to the impossibility to estimate relative prices and marginal rate of substitution either by the methodology of unity of knowledge or by the dialectical process-oriented evolutionary economics (Georgescu-Roegen, 1981), cannot be determined by the methods of stochastic surfaces in expected values or by the method of data envelopment analysis (DEA) for determining efficient consequences of resource allocation. The resulting simulations from the evolutionary learning method of circular causation as indicated by the evolutionary neighborhoods of event points in Figure 2.3 will cause shifting and changing evolutionary event paths. This will defy the measurement of efficiency ratios by using the stochastic surface analysis.

Instead of taking recourse to the above-mentioned kinds of analytical methods, the method of circular causation yields an approach that firstly is derived from the *Tawhidi* foundations of Islamic epistemology. Thereafter, by the choice of any of many appropriate statistical methods, mathematical specification of the circular causation model, and the use of simulation methods for normative reconstruction of the model coefficients, the multi-causal related variables yield their explanations and values. More on this will follow in subsequent chapters.

The meaning of economic value in Islamic methodological sense and its derivation from Islamic epistemological roots yields the evaluation criterion of social wellbeing (*maslaha*). The measurement of social wellbeing is carried out discursively in the perspective of life-fulfillment regime of sustainable development. This in turn is explained by degrees of complementarities between the intercausal variables of the circular causation system of equations. The degree of intervariable complementarities represents the quantitative sign of the degree of unity of knowledge between the variables included in the wellbeing objective criterion function. The evolutionary learning path of such intercausal relations between the variables conveys the meaning of sustainability.

The estimation and simulation of (relative) prices of inputs and outputs, quantities of goods and productive inputs, finance and money, physical and technological resources — in fact, the whole gamut of variables as required for the investigative study at hand, arise from the evaluation of circular causation equations. The concept of embedded economic value is the rate of change in the quantitative form of the social wellbeing function in terms of its component variables. Such numerical changes are taken for a given process or time. These are then summed. Thus, there is no reliance on marginal rates (e.g. of utility, production, inputs, social welfare alternatives, etc.) for the meaning of value. That is because the marginal rate as a mathematical formula cannot be quantitatively computed on a permanently corrugated surface caused by evolutionary learning under the epistemology of unity of knowledge and thereby with embedded moral and ethical forces.

Wellbeing function in the Islamic monotheism knowledge plane

We note the unified relationship between the goals of the wellbeing function in the light of the core of Islamic epistemology as Islamic methodology. Intercausal relations in unity of knowledge explained, estimated, and simulated in terms of econometric predictors by the circular causation equations lead to the study of degrees of inter-variable complementarities. Such estimated and simulated predictor values of variables explain the degree of sustainability in the system. The predictor values of the estimated and simulated variables feed into the social wellbeing function. Such an end result of the social wellbeing function is called *maslaha* in Islamic terminology. It is the evaluative function of the purpose and objective of the *shari'ah* (*maqasid as-shari'ah*) on conceptual and practical issues.

Methodology and method

Scientific methodology and method are different concepts to understand. Method represents analytical instruments and models that carry the epistemology inherent in methodology. The methods so chosen for scientific analysis must therefore be consistent with the scientific implications of the methodology. The conclusion is that methods, if conformable to the methodology, can be selected from the entire available categories in respect of such an appropriate choice of methods.

An example here is the circular causation model. Inherent in it are the methods of estimation, simulation, and evolutionary learning by deductive-inductive dialectical method of unison of causes and effects. All these cogently feed into the social wellbeing function to study the Islamic concept of value and life-sustaining criteria of socio-economic development. Yet, it is perfectly acceptable to use all *forms* of regression and simulation methods, mathematical forms, or otherwise denoting the system and cybernetic approach. Selected ones in such methods are ordinary least square method, maximum likelihood method, structural equations method, variance autoregression method, co-integration, spatial domain analysis method, etc. In the same way, various kinds of software for testing the circular causation system of equations by different acceptable methods can be used.

Contrarily, optimization and steady-state equilibrium situation cannot exist in the entire case of circular causation relations and evolutionary learning behavior across neighborhoods and expansionary historical paths. Therefore, mathematical methods like Lagrangian, construction of production possibility surface, linear programming, and some other ones can only be studied in respect of their critical evaluation. They cannot be used for the purposes of modeling and evaluating circular causation systems under the episteme of unity of knowledge.

As well, the dialectical method of evaluating conflict and competition scenarios as in evolutionary economic theory can be done by the use of the circular causation model to evaluate intervariable and intercausal differentiations. Yet, the results to be expected for such dialectical situations would not present the scenarios of unity of knowledge as fundamentally defined by the epistemological origin of $(\Omega, S) \to \{\theta\}$. Rather, the results will represent systemic and intervariable differentiations as by choices arising from rationalist background and neoclassical substitutions.

The same is the case for studying optimal and steady-state mathematical systems, as in mainstream economics. The intervariable signs of coefficients in the estimated circular causation system, if found to be negative, imply marginal rates of substitution (marginalism). This indeed is a consequence of resource scarcity and competition. The postulate of marginal rate of substitution between competing alternatives, returns back in this case of negative intervariable relations. The inference then is of the semblance of mainstream economic theory, especially of neoclassical axiom of economic rationality regarding marginalism.

What then is the nature of economic rationality, if any, for Islamic economics and socio-scientific reasoning? Any entrepreneurial and academic system that is defined on the epistemic basis of unity of knowledge, which is derived from the *Tawhidi* law and agrees with the extended nature of *maqasid as-shari'ah* (Choudhury, 2015), establishes the very different meaning of rationality as *fitra* in Islamic epistemology. Economics being an embedded academic enterprise with other multi-systemic disciplines reflects unity of knowledge by the positively complementary intervariable coefficients of the circular causation system. Figure 2.4 summarizes the relational epistemology of the Islamic methodological worldview. The entirety of evolutionary learning holism in such a case explains the meaning of Islamic rationality — in economics and other socio-scientific areas.

Pointwise identification of the postulates of Islamic socio-scientific (economic) rationality

Pointwise, the following postulates establish the meaning of Islamic socio-scientific (economic) rationality across the universal path induced by knowledge and exists in knowledge-induced space and time.

(1) There exists a functional concept of the *a priori* domain with the world, the *a posteriori* domain: unity of knowledge, $[(\Omega, S) \ni \{\theta; \wp(\theta)\}] \rightarrow \{(\theta, \mathbf{X}(\theta); \wp(\theta))\}$.

(2) The knowledge-induced vector, $\{(\theta, \mathbf{X}(\theta); \wp(\theta))\}$ evaluates the *maslaha* choices from *maqasid as-shari'ah*: Evaluation of $W(\theta, \mathbf{X}(\theta); \wp(\theta))$, subject to circular causation intervariable relations denoted by $\{f(\theta, \mathbf{X}(\theta); \wp(\theta))\}$ for examining intervariable complementarities or lack of these.

(3) The continuity axiom of events in knowledge, space, and time holds.

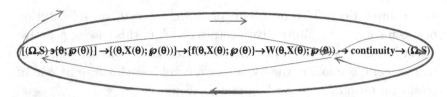

Figure 2.5. The continuous evolutionary learning field along the Sirat al-Mustaqim (straight but richly complex) path of *Tawhid* to world system to *Tawhid* in the Hereafter and the induction of this to the continuously learning experience in knowledge, space, and time dimensions.[15]

Figure 2.5 summarizes all the attributes of the continuously learning world system in terms of *Tawhidi* episteme of unity of knowledge. This is the major attribute of the participatory and complementary nature of evolutionary learning dynamics presented by *Tawhidi* methodological worldview. It applies universally and uniquely to all of Islamic socio-scientific thought, formalism, and application. In particular case of the general methodological world-view, the same methodology and its emergent formalism and methods apply to TIE.

This explanation gives the summary definition of the *Tawhidi* Islamic rationality axiom of structure and behavior. It is the opposite prototype of the combined axiom of transitivity in rational choice in mainstream economics (see exercise given below):

With three (and multiple) choices say, A, B, C.

If A is preferred to B, and if B is preferred to C, then A is preferred to C.

---

[15]The role of the mapping by the teachings of the Prophet was from the Qur'an as the chapter *an-Najm* (53:5) declares: "Nor does he speak of (his own) desire. It is only an Inspiration that is inspired. He has been taught (this *Qur'an*) by one mighty in power [Gabriel]." The role of the mapping "*S*" along with the extant of the *Tawhidi* law is essential to map the *Qur'an* into life and carry the cumulative experiences of life to the Hereafter, which is identical with the great Closure (Great Event) of *Tawhid*. Al-Hasani (2013) writes taking from Al-Bukhari and Muslim sources of *ahadith*: "He is the most knowledgeable of *Allah's* creation and the most well-acquainted of them with *Allah*...".

If A is preferred to B and also B is preferred to A, then A and B are mutually indifferent in choice.

Exercise 2

Answer the following questions:

(1) If A, B, C are knowledge-induced, can they be pre-ordered by preferences as in the case of the postulate of rational economic choice in mainstream economics? Explain.

(2) Can strict reversibility of choices hold true with knowledge induction as in the case of "indifference of preferences" in the axiom of rational economic choice? Explain.

(3) Why did Sen (1977) referred to the axiom of rational choice as the axiom of "rational fools"? — Read this paper by Sen (1977).

(4) Draw an indifference curve to show that knowledge induction of preferences cannot lie on a smooth and convex to the origin surface. Consequently, the consumer utility function cannot be well defined in such a case.

Conclusion

Epistemology as methodology is the soul of scientific thought. Epistemology deepens in socio-scientific discovery, as new intellection and problems and issues bring about fresh challenges to think far beyond normal science and paradigm shifts. The next domain of fresh epistemology coloring science is of the nature of "scientific revolution" as Kuhn (1970) called it. Yet, despite the great threshold of knowledge that scientific thought and application have contributed in the modern age, a large number of questions that are implicated, remain unresolved and unanswered. These are fundamental questions, the answers to which are essential to qualify the true purpose and goal of all of science — metascience.

The problem in this sphere is of a profound gap in understanding the metascientific enterprise. It arises from the methodological ineptness to answer certain great questions. Firstly, since all of mankind look up to a divine origin of life and uphold an ultimate reliance on this profound origin, yet the methodology of socio-scientific thought, and thereby, the applications thereof have failed to embed the divine law as a functional ontology in scientific methodology, methods, and thereby, towards understanding the overarching true reality.

The words of Wilson (1998, p. 264) are profoundly reflective on this topic: "Looked at in proper perspective, God subsumes science; science does not subsume God. Scientific research in particular is not designed to explore all of the wondrous varieties of human experience. The idea of God, in contrast, has the capacity to explain everything, not just measurable phenomena, but phenomena personally felt and sublimely sensed, including revelation that can be communicated solely through spiritual channels."

The post-modern age is one of search for that overarching scientific methodology that can embed religion with science. This would lead to the discovery of the methodology of metascience. It is in such a challenging methodological discovery that Islamic monotheism strides in with much to offer. The future of metascience with *Tawhidi* law embedded in it can offer the methodology that can be blended and analytically used for conceptual and practical applications by conformable methods of the monotheistic methodology as the final epistemology of the realm of metascience.

The *Tawhidi* epistemology derived from the *Qur'an*, the *sunnah*, and through enlightened socio-scientific discourse, thus unifying the *a priori* domain with the *a posteriori* domain of holistic reasoning, is full of analytical wealth. This describes and embeds all world systems and thereby economics with morality, ethics, and materiality in a unique and universal methodology having substantive depth and details that cut across the most advanced nature of new scientific search, discovery, and applications. The nature of analytics of the monotheistic embedding in metascience is mathematical in nature. Its application is the totality of the *a posteriori* domain by the instrumental forces of the discursive understanding interrelating God, men, intellect, and machines through learning models of unity of knowledge and its induction of socio-scientific generality and details. This is where epistemology and methods blend in their multi-intercausal organic pairing. Such will be the rendering of the

Islamic monotheistic episteme of unity of knowledge and its moral construction of the unified world system taken up in its generality and particulars. One such particular system is the field of TIE that is embedded with other ones.

This book will overarch across a comparative study of the embedded economic phenomena by the contrasting methodology between the *Tawhidi* methodological worldview with Occidentalism. We have already introduced the contrasting perspectives between these two methodologies in this chapter. Much remains to be covered in the subsequent chapters.

Students and scholarly readers would have covered the following essential topics of TIE in this chapter:

The foundational issues

1. Introduction.
2. TIE methodology in comparative perspectives.
3. The scope of TIE.
4. The nature of TIE introductory model.
5. Exercises and examples for establishing applications of TIE.

References

Al-Hasani, A.-M. (2013). *Muhammad (SWA) the Perfect Man*, Translated by Williams, K., Great Britain: Visions of Reality Books, p. 42.

Barrow, J. D. (1991). *Theories of Everything, the Quest for Ultimate Explanation*, Oxford, England: Oxford University Press.

Bartley, W. W. (1988). "Theories of rationality", in *Evolutionary Epistemology, Rationality, and the Sociology of Knowledge*, G. Radnitzky and W. W. Bartley, III (Eds.) LaSalle, Illinois: Open Court, pp. 205–213.

Blaug, M. (1968). *Economic Theory in Retrospect*, Homewood, IL: Richard D. Irwin, pp. 30–32.

Bohr, N. (1985). "Discussion with Einstein on epistemological issues", in *The Philosophy of Neils Bohr: The Framework of Complementarity*, H. Folse (Ed.), Amsterdam, the Netherlands: North Holland Physics Publications, p. 1988.

Cameron, A. and Palan, R. (1999). "The imagined economy: Mapping transformations in the contemporary state", *Millennium*, 28(2), 267–289.

Choudhury, M. A. (1996). "Economic integration in the sextet region and the Middle East Peace Accord", *International Journal of World Peace*, 13(2), pp. 67–78.

Choudhury, M. A. (2003). *Explaining the Qur'an, A Socio-Scientific Inquiry*, 2 Volumes, Lewiston, New York, USA: Edwin Mellen Press.

Choudhury, M. A. (2006). *Science and Epistemology in the Qur'an*, 5 Volumes (Different Volume Titles), Lewiston, New York, USA: The Edwin Mellen Press.

Choudhury, M. A. (2012). "On the existence of learning equilibriums", *Journal for Science*, 16(2), 49–62.

Choudhury, M. A. (2014a). *Tawhidi Epistemology and Its Applications in Economics, Finance, Science, and Society*, Cambridge, England: Cambridge Scholars Publishing.

Choudhury, M. A. (2014b). *The Socio-Cybernetic Study of God and the World-System*, Philadelphia, USA: Ideas Group Inc. Global.

Choudhury, M. A. (2015). "Res extensa et res cogitans de *maqasid as-shari'ah*", *International Journal of Law and Management*, 57(6), 662–693.

Choudhury, M. A. (2016). "Religion and economics", *International Journal of Social Economics*, 43(2), 134–160.

Descartes, R. (1954). "Discourse on method", in *The Philosophers of Science*, S. Commins & R.N. Linscott (Eds.), New York, NY: The Pocket Library.

Etzioni, A. (1988). "What is rational?" in *The Moral Dimension, Towards a New Economics*, New York, NY: The Free Press.

Georgescu-Roegen, N. (1981). *The Entropy Law and the Economic Process*, Cambridge, MA: Harvard University Press.

Hume, D. (1988). *An Enquiry Concerning Human Understanding*, Buffalo: Prometheus Books.

Hume, D. (1992). "Of the understanding", in *Treatise of Human Nature*, Buffalo, NY: Prometheus Books.

Kant, I. (1949). *The Philosophy of Kant*, Translated by Friedrich, C. J., New York, NY: Modern Library.

Kant, I. (1977). "Religion with the limits of reason alone", in *The Philosophy of Kant*, Translated by Friedrich C. J., New York: The Modern Library, p. 1988.

Kuhn, T. S. (1970). *The Structure of Scientific Revolution*, Chicago, IL: University of Chicago Press.

Nozick, R. (2001). *Invariances, the Structure of the Objective World*, Cambridge, MA: The Belknap Press of the Harvard University Press.

Palan, R. (2002). "The constructivist underpinnings of the new international political economy", in *Global Political Economy, Contemporary Theories*, Palan, R. (Ed.), London, England: Routledge, pp. 215–228.

Pheby, J. (1988). *Methodology and Economics, A Critical Introduction*, London, England: Macmillan.

Popper, K. (1998). *Conjectures and Refutations: The Growth of Scientific Knowledge*, London, England: Routledge & Kegan Paul.

Popper, K. (2004). *The Logic of Scientific Discovery*, London, England: Routledge.

Rawls. J. (1971). *A Theory of Justice*, Cambridge, Massachusetts: Harvard University Press.

Resnick, S. A. and Wolff R. D. (1987). *Knowledge and Class, A Marxian Critique of Political Economy*, Chicago, IL: The University of Chicago Press.

Romer, P. M. (1986). "Increasing returns and long-run growth", *Journal of Political Economy*, 94, 1002–1037.

Rucker, R. (1983). *Infinity and the Mind*, New York, NY: Bantam New Books.

Schumpeter, J. S. (1968). *History of Economic Analysis*, New York: Oxford University Press.

Sen, A. (1977). "Rational fools: A critique of the behavioural foundations of economic theory", *Philosophy and Public Affairs*, 6, 317–344.

Simon, H. (1957). *Models of Man*, New York, NY: John Wiley & Sons.

Smart, N. (2000). *Worldviews*, Upper Saddle River, New Jersey: Prentice Hall.

Solow, R. (1980). *Growth Theory, an Exposition*, Oxford, England: Oxford University Press.

Walras, L. (1954). *Elements of Pure Economics*, Translated by Jaffe W., Homewood, IL: Richard D. Irwin.

Walsh, M. J. (1985). *A History of Philosophy*, London, England: Geoffrey Chapman.

Wilson, E. O. (1998). *Consilience, the Unity of Knowledge*, New York, NY: Vantage Books.

Chapter 3

The Scope of *Tawhidi* Islamic Economics (TIE)

The general epistemological methodology of scientific investigation in the comparative perspectives of Occidentalism and Islam that was formalized in Chapters 1 and 2 is now brought forth to establish the nature and scope of *Tawhidi* Islamic Economics (TIE). The starting point is to note that in comparative methodological perspectives, like all other disciplines of study, economics too has been cast in the framework of its own differentiated specialization (Holton, 1992). Thereby, in the name of disciplinary specialization, mainstream economics has been deprived of its embedded methodological worldview along with the important human elements of concern. These elements are morality, ethics, and the crosscurrents of issues with other disciplines, whether by way of a unique methodology and methodical study, or by way of formalizing economics as a generalized human science (Boulding, 1968). Yet, quite evidently, the various disciplines lack the methodology and the attenuating method to blend morality and ethics with the material forms and considerations regarding the embedding. Thereby, even more damaging has been the fact that no methodical discovery has been attained that can analytically study morality and ethics as neural system studies and thereby draw policies, strategies, and institutional forms that can present a wider field of endogenous learning phenomena (Choudhury, 2014b).

In Chapters 1 and 2, we have explained why the estrangement of morality and ethics from socio-scientific studies occurred in respect of the differentiated worldview that was molded by the peculiar meanings given to rationalism and reason. Within this study was also constructed the conforming meanings of reason and economic rationality. Chapters 1 and 2 also pointed out the opposite meanings given to these methodological terms in *Tawhidi* scientific perspectives that are erected upon monotheism as the episteme of unity of knowledge, and according to it of the unity of the world system. Accordingly, economics as a sub-system of the wider ensemble of embedded systems has been deprived of what it used to be during the Greek world and which tapered off. Neither could it survive in the works of Walras despite the ethical views of human sciences that he upheld.

An example, beyond the different methodological ways of understanding and methodically applying the meanings of rational economic choice with and without ethics, was given in Chapters 1 and 2. We give another example here. This proves how the endogenous blending between ethics and economics, as with any other branch of science, cannot be attained in the existing theoretical structure. The intertemporal theory of resource allocation is necessarily between the real economy yielding rates of return and the financial economy yielding interest rates. By the neoclassical postulate of marginal rate of substitution which forms the core of economic theory treating resources as scarce, there always exists the inherent opportunity cost between real rates of return and interest rates, and between the real economy and the financial economy.

There is no ethical treatment in such an allocation of scarce resources over time to link up the financial sector with interest, and the real sector with real rates of return on spending. One of the prime reasons for this impossibility in using organic relational coherence between the two possibilities is caused due to the permanent prevalence of interest rate in individual and collective behavior and preferences. The intertemporal allocation of resources cannot be endogenously induced except by being ethically and morally induced with exogenous economic and social policies and regulations. When such exogenous actions are introduced into economic theory, market failures are argued to arise in terms of allocation of quantities of resources and prices via the incidence of tax rates.

The nature of morality and ethics in economic theory

The nature of morality and ethics arises from the rationalist background of taxation and charity. In Milton Friedman's case of subsidy for guaranteed income supplementation, every dollar so received, while increasing the household income, brings this nearer to the graduated taxation bracket. This kind of income distribution caused by subsidy as charity is known as "negative taxation". The moral and ethical meaning of subsidy as charity dissipates with the impact of negative taxation on household income.

In the case of a tax levy, the incidence of taxation and subsidy creates price distortion in the dented area of the production possibility curve caused by the tax/subsidy (inner point). Likewise, the market demand and supply curves shift due to the impact of the tax levy. Now, the net change in consumer and producer surplus is shared between the consumer and producer. The result is an inequitable impact of the tax levy either on the consumer or the producer. In the end, the tax instrument does not yield the ethical change that is expected of them.

The problem of the inequitable impact of government policies to correct market failures is a methodical consequence. The result of inequity points out that correction of market failures by non-market policy and regulatory instruments is a departure from the endogenous realization of ethical consequences in fair market dealing and instead the exogenous imposition of government intervention. In the latter case, the legal tenets play an important role in determining the direction and extent of intervention. The question is whether governments should raise taxes and apply fiscal expenditure directly affecting consumers, producers, and collective groups?

Or such general revenues should be spent in raising social consciousness to allow markets to correct themselves?

The above question is similar to the following ones: (1) Should governments and charities promote food stamps to address the problem of hungry and poor households? Or should the government tax revenues and charities raised for ameliorating the poor and hungry be given to the needy to spend on their own needs? The approach for market-driven adjustment would promote the latter case. (2) Would a lump sum of charity be preferred to a tax-adjusted household budget improvement? The answer is to opt for the first approach. Similar considerations are functions of the social and legal perspectives as to how these view the welfare context of taxation versus market-driven allocation.

Because the rationalist methodological approach is based primarily on government interventions in the case of market failures, the corresponding exogenous nature of policy intervention will necessarily cause market distortions. On the other hand, if spending is used as an instrument towards market adjustment as an endogenous action, then a different economic attitude towards market orientation is cogently effective. We will dwell on this point between mainstream economics and TIE to bring out the meaning of systemic ethics and what enables it as an endogenous force of social and economic actions.

Some necessary definitions

Morals and ethics

Morality is always the source of ethics, but ethics is not the same as morality. Ethics by and large is equated with humanism, which is derived from the rationalist roots of individual and collective free will. Consequently, as explained in Chapters 1 and 2, the derived meanings of reason and rationality under the canopy of rationalism in occidental epistemology as methodology also pursue economic differentiation and methodological individualism (Buchanan, 1999).

Yet again, ethics necessarily arise from the moral law which transcends the rationalist doctrinaire. When such equivalence occurs, ethics becomes an instrument carrying the moral law into experience.

Consequently, ethics cannot subsume the moral law. Epistemological foundation of TIE is found in the moral law. Ethics is a sign of good conduct according to the details of the moral law as textually provided and discursively extended. Yet, ethics that is revisionary of the moral law is unacceptable as the moral origin of ethics. Likewise, ethics that arises from the rationalist epistemic roots is unacceptable by the moral law. These conditions imply strongly that ethics is neither of the primal epistemic nature nor is it foundational in the realm of methodology.

A few examples will bring out the nature of essentiality of the moral law surpassing ethics in economic behavior and actions. Islamic charity like *zakat* is said in the *Qur'an* to be a claim of the poor on the wealth of the rich. Yet, the meaning of *"zakat"* goes into its literal meaning of purging and increasing wealth. By it the spirit and practice of the moral law yields amelioration of the needy in their productive transformation, in business and socio-economic development, and in proper choices of the good things of life. These and their like choices define the wellbeing criterion. The wellbeing attainment in turn establishes progress along the life-fulfilling regime of ameliorative socio-economic development.

How is the choice of the good things of life determined in the moral law? This is a matter of discerning the choice according to the precept of the monotheistic law of unity of knowledge by its intrinsic property of organic relational oneness by "pairing". This topic was covered in Chapters 1 and 2. We will return to this topic in greater depth later on. It is sufficient to point out at this time the following role of morality and ethics in the moral law: the *Tawhidi* law is the moral law of "everything". Its practice is discursively established on the details of life, experience, and applications of the moral law in and by the purpose and objective of the moral law — *maqasid as-shari'ah*. This field of intellection, application, and practices arises out of specific and social details by keeping focus on the *Tawhidi* law. The *Tawhidi* law as the moral law (*sunnat Allah*) is permanently assigned.[1] It is carried by the *sunnah* of the Prophet

---

[1] *Qur'an* (48:23).

Muhammad and the learned discourse of the community to determine the appropriateness of choices of goods and services, institutions, and the wellbeing criterion by the ethics of the moral law. The extant of ethics in such a domain of choices in accordance with the *Tawhidi* law comprises *maqasid as-shari'ah*. Thus, while the *Tawhidi* law comprises the primal moral law which is the indispensable epistemology of unity of knowledge, the *maqasid as-shari'ah* forms the ethical domain of the moral law. The *Tawhidi* law is established and unchangeable. The *maqasid as-shari'ah* is extendible (Mustafa, 2006; Choudhury, 2016).

In reference to the moral law that subsumes *zakat* and its ethics found in *maqasid as-shari'ah*, there is the critical element of the moral law as the principle of unity. It is signified by the joining of the hearts of the rich and poor to attain mutual (participated as unity) wellbeing. On the other hand, the ways of social distribution and usage of *zakat* in productive, sustainable, and extended ways of bringing about organic functioning of possibilities to enable the recipient and the donor in the grand social context is the ethical manifestation of *zakat*. Ethics is thus behavior and action that realizes on the relational plane based on the foundational epistemology of the moral law. The organization of *zakat* is of the nature of relational epistemology by constructing organic unity of knowledge between diverse possibilities for realizing sustainability of the common good contributed by *zakat*.

Exercise 1: In accordance with the verse of the *Qur'an* (2:275)

> *Those who devour usury will not stand except as stands one whom the Evil One by his touch has driven to madness. That is because they say: Trade is like usury. But Allah has permitted trade and forbidden usury. . . .,.*

Identify some ethics as examples of relational epistemology that can be derived as ways of relating trade with the inversion (abolition) of *riba*. (Hint: consider the various relational ways that relate trade (X_1, X_2) to the inversion of *riba* (R), as, $(1/R) = f(X_1, X_2, \theta); X_1$

denotes national income, X_2 denotes value of total international trade as (Export + Import)). $\{\theta\}$ is knowledge derived as relational epistemology based on *Tawhid* as the law of unity of knowledge.[2]

Many similar specific examples can be derived to prove that the underlying the precept of moral law is its permanence in governing over the order of things as the primal law.[3] But ethics is derived from the moral acts as the ways, instrumentation, and application of the moral law in all issues under study. Islam happens to be the only worldview wherein the moral law is codified. This enables the moral law and the derived ethics from it to co-exist without contradiction in purpose and objective of the common wellbeing of all. This fact is proved by the uniqueness and universality (Chapter 2) of the *Tawhidi* law as the ultimate law that governs all specifics. Contrarily, in the case of the rationalist methodology, the theory of overdetermination of epistemologies prevails. This renders any law based on rationalism to be random and conflicting in nature. Consequently, the domain of ethics derived from such random overdetermined laws remains undetermined as a moral edict of life, thought, experience, practicality, and application.

An example of the nature of overdetermination in rationalist moral law and the idea of ethics can be traced down to the definition of interest in this case. Mainstream economic theory of interest is strewn with many forms of interest rates. Among them are nominal rate of interest, real rate of interest, simple rate of interest, compound rate of interest, term structure of interest rates, effective rate of interest, own rate of interest, marginal efficiency of capital as interest rate, and so on. Many among Muslim economists argue that the real rate of interest, the own rate of interest, the marginal efficiency

---

[2] We write this as R^*, that is, $f(X_1, X_2, \theta) = $ constant. This implies that a percentage increase in *riba* decreases trade by the sum-total of elasticity coefficients of X_1, X_2, and θ-variable. Contrarily, a one percentage decrease in *riba* increases trade by the sum-total of elasticity coefficients of X_1, X_2, and θ-variable. The induction of the X-variables by θ-value will cause greater degrees of changes either of the two ways. θ-value thus introduces X-efficiency in the inter-variable relations (Liebenstein, 1966).

[3] *Qur'an* (2:117): "To Him is due the primal origin."

of capital, and the simple against compound rates of interest are permissible in Islam in the presence of inflation. The argument is also launched on the permissibility of less as against usurious rate of interest. Such ideas float around because of the absence of any legal edict that would unequivocally and conclusively rule on the moral theory of trade versus interest, and then leave this to human discourse under the ethics of understanding and applying the moral law via various ways of studying the truth of the *Qur'anic* verse relating trade and *riba*. This verse was mentioned above.

Interaction and integration

The other attribute of evolutionary economics and TIE is the property of interaction and integration. Though, these properties are understood and applied in different ways in these two economic theories. Besides, it is noted that neoclassical economics is not based on and therefore cannot explain the process nature of occurrence of economic events. For instance, optimization of the neoclassical "objective" function is a terminal condition of the first-order maximization of the Lagrangian resulting from the mathematical operation of constrained maximization. The terminal point of occurrence of the optimal state has no process dynamics to explain change as to how such optimal states are attained. It is just that the first-order conditions of optimization happen as mathematical necessity of a selected approach to problem solving, namely by the Lagrangian. Yet, underlying such necessity of optimization and the steady-state equilibrium, there remains the governing axiom of economic rationality. The underlying inter-relationships between rationalism, rationality, and reason in scientific problem solving venue were explained in Chapters 1 and 2.

The evolutionary learning world of processes and multi-causal organic relations as in the case of an embedded idea of economic theory and likewise of the entropy and evolutionary theory of economics rendered by Shackle (1972), Boulding (1981), and others, has not found their way into neoclassical economic theory. Where the process-orientation was forced into neoclassical economics, the result remained to be of the optimization character in the preferences of agents in public choice, rational expectation (Nelson and Winter, 1982). The axioms of scarcity, competition, and full information remained unchanged. Consequently, the concept of optimality and steady-state equilibrium remained as conditions of datum of preferences and economic rationality in all such neoclassical economic innovations.

Yet, the evolutionary learning perspective of organic unity of knowledge across multi-causal fields of entities, variables, relations, and systems is the natural result of the *Tawhidi* Islamic economic (socio-scientific) worldview. See Figures 2.3 and 2.4 (Chapter 2) in this regard. The consequences of resource allocation are thereby permanently probabilistic in nature. The consequences across knowledge-induced fields of actions and responses on given issues and problems to study, remained evolutionary learning points that converge toward but never attain what is referred to as the "nearest" points of the evolutionary learning equilibriums in the framework of a probabilistic idea of neighborhood of nearness. The continuity of the evolutionary learning phenomenon, as explained in Chapter 2 regarding the concept of continuity and reversibility (Figure 2.4) denies attainment of the evolutionary equilibrium points and the optimal point where novelty of learning and innovation as endogenous forces die, unless such points are applied exogenous shocks.

In occidental economic and political economy theory, the evolutionary learning context of the underlying methodology of over-determination, conflict, and undecidability in terminal decision-making altogether militate to establish the permanent conjecture without convergence. The moral law of unity of knowledge does not apply. Consequently, a permanent scenario of disequilibrium prevails. Such a socio-economic scenario was the rendering in Marxist political economy (Mandel, 1971; Cole, 1966).

At the end of this definitional sojourning, we note that abstraction *qua* abstraction *ad infinitum* does result into consensus by discourse. There remains permanently the randomness of discourse between contending epistemological thought and academe. Integration as consensus or convergence of views resulting from the

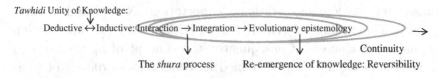

Tawhidi Unity of Knowledge:

Deductive ↔ Inductive: Interaction → Integration → Evolutionary epistemology →

Continuity

The *shura* process   Re-emergence of knowledge: Reversibility

Figure 3.1.   Co-evolutionary convolutions of the IIE-learning universe.

interactive pattern of a discursive milieu, governed by epistemic unity of knowledge and leading to ever more of the same pattern of discursive actions and responses is not to be found in the disequilibrium theory of political economy. Consequently, evolutionary learning though true yet occidental epistemic thought cannot yield an interactive leading to integrative, followed by co-evolutionary learning in the framework of unity of knowledge (see Figure 3.1).

In Islamic methodological framework (Chapter 2), the *Qur'anic* exegeses on universal "pairing" and convergence by means of consultation (discursive) *shura* dynamics (Choudhury, 2011) and re-origination of the world system in the light of the divine law (*khalq in-jadid* = moral consciousness), together establish the continuous interrelationship in the interactive, integrative, and evolutionary Learning (IIE) framework. These attributes comprise the properties of evolutionary learning of TIE and of the diverse knowledge embedded world systems.

Example 1

How are market prices set in the following three cases?

(1) The theory of market equilibrium.
(2) Non-convergent evolutionary dynamics (dialectics).
(3) IIE-learning dynamics leading to co-evolutionary equilibriums.

We denote by "p" prices of goods, services, inputs as the case may be. "q" denotes quantities of goods, services, inputs as the case may be. In the cases — Figures 3.2(a)–3.2(c), "p" and "q" are, respectively, neutral to θ, induced by θ-values of different kinds — in Figure 3.2(b) for non-convergent disequilibrium

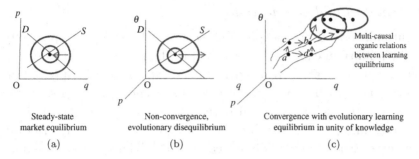

Figure 3.2. Perturbations of evolutionary equilibriums in resource allocation.

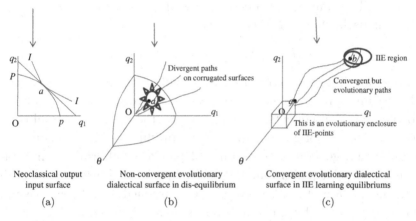

Figure 3.3. Contrasting forms of equilibriums and non-existence of optimality.

dialectical model, and in Figure 3.2(c) for convergent evolutionary equilibrium model of Islamic epistemic unity of knowledge. The output (input) spaces are also shown in these three cases correspondingly in Figures 3.3(a)–3.3(c). q_1, q_2 are quantities for the choices of goods, services, and inputs 1, 2. In the case of Figures 3.3(b) and 3.3(c), such bundles will be an increasing category. In Figures 3.3(b) and 3.3(c), optimum points and steady-state points cannot exist. Only evolutionary learning points of contrasting types exist.

The student needs to describe all the underlying methodological points that underlie the above contrasting equilibrium and non-optimal versus the optimal conditions of economic theory.

Optimality and equilibrium

Continuing on from the previous section, the study of optimality and equilibrium can now be extended to the intertemporal case with multi-causal variables. It was defined and explained in Chapter 2 that history is described by the continuous sequencing of events. In the Islamic case, such a historical path extends, as by the *Qur'an*, from the beginning to the end. The beginning of creation is the *Tawhidi* law of creation by the divine command.[4] The end is the Great Event of the Hereafter (*Akhira*) as the completion of the divine law (*Tawhid*).[5] Beginning is thus equivalent to the End and conversely as well. The universal trajectory now described by *Tawhid* is the straight path, the *sirat al-mustaqim*,

$$Tawhid \rightarrow \text{World System} \rightarrow Tawhid. \qquad (3.1)$$

Expression (3.1) is true both for the smallest continuous state of the IIE-learning processes as for the very large process of the beginning to the end. Consequently, as an example, the exchange equilibrium in every case — of goods and services, productive inputs, monetary equilibrium, general equilibrium and partial equilibrium, computational general equilibrium, full-employment equilibrium, and such like entities are all within the above-mentioned grand relationship. Thus, every one of such equilibrium states is induced by the knowledge variable that is derived from the epistemic origin of the *Tawhidi* law carrying with it the unity of knowledge and unification of goods and services in the exchange mechanism of markets.[6] Furthermore,

---

[4] *Qur'an* (2:117).

[5] *Qur'an* (6:75): "So also did We show Abraham the power and the laws of the heavens and the earth, that he might (with understanding) have certitude."

[6] The *Qur'an* exemplifies the entire universe of mind and matter as created and governed by the divine law (*sunnat Allah*) to be a fully established exchange order. In this complete domain, the signs of Allah (*ayath Allah*) are displayed and explained by *Tawhid* as the episteme of unity of knowledge both for the good choices as ordained, the bad choices that are forbidden, and the undetermined choices that need to be sorted out between the good and the bad ones. There is exchange and forms of equilibrium in everything that Allah has created by virtue of the synergistic model of unity of knowledge inter-connecting *haqq ul-yaqin* (*Tawhid* as law), *ilm ul-yaqin* (knowledge of *Tawhid* as law), and *ayanul-yaqin*

by the fact that all systems and sectors experience organic multi-causal relationships between them, therefore, evolutionary learning equilibriums characterize all the multi-systems in the IIE-process model.

Therefore, Relationship (3.1) is the grand containment of the generalized system of IIE processes as evolutionary epistemological relations lasting from the beginning to the end of history of the universe. The implication here is a deeply analytical and conclusive one. The universe of "everything" (Hawking and Mlodinow, 2010)[7] is structured in the framework of multi-causal and multi-dimensional unity of probabilistic relational epistemology. This indeed is the grand design conveyed by the relational and learning universe of the *Qur'an*. The *Qur'an* originally explains that such "pairing" also remains inherent between the false things of life, but in the context of their ultimate dissociation. In the midst of the IIE-process explanation of the multi-dimensional and multi-causal relationships between diverse systems, the only true depiction of the conscious universe is that of evolutionary learning from *Tawhid* to *Tawhid* through the processes of the intervening world system. The universe with its diversely unifying systems realizes itself in the midst of

---

(observations and reflection or *burhan aqli*). Consider many verses of the *Qur'an* regarding the central function of exchange as learning dynamics in everything from end-to-end of the universe of the *Qur'an*, mind, and matter. Of these verses is the following one: (*Qur'an*, 62:11): "Say: The (blessing) from the Presence of *Allah* is better than any amusement or bargain! And *Allah* is the best to provide for all (for all needs)." The universal persistence of trade and transactions by exchange in every matter concerning God, existence, mind, and matter and the contrariness of misguidance from the true path is found in the following verse (*Qur'an*, 2:16): "They have traded guidance for error, but their bargain has had no profit and they have missed the true guidance".

[7]Hawking and Mlodinow (2010, p. 80) wrote about similar learning (probabilistic general system) histories: "...for a general system, the probability of any observation is constructed from all the possible histories that could have led to that observation. Because of that (t)his method is called the 'sum over histories' or alternative histories' formulation of quantum physics".

evolutionary equilibrium denying steady-state equilibrium and all semblances of optimality.[8]

Take an example in the small-scale sub-universe of Expression (3.1). Consider an investor driven by economic rationality allowing perfect information predict an increasing price level and net capital gains. His cash flows are expected to increase over time because he assumes perfect or expected values of intertemporal cash flows to be known. This generates perfect information either by deterministic knowledge or probabilistic knowledge. So, the rational investor has to know his cash-flows fully well in these two cases at every point of time standing here and now with a financial binocular peering out into the future.

There comes the storm by the will of *Allah* that turns down his garden of expectation, wealth, and prospects of the overweening man who stood above *Allah*.[9] All these occur because the investor's rational behavior made him forget the various calamities that can come about if he did not include consciousness of *Tawhid* in his calculations of prospects and expectations. One such calamity that happens always is the depressive fluctuation of stock prices in the financial market where assets survive, continue, or die by unknown contingencies all the time.

So now, how will you predict or expect cash flows to behave? The conscious social system induces the cash flow by the epistemic knowledge arising from the monotheistic roots. How can cash flows be evaluated in this case? This is where the praises of *Allah* is raised at the "nearest" point of occurrence of an event, which is always knowledge-induced including those events that occur at any given point of time.[10] Yet, "time" is simply a recorder, not the cause of

---

[8]In respect of the pervasively probabilistic nature of events in the universe, Hawking and Mlodinow (2010, p. 72) write: "According to quantum physics, no matter how much information we obtain or how powerful our computing abilities, the outcomes of physical processes cannot be predicted with certainty because they are not determined with certainty."

[9]*Qur'an* (3:117); *Qur'an* (18:32–44).

[10]Value of asset=$W(\mathbf{x}(\theta)) = \Pi_{t=1}^{n}\text{Prob.}[(1 + r_t(\theta))^t]^*\mathbf{x}(\theta)_{t=0}$, subject to each $\{r_t(\theta)\}$ and $\{\mathbf{x}(\theta)_{t=0}\}$ being evaluated by the IIE-process model over the time

events. Only knowledge creates events and change by the will of *Allah* in the order and scheme of everything.[11] The student can explain the footnote formula and show how to calculate it with assumed values of the variables with and without θ-values.

Utility and welfare

According to our explanation of ethics as an instrument carrying with it either the moral law or rationalist behavior that yields the axiom of economic rationality, now the criterion of consumer utility function conveys satisfaction gained from the individualistic (household) or group enjoyment of a bundle of consumption goods. It is an ordinal psychological measurement of individualist consumption satisfaction. The ethics of utility function as a way of exercising individualistic preferences on the rational choices of a bundle of goods has no moral implications, in as far as economic rationality permanently pits the choices in the basket to compete with each other as marginal substitutes.

Although the idea of complements is invoked in neoclassical economic theory by way of determining the final satisfaction derived from the consumption of the bundle of goods, the theorem goes that in any three consumption goods or produced goods, two are substitutes. Or in any n-number of goods, there will always be some choices that are complements for attaining the final utility from the choices.

This is a flaw of understanding in terms of the principle of pervasive complementarities contrary to selected complements for the short-run. The reason is that in an economic system with embedded system-phenomena, with multi-causality and unity of

---

period for $\{r_t(\theta)\}$ over the vector of $\{\mathbf{x}(\theta)_{t=0}\}$. This is done by a special method called circular causation. In Chapter 1, we explained the idea of circular causation. We will deal with it more later on. The continuity of the conscious social and economic system conveys the meaning of consciousness and sustainability that arises from the ethics of the moral law.

[11] *Qur'an*(45:24): "And they say: 'What is there but our life in this world? We shall die and we live, and nothing but time can destroy us.' But of that they have no knowledge: they merely conjecture."

knowledge as interrelationships between them, there cannot exist long-run substitutions to engender social wellbeing as we have defined it.

Take an example. Say that tea and coffee are gross substitutes of each other, and sugar and milk are complements of these beverages. In that case, depending upon the size of the population of tea drinkers versus coffee drinkers, the increasing population of tea drinkers will draw on the stock of sugar and milk off the market. This would consequentially cause substitution between the sugar and milk for tea, and the sugar and milk for coffee. Such a substitution will be more pronounced by the long-term substitution effect on demand. What happens to the supply of tea and coffee and the stocks of sugar and milk? Answers here remain the same *ceteris paribus*.

The utility function is thus a criterion toward happiness and satisfaction by way of substitution. Whereas, we have argued oppositely that it is the complementing characteristic of resource allocation which is found to sustain life-sustaining wellbeing. The markets for the corresponding kinds of goods in the dynamic kinds of life-sustaining regimes of development and the market process in it stabilizes prices and expands quantities with an attenuating increase in population size. The implication on the demographic state is that the population remains young to generate and sustain the innovative and dynamic life-fulfillment regime of development and market processes.[12]

In the case of a pervasively complementary relation between the elements of wellbeing function replacing the utility function, both the individual and the social wellbeing functions as defined earlier reject substitution altogether. The result of pervasive complementarities is reversible rejection of marginal rate of

---

[12]In a dynamic basic needs caused by the incidence of θ-values, we note for wellbeing replacing the utility function, $W(\theta) = W(Q,p,P)[\theta].Q$ denotes output. p denotes prices of basic needs. P denotes population size. The stable population increase is characterized by a young population. Thereby, $d\overset{+}{W}/d\theta = (\partial\overset{+}{W}/\partial Q).(d\overset{+}{Q}/d\theta) + (\partial\overset{+}{W}/\partial p).(d\overset{\pm}{p}/d\theta) + (\partial\overset{\pm}{W}/\partial P)*(d\overset{+}{P}/d\theta) + \partial\overset{+}{W}/\partial\theta.$

substitution.[13] Consequently, relative prices or, equivalently, opportunity cost of the variables cannot be read off by the notion of marginal utility function of substitutes. As a result, the concept of value changes from that of marginal utility to complementary effect on wellbeing by the complementary variables in consumption and production. At the end, as explained by means of Figures 2.2 and 2.3, relative prices cannot be determined by the smooth convex-to-the origin surface.

The above result holds true for welfare function just as for utility function, because the welfare function is simply a map of the collection of consumer utility functions of individual citizens or households. Now, the same kind of explanation as above can be transferred to the case of substitution and competition between differentiated utility indexes as the variables of the welfare function.[14]

Example 2

As in the case of Figures 3.2 and 3.3, a higher-level analysis can be repeated for the relationship between allocation of goods by the utility function and evolutionary objective functions, and the utility allocation by the welfare function in the three cases as shown. The student can complete the formal steps for the three cases given the one case shown here.

---

[13]Note that the $\pm$ signs remain correspondingly paired — positive for positive, negative for negative. $(\partial W/\partial P)$ and $(dP/d\theta)$ are each positive in the life-fulfillment regime of development and by the fact that $W(\theta)$ and θ are monotonic transformations of each other in the sense of wellbeing.

Hence, $dW/d\theta > 0$ identically in the presence of complementary relations between the variables of $W(.)$. The result is the sustaining of the dynamic life-fulfillment regime of development and basic-needs markets in it. In the case of substitution, say between $X = (Q, p)$ and P, there is no presence of θ-values. The wellbeing function reverts to the utility function as $U = U(X, P); \partial X/\partial P < 0$, contrary to $W = W(X, P), (\partial W/\partial P)/(\partial W/\partial X) > 0$.

[14]In the case of welfare WL maximization, the result yields $(\partial WL/\partial U_1)/(\partial WL/\partial U_2) = -dU_2/dU_1 > 0$, implying that dU_1 and dU_2 are oppositely related, thus the case of marginal rate of utility substitution.

Wellbeing function (maslaha)

To reiterate, wellbeing is the functional explanation followed by its transformation of organic unity of relations between its component variables according to *maqasid*-choices. The wellbeing function while firstly being conceptual also assumes a measurable form in determining the degree of organic complementarities that exist between the variables. Such variables of choice in the wellbeing function represent the good things of life determined by the moral law, its derived ethics, and by the social discursive rule. In such a definition, the wellbeing function assumes the place of the maslaha objective arising from *maqasid as-shari'ah* and complying with the Imam Shatibi basket of goods in consumption and production. These are necessaries (*dhuruiyarh*), comforts (*hajiyath*), and refinements (*tahsaniyath*). Altogether, these categories of goods and services comprise the dynamic life-fulfillment regimes of development. They are dynamic by virtue of sustainability across dynamic regimes of development.

The wellbeing function is evaluated in terms of the circular causation relations between the *maqasid*-variables of the wellbeing function. In case of a deficiency in inter-variable complementarities signified by the negative sign of the inter-variables coefficients, the wellbeing function is simulated by changing such negative coefficients into plausible positive ones or less negative ones in a particular process of moral transformation, to be progressed onwards. The change in such values accords with the possibility of available resources over all expected changes that arise from the simulated choices, and by technical discourse on the appropriateness of the choices of complementary or less negative coefficients, is of the nature of activities of the Islamic consultation process called the *shura*.

So as explained in Chapter 2, the estimation and simulation of the wellbeing function, $(W(\mathbf{x}(\theta))$ with all the variables explained, and taken in its conceptual and quantitative forms, is represented in the following way. We use the term "evaluation" to mean both "estimation" and "simulation" performed sequentially in the quantitative model of wellbeing subject to circular causation relations:

$$\text{Evaluate } W = W(\mathbf{x}(\theta)); \ \mathbf{x}(\theta = \{x_1, x_2, \ldots, x_n\}[\theta]. \tag{3.2}$$

All variables are commonly induced by θ-knowledge value, $\theta = plim\{\theta_i\}$ by the use of the IIE-learning processes. This is referred to in the *Qur'an* as the *shura* consultation (discourse). Thereby, the permissible choices out of the moral law, its derived ethics, and extended discourse on choices according to the derived ethics, altogether form the discursively conscious basis of ethical determination of socio-economic things. The symbol $\{\mathbf{x}(\theta)\}$ represents such consciously determined variables induced by ethical consciousness denoted by $\{\theta\}$. The nature of $\{\theta\}$ is its derivation as epistemology of the *Tawhidi* law of unity of knowledge. That is $\{\theta\} \in (\Omega, S)$, etc. in its embedding of the economic variables (socio-scientific variables) $\{\mathbf{x}(\theta)\}$.

The evaluation of the wellbeing functional criterion (*maslaha*) is done by evaluating the circular causation relations in the $\{\mathbf{x}(\theta)\}$-variables. The circular causation equations are,

$$x_i = f_i(\theta, x_j(\theta)), \ (i,j) = 1, 2, 3, \ldots, n; \ i \neq j. \tag{3.3}$$

Expression (3.3) comprises n-number of equations in n-number of variables. Finally, there is the θ-equation,

$$\theta = F(\mathbf{x}(\theta)). \tag{3.4}$$

Clearly, Expressions (3.2) and (3.4) are "similar" functions (same type of functional forms). Hence, both are expressions of the wellbeing function. While Expression (3.2) is the conceptual form explaining the substantive meaning underlying the theoretical properties of the wellbeing function, Expression (3.4) is the empirical form in the actual measurement of the wellbeing function. Therefore, we can write $F(\mathbf{x}(\theta))$ as a positive function of Expression (3.2).[15] More on the empirical computation of the system of $(n+1)$ equations comprising Expressions (3.3) and (3.4) will be formalized later on in this book.

---

[15]Say that, $W = W(\mathbf{x}(\theta)) = f(\theta) = \theta^\alpha$. Then $\theta = {}^\alpha\sqrt{W(\mathbf{x}(\theta))}$, which is a transform of the wellbeing function. It is therefore a wellbeing function itself. Hence, W and θ are transforms of each other.

The socially embedded economic problem

Neither among process-oriented and epistemological-driven economic and social thinkers nor in Islamic epistemological approach are their fields of specialization any longer restricted to narrow areas that exclude the great moral and ethical issues. Such a comprehensive search and discovery interrelates diverse systems by interaction, integration, and continued co-evolutionary epistemology — IIE-learning processes.

In mainstream socio-economics, a type of social embedding is studied (Holton, 1992; Parsons, 1964) as being contrary to a differentiated system. Also a specific kind of embedded system can be derived from the neoclassical criticism by Sraffa (1960), by virtue of the fact that, in every given year of circular production of commodities by commodities, the output at the beginning of a time-period is distributed to factors of production. The output so distributed to productive factors forms a new chain of output production, and so on. Pasinetti (2001) writes on Sraffa's circulation of output as a criticism of neoclassical economics in the following words. In his words, "Four themes that appear as poison-arrows in Sraffa's critique of economic theory (are): (i) The marginalist theory of production and distribution; (ii) the theory of value, which the marginalists call price theory; (iii) the theory of marginal utility; and (iv) the theory of interest, when interest is presented as a reward for abstinence."

Exercise 2

The following exercise may be tried out: The following version of Sraffa's famous contribution to the circular causation idea underlying his *Production of Commodities by Means of Commodities* is extracted from Dorfman *et al.* (1958). The student/reader is asked to formalize the following questions embodied in the model presented:

(1) Explain the nature of Sraffa's model in the perspective of circular causation idea of endogenous output and input relationships in a model of economic resource allocation/distribution.

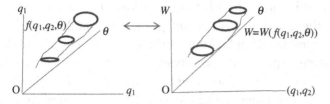

Figure 3.4. Wellbeing distribution of evolutionary learning choices.

(2) Incorporate in this model a diverse-system outlook for the study of interactive system-relations as the theory underlying embedded systems.

(3) How does Sraffa's model negate the neoclassical marginalist hypothesis in production and consumer choice theory as depicted in Figure 3.4, with fuzzy points on the production possibility curve and the consumer indifference curves?

Relational epistemology concept of ethics

The entire sequence of selected definitions of terms given above can now be summarized to explain the nature of TIE in comparison and contrast to mainstream economic thought. The central methodological worldview comprises the substantive meaning of morality. From this core of the divine law, ethics as relational epistemology is derived to convey the core meaning of unity of monotheistic knowledge and the unified world system.

Thus, the substantive meaning of ethics belongs to the domain of the world system that is depicted in Figure 3.1, in which there exist the interplay between the ontological (primal) order of unity of monotheistic law and the details of the constructive world systems. The underlying IIE-learning processes of embedded economic system are explained by means of the internal epistemological dynamics of unity of knowledge.

Thereby, ethics as derived from the moral law is neither an implement of humanism nor is it independent of the moral law. It is not the primal individual and collective preference of a rationalist design of civil conduct and its institutions. Instead, ethics is equivalent to the relational epistemological belief and its expression in the construction of embedded world systems. The methodology of the resulting explanatory worldview of unity of knowledge together manifests the nature and design of the *Tawhidi* believing world system. The systemic endogenous nature of ethics in Islam but which is also invoked by some heterodox economists (Sen, 1992; Boulding, 1968) presents the theory of embedded study of ethics in economics.

The total methodology, which is *Tawhidi* epistemology in essence, is referred to as the episteme of the system-oriented study of TIE. This reflects the totality of the knowledge-induced worldview. It comprises the knowledge-dimension of reality. But beyond this realization, the embedding of the knowledge-dimension with the dimensions of space and time comprises the study of phenomena as events occurring in the knowledge, space, and time dimensions. This comprehensive use of ethical dynamics in the totality of study of the unified world-system is referred to as phenomenology. In the *Tawhidi* epistemic context, phenomenology represents the combination of consciousness (*tasbih*) with the discursive investigation of the world system (*shura*) to know reality in generality and in particular issues, problems, and events. Taken together, the experience of the phenomenology of consciousness in the ethics-economics interrelations is thus causally related with *tasbih-shura*. In the *Tawhidi* epistemic theory of Islamic economics, the entire field of phenomenology is unraveled and applied in the mold of participation and complementarities between diverse entities, variables, relations, and systems, deductive and inductive reasoning, and *a priori* and *a posteriori* frames of mind and matter. Thereby, ethics implies the relational conception of unity of knowledge derived from the moral law.

Introducing the *Tawhidi* epistemology in developing the theory of financial economics

Initially defined, financial economics in mainstream terms marks the study of the interplay of conceptual and applied relationship between economic and financial theories. In such a definition, no academic demand is made regarding the study of interactive, integrative, and creative study of multi-disciplinary and multi-dimensional phenomenon of systemic interrelations caused by inter-causality between the representative variables. Thereby, for example, the study of social justice is considered as an exogenous (external) factor of social consideration. Such an ethical factor is at best influenced by government action, institutions, policies, and by sheer human choices of the good ones in society at large. There is no scope in such exogenous treatment of the theme of social justice and ethics to inculcate in society at large, a reaction towards consciousness caused by interaction between self, human preferences, and conscious experiences that together can automatically generate inter-causality between ethical character, actions, responses, belief, mind, and matter.

The embedding of knowledge with the generality and specifics of the world system, as in the case of financial economics, also conveys the idea of phenomenology. Phenomenology is the study of consciousness through the organic interrelationship between deontological (duty-bound) characteristics of self with its preferences and the creative actions and responses generated by relational experiences. The resulting attribute of ethics thus formed is explained as an endogenous actualization as opposed to ethics as exogenous behavior in mainstream financial economics.

An example of the meaning of ethics is based on the formation of preferences regarding ecological consciousness on matters needing ethical preferences as natural reaction. Such an attitude is contrary to being enforced by institutional policies. There is no conflicting enforcement in the interrelationship between action and response in a conscious framework of endogenous ethics. The conscious self in concert with the world system generates and sustains integrity between self, individual, and collective preferences and the sustainable ecological experience in our example. The result of endogenous ethical behavior is the generating of a system of interaction, integration, and evolutionary learning in the domain of unity of knowledge as episteme and its induction of the issues under study. In our study, such issues belong to the field of financial economics.

Finally, on the epistemological nature of TIE

With the above initial contrasting features between mainstream and Islamic epistemological worldviews in financial economics, we can now introduce the nature of TIE. This is the foundational methodological worldview of TIE that will be used throughout this book in terms of theoretical perspectives of economic issues, examples, and the imminent applications leading to inferences. Thus, the outlook of this book is thoroughly methodological as well as applied in the context of the *Tawhidi* methodology that has been brought out thus far and to be developed and explained throughout this book. This foundational methodological worldview establishes the bedrock of the revolutionary field of TIE and socio-scientific world-system studies.

Yet as we proceed on in various fields of economic reasoning, the approach of this book will be rigorously comparative with mainstream economic taken up in original reference to the *Tawhidi* epistemological worldview. Such an approach will allow both mainstream and *Tawhidi* Islamic economic reasoning to be examined and analytically tested to study specific economy problems through analytical formalism as this arises from the epistemic roots. In undertaking these directions of research, the methods (as opposed to methodological, which is universal) mathematical and empirical models will be invoked.

What is TIE?

From our methodological formalism revolving around the episteme of monotheistic unity of knowledge, which is equivalent to *Tawhid as divine law* projected in its complete phenomenology, we derived the distinctive nature of what is termed as the *Tawhidi* unity of knowledge functioning in the world system. Indeed, the extensive interpretation of the *Tawhidi* law by its function of organic unity of knowledge and the induced diversity of things can be read off from many verses of the *Qur'an*.[16]

---

[16] *Qur'an* (10:22): "He it is who enables you to traverse through land and sea; so that ye even board ships; — they sail with them with a favorable wind, and they

The central embedded role of *Tawhid* as law pervades the socio-scientific domain of "everything". Within this vast domain is the field of economics as an embedded socio-scientific study. The meaning of "everything" is that of the universal and unique nature of the imminent methodology that arises from the *Tawhidi* epistemology for all and every issues and problems. This is a fact despite variations in the diversity of issues, problems, theories, and applications in various disciplinary focuses.

The *Tawhidi* epistemology arises from its independent and substantive origin that is distinctive in the following three core contexts.

Firstly, the *Tawhidi* law is established irrevocably in the *Qur'an*. Secondly, there is the guidance of the Prophet Muhammad by his teachings called the *sunnah*. The third essential component of *Tawhidi* epistemology is the guidance of the learned ones based on the *Qur'an* and the *sunnah*. These three components taken together ground the true nature of *Tawhidi* methodology and the desired methods of analytical and applied formalism that are consistent with the nature of the methodology. Such methodical relevance arises from the nature of organic unity in the process of being and becoming underlying the problems under investigation. The methodological implication is very strong in the understanding and application of the Islamic *Tawhidi* worldview. In fact, there cannot be any thought, conception, inquiry, applications, and inferences without the conscious understanding of the *Tawhidi* methodological worldview. The *Qur'an* details such implications of reality.[17],[18]

---

rejoice thereat; then comes a stormy wind and the waves come to them from all sides, and they think they are being overwhelmed: They cry unto God, sincerely offering (their) duty unto Him, saying, "If Thou do deliver us from this, we shall truly show our gratitude!"

[17] *Qur'an* (41:53): "Soon will We show them Our Signs in the (furthest) regions (of the earth), and in their own souls, until it becomes manifest to them that this is the Truth. Is it not enough that your Lord does witness all things?"

[18] *Qur'an* (96:3–5): "Proclaim! And your Lord is Most Bountiful, — He Who taught (the use of) the Pen, — Taught man that which he knew not."

Thus, the *Tawhidi* methodological worldview as the primal and foundational Islamic epistemology of "everything" rests upon three irrevocable perspectives. Firstly, the *Tawhidi* episteme explains the organic unity of knowledge of the "paired" universe. Secondly, the singular *Tawhidi* precept of unity of knowledge constructs the world of unity of being and becoming. Thirdly, such things belong to the life-fulfillment needs. The universe of these divine and worldly attributes of the good things of life exists perpetually in the dimensions of knowledge, space, and time. They form the choices according to the *maqasid as-shari'ah* — the *maqasid*-choices.

The truly epistemological study of Islamic economics like all other worldly fields of study is embedded in the *Tawhidi* nature and design of the embedding universe within the knowledge, space, and time dimensions. The market is sensitized by endogenous ethics across interrelating systems. The institution is the body framework for the study and implementation of ethics and economic behavior with consciousness as a learned endogenous experience (*tarbiah*). Human economy and financial activity are entrenched in moral and ethical consciousness. The purpose and objectivity conceptualized and quantified by the wellbeing criterion of *maslaha* is in "everything" and is everywhere.

Understanding the knowledge, space, and time dimensions by the permanence of *Tawhidi* law[19]

Yet the three attributes of reality are not possible to be known in knowledge, space, and time conclusively by disclosed manifestation. That is because, the hidden reality (*ghayb*) is not manifest according to the meaning of knowledge in the *Qur'an* (3:190–191). The *Qur'an* declares regarding the unseen: "Behold! In the creation of the heavens and the earth, and the alternation of Night and Day, — there are indeed Signs for men of understanding, — men who celebrate the

---

[19] *Qur'an* (33:62): "(Such was) the practice (approved) of *Allah* among those who lived aforetime: No change wilt thou find in the practice (approved) of *Allah*. This practice is the divine manifestation of *Tawhid* as law from the beginning to the end of the knowledge, space, and time dimensions — the total reality."

praises of God, standing, sitting, and lying down on their sides, and contemplate the (wonders of) creation in the heavens and the earth, (with the thought): 'Our Lord! Not for naught have You created (all) this! Glory be to You! Give us salvation from the Penalty of the Fire' ".

An exegesis of these verses is the following: The *Tawhidi* law in its manifestation and explication of the universe comprehends "everything" ("Creation of the heavens and the earth"). This enables us to see and understand not the impossible divine attributes. Rather they are the cognitive and material unraveling of these attributes in things that are manifesting ("Behold!").

The extensive meaning of "Night and Day" embodies in it the meaning of the differentiation, the discernment of falsehood as darkness and truth as day. Such a criterion between truth and darkness advances the human comprehension of total reality. Such realization exists in a seamless and continuous way, across continuums of "everything". There lie the evidences as "Signs of God". The signs manifest the proofs arising from the primal ontology (moral law) and epistemology of the *Tawhidi* law and its deep explications.

In such a structure of creation, the *Tawhidi* law is reflected by its purpose and meaning: "Our Lord! Not for naught have You created (all this)". Such an encompassing universe, as far as human comprehension proceeds, is defined by the temporal and the final "Closure" in processes of evolutionary equilibrium trajectories that enclose the open evolutionary learning universe. We present this idea in Figure 3.5.

The nature of evolutionary equilibriums to be studied in *Tawhidi* Islamic financial economy *a la Tawhid*

Closure: $(\Omega, S) \leftrightarrow$ World System$(\theta, \mathbf{X}(\theta), t(\theta)) \leftrightarrow$ *Tawhid*: *Akhira*,

Open Universe (learning universe): World System$(\theta, \mathbf{X}(\theta), t(\theta))$.

(Ω, S) denotes the primal ontology of *Tawhid* (Ω: symbolically to represent the supercardinal (Chapter 2) topology of the *Qur'an*)

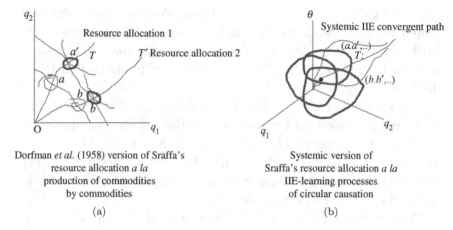

Figure 3.5. Nature of social embedding of the economic space.

mapped in degrees by the *sunnah* of Prophet Muhammad (S).
$\{\theta\}$ denotes worldly knowledge flows derived from the epistemology of (Ω, S).

$\mathbf{X}(\theta)$ denotes the mathematical ensemble of knowledge-induced variables.

$E(\theta, \mathbf{X}(\theta), t(\theta))$ denotes an event $(E(.))$ represented by the multi-systemic coordinate in knowledge (θ), space $(\mathbf{X}(\theta))$, time $(t(\theta))$.

Time, $t(\theta)$ is induced by knowledge because, it is knowledge not time, that causes an event to occur. Time reads the event and its systemic relations.[20]

The closure encompassing the open universe is a necessary and sufficient condition for the existence of a meaningful evolutionary equilibrium. The fixed point theorem (Brouwer, 1910; Kakutani, 1941; Nikaido, 1987) establishes the existence of equilibrium. Neighborhoods around equilibrium points within the fixed point closure (Choudhury *et al.*, 2007) establish the evolutionary nature of such equilibrium. In the *Tawhidi* epistemological formulation of Islamic financial economy, all equilibriums are evolutionary equilibriums

---

[20] *Qur'an* (76:1): "Has there not been over man a long period of Time, when he was nothing — (not even) spoken?" Thus, "time" was dysfunctional until functional knowledge dawned with the creation of man.

within the purposeful closure. Steady-state equilibriums are denied any relevance. They can be explained by the degenerate case of neoclassical economics and full-information assumption.

In Chapter 2, we defined event by $E(\theta, \mathbf{X}(\theta), t(\theta))$. Our worldly categories of events are diverse across systems and experiences. In regard to the study of economic issues and problems, the *Qur'an* points out several of these. From them the world can derive lessons for diverse human ends. Here are three specific cases in which the study of economics rests. These cases are events $E(.)$. Then there is the vector $\mathbf{X}(\theta)$ comprising consumption bundles along with consumer behavior; production along with production function and production diversification, and production, distribution, and ownership relations; wealth, money, and spending, and many more in detail. Over all such categories is the defining place of the conscious purpose, objectivity, and meaning (Masud, 1994).

The functional understanding of consciousness (θ) induced in consumption and production comprises the phenomenological study of the *Qur'an* in relation with the world system. Examples of such conscious behavior are moderation and balance for enjoying a happy self, the family, the community, and society.[21] On the theme of ownership and distribution, the *Qur'an* has declared fairness and equity[22]. The *Qur'an* has nonetheless left the equality not in terms of measure but in terms of justice. The theme of justice and spending is connected with abundance and sharing.[23]

---

[21] *Qur'an* (6:141–142): On production: "It is He who produces gardens, with trellis and without, and dates, and tilth with produce of all kinds, and olives and pomegranates, similar (in kind) and different (in variety): Eat of their fruit in their season, but render the dues that are proper on the day that the harvest is gathered. But waste not by excess: for God loves not the wasters." (141). On consumption and good things of life: "Of the cattle are some for burden and some for meat: Eat what God has provided for you, and follow not the footsteps of Satan: For he is to you and avowed enemy." (142).

[22] *Qur'an* (4:161): "That they took usury, though they were forbidden; and that they devoured men's substance wrongfully; — We have prepared for those among them who reject Faith a grievously penalty."

[23] *Qur'an* (2:261): "The parable of those who spend their substance in the way of God is that of a grain of corn: it grows seven ears, and each ear has a hundred

The matter of money is connected with resource mobilization.[24] All these activities of sustainability and the social economy are treated in an interconnected way of organic pairing and inter-causality. The extent of such interconnectivity is widely inter-systemic.[25]

The interconnectedness of the conscious attributes is exemplified by the sustainability of life-fulfillment regimes of development. Along such a trajectory of development, we note the complementarities and thereby participative functions over knowledge, space, and time dimensions of the organic inter-causal relationships between consumption and production and the underlying agential behavior in the reality of the ethically induced market process and market system. Preferences in such a market system are dynamic in nature, caused by the impact of θ-values. Individual ethical preferences are aggregated through the properties of interaction, integration, and creative evolution under innovation occurring along the evolutionary learning path of history. Every point of continuity of life-fulfillment regime of development is sustained by the equitable, just, and fair distribution of wealth, property, and ownership that a life-fulfillment regime of development ensues. That is because of the nature of needs and the stable prices and wages and returns on spending. These cause stable forms of the price—output relationship, the nature of appropriate technology, and returns on these activities to profit-sharing, wages, and rates of return. Now, when monetary expansion occurs along the life-fulfillment regimes of development, the continuous relationship between money and the real economy replaces interest rate with trade. The abundant rewards in the life-fulfillment regime of development come about. The social wellbeing

---

grains. God gives manifold increase to whom He pleases: and God cares for all and He knows all things."

[24] *Qur'an* (18:19): "Now send ye then one of you with the money of yours to the town: let him find out which is the best food (to be had) and bring some to you, that (you may) that (you may) satisfy your hunger therewith: and let him behave with care and courtesy, and let him not inform any one about you."

[25] *Qur'an* (13:3): "And fruit of every kind he made in pairs, two and two: He draws the Night as a veil Over the Day. Behold verily in these things there are Signs for those who consider!"

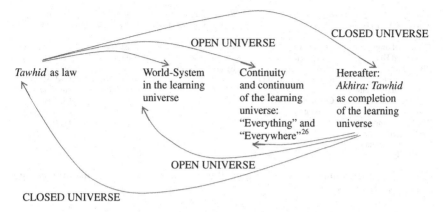

Figure 3.6. Closure of the complete universe of Signs of God in the order of "everything", "everywhere".

function (*maslaha*) is then simulated to higher levels by the force of continuous resource regeneration and its equitable ownership by all. Thus, by the impact of evolutionary learning in unity of knowledge as episteme, the nature of life-fulfillment regime of development becomes of the dynamic type. We refer to such a regime of change as the dynamic life-fulfillment regime of sustainability, or the dynamic basic-needs regime of participatory development.

The meaning of moral consciousness in TIE and science

In reference to the foregoing meaning of phenomenology and consciousness that results from the interrelationship between the *Tawhidi* law of unity of knowledge and the unifying world system, we can give it the analytical meaning. This is explained in Figure 3.6.

An overview of the book

This book is intended to be an original contribution to raise the young and reflective scholarly mind to the rigorous introduction of the study

---

[26] *Qur'an* (55:26–27): "All that is on earth will perish: But will abide (for ever) the Face of your Lord full of Majesty, Bounty, and Honour. Then which of the favors of your Lord will you deny? Of Him seeks (its need) every creature in the heavens and on earth: Every day in (new) Splendour does He (shine)!"

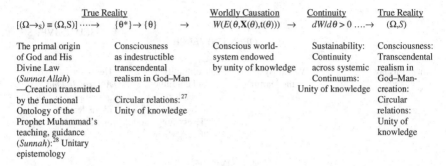

Figure 3.7. The analytical meaning of *Tawhidi* consciousness or phenomenology in the world system.

of *Tawhidi* methodology that is conceptually understood and applied to comprehensive issues and problems of economics and world system in generality and particulars (Fig. 3.7). The *Tawhidi* methodological perspective will thus be a contribution to the world of learning wholly. The erudition in it is global and transcultural in nature. Its findings and critical approach are not limited to the captioned "Islamic" economics of today. The book is a contribution to the realm of ideas where the *Tawhidi* law functions in formal, analytical, and applied ways of the epistemology of unity of knowledge and unity of the knowledge-induced world system.

Chapters 1–3 have laid down the foundational epistemological (methodological) worldview. On the basis of these initiating and foundational areas of economic reasoning, the preponderant area of *Tawhid* as the moral law and its dynamics in the evolutionary learning system of inter-causal relations between the good things of life can be studied. As well as the methodical derivation from such methodological foundations, known as circular causation, and the IIE

---

[27] *Qur'an* (42:52): "And thus have We by Our command, sent inspiration to thee: Thou knewest not (before) what was Revelation, and what was Faith; but We have made the (*Qur'an*) a Light, wherewith We guide such of Our servants as We will; and verily thou dost guide (men) to the Straight Way."

[28] *Qur'an* (3:109): "To God belongs all that is in the heavens and on earth: To Him do all questions go back (for decision)."

properties of this method derived from the foundational methodology become universal applications in economic problems.

We trust that this book will be an original contribution to a distinctive field of economic reasoning taken up in the inter-causal sense of unified world system by means of the episteme of unity of knowledge. This book is expected to project a methodical formalism derived from the foundational *Tawhidi* methodology for application to diverse economic issues. The approach throughout is comparative and contrasting with mainstream economics and the mainstream orientation of Islamic economics. Chapter 4 will lay down the principal instruments that arise from the participatory nature of Islamic economics in the light of the *Tawhidi* epistemic law of unity of knowledge in the field of financial economics. An analytical explanation of the avoidance of *riba* contra trade-related economic activities will be explained. The super-encompassing nature of the purpose and objective of the *shari'ah* taken within the divine law of unity of knowledge will be inter-causally linked with the *Tawhidi* principle of participation and the Islamic participatory economic instruments.

Chapter 3 needs to be studied by keeping the following areas of TIE in mind:

1. *Tawhidi* Islamic economic methodology.
2. The scope of TIE.
3. The formulation of *Tawhidi* Islamic economic model: An introduction.

References

Boulding, K. E. (1968). *Beyond Economics, Essays on Society, Religion, and Ethics*, Ann Arbor, Michigan: The University of Michigan Press.

Boulding, K. E. (1981). *Evolutionary Economics*, New York: Russell Sage.

Brouwer, L. E. J. (1910). "Uber un eindeutige, stetige Transformationen von Flachen in sich", *Mathematische Annalen*, 69, 176–180.

Buchanan, J. M. (1999). "The domain of constitutional economics", in *The Logical Foundations of Constitutional Liberty*, Indianapolis, IN: Liberty Fund.

Choudhury, M. A. (2011). "Dynamics of the shari'ah and the Islamic world-system", *King Abdulaziz University Journals-Islamic Economics*, 23(1).

Choudhury, M. A. (2012). *Islamic Economics and Finance: An Epistemological Inquiry,* Contributions to Economic Analysis, Vol. 291, Bingley, UK: Emerald Publications.

Choudhury, M. A. (2014a). *Tawhidi Epistemology and its Applications (Economics, Finance, Science, and Society),* Cambridge, UK: Cambridge Scholars Publishing.

Choudhury, M. A. (2014b). *The Socio-Cybernetic Study of God and the World-System,* Philadelphia, USA: Ideas Group Inc. Global.

Choudhury, M. A. (2016). "Res extensa et res cogitans de *maqasid as-shari'ah*", *International Journal of Law and Management,* 58(3).

Choudhury, M. A. and Hoque, M. Z. (2012). *An Advanced Exposition of Islamic Economics and Finance,* Lewiston, NY: Edwin Mellen Press.

Choudhury, M. A. and Zaman, S. I. (2006). "Learning sets and topologies", *Kybernetes: International Journal of Systems and Cybernetics,* 35(7), 1567–1578.

Choudhury, M. A., Zaman, S. I. and Sofyan S. H. (2007). "An evolutionary topological theory of participatory socio-economic development", *World Futures: Journal of General Evolutionary Systems,* 63(8), 176–180.

Cole, G. D. H. (1966). *The Meaning of Marxism,* Ann Arbor, Michigan: The University of Michigan Press.

Dorfman, R., Samuelson, P. and Solow, R. (1958). *Linear Programming and Economic Analysis,* New York, NY: McGraw-Hill Book Co., INC.

Hawking, S. W. and Mlodinow, L. (2010). "Alternative histories", in *The Grand Design,* London, England: Transworld Publishers, pp. 80, 82.

Holton, R. L. (1992). *Economy and Society,* London, England: Routledge.

Kakutani, S. (1941). "A generalization of Bouwer's fixed point theorem", *Duke Mathematical Journal,* 8(3).

Liebenstein, H. (1966). "Allocative efficiency vs. X. efficiency", *American Economic Review,* 56, 392–415.

Mandel, E. (1971). *The Formation of the Economic Thought of Karl Marx, 1843 to Capital,* Translated by B. Pearce, New York, NY: Monthly Review Press.

Masud, M. K. (1994). *Shatibi's Theory of Meaning,* Islamabad, Pakistan: Islamic Research Institute, International Islamic University.

Nikaido, H. (1987). "Fixed point theorems", in *The New Palgrave: General Equilibrium,* Eatwell, J., Milgate, M. and Newman, P. (Eds.), New York, NY: W. W. Norton, pp. 139–144.

Mustafa, O. M. (2006). "Objectives of Islamic banking: *maqasid* approach", *International Conference on Jurisprudence,* IIUM, August 8–10.

Nelson, R. R. and Winter, S. G. (1982). *An Evolutionary Theory of Economic Change,* Cambridge, MA: Harvard University Press.

Parsons, T. (1964). *The Structure of Social Actions,* New York, NY: The Free Press of Glencoe.

Pasinetti, L. I. (2001). "Continuity and change in Sraffa's thought", in *Piero Sraffa's Political Economy,* Cozzi, T. and Marchionatti, R. (Eds.), London, England and New York, NY: Routledge, pp. 139–151.

Sen, A. (1992). "Conduct, ethics and economics", in *On Ethics & Economics*, Oxford, UK: Basil Blackwell, pp. 88–89.

Sraffa, P. (1960). *Production of Commodities by Means of Commodities*, Cambridge: Cambridge University Press.

Shackle, G. L. S. (1972). *Epistemics & Economics*, Cambridge, England: Cambridge University Press.

Chapter 4

The Formulation of Islamic Economic Model

This chapter commences along the lines of application of the theory contrasting *Tawhidi* unity of knowledge and the rationalist world systems that we substantiated in Chapters 2 and 3. In this regard, we will first translate the premises of Chapter 2 in a formal model and explain all its details. Along with this task, this chapter will also explain several important concepts that emanate from the formal model and treat the essence of the Islamic instruments within such a formal model that carries with it the contrasting concepts, differentiating Islamic methodological worldview and the rejection of rationalism depicted in mainstream economics.[1] The same kind

---

[1]The oft-recited verse of the *Qur'an* (2:3) carries a deeper meaning. The verse is, "Who believe in the unseen, establish prayer, and spend out of what We have provided for them". The "unseen" here would encompass the abstraction that enables to fathom the recesses of meanings of praises of *Allah* (*Tawhid*) and the ways of conscious worshipping of the *Allah* in the functioning of the world systems (*tasbih*). The instruments to delve into such deep recesses of abstraction could be abstract mathematical concepts, cybernetic systems, and ontological inquiries. The part "establish prayer" is to extend intellection across the domain of consciousness to know the true reality (*Tawhid* and its illogical opposition by polytheism, see Chapter *Al-Haqqa*, 69). Thus, the conscious worshipper is perpetually and continuously in the presence of *Tawhid* (*Allah* and *Qur'an*).

of arguments and formalism applies to the generality of the world-system study and its details.

From Chapters 2 and 3, we bring forth the definitions and explanations of the critical terms that will be used all through. The following terms ought to be well understood, premised on the epistemology of *Tawhidi* unity of knowledge.

1. We will increasingly refer to this epistemic premise of socio-scientific study in general as consilience (Wilson, 1998) in the English masterpiece, and as *Tawhid* as the cardinal basis of belief and the core of Islamic methodological worldview along with its methodical functional applications in analytical depth (Choudhury, 2014a).

2. Rationalism is the opposite of *Tawhid* though necessarily of the nature of consilience. That is because other than unity of knowledge and its induction of the good things of life and the essence of the pairing universe, *Tawhid* does not accept any other way of defining unity of "being" and "becoming" on the generality and details of "everything" (Barrow, 1991). Rationalism is the humanly concocted idea that bases its explanation of universal phenomena on scarcity, conflict, competition, differentiation, and marginalism. These conditions are treated as humanly designed and postulated in mainstream economic science. They are untenable in the understanding of the *Tawhidi* methodological worldview that is conceptualized and applied to Islamic economics, finance, science, and society, and their various intellectual diversities.

3. Complementarities and participation refer to the organic unity between things, which in the *Tawhidi* sense must comprise the

---

The part "spend out of what We have provided for them" means the divulging and dissemination of the experience of conscious worshipping by all the means and awakening of righteous acts. These would involve both the dissemination of *Tawhidi* worldview and the material spending in the way of *Allah* by exerting the efforts of mind and matter. This is the pursuit of *Tawhid* as divine *law* of monotheism in action in the generality and details of the world system. The *Qur'an* (29:69) says, "And those who strive for Us, We will surely guide them (to) Our ways. And indeed, *Allah* surely (is) with the good-doers."

good things of life. Hence, these emanate from the domain of the purpose and objective of the Islamic law that is derived from the divine law (*sunnat Allah*) and then discoursed among the learned ones (*ulul amr*).[2] In the general sense of the world system, complementarities are between all things approved by the *sunnat Allah* and reflected on decisions in the discursive medium of the *maqasid as-shari'ah*. This is the *Qur'anic* idea of consilience that invokes unity of "being" and the dynamics of "becoming" as representing the organic dynamics by way of pairing[3] or unification. While complementarity applies to things symbolized by their variables, participation is the attribute of the same nature that may be appropriately applied by the meaning of complementarity between agents and agencies. The *Tawhidi* worldview of unity of knowledge and the process of unification between all good things of life (*halal at-tayyabah*) — i.e. in "being" and "becoming" — form the *Tawhidi* organic unity of knowledge and of unification. The dynamic process of becoming' comprises the dynamics of interaction, integration, and evolutionary (IIE) learning over the knowledge, space, and time universe. Of these co-ordinates of the non-Cartesian universe so spanned, knowledge is the most substantive. On knowledge derived from the *Tawhidi* epistemology of unity of knowledge, both space and time depend for their configuration. Time cannot create or originate anything. It simply records events that happen continuously. Events happen, appear, disappear, and unravel intertemporally by the causation of knowledge flows derived from the *Tawhidi* ontological origin. This point was explained in Chapters 2 and 3 in terms of the supercardinality concept.[4]

---

[2] *Qur'an* (4:59): "O ye who believe! Obey God, and obey the apostle, and those charged with authority among you. If ye differ in anything among yourselves, refer it to God and His Apostle, if ye do believe in God and the Last Day: That is best and most suitable for final determination."

[3] *Qur'an* (36:36): "Glory to God, Who created in pairs all things that the earth produces, as well as their own (human) kind and (other) things of which they have no knowledge."

[4] Because time is premised on the primacy of knowledge flows that arise and continue on the basis of $\{\theta\} \in (\Omega, S)$, we therefore write time as $t(\theta)$. A saying

4. Wellbeing is the objective criterion function that measures the degree to which complementarities or participation exists between the variables, agents, and agencies representing the good choices of life and rejecting the false and unwanted ones. The wellbeing function is therefore a criterion of pairing, equivalently unity of knowledge premised on *Tawhidi* consilience. This quantification of the wellbeing function is firstly taken up in the "as is" state of complementarities between the choices. The "as is" state is then improved to the normative "as it ought to be" state by appropriately changing the estimated coefficients into simulated coefficients of a system of circular causation structural relations. See below for a definition of circular causation as the modeled quantification of the degree of unity of organic relations between representative variables.

A similar kind of estimation and simulation also exists for the opposite kinds of choices. These reflect extensive differentiation between the choices made. An example is conveyed by the conflict and differentiated model based on the dialectical property of rationalism. In this case, the coefficient of relationship between

---

(*hadith*) of the Prophet as the inspired one called *hadith al-qudsi*, goes as follows (narrated by Al-Bukhari and Al-Muslim cited in Ibrahim and Johnson-Davies (n.d.)): "Sons of Adam inveigh against (the vicissitudes of) Time, and I am Time; in My hand is the night and the day". The exegesis of this hadith is that time belongs to *Allah* who is the absolute in knowledge. Thus, time belongs to knowledge that is *Allah's*. It can therefore be written, $t(\theta \in (\Omega, S)) = t(\theta)$. Thus, the dimension of knowledge, space, time is written in the non-Cartesian co-ordinate as $\{\theta, \mathbf{x}(\theta), t(\theta)\}$, with $\{\mathbf{x}(\theta)\}$ as the continuum spanned by *Tawhidi* knowledge. $\{\mathbf{x}(\theta)\}$ spans the entire continuum of space induced by the primacy of knowledge. But the events in the universe unravel a little at a time as knowledge evolves and proceeds on.

The non-Cartesian nature of the *Tawhidi* universe of the Signs of *Allah* is defined by the non-commensurate nature of the topology denoted by $\{(\Omega, S) \to \theta\}$. From this is defined the equally non-Cartesian nature of space and time premised on knowledge flows. Thus, any good is measured by the service it provides to be of relational importance. Mere size does not matter in the valuation of goods (e.g. land). "$\{\mathbf{x}(\theta)\}$" can thus be interpreted as the total valuation of the goods by the unity between essence and materiality. This integration yields the consciousness of total evaluation of things.

the good and the bad choices will be indicated by a negative coefficient. This will require a normative approach to improve the choice of the good thing by reducing and replacing the unwanted one. Likewise, the relationship between the bad choices will be indicated by a positive sign of the coefficient in their negative sense of organic relations. The simulation focus would then be to reconstruct the choices such that the coefficient moves towards zero.

5. The circular causation equations appear in their structural form so as not to generate problem of multicollinearity in the econometric estimation. These equations explain interdependencies between the variables of the relations as they exist (estimation) and as they ought to be related (simulation). Such a system of circular interrelations explains the pairing and complementary (participatory) properties of the *Tawhidi* postulate of unity of knowledge and unification between the particular choices.

6. The multiverse extension of a single systemic circular causation relationship denotes the particular methodological superiority of the *Tawhidi* postulation contrary to rationalism that is embedded in mainstream economic theory. Multiverse system of IIE learning relations point out the multi-dimensional pairing (complementary, participatory) relationship between diversely distributed systems.

An example here is the sub-system of the grand world system as markets and economy related with the physical systems of energy, cosmology, and interdisciplinary fields. An example of such multiverse circular causality is depicted in the *Qur'anic* Chapter, R'ad.[5]

---

[5] *Qur'an* (13:1-5): "Alif, Lam, Meem, Ra. These are the verses of the Book; and what has been revealed to you from your Lord is the truth, but most of the people do not believe. It is *Allah* who erected the heavens without pillars that you [can] see; then He established Himself above the Throne and made subject the sun and the moon, each running [its course] for a specified term. He arranges [each] matter; He details the signs that you may, of the meeting with your Lord, be certain. And it is He who spread the earth and placed therein firmly set mountains and rivers; and from all of the fruits He made therein two mates; He causes the night to cover the day. Indeed in that are signs for a people who give thought. And within the land are neighbouring plots and gardens of grapevines and crops and palm trees, [growing] several from a root or otherwise, watered with one water; but We make some of them exceed others in [quality of] fruit. Indeed in that are

Here the multiverse systems are exemplified by, but not limited to, the following ones: the earth, cosmology, environment, geography, and diversity in relational unity of "being" and "becoming".

The multiverse concept is also a multi-dimensional one spanned across knowledge, space, and time. Consequently, the multi-systems of the unifying multiverse and the formal method of circular causation and wellbeing remain valid for the measurement of intensity of unity of knowledge in knowledge-embedded pairing things. Such a phenomenon is spread out in all dimensions, each and all being spanned by knowledge, space, and time.[6] Thus, the unique and universal methodology of *Tawhidi* unity of knowledge conceptualizes the Islamic worldview and is applied over all details of the multiverse.

It can be inferred from the above summary of certain key points in Islamic economics and the general socio-scientific work that the evidence of degrees of unity of knowledge and simulated unification between critical variables is given by measured complementarities (participation). This is signified by the various coefficients of the circular causation system of equations.

The other inference drawn from the above discussion on unity of knowledge, complementarities (participation), and estimated (simulated) wellbeing functions, subject to circular causation system of equations, is the following particular one. The degree of complementarity or participation is the most significant social indicator as concept and empirical measure regarding unity of knowledge. *Tawhidi* Islamic economics (TIE) differs significantly from mainstream economics in terms of its permanent axiom of participative resource mobilization on the good choices as opposed to the permanence of

---

signs for a people who reason. And if you are astonished, [O Muhammad] — then astonishing is their saying, 'When we are dust, will we indeed be [brought] into a new creation?' Those are the ones who have disbelieved in their Lord, and those will have shackles upon their necks, and those are the companions of the Fire; they will abide therein eternally."

[6] *Qur'an* (65:12): "It is *Allah* who has created seven heavens and of the earth, the like of them. [His] command descends among them so you may know that *Allah* is over all things competent and that *Allah* has encompassed all things in knowledge."

the postulate of scarcity in mainstream economics. Chapter 3 has explained this critical difference on the basics of the two economic systems. The policy, institutional, social, and scientific implications are vast as well. We will return to this important point as we move along in this book.

Example 1

Consider capital formation by means of two opposite ways — firstly by ways of trade, and oppositely by way of interest rate. We denote the corresponding relative price by (r/i), where "r" denotes the rate of return on trade (market exchange) and "i" denotes the real rate of interest. The wealth equation is given by $W = X_1 \cdot r + X_2 \cdot i$. X_1 and X_2 are trade versus interest bearing outlays, respectively. The indifference curve between X_1 and X_2 in mainstream economic theory implies that both trade and interest are acceptable good activities. Such a choice is reprehensible to Islam. It is also an illogical one. For, interest impedes investment and favors bank savings. On the other hand, investment is spending in trade-related activities. Savings is withdrawal (Ventelou, 2005). Investment is spending today for future rewards of "$r \cdot X_1$". Savings is present withdrawal for future spending of "$i \cdot X_2$".

In the state of optimal allocation of wealth, we would have, $dW = r_1 \cdot dX_1 + i \cdot dX_2 = 0$. The result then is this: as "r" increases relative to "i", then X_1 increases relative to X_2. Consequently, $dr/di = -dX_2/dX_1 > 0$. But such a result remains similar when X_2 increases relative to X_1. Consequently, the Islamic significance to the avoidance of interest is not explained by the neoclassical economic postulate of marginal rate of substitution.

Furthermore, in the optimal state of allocation of wealth between the two sources of wealth we would have the result

$$-d(r \cdot X_1)/d(i \cdot X_2) = -(rdX_1 + X_1 \cdot dr)/(idX_2 + X_2 \cdot di) > 0,$$

in either case of r and i increasing in opposite forms of allocation of wealth between X_1 and X_2. The Islamic case of avoidance of interest for the favor of trade is thus not addressed in mainstream economics.

In the TIE and ethical case, the principal factors underlying the avoidance of interest are an integrated combination of economic and ethical factors. These two factors are endogenously interrelated in the sense of unity of knowledge and positive complementarities between two possible ways of generating wealth. These ways ought to remain complementary to each other. This means that, the financial instrument to use must be a participatory one between two instruments of trade, so as to produce positive socio-economic returns of spending in such good choices.

Examples in such a case would be of the following kinds and many more:

(1) Complementing the instruments of profit-sharing and equity-participation, trade financing and return on trade as market exchange, cost-plus pricing and yield on real assets. These are economic and financial complementarities.

(2) The ethical factor realized together with the economic activities would be poverty alleviation by complementing this goal in respect of the resources of the participants (X_1, X_2), increasing worker empowerment by means of cooperative production and decision-making between workers and management, the rich and the poor.

(3) Participation between the largest possible nexus of participants would be implemented as stakeholders' group activity. The resulting risk diversification and production diversification would further enhance appropriate technology, innovation, and all that these yield.

The complementarities between X_1 and X_2 by various ethico-economic factors are encapsulated in the knowledge parameter, say "θ". The **X**-vector of variables is now changed into $\{W, X_1, X_2, r_1, r_2\}[\theta]$, all variables being commonly induced by "θ" to establish a fully circularly causal participatory system of choices and allocations. "r_1" and "r_2" are the rates of return in two complementary financing and ethical choices. Note, the word ethics here stands for the degree of complementarity gained from the participatory financing instruments of allocating wealth.

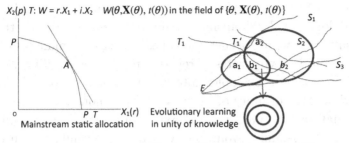

Figure 4.1. Contrasting resource allocation between Islamic and mainstream economic formulations.

Figure 4.1 shows the two opposite cases of allocation of wealth in mainstream and Islamic cases, respectively. As pointed out in Chapter 3, there cannot logically be any optimum and steady-state equilibrium point for the Islamic case of resource allocation in its continuous evolutionary learning property of unity of knowledge. The Islamic case, based on its perturbation effects (Choudhury, 2013) caused by ethical factors that remain embedded as knowledge induction in the economic variables and all other kinds of socio-scientific variables cause probabilistic fields around the points of occurrence of events. Such perturbations cannot be removed by methods like data envelopment analysis (DEA) and stochastic surfaces method. The reason is the persistence of continuous field of simulacra of perturbations and the unattainability of the specific optimum point. The optimum and steady state point remains in the core of economic processes (Debreu, 1959). The core is not accessible, and therefore, not real in treating the conjoint learning interrelations between unity of knowledge and the knowledge-induced variables at hand that are scattered over knowledge, space, and time. Consequently, as pointed out earlier, the mainstream postulates of scarcity, marginal rate of substitution or opportunity cost, competition, conflict, and methodological individualism in mainstream dialectics, and thereby, the results that we are accustomed of assigning to formulas of pricing, marginal productivity, rates of return, and general equilibrium models, all these cannot be copied into Islamic economic formulations by its methodology of unity of knowledge. Now, none of the postulates of rationalism that influence the axiom of economic rationality can abide in the Islamic evolutionary learning formulation, invoking knowledge, space, and time dimensions of the vector of variables $\{\theta, \mathbf{X}(\theta), t(\theta)\}$, and in the functions of such vectors, such as the wellbeing function, $W(\theta, \mathbf{X}(\theta), t(\theta))$, and the system of circular causation relations that explains organic interrelationships in respect of the states of complementarities between the variables, or otherwise.

Detailed formal model of *Tawhidi* consilience: Single system

How does each of the evolutionary paths ES_i correspond with the single-system depiction of *Tawhidi* ethico-economic learning universe? We will now formalize this one-system explanation under the precept of *Tawhidi* unity of knowledge. Following this, the multi-system case will be taken up. We exemplify the one-system case with the example of sustainability in socio-economic development. The sustainability concept is different from sustainable development. Very briefly, we note the differences here in order to then formulate the sustainability index as an example of the wellbeing function defined above.

Sustainability is the organic unity between the knowledge-induced choices of development showing the IIE learning experience in an ever-widening domain of life-sustaining systems. This is also the meaning of the multiverse unity that is set by complementarities between the good things as life-sustaining choices. These are the *maqasid*-choices. Sustainability is based on the concepts of social and spiritual capital (Halpern, 2005; Zohar and Marshall, 2004). Such concepts of capital and wealth, growth, development, and social choice depend upon the IIE learning processes of ethico-economic choices to sustain wellbeing at large. In this sense of being an organic relationship between ethics and diversity of capital with the idea of consilience in it, the meaning of sustainability comes near to the idea of organic unity of morality in choices of capital, and thereby of the artefacts wherein capital is used for moral construction. In such respects of the nature of continuously replenished capital within the life-sustaining concept, the nature of capital is an output of relational unity of knowledge. The property of evolutionary learning under sound consciousness, which is the function of knowledge derived from *Tawhidi* epistemology automatically (endogenously), sustains capital by its wider field of organic interrelationship with wealth, technology, innovation, and the life-fulfillment development outlook. Capital may depreciate but is continuously replenished by such vastly complementary relationships between diverse possibilities according to the episteme of unity of knowledge.

Sustainable development (World Commission for Environment and Development, 1987) treats capital as depreciable good. Although the role of ethics and consciousness is invoked, yet this is not of the self-motivational type. Endogeneity of evolutionary learning and the induction of unity of knowledge are not embedded in choices. Policies and regulations become externally induced ways of directing recovery of capital depreciation. Consequently, the ethical imposition being externally applied, the policy and regulatory instruments are exogenous in nature. This is contrary to the case of organic relationship of capital in the concept of sustainability.

Example 2

The case of sustainable development is a mainstream concept and its welfare concept is a utilitarian one. In Figure 4.1, we can think of two substitutes (X_1, X_2), which can be X_1 denoting environment and X_2 denoting employment. In mainstream economic parlance of opportunity cost, as environment conservation (X_1) increases, forest employment (X_2) drops as clearcutting drops. The reverse case is also true. These manifest the opportunity cost and marginal rate of substitution underlying resource allocation between X_1, X_2 as competing alternatives.

Contrarily, in the case of TIE formulation, X_1 and X_2 are endogenously embedded with the ethical and appropriate technological and innovation effects. This means that environment conservation or clearcutting can increase, but the use of seeding and replantation by the discursive learning between foresters and management will continuously diversify plantation and replant trees, as the case may be. The three factors, namely, $\{\theta_{\text{discourse}}, X_1(\theta), X_2(\theta), t(\theta)\}$ are thus interactive, integrative, and continuously evolutionary through the discursive medium of innovation creating θ-flows by induction. The Islamic diagram of Figure 4.1 now explains the Islamic case of sustainability. Many other cases of environment conservation studied intertemporally can be formulated. The student can try the following exercise.

Exercise 1

Formulate the contrasting cases of sustainability issue in mainstream economics and Islamic economics for the following problem: allow for forest clearcutting but diversify the forest into fruit-bearing that can generate a secondary-linked industry. Consequently, show how the revenue flow takes place among the fruit industry, the forestry industry in diversifying products, and the producers and managers as shareholders. Use a system diagram for explanation.

Formulation of single-system *Tawhidi* epistemological model for unity of knowledge

The commencing point of the knowledge-induced world system in which economics is one is the absolute and perfect law of unity of knowledge, *sunnat Allah*, the divine law. Thus, by *Tawhid* in the socio-scientific intellection, we do not associate the theology of *Allah* and the metaphysical implications of *Allah's* oneness, the "*dhat*" or essence "*a'sas*". Such quiddity is beyond human understanding and stand to sheer speculations without benefit in living experience. We avoid all such metaphysical queries. Instead, we associate *Tawhid* with the unity of the law of *sunnat Allah* and its induction in the process of unification of the generality and details of the world system. In the case of economics, for instance, the precept of unity of knowledge is explained by the organic complementarities between the chosen artefacts in the light of the nature of the Signs of *Allah* (*ayath Allah*)[7] that unravel the unity of "being" and "becoming" and its negation of falsehood to establish the truth.

Allah is not a metaphysical being in Islam as if removed from the world system and its details. Rather, He makes Himself known through His Signs in the order of reality, which comprises *sunnat Allah* in its completeness. *Sunnat Allah* is washed and explained by the Signs of *Allah* (*ayath Allah*) incrementally to human comprehension. Therefore, we take the domain of *sunnat Allah* as the complete and absolute knowledge that creates everything. Yet, by itself, it remains uncreated.

Sunnat Allah as the law of complete and absolute unity of knowledge assumes a non-dimensional mathematical precept. This is referred to as the topology of the supercardinal order (Chapter 2).[8] We will refer to it as the topology, that as the mathematical concept has no dimension and encompasses all of knowledge. We denote this supercardinal topology by the symbol, Ω. The unraveling of the *sunnat Allah* through the message of the *Qur'an* is done by the *sunnah* (teaching) of the Prophet Muhammad. Let the *sunnah* as mapping of the *Qur'an* to the details of the world system be denoted by "s". Then the further discourse among the learned in

---

[7]The signs of *Allah* (*ayath al-Allah*) are all-pervasive over the knowledge, space, and time dimensions. Nothing is left out either in generality or details. The world-system (*a'lameen*) comprises the signs of *Allah*. They encompass the universe of mind and matter in their details of conceptions, formalism, empirical nature and inferences for the construction of the generality and details of the world system. The *Qur'an* (55:13) declares in this regard: "Which then of the bounties of your Lord will you deny?" Furthermore, the *Qur'an* (41:53) declares: "Soon will We show them our Signs in the (furthest) regions (of the earth), and in their own souls, until it becomes manifest to them that this is the Truth. Is it not enough that thy Lord doth witness all things?"

[8]*Qur'an* repeatedly declares like "Verily with God is full knowledge and He is acquainted (with all things)." Also, man has been given a small part of this knowledge as Mercy, and the totality of which is with *Allah*.

Islam (*ulul umri*) is denoted by $\{f\}$. The compounding between $\{s\}$ *unnah* and $\{f\}$ is denoted by, $s \bullet \{f\} = S$, say.

We have shunned away from identifying Ω with the *Qur'an*, because as a functional artefact of the world system it is part of the *Qur'an*. It presents *sunnat Allah* that is functional as a conceptual and an observational category in its operation. Also note that, the *Qur'an* includes certain verses of "*muqatt'at*", divinely secret meanings. These meanings are in the realm of the hidden (*ghayb*), about which the *Qur'an* forbids belaboring to extract meanings regarding them. Those who indulge in this kind of futile speculation are among the weak in belief. Yet, the *Qur'an*, *Tawhid*, and the *Hereafter* (*Akhira*) are relationally identically precepts of belief as the *Qur'an* declares in the chapter, *Naba*. Thus, the unraveling of unity of knowledge as the meaning of the *Tawhidi* epistemology (theory of knowledge) is denoted by[9]

$$[\Omega \rightarrow_{(s\bullet f)} = S \rightarrow \{\theta\}]. \tag{4.1}$$

The function of the flow of knowledge, $\{\theta\}$ derived as shown in Expression (4.1) is to unravel the *ayath Allah* in its generality and details as between the heavens and the earth.[10] Yet, because $\{\theta\}$ is incrementally derived, and so also the "de-knowledge" $\{\theta'\}$ is incrementally rejected with the growth of certainty of knowledge, therefore, the *ayath Allah* manifest themselves surely but incrementally to our human limitations in acquiring full knowledge. We thereby write

$$\{\theta\} \rightarrow \mathbf{X}(\theta) : \{\theta, \mathbf{X}(\theta)\},$$

---

[9] *Qur'an* (78:1-5): "About what are they asking one another? About the great news — that over which they are in disagreement. No! They are going to know. Then, no! They are going to know." Yusuf Ali explains the Great Event as the equivalence, The Hereafter $\approx$ *Qur'an* $\approx$ The Prophetic Message of *Tawhid*.

[10] *Qur'an* (42:52-53): ".... We have made the (*Qur'an*) a Light, wherewith We guide such of Our servants as We will; and verily thou dost guide (men) to the Straight Way, — The way of God to Whom belongs whatever is in the heavens and whatever is on earth. Behold (how) all affairs tend towards God!"

where $\mathbf{X}(\theta)$ denotes the observational entities as multi-variates of *ayath Allah* (being positively induced by knowledge $\{\theta\}$ or by "de-knowledge" $\{\theta'\}$ in order to unravel the truth of knowledge).

We write in combined form

$$[\Omega \rightarrow_{(s \bullet f)} = S \rightarrow \{\theta\}] \rightarrow (\mathbf{X}(\theta), t(\theta)) : \{\theta, \mathbf{X}(\theta), t(\theta)\}. \qquad (4.2)$$

The wellbeing conveyed by the blessings ensued from the *ayath Allah* is a functional criterion explaining and unraveling the degree to which complementarities exist or fail to exist so as to be corrected into moral reconstruction. We write the wellbeing function as

$$W(\theta) = W(\theta, \mathbf{X}(\theta), t(\theta)). \qquad (4.3)$$

Altogether by combining the above expressions we can write

$$[\Omega \rightarrow_{(s \bullet f)} = S \rightarrow \{\theta\}] \rightarrow (\mathbf{X}(\theta), t(\theta)) : \{\theta, \mathbf{X}(\theta), t(\theta)\}$$
$$\rightarrow W(\theta, \mathbf{X}(\theta), t(\theta)). \qquad (4.4)$$

We denote Expression (4.4) as the start and end of one process of evolutionary learning under the precept of unity of knowledge shown in the bracketed, $[\cdot]$.

The commencement of the second process of evolutionary learning follows evaluation of the wellbeing function under the condition of circular causation that represents degrees of complementarities between the variables as expressed by the coefficients of the inter-relating variables $\{\mathbf{X}(\theta)\}$. The resulting equations bringing out the intercausal dependencies between the variables are the circular causation relations (Toner, 1999a, 1999b). We write these as say, $\mathbf{X}(\theta) = \{X_1, X_2, \ldots, X_n\} [\theta]$.

The circular causation equations for this vector are

$$\left. \begin{array}{l} X_1(\theta) = f_1(X_2, \ldots, X_n)[\theta], \\ X_2(\theta) = f_2(X_1, \ldots, X_n)[\theta], \\ \qquad \vdots \\ X_n(\theta) = f_n(X_1, \ldots, X_{n-1})[\theta]. \end{array} \right\} \qquad (4.5)$$

These equations are used as structural ones (not reduced forms) to estimate the wellbeing function by statistically observing the coefficients of the various equations of (4.5). The "as is" functional form of the wellbeing function is thus generated by the following estimation exercise:

Estimate $W(\theta) = \theta$(say by linear approximation,

but this can be nonlinear), $\qquad\qquad$ (4.6)

subject to Equation (4.5).

There are now $(n + 1)$ equations in $(n + 1)$ variables. While the observations of $\mathbf{X}(\theta)$-variables can be obtained from the actual data base, the values of $\{\theta\}$ for each of the $\mathbf{X}(\theta)$-variables must be assigned in accordance with the ranking and averaging across the data set. We show this kind of ranking and averaging in the appendix to this chapter.

When estimation does not show an appropriate degree of complementarities between relevant variables in accordance with the precept of unity of knowledge, then simulation for a better moral reconstruction can be carried out. This is done by discursively changing the estimated coefficients into better complementary values. The theoretical meaning underlying this transformation is that, coefficients are dynamic under repeated simulations (simulacra) while leaving the data set at the observed level. The economy and economic problems in microeconomics are thus affected by the ethico-economic embedding by way of the perturbations caused by $\{\theta\}$ inducing the $\mathbf{X}(\theta)$-variables. The resource allocation consequences are of the nature shown in Figure 4.1.

With the above explanation of estimation and simulation of wellbeing function subject to circular causation Equation (4.5), the complete one-process P_1 of the *Tawhidi* epistemic explanation of Islamic economic formulation can be written down as

$$P_1 : [\Omega \to_{(s \bullet f)} = S \to \{\theta\}] \to (\mathbf{X}(\theta), t(\theta)) : \{\theta, \mathbf{X}(\theta), t(\theta)\} \to W(\theta, \mathbf{X}(\theta), t(\theta)).$$

$$\tag{4.7}$$

$\qquad\qquad\downarrow \qquad\qquad\qquad\qquad \downarrow$ subject to Equation (4.5)

$\qquad$ interaction $\quad$ interaction leading to integration

At the end of every process, thus P_1, evolutionary learning commences to engender P_2, and then likewise P_3 following P_2, etc. At the commencement of every process, the primal ontology denoted by [.] must repeat to refer back everything to *Tawhid* once again and so on, continuously along the evolutionary learning paths.

Expression (4.7) is now completed along IIE learning processes as

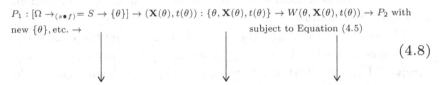

$$P_1 : [\Omega \to_{(s \bullet f)} = S \to \{\theta\}] \to (\mathbf{X}(\theta), t(\theta)) : \{\theta, \mathbf{X}(\theta), t(\theta)\} \to W(\theta, \mathbf{X}(\theta), t(\theta)) \to P_2 \text{ with}$$

new $\{\theta\}$, etc. $\to$ subject to Equation (4.5)

$$(4.8)$$

interaction   interaction leading to integration $\to$ evolutionary learning

Note that the process meaning of including [.] in every evolutionary learning process indicates simulated levels of comprehending the *Tawhidi* unity of knowledge, and thus the moral reconstruction of the economic system (world system).

Expression (4.8) is the final single-system formulation of Islamic economy in its microeconomic and macroeconomic states under the theory of *Tawhidi* unity of knowledge. Yet, the same string relation also holds for the "de-knowledge" case. Take the example of dialectical models of rationalist genre as in Marxism/Hegelianism (Resnick and Wolff, 1987). According to Marxist theory of economic planning, the price relatives are set by central planning. Hence, the resource allocation trajectory follows a given path over the planning period. The production possibility curve *PP* in Figure 4.1 becomes kinked in shape. The variables become perfect complements but not endogenously, rather by the command of central planning.

The nature of microeconomics and macroeconomics in *Tawhidi* methodology

It is worth noting how microeconomics and macroeconomics are treated by the *Tawhidi* String Relational formulation of Expression (4.8). In TIE formulation by the *Tawhidi* string relation (TSR)

of Expression (4.8), most importantly the method of aggregation by IIE learning determines the level of economic analysis. An example here is of preference formation from the individual to the level of social preference. In mainstream economic theory, social preferences and thereby the social welfare function are established by linearly independent individual preferences by virtue of the fact that methodological individualism determines all forms of choices in mainstream economics.

The household welfare function is determined by the competing preferences of husband and wife, so as to explain why the marriage survives? Becker (1989) sought the answer in the following household payment arrangement: if the monetary perk that the husband adds to the wife's earned income causes her marginal utility of income along the shifted curve, to be higher than the marginal utility of earned income, then the marriage survives. Otherwise it breaks down. On the other hand as well, the "real" marginal household utility before and after the income transfer remains equal for the husband and the wife, then the marriage remains in balance (social equilibrium). Otherwise the family breaks down. Such a result remains independent of children in the family. In the sense of social welfare, this welfare function becomes a linearly additive function of the totality of society's husbands and wives. Now, there are two competing groups of welfare functions. The above utilitarian criterion for the national family welfare applies.

In the *Tawhidi* formulation of social choices with Islamic values, aggregation is done by interaction, integration, and sustainability conferred by evolutionary learning processes. The family aggregate preference is determined by the common agreement reached between all family members on any decision undertaken. The common agreement represents the interaction leading to consensus (integration). The family furthers its discursive value onwards as the maturity of knowledge seeking for the common good continues by evolutionary learning in continuums.

When such household IIE learning values are promoted at the societal level, a greater nexus of behavioral patterns takes place along the same line. Now, the wellbeing function represents the tree of nexus of interrelationships for the common good. The *Qur'an* declares that divorce is the worst of the permissible acts in the eyes of *Allah*. On the other hand, ceremonious prayer at its appointed time is the most liked by *Allah*. The implications of such declarations are that knowledge-gaining activity by prayer cements participation and pairing in and across families in the social order (Choudhury, 2011).

The microeconomic nature of the family in the case of main-stream economics now disappears by the presence of the knowledge-induced interrelations that extend from the family to society at large. Likewise, the macroeconomic nature of an estranged nation in familial agreements is replaced by the IIE learning preferences that are induced by ethical behavior denoted by knowledge flows $\{\theta\}$ within families and across the families of the nation as a whole. An aggregate social ideal thus arises out of such evolutionary learning behavior.

Exercise 2

In the case of economic planning by keeping capital/labor ratio fixed how would you use Figure 4.1 to explain the three cases: (1) mainstream neoclassical case with X_1, X_2; (2) Marxist fixed endowment case with X_1, X_2; and (3) the Islamic case using the complementary case of evolutionary learning.

Example 3

Let us now take parts of the Human Development Index to fit into the Islamic formulation by Expression (4.8), while undertaking a critical view of HDI. HDI (see UNDP) is a geometric mean of the three critical indicators — real GDP, life expectancy, and years of schooling by levels of education. These indicators can be further disaggregated as by age, gender, and sources of incomes (earned, wealth, and transfer by poor brackets). Such disaggregation however is not done. Rather different indexes are developed such as poverty index, gender empowerment index. HDI as it is used to rank countries not only according to income levels but also by social causes is a mono-causal indicator. Contrarily, if we were to treat the HDI as a wellbeing index, then this would be estimated and simulated firstly as one-process and then in a more complex undertaking by subsequent evolutionary processes. In each such case, circular causation equations will be used as the relations signifying degrees of existing complementary relations and the expected complementarities that can be induced via the coefficients of the variables.

Now, using the TSR of Expression (4.8), we denote the following indicators:

1. X_1: real GDP per capita; thus, $X_1(\theta)$ would denote a degree of complementarity with the other variables.
2. X_2: life expectancy; thus, $X_2(\theta)$ would denote a degree of complementarity with the rest of the variables.
3. X_3: enrolment ratio; thus, $X_3(\theta)$ will denote a degree of complementarity with the rest of the variables.
4. The wellbeing function replacing HDI would be $W(\theta) \approx \theta = W(X_1, X_2, X_3)[\theta]$.
5. The estimation and simulation of the wellbeing function subject to circular causation equations are given by

Evaluate $\theta = W(X_1, X_2, X_3)[\theta]$,
subject to

$$\left. \begin{array}{l} X_1 = f_1(X_2, X_3), \\ X_2 = f_2(X_1, X_3), \\ X_3 = f_3(X_1, X_2). \end{array} \right\} \tag{4.9}$$

Each of these equations and the wellbeing function can be taken in linear, log-linear, and other complex forms. For reasons of interpreting the coefficients as elasticity of wellbeing in respect of each of the variables, it is preferred to estimate in the log-linear form.

In the light of the *Tawhidi* epistemology, the HDI estimation in respect of the intervariable causality means that a balance ought to be established between the list of critical variables to impart wellbeing as a common good to all. This too is the idea of sustainability that was explained earlier. The variables can be disaggregated further. Without the *Tawhidi* epistemic foundation, the need for circular causation, complementarity, and the meaning of wellbeing (*maslaha*) would not arise. The entire problem would then devolve into the HDI as the mainstream mono-causal problem.

Next, we fit in all the different parts of the multi-causal meaning of HDI as wellbeing as follows:

$$
\begin{array}{c}
\text{Unity of knowledge } \{\theta, X_1(\theta), X_2(\theta), X_3(\theta); (t(\theta))\} W(\theta) \approx \theta = W(\{\theta, X_1(\theta), X_2(\theta), X_3(\theta); \\
(t(\theta))\}, \text{etc.,} \qquad \qquad \qquad \qquad \qquad \qquad \qquad \text{subject to Equation (4.9)} \\
P_1 : [\Omega \to_{(s \bullet f)} = S \to \{\theta\}] \to (\mathbf{X}(\theta), t(\theta)) : \{\theta, \mathbf{X}(\theta), t(\theta)\} \to W(\theta, \mathbf{X}(\theta), t(\theta)) \to P_2 \text{ with} \\
\text{new } \{\theta\}, \text{etc.} \to \qquad\qquad\qquad\qquad \begin{array}{c}\text{subject to}\\ \text{Equation (4.5)}\end{array} \qquad (4.10) \\
\text{interaction} \quad \text{interaction leading to integration} \to \text{evolutionary learning}
\end{array}
$$

Extension of Islamic economic formulation to multi-systems

Consider two-system construction of the TSR formulation of TIE (world system) — heavens and earth. As the *Qur'an* declares, *Allah* is the Lord of the heavens and the earth and all that are in between. In mainstream economic theory, the nexus of relations between different variables belong to a single-system process relation divided into sectors. Thus, in the generalized system of organic interrelations, the product market, the labour market, the fiscal sector, and the monetary sector — all these sectors and their variables form the interacting sub-systems within the same economic system. This can be further expanded to the open economy case with trade and international factors and services as interrelations. Nonetheless, in the widest form of the generalized system model, there are exogenous variables, such as fiscal and monetary policies importantly, and all other policies that are exogenously applied in mainstream economics. Consequently, unlike this case, in the Islamic self-regulatory case, the circular causation relations generate pervasively endogenous variables including the endogenous-type policy variables. Preferences of all kinds we have shown are not datum, being θ-induced. Technology and innovation are all θ-induced. Only a free choice stands out under conditions of conscious decision-making with righteous guidance. The *Qur'an* says in this regard that only truth stands out. Truth is the principle of unity of knowledge and its induction of the good things of life — the *maqasid*-choices.[11] Policies must therefore interrelate with all other endogenous variables and thus become endogenous themselves by the force of the underlying principle of organic "pairing" that reflects the Truth of the *Tawhidi* episteme of unity of knowledge and its induction of the unified economic sub-system.

Besides, the multi-system TSR in the formulation of the *TIE* system points out that the economy and its variables and functions are only a part of the nexus of systemic interrelations. Indeed, as we will explain towards the end of this book, science and economics span the entire universe with meaning and consciousness. Thereby, the universal design of the *Tawhidi* law is indeed that of science and economics. These mind spaces form the grand design of the science of the Signs of *Allah* and of the comprehensive order and scheme of embedding of *Tawhidi* economic science with every other discipline and conduct of life. This life experience embraces the moral and ethical order. It is the order of *maqasid as-shari'ah* derived in, from, and towards the deepening knowledge of the *Tawhidi* law and its induction of the world system in its generality and details. Because of the multi-systemic depiction of the consciously evolutionary learning, the world system becomes the true depiction of reality. Therefore, TIE does not stand alone as an isolated system. It cannot be studied as such. The meaning of knowledge flows, "θ" derived from the divine source, (Ω, S), as we have explained, now implies the unity of all IIE systems, both intra-systems and inter-systems in the entire nexus of experience.

---

[11] *Qur'an* (10:32): "Such is God, your real Cherisher and Sustainer: Apart from Truth, what (remains) but error? How then are ye turned away?"

Multi-system model formulation: Islamic political economy contra mainstream political economy

A depiction of such an internexus of unifying relationships is conveyed by the discipline of Islamic political economy and world-system study (Choudhury, 2014b). Here too there is a substantive difference between the mainstream study of political economy and Islamic political economy. In either case though, the study of political economy encompasses a broad field of interactive study across a nexus of factors that impinge on economic activities. Among such extraneous forces impressed exogenously on economic variables, mainstream economic thought adds on political, social, cultural, and recently religious forces (Witham, 2010). Such is the impossibility of the problem of heteronomy departed away from consciousness as intrinsic value.

Political economy in its mainstream context (Staniland, 1985) is a study of the dynamics of conflict and strategies underlying the nature, formation, and distribution of wealth among its contending claimants. These can be groups within countries, regions, and among countries in the global economy, which is the study of world system in its capitalistic and socialistic meanings of conflict and competition, and acquisition and deprivation. Thus, there is the classical political economy and the global political economy that grew on the spur of capitalist globalization (Nizan and Bichler, 2000). Political economy taken in the context of global conflicts also addresses the deeply theoretical issues of epistemology (Ruggie, 2003a, 2003b). It reflects the alternative views of social reality across nations, culture, and historical developments.

Nitzan and Bichler contrast the better picture of global political economy against the neoclassical political economy (Srinivasan, 1985) and the neoliberal political economy (Nitzan and Bichler, 2000, p. 67) in the following words: "And so from Smith onward, it became increasingly customary to separate human actions into two distinct spheres, 'vertical' and 'horizontal'. The vertical dimension revolves around power, authority, command, manipulation, and dissonance.

Academically, it belongs to the realm of politics. The horizontal axis centers around wellbeing, free choice, exchange, and equilibrium — the academic preoccupation of economists. The consequence of this duality was to make modern political economy an impossible patchwork: its practitioners try to re-marry power and wellbeing, but having accepted them as distinct spheres of activity to begin with, the marriage is inherently shaky."

Islamic political economy of the *Tawhidi* epistemological genre is substantively different from the mainstream study. But its methodology subsumes the mainstream one by a change of the knowledge model into a "de-knowledge" model that is based on methodological individualism, conflict, competition, and the belief on the scarcity of resources that otherwise can be shared. *Tawhidi* Islamic political economy as an epistemological study is premised on unity of knowledge across diversity of partners who can complement the claims on resources, wealth, and markets. Such a foundation of *Tawhidi* Islamic political economy rests on the *Tawhidi* epistemology of unity of knowledge. This methodology was explained earlier. In the multi-system extension of the TSR, the IIE learning properties of this formulation applies to the learning dynamics of multi-group cooperation, intra-country political and institutional cohesion, globalization with a human face, and institutional global governance for common wellbeing.

Examples of *Tawhidi* Islamic political economy studies are economic integration of the *ummah*, the world nation of Islam via trade, development, resource sharing, and common institutional policies and strategies such as monetary and development policies, and shared spirit and practice of discourse (*shura*). *Tawhidi* Islamic political economy can contribute significantly to global wellbeing by suggesting such cooperative (participatory) models to the United Nations Organization, UNCTAD, World Bank, IMF (Commission on Global Governance, 2005). The Islamic worldview can also contribute to the goal of development of the South. The South Commission (1990, p. 13) writes: "To sum up: development is a process of self-reliant growth, achieved through participation of the people acting in their own interests as they see them, and under their own control." In the light of such a broad perspective of political economy as cooperation, participation, and complementarities in the common heritage of man and global society, the *Tawhidi* multi-system model has much to offer.

Yet in the multi-system framework of *Tawhidi* Islamic political economy, there are a number of critical details that need to be studied. Firstly, there is the theory of the *shura* evolutionary learning process and institution. The *shura* means the *Qur'anic* medium of consultation.[12] But the *shura* broadly means discursive process of multi-system enlightened discussions and decision-making at all levels. There is an even further broad meaning associated with the *shura*. This is regarding what the *shura* consults about. At this stage of the Islamic existence, the *shura* becomes a discursive process that studies and consults mutually within and across it on the substantive issues of diverse depth and meaning of enlightened arguments. Such *shuras* belong to diverse ranks of scholarly discourse as also of policy-makers. In this way, the *shura* model extends to all levels of the social order — the family, community, society at large, institutions, the marketplace, and all the smaller and larger bodies that these endure. This comprehends the totality of the TIE and science. The *shura* thus discourses on the details of the mind and matter interrelated issues. These are equivalent to investigating the nature of the worshipping world system in its generality and details. The recognition of the conscious world system in perpetual abeyance to *Allah* is termed as *tasbih*. The *Qur'an* (42:53) says in this regard: "The Way of God, to Whom belongs whatever is in the heavens and whatever is on earth. Behold (how) all affairs tend towards God!" The central role of *tasbih*, consciousness of the worshipping world of matter and mind in *shura* process is brought out elsewhere in the *Qur'an* (21:79).[13] Also see *Qur'an* (59:24).[14]

---

[12] *Qur'an* (42:38): "Those who hearken to their Lord, and establish regular prayer; who (conduct) their affairs by mutual consultation . . . . ."

[13] *Qur'an* (21:79): "To Solomon We inspired the (right) understanding of the matter: to each (of them) We gave judgment and Knowledge; it was Our power that made the hills and the birds celebrate Our praises, with David: It was We Who did (all these things)."

[14] *Qur'an* (59:24): "He is God, the Creator, the Evolver, the Bestower of Forms (of Colours). To Him belong the Most Beautiful Names: Whatever is in the heavens

Multi-system formulation of *Tawhidi* Islamic political economy

Let S_1 denote the system comprising heavens, and S_2 denote the system comprising the earth. The multi-system TSR is shown by

$$\rightarrow \{\theta_1\}] \rightarrow (\mathbf{X}_1(\theta_1), t(\theta_1)) : \{\theta_1, \mathbf{X}_1(\theta_1), t(\theta_1)\} \rightarrow W(\theta_1, \mathbf{X}_1(\theta_1), t(\theta_1)) \rightarrow P_2$$

with new $\{\theta_1\}$, etc.

$$[\Omega \rightarrow_{(s \bullet f)} = S \rightarrow \{\theta_1, \theta_2\}] \tag{4.11}$$

$$\rightarrow \{\theta_2\}] \rightarrow (\mathbf{X}_2(\theta_2), t(\theta_2)) : \{\theta_2, \mathbf{X}_2(\theta_2), t(\theta_2)\} \rightarrow W(\theta_2, \mathbf{X}_2(\theta_2), t(\theta_2)) \rightarrow P_2$$

with new $\{\theta\}$, etc.

According to the *Qur'an*, the heavens and the earth are paired realities in the worship of *Allah*. They therefore share a common law, which is derived from the divine law (*sunnat Allah*) that governs the domains of the heavens and the earth. Exemplars of such domains include solar energy, rain, and taming and tapping the wind and the cosmic environment. These elements are associated with the cosmic domain. The earth as the other domain has its vegetation, produce, markets, and yields as rewards. These belong to the economic and social domains. While these domains have their distinct dynamics of learning (*tasbih*), yet they collectively unite to define the common wellbeing of the multi-system universe through their common worship of *Allah* in terms of *sunnat Allah*.[15]

Thus, the expressions in (4.11) are combined together according to the dynamics of IIE learning. The resulting system of circular causation system comprises the computational general equilibrium model of the multi-system universe.

---

and on earth, do declare His Praises and Glory: And He is the Exalted in Might, the Wise."

[15] *Qur'an* (22:18): "Seest thou not that to God bow down in worship all things that are in the heavens and on earth, — the sun, the moon, the stars; the hills, the trees, the animals; and a great number among mankind..."

The multi-variates are denoted by the vector, $\mathbf{X}(\theta) = \{\mathbf{X}_1, \mathbf{X}_2\}[\theta]$, where $\theta = (\theta_1 \cap \theta_2)$. This implies the wellbeing function to assume the form $W(\theta) = W(\mathbf{X}(\theta))$. The circular causation model is given by, $\mathbf{X}_1(\theta) = f_i(\mathbf{X}_2(\theta))$, where the vector variables are expanded over as many elements as they can possibly have, say n_1 — number for $\mathbf{X}_1$, n_2 — number for $\mathbf{X}_2$. Thus, the various functional relations are structural equations for $i = 1, 2, \ldots, n_1, \ldots, n_2$ (say). There are $(n_1 + n_2)$ number of circular causation equations. The final $(n_1 + n_2 + 1)$th equation gives the *quantitative* empirical form of the wellbeing function as defined earlier: $\theta = W(\mathbf{X}(\theta))$, say by a linear approximation obtainable by the implicit function theorem of differential calculus. We will explain the assignment of θ-values in the appendix to this chapter.

One form of these various equations can be log-linear. This form helps in a ready interpretation of the estimated and simulated coefficients as elasticity coefficients of the dependent variable in respect of the independent variables. The quantitative form of the wellbeing function can be taken in the product for $\theta = \Pi_{i=1}^{(n1+n2)} \mathbf{X}_1{}^{\mathbf{a}} \mathbf{X}_2{}^{\mathbf{b}}$; $\mathbf{a, b}$ are vector coefficients of the various variables of the vectors as shown. They explain the degrees of complementarities between θ-values and the variables, and between the variables as shown in the circular causation estimates and simulated values. Thereby the coefficients "$\mathbf{a}$" and "$\mathbf{b}$", because of their simulacra of variations according to the policy-theoretic changes in θ-values, are themselves also θ-induced. The result now is that the entire system of simulation of wellbeing, subject to the system of intervariable circular causation relations becomes a nonlinear and dynamic functional.

Exercise 3

Adapt the multi-system formulation of the TSR (4.11) to the verses 1–5 of the Chapter *R'ad* of the *Qur'an* and explain all details. Particularly in reference to verse 5, set up and explain the "*de-knowledge*" model of rationalism of mainstream multi-system in terms of its characteristics of differentiation, methodological independence and individualism, competition, and both denial or exogeneity of moral and ethical values in socio-economic methodology.

Appendix

Assignment of θ-values for circular causation estimation/simulation

The following tabulation shows how θ-values corresponding to the socio-economic values are assigned to represent the ranking of knowledge both within given columns and across rows of variables by averaging. Within given columns of the socio-economic variables that are considered admissible according to the *shari'ah*, the best selected θ-value may be assigned to say $\theta = 10$. Rest of the θ-values are prorated by the formula: $\theta_s = (10/x_c{}^*)^*x_s$, where $x_c{}^*$ denotes the socio-economic value corresponding to the selected one for $\theta = 10$. "x_s" denotes the other socio-economic values, $s = 1, 2, \dots$. θ_s denotes the pro-rated θ-values for the socio-economic variables $s = 1, 2, \dots$. Note that the attributes of *asma al-husna* are used to qualify the kind of moral and ethical values and their levels of significance in this respect that are reflected by the given socio-economic variables.

For instance, variables by columns representing peace (*salam*) for stability, bestower of forms (*bariul musawwir*) representing diversification, strength (*matin*) representing growth, safety (*muhaimin*) representing sustainability, etc. Such attributes associated with the characterization of socio-economic variables may also be surveyed. An example of such a case is the survey of managers on their managerial qualities responding to selected attributes of *asma al-husna*. The responses can be ranked.[16]

In multi-system estimation and simulation using the circular causation method responding to the *Tawhidi* methodology of unity of

---

[16]Let $i = 1, 2, \dots, m$ denote number of managers surveyed cross-sectionally in respect of specified socio-economic variables, $j = 1, 2, \dots, n$ to respond to a given attribute of *asma al-husna* corresponding to the socio-economic variable by the quality of managers' responses. Let such responses be ranked as $\theta_{ij} = 1, 2, \dots,$ 10 along with fractions between these numbers. The averages across the columns represent row-averages: $[\Sigma_{j=1}^{n}\theta_{ij} \cdot j]/n = \theta_i\text{avg}, i = 1, 2, \dots, m$.

Table A.1. Primary/secondary data tabulation.

Socioeconomics Variables: Activities	Attributes from *asma al-husna* (a_i)	Responses by Numbered Responses	Averaged to Denote θ-values
x_1^k	$i = 1$	θ_{11}^{k}	
	2	θ_{12}^{k}	
	.	.	$\theta_1^k = \mathrm{Avg}(\theta_{11}^{k}, \ldots, \theta_{1n1}^{k})$
	.	.	
	n_1	θ_{1n1}^{k}	
x_2^{k}	$i = 1$	θ_{21}^{k}	
	2	θ_{22}^{k}	
	.	.	$\theta_2^{k} = \mathrm{Avg}(\theta_{21}^{k}, \ldots, \theta_{2n1}^{k})$
	.	.	
	n_1	θ_{2n1}^{k}	
x_n^{k}	$i = 1$	$\theta_{n,1}^{k}$	
	2	$\theta_{n,2}^{k}$	
.	.	.	$\theta_n^{k} = \mathrm{Avg}(\theta_{n,1}^{k}, \ldots, \theta_{n,n1}^{k})$
.	.	.	
.	n_1	$\theta_{n,n1}^{k}$	

Table A.2. Tabulations with socio-economic values and θ-values.

t	x_1^{t}	x_2^{t}	$\ldots$	x_n^{t}	θ_1^{t}	θ_2^{t}	$\ldots$	θ_n^{t}	$\theta^{t*} - \mathrm{Avg}(\theta_1^{t}, \theta_2^{t}, \ldots, \theta_n^{t})$
1	x_1^{1}	x_2^{1}	$\ldots$	x_n^{1}	θ_1^{1}	θ_2^{1}	$\ldots$	θ_n^{1}	θ^1
2	x_1^{2}	x_2^{2}	$\ldots$	x_n^{2}	θ_1^{2}	θ_2^{2}	$\ldots$	θ_n^{2}	θ^2
.									
.									
T	x_1^{T}	x_2^{T}	$\ldots$	x_n^{T}	θ_1^{T}	θ_2^{T}	$\ldots$	θ_n^{T}	θ^T

knowledge, the tabulation is done in Table A.1. Table A.2 shows this with θ-values. This is an example that is applicable to both the single-system and multi-system cases. It is also an example applicable for cross-sectional and time-series values of socio-economic variables, and for cross-sectional questionnaire survey responses on socio-economic variables as these are tallied with given qualities reflected by *asma al-husna*. Among the cross-sectional cases, there can be regions and countries as in trading blocs. There can be firms, corporations, and small and medium size enterprises and their managers.

Data can also be generated by panel. In this case, cross-sectional variables can be first averaged by time series and θ-averages developed as discussed above. The time series of θ-averages can be next used for running the time-series circular causation equations. The final results in every case now involve the estimation and simulation of the following circular causation model:

Estimate/simulate $\theta = W(\mathbf{X}(\theta_{avg}))$,   (A.1)

subject to circular causation equations in the elements

of the vector variables $\mathbf{X}(\theta_{avg})$

corresponding to the $\mathbf{X}(\theta_{avg})$-variables for every θ_{avg}-value.

Note that in estimating/simulating the circular causation equations, it is not absolutely necessary to use the θ_{avg}-values. These equations may be estimated/simulated as structural relations between the socio-economic variables solely without θ-variable. But in the estimation/simulation of the wellbeing function, θ_{avg}-values are required to be one column of observations corresponding to the socio-economic variables. Without this column of values, the coefficients of the variables in (A.1) cannot be estimated/simulated.

Furthermore, the phases of simulated θ-values over stages of evolutionary learning are depicted in Table A.3. Likewise, the simulacra of simulated socio-economic variables corresponding to series of θ_{avg}-values are shown in Table A.4.

Table A.3. Simulated θ_{avg}-values over phases of evolutionary learning.

θ_1	$\rightarrow$	θ_2	$\rightarrow$	θ_3	$\rightarrow \ldots\ldots \rightarrow$	θ_n
$\downarrow$		$\downarrow$		$\downarrow$		$\downarrow$
θ_1^*	$\rightarrow$	θ_2^*	$\rightarrow$	θ_3^*	$\rightarrow \ldots\ldots \rightarrow$	θ_n^*
$\downarrow$		$\downarrow$		$\downarrow$		$\downarrow$
θ_1^{**}	$\rightarrow$	θ_2^{**}	$\rightarrow$	θ_3^{**}	$\rightarrow \ldots\ldots \rightarrow$	θ_n^{**}

Table A.4. Simulated socio-economic variables in respect of simulated θ_{avg}-values over phases of evolutionary learning.

$$x_1(\theta_1) \rightarrow \qquad x_2(\theta_2) \rightarrow \qquad x_3(\theta_3) \rightarrow \dots\dots \rightarrow \qquad x_n(\theta_n)$$
$$\downarrow \qquad\qquad\qquad \downarrow \qquad\qquad\qquad \downarrow \qquad\qquad\qquad\qquad\qquad \downarrow$$
$$x_1{}^*(\theta_1{}^*) \rightarrow \qquad x_2{}^*(\theta_2{}^*) \rightarrow \qquad x_3{}^*(\theta_3{}^*) \rightarrow \dots\dots \rightarrow \qquad x_n{}^*(\theta_n{}^*)$$

$$x_1{}^*(\theta_1{}^*) \rightarrow \qquad x_2{}^*(\theta_2{}^*) \rightarrow \qquad x_3{}^*(\theta_3{}^*) \rightarrow \dots\dots \rightarrow \qquad x_n^*(\theta_n{}^*)$$
$$\downarrow \qquad\qquad\qquad \downarrow \qquad\qquad\qquad \downarrow \qquad\qquad\qquad\qquad\qquad \downarrow$$
$$x_1{}^{**}(\theta_1{}^{**}) \rightarrow \quad x_2{}^{**}(\theta_2{}^{**}) \rightarrow \quad x_3{}^{**}(\theta_3{}^{**}) \rightarrow \dots\dots \rightarrow \quad x_n{}^{**}(\theta_n{}^{**})$$

Exercise 4

(i) Fit the variables shown in Tables A.1–A.4 into the multi-system model explained in Expression (4.11).

(ii) Explain the steps in the multi-system construction of the *Tawhidi* string relations. Use either of (i) time-series data; (ii) cross-sectional data; and (iii) panel data approach.

(iii) In each case, write down and explain the corresponding circular causation model.

Conclusion

Throughout the earlier chapters, and it will be the same throughout this book, the central methodology of TIE in particular and Islamic world system in general is the *Tawhidi* methodology. It has its deep analytical premise that takes its shape and form in describing the multi-causal world system with economics as a particular but most profound study of intervariable circular causal relations with the nexus of multi-systems. Nothing escapes this methodology. The results borne out by the circular causation based on the epistemology of unity of knowledge arising from the *Tawhidi* methodological worldview are profound.

The *Tawhidi* methodology of unity of knowledge explained and quantitatively reflected through the model of circular causation is found also in the books of the sociological thinkers. On the circular causation issue Fitzpatrick (2003, p. 128) writes "everything is a reproduction of other reproductions. Society explodes in on itself and we cannot liberate ourselves from the *simulacra*...". In science likewise, Hawking and Mlodinow (2010, p. 80) writes regarding the scientific method with the property of simulacra: "Feynman showed that, for a general system, the probability of any observation is constructed from all the possible histories that could have led to that observation. Because of that his method is called the "'sum over histories' or 'alternative histories' formulation of quantum physics".

This and the earlier chapters have derived the *Tawhidi* methodology from the *Qur'an* and the *sunnah*. They have provided several examples and have set several exercises for general readers to work out in detail. It is necessary for the serious readers and students to understand the nature of and scientific discovery by the *Tawhidi* methodology that is universally and uniquely reflected by the method of circular causation. This method describes and analytically calculates the degrees of complementarities (partnership, participation) between the variables representing the good things of life.

By the same methodology, the circular causation method can also explain the behavior of the "de-knowledge" model. This is the model that arises from the epistemology of rationalism as defined in this and earlier chapters. Consequently, the *Tawhidi* methodology of unity of knowledge is in most cases contrary to the axiom of mainstream economics. The results and consequences of this contrariness remain unique yet universal to the case of TIEs in particular and the *Tawhidi* Islamic world system in general.

References

Barrow, J. D. (1991). *Theories of Everything, the Quest for Ultimate Explanation*, Oxford, England: Oxford University Press.

Becker, G. S. (1989). "Family", in *The New Palgrave: Social Economics*, Eatwell, J., Milgate, M. and Newman P. (Eds.), New York, NY: W.W. Norton, pp. 64–76.

Choudhury, M. A. (2011). "Family as socioeconomic management system", *International Journal of Management Systems*, 18(1), 99–115.

Choudhury, M. A. (2013). "Perturbation theory in cognitive socio-scientific research: Towards sociological economic analysis", *Mind and Society*, 12(2), 203–217.

Choudhury, M. A. (2014a). *Tawhidi Epistemology and Its Applications: Economics, Finance, Science, and Society*, Cambridge, England: Cambridge Scholarly Publishing.

Choudhury, M. A. (2014b). "Islamic Political Economy: A Methodological Inquiry", *Social Epistemology. Review and Reply Collective (SERRC;* http://social-epistemology.com).

Commission on Global Governance (1995). "Global Civic Ethic", in *Our Global Neighbourhood, A Report of the Commission on Global Governance*, New York, N.Y: Oxford University Press.

Debreu, G. (1959). *Theory of Value, an Axiomatic Analysis of Economic Equilibrium*, New York: John Wiley.

Fitzpatrick, T. (2003). "Postmodernism and new directions", in *Social Policy*, Alcock, P., Erskine, A. and May, M. (Eds.), Oxford, England: Blackwell, pp. 125–133.

Halpern, D. (2005). *Social Capital*, Cambridge, England: Polity Press.

Hawking, S. W. and Mlodinow, L. (2010). "Alternative histories", in *The Grand Design*, London, England: Transworld Publishers, pp. 80, 82.

Ibrahim, E. and Johnson-Davies, D. (n.d.). *Forty Hadith Qudsi*, Translated and Personal Publication.

Nitzan, J. and Bichler, S. (2000). "Capital accumulation: Breaking the dualism of 'economics' and 'politics', in *Global Political Economy, Contemporary Issues*, Palan, R. (Ed.), London, England: Routledge, pp. 67–88.

Resnick, S. A. and Wolff, R. D. (1987). *Knowledge and Class, A Marxian Critique of Political Economy*, Chicago, IL: The University of Chicago Press.

Ruggie, J. G. (2003a). "Introduction: What makes the world hang together? Neo-utilitarianism and the social constructivist challenge", in *Constructing the World Polity*, London, England: Routledge, pp. 1–40.

Ruggie, J. G. (2003b). "The new institutionalism in international relations", in *Constructing the World Polity*, London, England: Routledge, pp. 45–61.

South Commission (1990). *The Challenge to the South*, Oxford, England: Oxford University Press.

Srinivasan, T. N. (1985). "Neoclassical political economy, the state and economic development", *Asian Development Review*, 1(1), 38–58.

Staniland, M. (1985). "The fall and rise of political economy", in *What is Political Economy? A Study of Social Theory and Underdevelopment*, New Haven, CT: Yale University Press, pp. 10–35.

Stehr, N. (2002). "Knowledge societies", in *Knowledge & Economic Conduct, the Social Foundations of the Modern Economy*, ON, Canada: University of Toronto Press Toronto, pp. 63–73.

Toner, P. (1999a). "Gunnar Myrdal (1898–1987): Circular and cumulative causation as the methodology of the social sciences", in *Main Currents in Cumulative Causation, the Dynamics of Growth and Development*, Chapter 5, Houndmills, Hampshire: Macmillan Press Ltd.

Toner, P. (1999b). "Conclusion", in *Main Currents in Cumulative Causation, the Dynamics of Growth and Development*, Chapter 7, Houndmills, Hampshire: Macmillan Press Ltd.

United Nations Development Program (UNDP) Several Annual Reports. *Human Development Report*, New York, NY: Oxford University Press.

Ventelou, B. (2005). "Economic thought on the eve of the General Theory", in *Millennial Keynes*, Chapter 2, Armonk, New York: M. E. Sharpe.

Wilson, E. O. (1998). *Consilience, Unity of Knowledge*, New York: Vantage Press.

Witham, L. (2010). *Marketplace of the Gods, How Economics Explains Religion*, Oxford, UK: Oxford University Press.

World Commission for Environment and Development (Brundtland, G.H. Report) (1987). *Our Common Future*, Oxford, England: Oxford University Press.

Zohar, D. and Marshall, I. N. (2004). *Spiritual Capital: Wealth We can Live By*, Francisco, CA, USA: Berett-Koehler.

Chapter 5

Islamic Participatory Instruments and the Ethical Dimensions

Introduction

An intellectual critique is launched on the prevalent nature of knowledge and scope of thinking in Islamic economics and finance. Such thought and the practices that emanate with them have resulted in a poor Islamic showing by the development of the present state of Islamic knowledge and financial institutions worldwide. No revolutionary worldview has arisen. The missing paradigm in intellection, application, and practice is the distinctive Islamic worldview concerning the functional nature of the epistemology of unity of knowledge that emanates from the monotheistic law in the *Qur'an* and is guided into action by the *sunnah*, and thereby, by Islamic discourse. The chapter recommends that the worldview of unity of knowledge (*Tawhid*) by its epistemology and functionalism be formalized and applied at the highest educational and institutional levels. Along the path of such intellectual and applied reconstruction, the chapter rejects the validity of the *traditional practice* of *fiqh*, religious interpretive knowledge. Yet, we uphold the importance of *fiqh* in Islamic jurisprudence. Thus, the chapter recommends returning every inquiry to the *Qur'an*, the *sunnah*, and Islamic discourse for ever fresh search and discovery in all socio-scientific matters every time an issue is raised. The scope of the *maqasid as-shari'ah* is thus broadened out into the widest socio-scientific inquiry to help in developing *muamalat* (socio-economic affairs).

The chapter then gives an example showing the institutionalizing possibility of an integrative financing instrument in trade and development in the *ummah* according to the theory of unity of knowledge and unity (*Tawhid*) of the knowledge-induced (*Tawhidi* knowledge-induced) specific case of the participatory instrument. This foreign trade financing certificate (FTFC) can be commercially viable and academically rewarding according to the underlying theory of unity of knowledge and the unitary world system (*Tawhidi*).

Background

There is a debate being waged for a considerable time now by Islamic economists and finance experts calling for resorting to mainstream methods and models of these fields with some *fiqhi* coloring to them. *Fiqh* means canonical Islamic jurisprudence or rules of the *shari'ah*, the Islamic law, based on religious interpretation. *Fiqhi* inferences color what the protagonists would like to qualify as "Islamic". The retrogressive results have been that Islamic financial institutions have embraced this mechanistic approach to label what they call is Islamic economic and financial instruments and *shari'ah* compliance.

There are multiple methodological errors in such an approach to what has come to be referred to as "Islamic Economic" and "Islamic Finance" activities and the many themes they comprise. In the end, the result of the intellectual enterprise leaves the observer in a deep predicament of intellectual poverty and loss of self-reliance toward establishing a *Qur'anic* worldview transcending both mainstream imitation (*taqlid*) and also sheer *fiqhi* (interpretive) origin of Islamic thinking.

In regard to the latter case, Asad (1987) writes: "In consequence, our current theology (*kalam*) and canonical jurisprudence (*fiqh*) now resemble nothing so much as a vast old-clothes shop where ancient thought-garments, almost unrecognizable as to their original purport, are mechanically bought and sold, patched up and re-sold, and where the buyer's own delight consists in praising the old tailors' skill."

Such problems multiply during the new millennium even with the rise of post-modernist questioning in intelligentsia and with deepening Islamic crisis with the Western world. We want to address this problem of the Muslim predicament as it is presently premised in the mainstream mold against the backdrop of what otherwise can be truly an Islamic approach and worldview to problems of economics, finance, institutions, social ordering, and the whole world system of Islam (Choudhury and Hoque, 2004).

Objective

This chapter argues that the submissive attitude and advice on equating the Islamic and mainstream *methodologies* and even empiricism, thereby calling for adopting mainstream *methods* of analysis, constitute a flawed reasoning and a defeated apologia.

To revert to Islamic economics and finance as an embedded study in the ethico-epistemology of divine oneness as the foundation of Islamic Law, is the principal objective of this chapter. This critical examination is built up by an examination of the idea and practice of Islamic economics and finance during present times. Epistemological issues are examined in the socio-scientific reconstruction of what this chapter surmises should be the true methodology in Islamic economics and finance.

Critical methodological issues of Islamic Economics and Finance

This chapter makes a major difference between the concepts of *Methods* and *Methodology*. Choudhury (1999) explains that methodology and methods are interrelated scientific primitives. They are together used for understanding the praxis and applying this to inferential consequences arising from the methodological premise by the corresponding analytical methods that apply.

The original praxis is invariably epistemological in nature. Epistemology is subsequently integrated by a scientific discursive approach with applied models, and thereafter deriving the evidences from the models and analysis of applications. Methods belong to the engineering (functional) ontological domain (Gruber, 1993) and the evidences form Heidegger's consequences of "being" (Heidegger, 1988), when the analysis and application of the original methodological premise is to be formulated and applied for understanding real-world facts.

Yet, in the absence of the epistemological methodology, it is possible for methods to be used independently of the methodological understanding. When this is the case, methods fail to have substantive relevance in the light of methodology. They exist merely as procedural artifacts for conducting an analysis, but not necessarily the true and relevant one. Choudhury (1999, p. 348) writes, "Methods can exist without methodology as was explained in the earlier chapters for the case of the reductionist design of rationalism. Yet, methodology cannot exist without the corresponding determined methods. Such methods must be derived from the essence of the methodology itself. They must be such instruments that mobilize the entire methodological nature of divinely unified systems into explanatory relations". We referred to this premise of reasoning as the *Tawhidi* epistemology of unity of knowledge. In this chapter, we will explain the difficulties that are encountered in such academic ventures from the Islamic side.

Contrary to this assertion is the felt distancing of the prevailing Islamic socio-scientists from a substantive reference to the *Qur'anic* worldview, its epistemology of oneness of the divine law (*Tawhid*), the intercausal understanding of unification of knowledge in issues of world systems by the epistemological methodology that remains embedded in the generality and details of such world systems. The field of economics and finance are subsets of the grand domain of the Islamic world system. Consequently, there has remained an utter vacuum in the construction of the Islamic phenomena *vis-à-vis* its epistemology, the reality in the world system, and the moral reconstruction of a socio-scientific normative module. Such normative questions are empirically studied by what we have explained to be the circular causation model of estimation and simulation of wellbeing. Such an approach can result in simulacra of possibilities in converting the normative picture into a positive picture (Choudhury, 1998).

Within the broad arena of human inquiry are massive questions that span methodology, methods, and both normative and positive constructions in the light of the *Qur'an* and the *sunnah*. Without this fundamental epistemological reference, there cannot be an authentic building block of the Islamic revolutionary paradigm of socio-scientific worldview. We have explained this fact in good details in Chapter 4. Within the *Tawhidi* methodological worldview, there is the embedded field of *Tawhidi* Islamic economics and finance as a subset of the generalized study of the generality and particulars of the world system. Precisely for the *Tawhidi* intellectual gap in an otherwise rationalist development of Islamic economics and Islamic finance, the last 70 years of their existence and the last 30 years of Islamic banking and Islamic development finance organizations have produced no great positive challenge and transformation in the Muslim World as she slips into intellectual decadence. No revolutionary reconstruction of the socio-scientific methodological worldview could be rendered. Thus, the *Tawhidi* epistemological foundation along with its methodological applications in the generality and details of "everything" remains the decisive criterion of Islamic reality.

An example: Ambivalence of Tawhidi methodological goals in Islamic financing institutions

As an example, the ambivalence of the goal of Islamic intellectual world system in the light of the *Qur'an, sunnah,* and the *Tawhidi* methodology is proved by the case of a cursory and unplanned use of Islamic charity for human uplift. A haphazard approach presently exists despite much talk on the issues of human development in the drawing boards of the Islamic intellectuals and practitioners. The same state of Islamic thought and practice has prevailed for quite some time now. There is hardly any will to change despite gigantic flaws of Islamic economics and finance otherwise in the absence of the *Tawhidi* methodological worldview.

High announced rates of return on earning, rates of return on assets, and profitability and stability of Islamic banks still do not point toward social wellbeing. Islamic banks make large profits to safeguard shareholders' wealth, but remain distanced from the Islamic philosophy of financing assets in the real economy within market integration and commonly spread-out capital that can be shared by stakeholders. The complementary and participatory nature of Islamic financing, capital formation, and banking and non-banking activities without sound stakeholding activity causes the ultimate objective of maximizing shareholders' wealth. These approaches remain unchanged from the conventional corporations and banking practices.

On the other hand, only by the participatory spread of capital and investment in society at large, and by deepening financing in the real economy, the rate of interest can be decreased. Such a possibility comes about by replacing loan capital with share capital among stakeholders at large, and expanding the nexus of intersectoral and interfirm participation with a broad diversified investment portfolio. The result at the end would then be a market-driven injection of capital and financing into the money-real economy linkage for the general participatory framework.

Such a broadened perspective of stakeholding across a wide nexus of participation is equivalent to adopting the proven meaning of the *Tawhidi* unity of knowledge and knowledge-induced activities in terms of wellbeing (*maslaha*). Without such an approach, Islamic banks are in permanent misunderstanding regarding the objective and goal of Islamic financial transformation that ought to realize social transformation by adopting the *Tawhidi* principle of unity of knowledge and the knowledge-induction of the social economy. The pronounced cases of the social economy would be caused by the organic linkages between money and the real economy, and engaging society at large and the nexus of enterprises big and small sharing in diversified production and risk. The particular instruments that can bring about such participatory socio-economic changes ought to be also of the participatory type between the nexus of producing firms and financing enterprises. The participatory realization of *Tawhidi* Islamic economic and financial change would require the correct portfolio of all such single instruments that can be organically unified together in the form of development-financing instruments.

Yet, the Islamic development-financing portfolio today is very weakly diversified. Much of the portfolio remains concentrated in cost-plus financing instrument, equity-financing, and foreign trade financing (FTF). The role of profit-sharing financing instrument (*mudarabah*) has declined. The accumulation of funds in equities (*musharakah*) and mark-up financing (*murabaha*), and securities in the secondary financial market that revolve around the above-mentioned secondary ones has caused lack of risk-diversification and production-diversification in the face of a concentration of FTF of short-term funds. In the end, the efficiency ratios quoted by Islamic banks fail to bring out the true status of the social effects of Islamic bank financing. The social effects in fact remain very weak. Complementary relations are required between the economic and financial variables on the one side, and the social variables together with the economic ones. Most important of these are self-reliant human development and sustainability of development and growth in human resources. In the absence of these important social factors for the common stakeholders, the financial results of many of the high ratios only projects the benefits in terms of private depositors' returns with the high equity/liability ratios. Consequently, the goal of social wellbeing (*maslaha*) that we highlighted in Chapter 4 could not be realized.

The above-mentioned empirical facts — see Table 5.1 — point out that Islamic banks to date have failed to attain the participative complementarities between the economic goals as well as social goals. The complementary kind of organic embedding of unity between all good things of life arises from the episteme of unity of knowledge and of its knowledge-induced issues of the world system. This is the essential principle underlying the *Tawhidi* worldview, and thereby *Tawhidi* Islamic economics, finance, and the social order. Such kinds of complementary interrelations between the *shari'ah*-driven possibilities mark the *functional* ontology of unity of knowledge. Such a functional ontology forms the *Tawhidi* epistemological applications of the *Tawhidi* methodological worldview that we explained in all of the previous chapters. The *Tawhidi* epistemological premise is the end-all and the be-all of the Islamic worldview. It equally grounds *Tawhidi* economics and finance as well as society and science in it.

Table 5.1. Islamic bank financing, Malaysia, millions ringgit.

End of Period	Bai Bithaman Agil	Ijara	Ijara Bai	MUR	MUSH	MUD	Istisna	Total
2006 (Dec)	15,822	499	9,518	3,501	157	148	494	30,139
% share	52.50	1.65	31.58	11.62	0.52	0.49	1.64	100
2009 (Dec)	42,732	4017	38,353	23,016	1,875	376	1487	111,856
% share	38.20	3.59	34.28	20.58	1.68	0.34	1.33	100
2010 (Dec)	52,642	2,834	43,487	23,296	3,958	275	1,615	128,107
% share	41.09	2.21	33.49	18.18	3.06	0.21	1.26	100
2011 (Dec)	83,148	6,332	62878	56,940	15,817	146	696	260,476
% share	26.07	2.43	24.14	21.85	6.07	0.05	0.26	100
2014 (Jan)	83,452	6,526	63,812	58,746	16,636	148	900	284,616
% share	29.32	2.29	22.42	20.64	5.84	0.05	0.31	100

Sources: Bank Negara Malaysia 2014.
http://www.bnm.gov.my/index.php?ch=en_publication_catalogue&pg=en_
publication_msb&eId=box1&mth=1&yr=2011&lang=en.

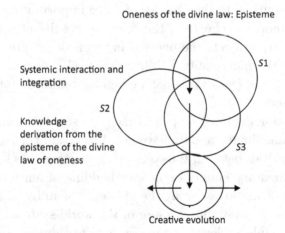

Figure 5.1. Systemic expression of knowledge-induced unity of knowledge as episteme.

Figure 5.1 depicts the knowledge-induced embedding of systems according to the ever-expanding discursive impact of learning in *Tawhidi* unity of knowledge on issues of the world system. This, though, is not the nature of Islamic financing as it prevails today.

For published data of Islamic Bank Bangladesh (IBBL Annual Report, 2007), considered among the best one internationally according to the Global Finance Forum, *murabaha* (mark-up financing) financing comprised almost 51% of total financing in the year 2007. PLS financing (*mudarabah* and *musharakah*) held a distant 0.13% financing ratio. No data on social spending (Islamic *zakah* and *sadaqah* on the needy) are available in the bank balance sheets or otherwise. This is one of the persistent problems of disclosure and transparency of Islamic banks in declaring their social spending and social assets. If we approximate microenterprise development financing as a rough representation of a kind of social spending, the ratios held by the Islamic Bank Bangladesh were as follows: 0.02% of total investment in 2007 and 0.005% in 2006. These are despicable figures on social spending. In spite of these low social standings and in the absence of transparency and disclosure and the inadequacy of the balance sheets of Islamic Bank Bangladesh, its return on equity (ROE) ratio stood at a high 13.42% in 2006 and 13.00% in 2007. The conclusion is reinforced: such efficiency ratios, while they speak out in favor of shareholders' returns and wealth positions, are not representative of the social and ethical meaning of *Tawhidi* Islamic economics and finance.

In the case of Islamic banks in Indonesia, published data (Bank Indonesia, 2009) indicates a slightly better but yet questionable financing trends for microenterprises. Medium and small-scale microenterprises (MSMEs) financing ranked at approximately 15% of total financing in 2008, up from approximately 9% in 2007. Yet, Islamic financing of rural sector projects ranked between 4.00% and 4.50% between the years 2006 and 2008. The ROE was a large range, 37% to 68.85% between 2006 and 2008. Thus, once again the inadmissibility of Islamic bank financial reporting in respect of the ethical social context remains unchanged.

In the case of Malaysian Islamic banks, published data show that the Islamic bank social financing ("community, social, and personal services") stood at 0.69% in January 2005 and 0.91% in December 2005. This ratio decreased to 0.88% in March 2006. Given the high watermark of Malaysian Islamic banks in Islamic banking and finance in the secondary financing markets, the social financing figures, shown in their consolidated balance sheets, augur poorly for the ethical and social objectives.

The trend towards secondary financing in Malaysia is significantly away from the main basis of Islamic participatory financing, which comprises the profit–loss instruments: $M1 = mudarabah$ and *musharakah* $= M2$. The overwhelming concentration is in *bai bithaman agil, ijara thumma bai*, and *murabaha*, all of which are secondary financing instruments. Besides, there is debate now around the overconcentration of *murabaha* at the expense of PLS-portfolio diversification. We note this trend as the usual feature of Islamic financing structure over the time period 2006–2014. Such a trend throughout the time period proves that the Islamic portfolio has remained non-diversified.

The inference derived from Islamic bank financing on the ethical front

Over the expanse of time from 2001 to present time, the Islamic bank financing facts point out a clear pattern. This means that Islamic financial institutions are evolving along a line of activities based on a mechanistic understanding of the *shar'iah*. In fact, the *shar'iah* conception based on learning dynamics did not evolve in Islamic banks by a participatory discourse of the learned with diverse agencies of the Muslim community. There is no effective process in place in the Islamic institutions to understand the foundational methodology of the *Tawhidi* worldview. This is unity of the knowledge emerging from the *sunnat Allah* (*Tawhid*) in action in the world system in all details of problems and issues. The *shura*, Islamic consultative medium, which generates an extensive learning process spanning all of human order including science and complexity, is not a mechanistic institutional consultation. Rather, the *shura* learning process is premised on knowledge reproduction by developing insight into the intellection process of unity of knowledge integrated with intellectual discourse. These two directions together evolve directions and rules on how the *Tawhidi* episteme of unity of knowledge can be actualized in the problems and issues at hand (*Qur'an* 42:38, 49–53).

A sheer literal interpretation of a particular injunction of the *shar'ah* to safeguard shareholders' wealth, and thus the preservation of the net worth of the Islamic institution, despite being a necessary condition of justice, fairness, and accountability, remains devoid of the purpose and objective of the *shar'iah* (*maqasid as-shari'ah*). This happens when the understanding of complementary and causal relations between different parts of the economic, financial, and social orders for attaining wellbeing is not understood as belonging distinctively to the episteme of unity of the divine law in action with issues concerning the world system.

Exercise 1

Search the internet for financing data on various primary, secondary, and ethical instruments to bring out the current state of relative financing being carried out by Islamic banks to attain the endogenous mix between economics, financial, and ethical goals.

The principle of pervasive complementarities applied to Islamic financial instruments

The resulting state of tradeoff in resource allocation and decision-making *vis-à-vis* mainstream economic roots of the prevailing thinking in Islamic economics and finance is contrary to the principle of the paired universe presented by the *Qur'an* (36:36). The *Qur'anic* pairing of entities in world systems is the defining basis of what we refer to here as the *Principle of Pervasive Complementarities* across diversity. This is the principle that arises from the episteme of *Tawhidi* unity of knowledge and explains that all the good things of life are complemented together in pairs, being unitary.

Also, by the same principle and the ensuing model of circular causation explaining *Tawhidi* consilience of unity of knowledge also explains the "de-knowledge" model in terms of its characteristics of association between the rejected things according to the *Tawhidi* methodological worldview. The difference between the knowledge worldview and the "de-knowledge" worldview is that, in the former case, the central perspective is of unity between the good things of life (*halal at-tayyabah*) creating consilience. In the latter case, the association is between the rejected things from the domain of goodness. The dynamics are now characterized by the increasing conflict, competition, methodological individualism and independence between the groups of rejected things. In the absence of understanding and applying the principle of pervasive complementarities for Islamic transformation, Islamic economics and finance and the Islamic organizations, have lost their way by still holding on to the principle of marginal rate of substitution and trade-off as of mainstream economics.

In the earlier chapters, we have explained the rejection of this latter postulate in Islamic economics by virtue of the interactive, integrative, and evolutionary learning dynamics according to the *Tawhidi* methodological worldview. When these properties cease to exist, the entire economic system relents on the postulate of marginal rate of substitution. This postulate is linked with the axioms of scarcity of resources, competition, optimization, and steady-state equilibrium conditions. On the other hand, even in the dialectical nature of the rationalist world system, there is no dynamics left to extend such a dialectical process of evolutionary learning to the *a priori* domain of *Allah* and thereby the derivation of knowledge therefrom. The result is the problem of heteronomy. It partitions the moral domain of the *a priori* from the material domain of the *a posteriori*. Without realizing these foundational *problematique* of mainstream economics and finance and of the entire generality and details of the world system, the carriage of Islamic economics within such axioms has severed itself from the true Islamic epistemic roots, which is the *Tawhidi* methodological worldview.

The *Qur'an* clearly differentiates the dialectical befriending nature of truth from falsehood. The *Qur'an* (21:92) declares regarding the brotherhood of Truth: "Verily, this Brotherhood of yours is a single Brotherhood, and I am your Lord and Cherisher: therefore serve Me (and no other)." Regarding the brotherhood of Satan with its false attitude of human conflict the *Qur'an* (4:119–120) declares: "I will mislead them, and I will create in them false desires; I will order them to slit the ears of cattle, and to deface the 'fair' nature created by God! Whoever, forsaking God, takes Satan for a friend, hath of a surety suffered a loss that is manifest. Satan makes them promises, and creates in them false desires; but Satan's promises are nothing but deception."

The true nature of Islamic economic and financial studies

The above set of arguments gives an illustrative example, though not meant to be exhaustive in so many details that can be objectively launched against the present state of Islamic economics and finance. Yet, the field of *Tawhidi* Islamic economics and finance bears a revolutionary mastery in the world of learning. This intellection must be pursued as the final ideal of moral reconstruction in this field.

This leads to a critical review. We reiterate here the nature of *Tawhidi* Islamic economic and financial studies in a different light in reference to the *Qur'an* and the *sunnah* as the basis of the *Tawhidi* epistemology. By *Tawhidi* epistemology, we mean the epistemology of organic unity of divine knowledge in relation to the schemes of issues of the world system, particularized here to economics and finance. The same analytical design stands true for the most general nature of the world system by virtue of the methodological worldview of *Tawhidi* universality and uniqueness.

We therefore need to examine the nature of Islamic economics as an interdisciplinary paradigm that explains interaction over the domains of moral guidance, *Tawhidi* law, and their impulses in the issues of world systems. These elements are evolved according to discursive impulses and learning processes. Such interactive and inte- grative learning systems governed by evolutionary learning *processes* have remained outside mainstream economic analysis. Mainstream economic doctrine, yet not the epistemological worldview of unity of knowledge, has been thoroughly imported into the enterprises of Islamic economics and Islamic finance. Such an imitation rendered Islamic economics and finance incapable of being any different from mainstream economic and financial ideas, wherein deep methodolog- ical concerns abound.

The *fiqh* (juridical interpretation) tradition has succumbed to this catching-up fervor in the midst of the tenor of capitalist globalization and the resulting inadequate kind of human resource development. These problems today influence the Islamic institutions and its mainstream-oriented intellection. Yet, this is not to be the true nature of the Islamic intellection and its methodological implementation according to the *Tawhidi* worldview of consilience in the revolutionary world of learning.

The substantive question of interaction, integration, and creative evolution by learning between diverse issues of embedded social, economic, and scientific systems in accordance with the epistemology of oneness of God is equivalent to the invoking of the unity of divine knowledge. This approach is particular to the Islamic worldview and is fundamental in understanding the nature and logic of economic behavior and Islamic transformation in embedded systems with endogenous variables of circular causation relations. Such a knowledge-centered process model transcends the level of the individual, family, and shareholders into society, markets, stakeholders, institutions, and the global order (Choudhury *et al.*, 2003). Foucault (1972) exalted such a model of discursive society.

Without the *Tawhidi* episteme spearheading Islamic economic, financial, and social investigations, and thereby the delineation and analysis of the emergent problems, there cannot emerge Islamic reasoning regarding the abolition of interest rate, money, finance, and real economy; and institutional, social, and Islamic global orders. Consequently, the mainstream model of money and macroeconomic dynamics will continue to prevail. The mainstream microeconomics of Islamic behavior will prevail. Yet, the *Tawhidi* and mainstream approaches of *Tawhidi* Islamic economics and finance are fundamentally different.

Other Islamic economists in this group have continued on to force deductions from the works of the scholastic Islamic scholars to fit the mainstream model and thought. On this issue, see Oslington (1995) for a criticism of Ghazzanfar and Islahi's (1990) mainstream historical orientation of the Islamic scholastic scholars, notably Imam Ghazali. In none of these studies there has been any attempt to critically study the history of economic thought and of Islamic economic thought from the *Qur'anic* point of view *vis-à-vis Tawhid,* its methodology, and impact on the moral construction of the economic and financial world system.

Instead, the Islamic world system is truly established and its analytics constructed on the basis of the *Tawhidi* worldview as unity of divine knowledge spanning inter and intra-systems that continuously interact, integrate, and evolve. They thus learn in concert with the existential phenomenon of discourse, participation, and paired organic linkages. These properties of the learning processes realize the worldview of unity of the *sunnat Allah* in relation to the unified nature of variables and issues in the economic and financial multi-causal world systems. The model of such multi-causal *Tawhidi-* induced world system in unity of knowledge was explained in detail in Chapter 4.

The principle of pervasive complementarities as the explanatory form of intercausal participation and organic unity of knowledge initiates the discursive *tasbih-shura* process of evolutionary learning through the dynamics of the *shuratic* process. Such elements and their characteristics are discovered by the application of the circular causation model. The underlying intercausal relations between the selected variables explain the formulation and application of the functional or engineering ontology (Maxwell, 1962). Functional ontologies are explanatory functions derived from the *Tawhidi* methodology of consilience in unity of knowledge. This is the way to extract the implications of the paired universe of pervasive interaction, integration, and evolutionary learning in unity of knowledge, as was explained in previous chapters.

How do we get to the *Tawhid* methodological formulation from the imitative Islamic mainstream economic approach?

Firstly, education along lines of the *Tawhidi* epistemology of global change with particular emphasis placed on the dynamics of economics and finance must instill such awareness and education at the intellectual and practitioning levels. Specifically, we will deal with the theme of money, finance, and real economy later on in this book, as a major example of the concept and application of the *Tawhidi* methodological worldview applied by using the circular causation model derived from the *Tawhidi* methodological worldview. The Islamic Research and Training Institute (Jeddah, Saudi Arabia) in concert with seats of higher education in the Muslim world and the Islamic banks, ought to spearhead such discourses. The right kind of Islamic world intellectual and scientific leadership with the correct form of human resource development would be adopted along lines of the grand program of *Tawhidi* methodological, analytical, and applied worldview. A critical examination of the comparative studies both in mainstream and existing Islamic economic and finance studies would be adopted. Such original and revolutionary approaches do not exist now. Yet, they are of the utmost importance for the world of learning and true Islamic transformation in the socio-scientific order.[1]

Secondly, a conglomerate of pilot projects can be established. Examples are a diversity of processes interrelating primary goods with agrarian and petroleum production. Such interfaced goods would be developed and traded internationally. In international trade, the gold standard will become the basis of intercommunal trade agreement in the Muslim world. The Islamic development

---

[1]Kuhn (1970), the historiographer of science, writes regarding the nature of scientific revolution, on which the *Tawhidi* methodological worldview shares: "... scientific revolutions are here taken to be those non-cumulative developmental episodes in which an older paradigm is replaced in whole or in part by an incompatible new one." In our present times, the birth of a new, more inclusive and extant, meaningful and beneficial way of looking at science and the world system in terms of an organic and holistic model rests on the emergence of a new epistemology. Einstein (1954) writing to his friend Niels Bohr remarked that there cannot be science without epistemology. Likewise, there cannot be a new science without a new epistemology. Indeed, it appears that the intellectual vision of the new millennium is essentially such a search and discovery of the new epistemology. But when any particular discipline is awakened by the touch of a new epistemology, all other disciplines are equally awakened. This was the way that economics was touched by the mathematical novelty of the 18th Century enlightenment.

bank (IDB) will establish such a pilot mechanism on the basis of maintaining the principle of 100% reserve requirements monetary system between the central bank and the Islamic banks in the trading countries (Choudhury, 1997). The pilot project can be subsequently expanded to include many traded items of similar kinds of diversified goods. We will have occasion to explain the nature of the 100% reserve requirement monetary system in the macroeconomic part of this book.

There will be a special need to protect such expanding segmented markets of goods, services, and financial instruments. This can be done by targeting specific markets for trade promotion in goods and services that can be generated in the pilot project and traded by the 100% reserve requirements monetary system with the gold standard (Choudhury and Hoque, 2004).

A value contract will be established between the central bank and the commercial bank on holding a residual (small) amount of gold, which IDB will guarantee. This gold stock will support the "residual" amount of unmobilized currency (say the IDB Dinar in the gold standard) that may remain unutilized after a maximum quantity of money is mobilized into the real sector (i.e. trade and development) by means of Islamic financial instruments. This "residual" amount of the IDB Dinar needs to be backed up by a quantity of gold that will be sufficient to assign value to the unit of currency in circulation in the real economy (i.e. resources mobilized in market exchange, trade, and development).

Consequently, the quantity of gold required for shoring up the value of currency in circulation will be small as resource mobilization remains inversely proportional to the quantity of gold required to shore up the residual unmobilized resource. The amount of gold held in the central bank for shoring up the value of residual unmobilized monetary resource would thus be inversely related to the speed and quantity of finances mobilized into the real economy. On the structure of 100% reserve requirement monetary system, see Choudhury (2004b). On the gold standard respecting "residual" quantity of gold required to lubricate trade and development, see Mydin (2004) and Mydin and Larbani (2004). While these explanations may be too advanced for the student and readers, the dynamics underlying them in respect of the *Tawhidi* methodological worldview will be explained in detail in the macroeconomics part of this book.

Example 1

A small amount of gold is required to maintain the value of monetary circulation in the real economy.

Here is a formal explanation of the gold-backing or real asset-backing of currency as an essential choice of prescribed medium in Islamic economics and finance kept in active in circulation in relation to the real economy.

Let *the* total of monetary resources be $R = R_c + R_e$,

where R_c is unmobilized and thus with central bank, and

R_e is mobilized into the real economy.

Let G be the quantity of Gold required for shoring the total monetary resource (stock R_c and flow R_e).

Let the central bank set, $R/G = a$, be the money/gold ratio. If all of money is measured in terms of gold standard, then $a = 1$.

Now, $d(R/G) = 0 = d(R_c/G) + d(R_e/G)$, implying, change in the gold value of money in reserve is cancelled by the change in the gold value of money in circulation. In other words, the higher the need for the gold value of money in circulation, the lesser is the need to hold an equivalent gold value of money with the central bank and *vice-a-versa*.

Furthermore, $[d(R_c/G)]/(R_c/G) = [d(a - R_e/G)]/(a - R_e/G)$. Therefore, the monetary elasticity coefficients ($\varepsilon(.)$) between the central-bank holding and circulation yield, $\varepsilon(R_c/G) = \varepsilon(a - R_e/G)$ is an inverse relationship in terms of the gold standard of monetary valuation. Thus, decreasing amounts of gold are required for shoring the money in circulation. Figure 5.2 explains this case on the two sides of G affecting R_c and R_e.

The opposite signs of elasticity coefficients further establish the fact on the smaller scale of gold to shore R_c in terms of the gold standard as R_e increases and *vice-a-versa*. Thus, the response to an increase in gold to shore the value of R_e mobilized in the real

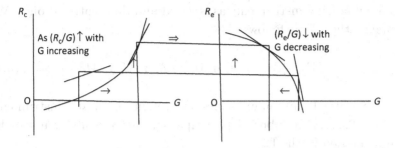

Figure 5.2. Central Bank relations on shoring currency in circulation.

economy is negligible when full mobilization of R is realized into the real economy, with $a = 1$ in this case.

Obviously, the above result is true also in the case of partial mobilization of monetary resources into the real economy with $a > 1$. The amount of G remains between zero and a small amount with the central bank, under the condition of full to partial mobilization of monetary resources in the real economy. With a further impact of knowledge, technology, and innovation in financial resource mobilization, the curves as shown will shift rightwards for (R_c, G) and upwards for (R_e, G). One such case is the joint mobilization of financial resources by the pooled fund (PF) idea. This is formalized blow. The converse case is also true.

A *Tawhidi* epistemological application to unified Islamic financing portfolio: PF Model

The *Tawhidi* epistemology of unity of knowledge can be applied to the construction of a complementary portfolio of Islamic financing instruments. We call it the PF *vis-à-vis* the amounts floating in Islamic financing instruments (M_i); $i =$ *mudarabah, musharakah, murabaha, ijara, sukuk, FTF, bay-muajjal,* and various other secondary participatory financing instruments. These together mobilize funds across the real economy with both secondary portfolio diversification and production diversification in the real economy in respect of serving the international trade and development goal for the benefit of the *ummah* and otherwise. The PF negates the treatment of

Islamic financing instruments as isolated and differentiated ones. We formalize the PF as follows:

$$PF = \{M_i\}_i, \text{ with } M_i \leftrightarrow M_j; \; M_i \geq M_i^*. \tag{5.1}$$

M_i^* are critical minimum values for retention in ith instrument; $i, j = 1, 2, \ldots, n$ number of participatory instruments that can be complemented in the PF.

M_i funds are required to be complemented together in order to diversify PF. This would serve a number of financing benefits. The risk and production in relation to the real economy financing will be effectively diversified. The medium to attain such diversifications can be realized by means of FTF in relation to economic development for product diversification in the real sector in agreement with the *shari'ah*.

In this way, each M_i and the PF ensemble are maintained by interflow of returns between FTF and PF through the medium of production (Q) and unit-risk diversification (Risk/Q). Production and unit-risk diversifications are further spread across various sectors $(s = 1, 2, \ldots, S)$ and projects $k = 1, 2, \ldots, K$. Hence, $Q = \{Q_s\}$; Risk/$Q = \{(\text{Risk}/Q)_s\}$. The diversification bundle (D) is the tuple of production (return) and unit-risk diversification, i.e. $D = \{Q_s, (\text{Risk}/Q)_s\}$. In the more diversified form of sectors by projects, the diversification bundle would be $D = \{Q_{ks}, (\text{Risk}/Q)_{ks}\}$; $k = 1, 2, \ldots, K; s = 1, 2, \ldots, S$.

The characteristic interrelations between the participatory variables are shown by

$$PF = \{M_i \leftrightarrow M_j\} \leftrightarrow D = \{Q_s, (\text{Risk}/Q)_s\}. \tag{5.2}$$

Exercise 2

Put the Expression (5.2) in its matrix form with projects by sectors in the real economy conformable to the *shari'ah at-Tawhid*.

$$PF = \{M_i \leftrightarrow M_j\}_{ks} \leftrightarrow D = \{Q, (\text{Risk}/Q)\}_{ks}. \tag{5.3}$$

Now, use the *Tawhidi* functional ontology (function based method-ologically on a given epistemology) to explain the (k, s)-matrix construction in the *Tawhidi* methodological context.

Stakeholding and shareholding in the PF for purposes of risk and production diversifications

Shares in unit amount (S_{PF}) are sold revolving around PF for the purpose of achieving Expression (5.2). S_{PF} is spread over PF without it being necessary to identify which particular S_{PF} is locked into specific instruments. S_{PF} as financial resources are allowed to flow freely across the instruments that are complemented in PF for the purpose of realizing the diversification bundle denoted by D so as to sustain the relationship shown in Expression (5.2).

The interactive, integrative, and evolutionary interrelations of the *Tawhidi* methodological genre acting by circular causation between all the variables are denoted by

$$S_{PF} \leftrightarrow PF \leftrightarrow D, \text{ i.e.}$$
$$S_{PF} \leftrightarrow \{M_i \leftrightarrow M_j\} \leftrightarrow \{Q_s, (\text{Risk}/Q)_s\}. \tag{5.4}$$

Production, development, and innovation effects in Expression (5.2) are shown by value imputation of a qualitative θ-variable, which is shown to acquire ordinal values in respect of the other variables of the system of interrelations. Expression (5.4) is now written in its θ-induced form as follows:

$$\theta \leftrightarrow [S_{PF} \leftrightarrow \{M_i \leftrightarrow M_j\} \leftrightarrow \{Q_s, (\text{Risk}/Q)_s\}][\theta]. \tag{5.5}$$

That is, "θ", which is derived from the *Tawhidi* epistemological roots influences all the variables uniquely as the enabling and responding variable to put the FTF system in its interactive, integrative, and creative dynamics. Because of this primal influence of θ-variable on all the variables by virtue of the principle of pervasive complementarities and choices in the context of *maqasid as-shari'ah*, the induced consequences acquire an ethical dimension. Such an ethical dimension comprises the actualization of sustainable development and growth with equitable distribution of resources across diverse interlinked economic sectors. The social consequence is also poverty alleviation by developing microenterprises and activating medium and small enterprises (MSMEs), realizing productivity and production and risk diversifications as gains to diversify the economy, and increased participation in the economy induced now by ethical value. See below for further explanation regarding sectoral linkages. In this way, the resulting wellbeing criterion becomes a conceptual and empirical measure of degrees of complementarities between the variables. This is the empirical manifestation of the *Tawhidi* methodological application at work in the midst of ethical construction of the Islamic financing instruments to realize economic and social complementarities by virtue of linkages as organic unity of knowledge and knowledge-induced artifacts.

Thus, the episteme underlying θ-value is in the learning processes generated by it and its induction of the variables of the entire system of relations defined by Expression (5.4). Such a systemic interrelationship conveys the meaning of organic unity between the different parts of the total system of variables-specific interrelations. The interrelations are implied by $\leftrightarrow$.

Consequently, the origin of such a system of organic unity as a learning system of interrelations must epistemologically arise in reference to a certain methodological foundation that fundamentally defines the knowledge-induced function of organic unity. The underlying epistemological foundation of the complementary relations of the selected *maqasid as-shari'ah* choices is the *Tawhidi* law of unity of knowledge. *Tawhid* as the unitary law maps on to the world system of "everything" in the framework of unity of knowledge and knowledge-induced unified systems. We denote the epistemological foundation of *Tawhid* in terms of its fundamental knowledge base, namely the *Qur'an*, the *sunnah*, and the discourse of the learned ones through the medium of the *shura* and *ijtihad* (practice of deducing knowledge from the epistemological sources).

We denote this foundational basis of θ-value by $\Omega = (Q, S)$, Q as the knowledge universe of the *Qur'an*, and S as the ontological mapping of the *sunnah* on to the world system. That is, $\theta \in [\Omega = (Q, S)]$ as this formulation was explained in the earlier chapters.

Expression (4.5) is now extended to its comprehensive primal form

$$[\Omega = (Q, S)] \rightarrow \theta \leftrightarrow [S_{\text{PF}} \leftrightarrow \{M_i \leftrightarrow M_j\} \leftrightarrow \{Q_s, (\text{Risk}/Q)_s\}][\theta].$$
(5.6)

In the circular causation system (5.6) of learning interrelations between the variables, every variable including θ-variable is endogenously interrelated. The exception is of $[\Omega = (Q, S)]$, which remains primal, and hence exogenous in defining the rest of the relations. This is the picture of the small-scale universe, as of a project such as FTF. But if the objective of any project is extended with its ultimate objective and purpose of the *shari'ah* (*maqasid as-shari'ah*) to comprehend the beginning until the end of worldly experiences, then the Closure (see earlier chapters) is created by the very large system of learning interrelations extending up to the Great Event of the Hereafter (*Akhira*). We denote this kind of completion of Expression (5.6) by the Closure as

$$[\Omega = (Q, S)] \rightarrow [\theta \leftrightarrow [S_{\text{PF}} \leftrightarrow \{M_i \leftrightarrow M_j\} \leftrightarrow \{Q_s, (\text{Risk}/Q)_s\}][\theta]]$$
$$\leftrightarrow \text{ repeat the sequence } [..] \text{ in continuum until } \leftrightarrow [\Omega = (Q, S)].$$
(5.7)

In this form of the complete learning system in unity of knowledge and its induced world system generated by $[\Omega = (Q, S)]$ through θ, the *maqasid as-shari'ah* becomes (θ)-derived from $[\Omega = (Q, S)]$. The *maqasid as-shari'ah* thereby actualizes the world system. We note that with Mq denoting *maqasid as-shari'ah* $Mq \subset (Q, S)$ and $\theta \in (Q, S) \Rightarrow \theta \in Mq$,

$$[\theta \in [\Omega = (Q, S)] \leftrightarrow [S_{\text{PF}} \leftrightarrow \{M_i \leftrightarrow M_j\} \leftrightarrow \{Q_s, (\text{Risk}/Q)_s\}][\theta]].$$
(5.8)

Conversely, the pursuit of the PF and D with all forms of complementarities in them, as the *Tawhidi* Islamic economic and financial sub-system of the grand world system attainable by the learning experience, regenerates new means and learning through fresh evolutionary θ-values. Hence, unity of knowledge embodied in the *maqasid as-shari'ah*, $\{\theta\}$, is regenerated through the evolutionary learning processes in unity of knowledge. This process of unity of knowledge and its social reconstruction of the world system never ends until the end of worldly time, that is, at the Great Event of the Hereafter (*Akhira*). The learning process in unity of knowledge arising from $[\Omega = (Q, S)]$ and closing on itself through the learning processes of the finite world system is referred to in the *Qur'an* as the learning mediums of *shura* and *ijtihad*.

Underlying the system of interrelations given by (5.4), there are the functions played by the institutions. These comprise the private sector further divided between the urban and rural sectors in order to actualize the developmental effects and social consequences on poverty alleviation. Other categories of sectoral diversification would be the development of non-banking institutions like finance houses, corporations interrelated with microenterprises, small and middle size enterprises (MSMEs), and industrial sectors and various other projects according to the context of *maqasid as-shari'ah*. The public sector will comprise the government, central bank, Islamic banks, development banks, and organizations. The stakeholders will be both national and international ones as in terms of integration within the *ummah* and otherwise. The above-mentioned categories of sectors will all be sources of gaining participatory holdings and projects for embedding economics, financial, and social results. The Islamic banks ought to act as the brainchild of such an idea and generate the synergistic relations as pointed out in (5.4).

The circular causation system of the complete system of interrelations given by Expression (5.8) is shown in Figure 5.3.

Exercise 3

(1) Reformulate Expression (5.8) in terms of projects by sectors in matrix form as in Exercise 1.

(2) Explain the *Tawhidi* ontology underlying the interaction, integration, and evolutionary learning characteristics of unified systems in terms of PF and D as explained.

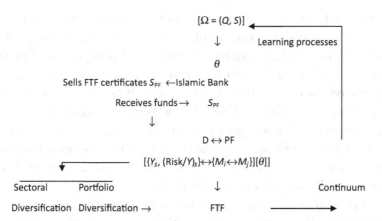

Figure 5.3. Circular flow of resources for sustaining FTF in the economic development process.

FTFC in the PF formalism

Why is the above formalism particularly attractive for FTFC? Although the mechanism and arguments in favor of *Tawhidi* Islamic financing is true of any particular tradable instrument replacing interest rates, it has a particular appeal for FTFC. Tradability under FTF is of the nature of merchandise, capital, and contracts supported by real assets. Consequently, the rates of return on FTF are short-term, fairly risk-free yield rates (r_f). This prospect of the yield rates causes short-term risk-free effects on the other variables. When further induced by θ-values, the real economy advances with production and risk diversifications. Circular causation is generated between r_f and the returns on the other variables according to the same principle of pervasive complementarities between Islamic financing instruments. Thus, for example,

$$r_f \leftrightarrow [\{Y_s \uparrow, (\text{Risk}/Y)_s \downarrow\} \leftrightarrow \{M_i \uparrow \leftrightarrow M_j \uparrow\}][\theta]]$$
$$\equiv [\{r_{Ys} \uparrow, r_R \downarrow\} \leftrightarrow \{r_{Mi} \uparrow \leftrightarrow r_{Mj} \uparrow\}][\theta]. \qquad (5.9)$$

The r's stand for growth rate of output (r_{Ys}), rate of decrease in unit risk (r_R), and yield rates (r_{Mi}, r_{Mj}). The foundational effect of θ-value as the way of understanding and enacting the development regimes of unity of knowledge between the variables by economic, institutional, and social reconstruction, applies extensively. The institutional reconstruction implies endogenous relationship of the discursive nature of evolutionary learning and policy-making through the process of *shura* (institutionalism) in cognizance of the principle of pervasive complementarities (development participation). Because of the flexible nature of the FTF relations between the tradable and financing variables, participatory development along with the ethical injunction of pairing implied by θ-values implies a grassroots access towards involving the marginal traders and the principal ones, interrelated between large and small firms.

This kind of a social effect has strong bearing on raising the capability of the poor through participatory productive activities. The result then is poverty alleviation. Sectoral linkages, rural-urban linkages, and other forms of developmental synergy are enhanced for realizing micro–macro unified complementarities in participatory development planning. Microenterprises and small and medium size businesses prosper along with large corporations that complement each other. A dynamic grassroots interactive and integrative development regime is promoted with endogenous technological induction through the organic evolutionary learning processes of systemic pairing. Pairing as cause and effect that are circularly established in the learning processes of participatory development implies strong endogeneity of unity of knowledge (θ) and unity of the system comprising FTF in relation to the real economy along with the proper direction of institutional strategic and policy variables.

Conclusion

After 70 years of Islamic economics and finance since its inception and 30 years of the inception of Islamic banks, there still remains a great gap in true Islamic intellection in the scholarly field that Islamic economics and finance can potentially give to the world. Thus far, it is only the goals of capital formation, organizational survival by competition in the capitalist globalization scene, profit-making in an intensifying global financial competition, and the protection and maximization of shareholders' wealth by Islamic banks that have activated the motivations and activities of the Islamic financing institutions and development organizations. The study of Islamic economics and finance has thus remained a "normal" science imitating mainstream economics and finance lock stock and barrels. Contrary to this state of Islamic economics and finance, what these truly ought to be is a "scientific revolution" (Kuhn, 1970). Such a contribution would bestow something new and challenging to the world of learning as a whole by concept, methodology, and applications. This emergent field would also bestow wellbeing on all at large.

Likewise, on the academic side, the absence of the epistemological worldview in Islamic economics and finance has failed to treat the study of endogenous ethics and economics as a substantive scientific theme (Edel, 1970) of Islamic economics and finance. Such a failure has been due to the subservience of vision and intellect to the mainstream rationalist thought that is already subject to questioning on the theme of ethics and unity of knowledge and consilience contra heteronomy. Consequently, the true intellection of *Tawhidi* Islamic economics and finance is lost to the mainstream rationalist and rationality postulates. The *Tawhidi* methodological worldview of unity of knowledge and the knowledge-induced world system have been increasingly taken away from the *Tawhidi* methodological worldview by its mainstream mold of thinking, analytics, and applications. The vision, mission, understanding, and use of Islamic economics and financial instruments and Islamic institutions have thus been misplaced. New and fresh directions are required in terms of the *Tawhidi* worldview. This is the cardinal foundation of Islam and its uniqueness and universality in the world of intellection and applications.

One can still ask the question: Why is it necessary to invoke the *Tawhidi* unity of knowledge and God and the study of the world system in the plane of socio-scientific inquiry? The answer to this query will be unraveled throughout this book. For the present, it may simply be noted that, without *Allah* and *Tawhid* in the highest echelons of socio-scientific thought, human inquiry will be forever trapped in the belief of methodological independence and differentiation between the economic and financial interests on the one side and the moral and social wellbeing on the other. Consequently, neither the conceptual background nor its dissemination in intellection and its practical results, would be realized. Such is the moral heteronomous picture regarding the conflict and competition over scarcity over resources between marginalist substitutes. These kinds of postulates of economic rationality make up the core axioms of mainstream economics. Contrarily, the reality of evolutionary learning in the *Tawhidi* context of organic pairing, distributive sharing, and complementarities offers the possibility of abundance, and thus the emergence of embedded economic and moral possibilities.[2]

In this chapter, the important areas to focus upon as mentioned in Chapter 1 are as follows:

1. The formulation of *Tawhidi* Islamic economic model.
2. Islamic participatory instruments and the ethical dimensions.

The teacher will be required to extract the essential elements of these topics, though the chapter expounds a vastly many rigorous issues of *Tawhidi* Islamic economics and finance.

References

Asad, M. (1987). *This Law of Ours*. Gibraltar: Dar Al-Andalus.

Choudhury, M. A. (1997). *Money in Islam*. London, England: Routledge.

Choudhury, M. A. (1998). *Studies in Islamic Social Sciences*. London, England: Macmillan.

Choudhury, M. A. (1999). "Methodological conclusion", in *Comparative Economic Theory: Occidental and Islamic Perspectives*, Chapter 21, Norwell, MA: Kluwer Academic Publishers.

Choudhury, M. A. (2004a). *The Islamic World-System: A Study in Polity-Market Interaction*. London, England: Routledge.

Choudhury, M. A. (2004b). "Islamic political economy", *Review of Islamic Economics*, 13(1), 67–90.

Choudhury, M. A. and Hoque, M. Z. (2004). *An Advanced Exposition in Islamic Economics and Finance*, Lewiston, Maryland: Edwin Mellen Press.

---

[2] *Qur'an* (17:20): "Of the bounties of thy Lord We bestow freely on all — these as well as those: The bounties of Thy Lord are not closed (to anyone)."

Choudhury, M. A., Umar, Y. and Al-Ghamdi, M. (2003). "*Ummatic* globalization versus neoclassical capitalist globalization", *Review of Islamic Economics*, 12(1), 5–45.

Edel, A. (1970 Reprint). "Science and the structure of ethics", in *Foundations of the Unity of Science*, Neurath, O., Carnap, R. and Morris, C. (Eds.), Vol. II, Nos. 1–9, Chicago, ILL: The University of Chicago Press, pp. 273–378.

Einstein, A. (1954). "Considerations on the universe as a whole", in *Relativity, the Special and the General Theory*, Translated by Lawson R. W., London, England: Methuen.

Foucault, M. (1972). *The Archeology of Knowledge and the Discourse on Language*, Translated by Sheridan, A. M., New York: Harper Torchbooks.

Ghazzanfar, S. M. and Islahi, A. Z. (1990). "Economic thought of an Arab Scholastic, Abu Hamid al-Ghazali", in *History of Political Economy*, 22(2), 381–403; Reprint (2003). *Medieval Islamic Economic Thought, Filling the "Great Gap" in European Economics*, Ghazzanfar S. M. (Ed.), London, England: Routledge.

Gruber, T. R. (1993). "A translation approach to portable ontologies", *Knowledge Acquisition*, 5(2), 199–200.

Heidegger, M. (1988). *The Basic Problems of Phenomenology*, Translated by Hofstadter, A., Bloomington and Indiana: Indiana University Press.

Islamic Bank Bangladesh. *Annual Report 2007*. Dhaka, Bangladesh: Islami Bank Bangladesh (IBBL).

Kuhn, T. S. (1970). *The Structure of Scientific Revolution*, Chicago, IL: University of Chicago Press.

Maxwell, G. (1962). "The ontological status of theoretical entities", in *Minnesota Studies in the Philosophy of Science, Vol. II: Scientific Explanation, Space and Time*, Feigl, H. and Maxwell, G. (Eds.), Minneapolis, Minnesota: University of Minnesota Press, pp. 3–27.

Mydin, A. K. (2004). *The Theft of Nations*, Kuala Lumpur, Malaysia: Pelanduk.

Mydin, A. K. and Larbani, M. (2004). "The gold dinar: The next component in Islamic economics, banking and finance", *Review of Islamic Economics*, 8(1), 5–34.

Oslington, P. (1995). "Economic thought and religious thought, a comment on Ghazzanfar and Islahi", *History of Political Economy*, 27(4), 781–785; Reprint (2003). Ghazzafar S. M. (Ed.), *op cit.*

Chapter 6

The Dual Theories of Consumer Behavior and Markets

In the previous chapters, the foundational topics of Islamic methodology and some of the methods and formulations arising from it were laid down in terms of the *Tawhidi* theory of knowledge. This theory was laid down in terms of firstly, ontology. Ontology means the theory of existence, as of the primal origin of knowledge being the *Qur'an* and its instrumentation by the *sunnah*. Secondly, there is epistemology, meaning the theory of knowledge. In Islamic intellection, epistemology is derived from the *Qur'an* and the *sunnah* in terms of the cardinal law of *Tawhid*. It is logical for the purpose and establishment of an abiding theory of *Tawhidi* Islamic economics (TIE) and broadly of *Tawhidi* socio-scientific intellection to utilize the foundational topics. The analytical results so arising from the methodological foundations will then be carried over into quantitative perspectives. This last part of the comprehensive theory of TIE is referred to as the unraveling element of consciousness. In scientific language, this last part that integrates ontology and epistemology in a methodological way leading to the methods of analysis is referred to as phenomenology.

The all-encompassing robust theory of any scientific endeavor, and thereby of TIE, is to establish the continuity of intervariable

161

relations by circular cause and effect across diversity of specific problems. In TIE therefore, we invoke the study of analytical economics in the perspective of the Islamic theory of moral, ethical, and material valuation for the common good of all. The *Qur'an* is clear on such an analytical formulation, but which the *Qur'anic* exegesis must extract out and develop upon. There is firstly the Belief in *Tawhid* as the Purity (*Iqhlas*) of *Allah* as the One. Secondly, there is the derivation of *Tawhid* as Law. This explains the world system (*a'lameen*) in terms of the nexus of unity of things caused and continued by extension of the unity of knowledge affecting the organic connectivity, continuity, and extendibility of the attributes of organic relational unity in and across systems.

The *Qur'an* (36:36) deepens human intellection in the principle of organic pairing. The multi-systemic connectivity by means of the organic complementarities, also meaning participative systems represented by their multi-entities and variables, can be derived by the exegesis of the following *Qur'anic* verses: *Qur'an* (13:1–5) points out the embedded moral and material realities of the *Tawhidi* law in terms of multi-systems of interrelations with their intercausal multivariates, signifying the *Tawhidi* unity of knowledge by organic causality. On dimensions of reflection that ignite extended human intellection and that enter the study of economics and socio-scientific systems, there is the *Qur'anic* verse (45:36): "All praise belongs to *Allah*, the Lord of the heavens and the Lord of the earth, Lord of all the worlds". The multi-system and multi-stage denoted by their variables as observations embedded in the moral actualization, there is the verse of the *Qur'an* (81:15–21) raising the consciousness of the morally embedded material reality. Then there is a further deepening realization of the worshipping world that consciously recognizes the oneness of *Allah* as conscious worship (*tasbih*) in the scheme and order of all things (*Qur'an*, 59:24): "Whatever is in the heavens and the earth, do declare His Praises and Glory: and He is the Exalted in Might, the Wise." Over all these attributes of the nature of existence is the intrinsic learning property of all things, animate or inanimate, caused by the process of organic pairing as well as by the human intervention to learn and discover the truth.

The *Qur'an* says in this regard in many verses, of which some are the following ones:

"....see in the creation of the Most Merciful any inconsistency. So return [your] vision [to the sky]; do you see any breaks?" (67:2–3).

"Have they not considered how *Allah* originates creation and then repeats it? Indeed that, for *Allah*, is easy." (29:19).

"Indeed, in the creation of the heavens and earth, and the alternation of the night and the day, and the [great] ships which sail through the sea with that which benefits people, and what *Allah* has sent down from the heavens of rain, giving life thereby to the earth after its lifelessness and dispersing therein every [kind of] moving creature, and [His] directing of the winds and the clouds controlled between the heaven and the earth are signs for a people who use reason." (2:164).

"And how many a sign within the heavens and earth do they pass over while they, there from, are turning away." (12:105).

"Do they not contemplate within themselves? *Allah* has not created the heavens and the earth and what is between them except in truth and for a specified term. And indeed, many of the people, in [the matter of] the meeting with their Lord, are disbelievers." (30:8).

"Or were they created by nothing, or were they the creators [of themselves]? Or did they create the heavens and the earth? Rather, they are not certain." (52:35–36).

"Indeed, We created man from a sperm-drop mixture that We may try him; and We made him hearing and seeing." (76:2).

The above verses and many more of their kind point out the properties of the essential building blocks of the *Tawhidi* theory of unity of knowledge that governs over all morally embedded constructs of mind–matter reality. The unity of the world system in its generality and particulars is then pointed out as the unique truth by the following properties:

(i) Organic pairing in unity of knowledge. This is explained by the discursive process of discovering and reconstructing the

mind–matter reality along the precept of pervasive complementarities, as also participation between all the good things of
life — the *maqasid*-choices. The process in diversity as the
principle of *interaction* leads to convergence as the principle of
integration.

(ii) The principles of *interaction* leading to *integration* are followed
by the continuity and extendibility across systems represented
by their multivariates. This marks the principle of evolutionary
learning.

(iii) Thus *interaction, integration, and evolutionary* (IIE) *learning
process* mark out the continuous and extended intercausal
properties of the *Tawhidi* methodology of incessant organic
learning in unity of being and becoming of the phenomenological
essence of mind and matter occurring in "pairs".

(iv) The phenomenological attribute, i.e. scientific consciousness,
combines conception with application, quantitative or discursive, to lead into an evaluative stage of completion followed by
regeneration of the whole evolutionary process intertemporally
across processes and within processes cross-sectionally or over a
given period of time.

It was proved in the previous chapters that the above-derived
properties of the *Tawhidi* methodological worldview, as the only
possible foundation of all Islamic disciplines including economics and
finance, science and society, leads to the formulation of a unique and
universal formalism arising from the inner properties of *Tawhid* as
law applied to systemic study. We recapitulate it, a good deal of
detail having been given earlier.

First, we note the following description of the multivariate
construct in the embedded field of the *Tawhidi* law of unity
and its induction of materiality. We also note in the summary
representation in Figure 6.1 the recursive interrelations between
ontology, epistemology, and phenomenology as the scientific properties of the nature of *Tawhidi* law of unity of knowledge acting in
material cognates. Inherent in the representation of Figure 6.1 is also
the process-oriented nature of Islamicized disciplines of knowledge
including Islamic economics.

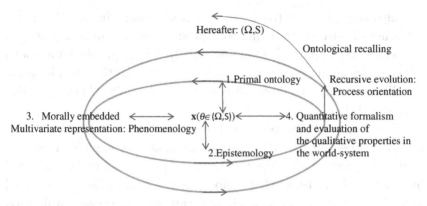

Figure 6.1. Circular interconnectivity (complementarities) by recursive evolutionary evaluation.

Section 4 of Figure 6.1 is formalized as *evaluation* of the social wellbeing function, $W(\mathbf{x}(\theta))$, which measures the degree of complementarities between the selected variables $\mathbf{x}(\theta)$ that are embedded in the moral consciousness denoted by "θ" derived from the primal ontology of *Tawhidi* unity of knowledge. This law was denoted by (Ω, S). These symbols were explained in the previous chapters.

The recursive or continuous re-emergence of the evolutionary learning process in unity of knowledge is shown by the circular causal paths moving to its terminal, equilibrium, and optimal point only in the Hereafter and at the very Beginning,[1] and nowhere else along the IIE-learning processes spanning out in knowledge, space, and time. The Hereafter as the Great Event in the *Qur'an* (*surah* 78) equates this End as the only other point of perfect completion besides the *Tawhidi* Beginning. There is no other such point in any issue and problem of the entire world system. Thereby, the theory of TIE, and likewise of all such specific studies, have no optimality and steady-state equilibrium, although only "expectational" evolutionary learning equilibriums remain. Yet, the attainment of any event within the universal history of $[(\Omega, S) \rightarrow$ World system $\rightarrow (\Omega, S)]$ must have a *closure* for completion of a learning process across IIE-learning processes. On the other hand, there is the final *Closure*, which is

---

[1] *Qur'an* (57:3): "He is the First and the Last, the Evident and the Imminent: and He Has full knowledge of all things."

the ultimate point of the learning world system in the Hereafter. All other closures within the world system are evolutionary ones of the punctuated kinds (Grandmont, 1989). In the physical and social sciences, such non-convergent, continuously evolutionary biological equilibriums are of recent discovery (Hull, 1988; Thurow, 1983; Burstein, 1991).

The intercausality between the representative variables of the systems experiencing IIE learning processes is explained by the recursive gyration of Figure 6.1. Such intercausality is evaluated by what we have referred to before, as the evaluation of the social wellbeing function, subject to circular causation relations. Evaluation includes estimation followed by simulacra of simulations. This complete quantitative formalism is included in step 4 of Figure 6.1 and its evolutionary continuity across knowledge, space, and time dimensions marking the evolutionary learning processes.

We write the above phenomenological nature of socio-scientific thought according to the *Qur'an* in the following formalism. It is written down here once again as in the previous chapters.

$$\text{Evaluate } W(\mathbf{x}(\theta)), \tag{6.1}$$

$$\text{subject to } x_i(\theta) = f_i(\mathbf{x}_j(\theta)); \; \{\theta\} \in (\Omega, S);$$

$$\theta = \lim\nolimits_{\text{interaction, integration}} \{\theta\}, \tag{6.2}$$

$$i, j; \; i \neq j = 1, 2, 3, \ldots.$$

$\mathbf{x}_j(\theta)$ denotes the vector of variables excluding the interrelated variable $x_i(\theta)$ by way of testing the degree of complementarities between all the variables. The degrees of intervariable complementarities are denoted by the signs of the estimated coefficients in the system of circular causal relations denoted by Expression (6.2).

We have noted earlier that the social wellbeing function given by Expression (6.2) cannot be empirically evaluated. This is because, we do not have observation values for $W(.)$. For such values of the social wellbeing, we need to depend on ordinal assignment of θ-values. Such ordinal θ-values are computed pro rata according to the $\mathbf{x}(\theta)$ observations. A specific $\mathbf{x}(\theta)$ observation is fixed, say $\mathbf{x}^*(\theta = 10)$ is selected along the column values for each of the different columns of $\mathbf{x}(\theta)$-values. Then the rest of the column θ-values are generated pro rata with the corresponding $\mathbf{x}(\theta)$-values.

The following formula can be used for computing the final computation of θ-values:

θ_{ic} corresponding to $\{x_i(\theta_i)_c$

$$= [\theta^*(\text{say} = 10)].(x_i(\theta_i)/x*(\theta = 10))\}_{\text{given columns, } c}, \quad (6.3)$$

$$\theta_i = \left[\sum_c \theta_{ic}\right]\Big/ \#c, \ i = 1, 2, 3, \ldots, \quad (6.4)$$

by observations over all columns to generate the final average column of θ_i-values.

The table of complete vector values (bold notations) would now appear as follows:

$$\boxed{\mathbf{x_i}(\theta_1) \quad \theta_i \quad \theta} \quad (6.5)$$

In the process of evaluation by regression relations with the learning coefficients, Expression (6.5) can be written down as the following relationship:

$$\theta = F(\mathbf{x}(\theta)). \quad (6.6)$$

Expression (6.6) is a "similar" function with Expression (6.1), being functions of the same variables and explaining the phenomenon of unity of knowledge. This derivation also means that, because of the continuity and non-zero property of the wellbeing function in terms of θ-values, the implicit function theorem of differential calculus will apply to result into Expression (6.6). The estimation and simulation by policy-theoretic changes in the estimated coefficients to generate desired complementarities between the variables and thus improving the estimated values, and which together perform the evaluation of the wellbeing function, can now be completed by the system comprising Expressions (6.2)–(6.6).

The attributes of the *Tawhidi* unity of knowledge and its applications now conclusively state that the axioms of mainstream economics of optimization and steady-state equilibrium along with its postulates of scarcity, rational choice, full information, competition, and optimal allocation of resources between competing ends cannot hold up for the case of Islamic economics, which, by its *Tawhidi* axiom and attributes of unity of knowledge, we refer to as TIE.

The mainstream economic assumptions are all replaced by the postulates of continuous evolutionary learning with interaction and integration in circular causation between the selected variables. The analytical explanation underlying all these inferences arising from the *Tawhidi* epistemology, contrary to the mainstream rationalist assumptions, was given in the earlier chapters. The present chapter will investigate the imminent differences between the *Tawhidi* epistemological approach and the mainstream rationalist approach. Regretfully, the latter case has been blindly followed by the existing study of Islamic economics that has no socio-scientific novelty to offer to the world of learning as can be discovered in the *Tawhidi* methodological worldview of unity of knowledge and its application to the unity of organic relations between systems and their representative variables.

In the case of differentiated systems, especially those characterized by methodological individualism and rational choice axioms of mainstream economics, the same system of evaluation comprising Expressions (6.2)–(6.6) would apply. However, the ontologically determined choices would be differentiated from the good choices as recommended by the *Tawhidi* law. Besides, the estimated coefficients will show to be negative or weakly positive showing marginal substitution between the variables and their corresponding entities. Finally, many of the variables, such as technology and innovation, will be exogenous in character. Consequently, the organic evolutionary behavior will be annulled in the system of intervariable circular causation.

Exercise 1

(i) Explain in your own words the evaluation method of the social wellbeing function, subject to circular causation relations given by Expressions (6.1)–(6.6).

(ii) Take the case of continuous reproduction of household income with human capital and innovation as forms of resources in formulating a model of the type (6.1)–(6.6).

(iii) What is the exogenous and endogenous nature of technological change in equating seller's revenue with household income in mainstream economics and TIE?

We will now use the contrasting approaches of Islamic *Tawhidi* methodology against the mainstream methodology of rational choice on the topic of the theory of consumer choice. We will use the method and models laid out above and in the previous chapters. At the outset, we lay down definitions of some terms and concepts that will be used to develop the theory of ethically oriented idea of consumer choice and individual and collective behavior in *Tawhidi* perspectives.

Definitions

1. *Economic choice among complementary "possibilities" rather than among marginalist "alternatives"*

The ethically/morally embedded vector of variables in the *Tawhidi* sense explained in Figure 6.1 forms possibilities rather than alternatives in their state of extensive complementarities rather than marginal substitutes. Even local complements between goods are replaced by extensive complements between the good things of life intra-system followed by extension to inter-systems. The good and bad things cannot form substitutes, and of course not complements. Allowing for imperfect learning about the nature of goods between good and bad, that is the hybrid, which the *Qur'an* refers to as *mutashabihat*, the role of knowledge flows derived from the *Tawhidi* ontological law through the enabling medium of the *sunnah* and social discourse, i.e. $\theta \in (\Omega, S)$, soon separates the good and the bad into disjoint baskets. Thereby, the progress of knowledge of unity of being through the process of discourse completely removes the bad from the consumption basket. National and *ummah* policies and regulations must then be made to eradicate such "bads" from the consumption basket.

Examples of the process of removing the bad through a discursive separation in reference to the *Tawhidi* law, as in the case of the *maqasid as-shari'ah*, are avoidance of smoking, eliminating environment degradation, and the gradual avoidance of acts such as temporary marriages (*mutah*), alcohol consumption, and slavery according to the *Qur'anic* law. In the end, when a clear distinction is ascertained between truth and falsehood, good and bad, permissible and forbidden through social discourse, the *Qur'an* then bans the bad. Individuals, communities, nations, and the *ummah* are collectively asked to ban the bad by the force of legislation, regulation, and public policy. These are discursively set by the gaining moral consciousness of learning from lesser to higher levels of certainty. The *Qur'an* (2:42) says in this regard: "And cover not Truth with falsehood, nor conceal the Truth when ye know (what it is)". There are many other similar commands and evidences in the *Qur'an*.

2. *Choice in terms of cost and benefit mechanism in mainstream economics and otherwise*

The term "choice" in Islamic consumer behavior is therefore not based on the sheer material assessment of cost and benefit (pain and pleasure). For example, this notion is explained by the pleasure of social smoking and drinking and the pain of losing social friends caused by not indulging in these in group mingling together.

Economic wealth is massively raised from smoking, drinking, and pornography. Governments raise heavy tax revenues from the profits of the corresponding businesses. Governments claim that such taxes can be recycled for spending in social welfare. These are assumed in economic perspective to be the benefits raised from social oddities. Yet, the pain from them is the sustained culture of environmental decadence, health problems, and a sexually devastated society that cannot be reformed over time after the ravages of social destruction have run their course. The cost and benefit formula of rational consumer and social choice must therefore be rejected as an acceptable approach for social evaluation, within which are the embedded individual choices. The idea of "alternative" between "responsible" drinking, "responsible" smoking, "consensual" sex, and "adult" pornography as benefits allowing resource allocation in these at the level of consumption and production, form untenable social practices. They fall off reasoned behaviors.

The oppositeness of the concepts of possibilities and alternatives is inherent in the nature of moral/ethical embedding versus marginalism, respectively. In *Tawhidi* framework, the consumer choices of possibilities annul the regime of marginal substitution found in consumer rational choices. Thereby, the axioms of rational choice behavior become untenable in the morally embedded case of pervasive complementarities between the good things of life and avoidance of the bad choices. Sustainability and ethico-economic possibility can only be possible in this kind of regime of social and individual choices. These attributes of a good society are degraded to oblivion in the differentiated economic and social orders of marginalism determining cost-benefit mechanism of alternatives oppositely poised between economic transactions and social wellbeing.

In the above contrast in meaning between truth and falsehood, the same model and method of *Tawhidi* methodology of unity of knowledge apply. But the limiting trend of "de-knowledge" (falsehood by differentiation and methodological individualism) (Holton, 1992) is towards differentiation arising from marginal substitution of economic rationality. Consequently, the moral, ethical, and social effects of choices of "alternatives" lead to methodological individualism that becomes a logical effect of rational choice axiom universally in respect of mainstream economic doctrines (Buchanan, 1999).

The system model given by Expressions (6.1)–(6.6) will apply as well in the perverse sense of negative coefficients signifying marginalist substitution as the mark of differentiation and showing the parting knell of complementarities. The epistemological praxis of unity of knowledge is denied in this system in the limiting case of "de-knowledge" increasingly deepening the marginalism of resource allocation.

Even local forms of complementarities that are considered in mainstream economic theory of consumer behavior cannot be acceptable in the case of *Tawhidi* episteme of unity of knowledge. The TIE resource distribution results in pervasive complementarities between the good things. The same method of circular causation explains the limiting case of complements departing in the limiting case into marginalist disjoint states, conflict, competition, and cost-benefit notions of rational choice of allocation of resources between scarce alternatives.

In the above-mentioned examples, *Tawhidi* methodology premised in unity of knowledge resolves the cost-benefit problem of "alternatives" of mainstream economics by inducing evolutionary process learning that continuously and endogenously learn with the knowledge-induced variables. This attribute of TIE is explained in Figure 6.1, showing continuous reproduction of resources under θ-induction. Consequently, the core axiom of scarcity in mainstream economics is replaced by abundance in the good things of life in TIE. Consequently, a continuous reproduction of this kind can flow into increased payments and usage of inputs of production and enjoying of different consumption goods of life-sustaining type. Marginal substitution and limited complementarities between the good and the productive inputs are together annulled all along the expansion path of resources, outputs, and payments. Even though this kind of distribution and ownership of goods and resources may have *differential* increments pertaining to the consumer goods, inputs, and production outputs, these are positively acquired as the good things of life. It was explained in the earlier chapters that evolutionary learning processes in unity of knowledge by pervasive complementarities between the knowledge-induced resources, goods, inputs, and outputs leave the decision-making points to be perturbation points due to evolutionary learning in complementarities.

3. *Marginalism, priorities, and complementary possibilities*

Consider Figure 6.2 in regard to the above-mentioned topics to prove that the idea of "priorities" in choices by marginal substitution is

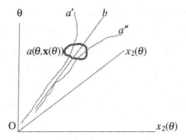

Figure 6.2. Complementarity versus marginalism and priorities.

untenable in *Tawhidi* methodology. Priority of resource allocation among possibilities carries a different meaning in the case of continuously reproduced resources.

Here is how the concept of allocation among priorities is explained contrary to the marginal substitution idea of neoclassical economics.

Let $(x_1(\theta), x_2(\theta)) = (10, 20)$ at the point "a" for a given θ-value within a system of relations under the Expressions (6.1)–(6.6).

Let $(x_1(\theta), x_2(\theta)) = (5, 25)$ at the point "a'" for a given θ-value within a system of relations under the Expressions (6.1)–(6.6).

Let $(x_1(\theta), x_2(\theta)) = (15, 25)$ at the point "a''" for a given θ-value within a system of relations under the Expressions (6.1)–(6.6).

Let $(x_1(\theta), x_2(\theta)) = (15, 30)$ at the point "b'''" for a given θ-value within a system of relations under the Expressions (6.1)–(6.6).

1. Now,

$$[dx_1(\theta)/d\theta]_{a-a'} = -5; [dx_2(\theta)/d\theta]_{a-a'} = 5;$$

$$[dx_1(\theta)/dx_2(\theta)]_{a-a'} = -1.$$

This is the case of substitution in the mainstream frame, but only if a steady-state point is maintained at "a" and "a'". But this is impossible within the perturbation set "a" and along the nonlinear expansion path Oa'.

Hence the meaning of "evaluation" of the wellbeing function as conveyed, subject to simulation of the coefficients of the circular causation relations, becomes an effective way of policy and strategy changes affecting Oa' toward a social reconstruction of consumption, toward attaining greater degrees of complementarities between the good things of consumption while avoiding the bad consumptions.

2. By calculation from the above data on diverse points,

$$[dx_1(\theta)/d\theta]_{a-a'} = 5; \quad [dx_2(\theta)/d\theta]_{a-a'} = 5; \quad [dx_1(\theta)/dx_2(\theta)]_{a-a'} = 1.$$

This is the case of complementarity between $x_1(\theta)$ and $x_2(\theta)$ with the possibility of resource reproduction from a to a''. But this is impossible within the perturbation set "a" and along the nonlinear expansion path Oa'. Hence, the meaning of evaluation of the wellbeing function is conveyed, subject to simulation of the coefficients of the circular causation relations. In the idea of "evaluation", simulation of the wellbeing function becomes an effective way of policy and strategy changes affecting Oa'' toward gaining greater degrees of complementarity.

3. The same implications as above remain true of complementarity and evolutionary learning across nonlinear regimes of possibilities along the Ob path. This path cannot remain linear, as shown within evolutionary learning regions that engulf the linear path shown despite the complementarity between $x_1(\theta)$ and $x_2(\theta)$ for increasing θ-values.

The above-mentioned conditions of complementarities and changes made to the marginalist path by policy induction endogenously affecting the $\mathbf{x}(\theta)$-variables holds strictly in the topological space. A topological space is non-Cartesian in geometric coordinates. Therefore, the inferences drawn above hold true everywhere in the positive quadrant of Figure 6.2, now configured as a non-Cartesian topological space.

Case 2 negates the idea of priorities according to *Tawhidi* methodology as long it is equivalent to invoking the marginalist condition as shown. But the idea of priority can be interpreted along the policy-induced reconstructed path of Case 1, causing the marginalist condition to change into complementarity by θ-induction. In this case, the following results are found: $[dx_1(\theta)/d\theta] > 0$; $[dx_2(\theta)/d\theta]$; but it is possible that, $[dx_1(\theta)/d\theta] > 0$ and $[dx_1(\theta)/d\theta] > 0$; yet, $d^2x_1(\theta)/d\theta^2 >$ or > 0 and, oppositely, $d^2x_2(\theta)/d\theta^2 <$ or > 0.

Here, take an example in respect of Case 2 above: $[dx_1(\theta)/d\theta]_{a-a'} = 5$; $[dx_2(\theta)/d\theta]_{a-a'} = 5$; furthermore, $[dx_1(\theta)/d\theta] = 2$; $[dx_2(\theta)/d\theta] = 7$. Then, $(d/d\theta)[dx_1(\theta)/d\theta] = d^2x_1(\theta)/d\theta^2 = -3$; $(d/d\theta)[\ dx_2(\theta)/d\theta] = d^2x_2(\theta)/d\theta^2 = 2$.

Since the above possibilities occur everywhere in the non-Cartesian space spanning the positive "quadrant", by taking away the axes, therefore, both marginalist allocation of resources by competing choices of mainstream economics and its correction to complementary choices can be explained. *Tawhidi* methodology and the imminent method encased in Expressions (6.1)–(6.6) can therefore explain both the mainstream case of optimality and steady-state equilibrium, and oppositely the case of evolutionary learning by processes in unity of knowledge.

The idea of priority in scarce allocation of resources as marginal substitution between "possibilities" has been erroneously upheld in the existing mainstream orientation of Islamic economics. Even in the Islamic literature, such an idea has been upheld but it is flawed, unless explained in the technical way. Examples of such flawed idea of "priority" is that of "consequentialist rationality" that was upheld by Imam Shatibi (Attia, 2008) as an inductive thinker of *maqasid as-shari'ah*. He viewed the legitimacy of choices in terms of cost-benefit conception. The mistaken concept of priority has been used by Islamic economists without explaining a technical basis of how priority can be explained not in the neoclassical economic sense.

Exercise 2

Take the case of allocation of household budget between tea and coffee. Since both of these goods are considered as acceptable under the *shari'ah*, therefore they can be abundantly marketed for consumption.

(i) Name some of the complementary variables that would keep the prices of these goods stable and affordable as basic commodities.

Give especial consideration to advertisement of the benefits from the complementary goods under the *shari'ah.*

(ii) Resources for consumption can then be socially used in these kinds of consumptions. Would then the case of marginal rate of consumption be true? Would the axiom of scarcity of resources and thereby its allocation in competing alternatives be true in reality?

(iii) Explain the consumer choice problem of tea and coffee in respect of the *Tawhidi* methodology underlying Equations (6.1)–(6.6) in the case of these goods.

Consumer preference and social preference formation according to *Tawhidi* circular causation theory

With the rejection of the axioms of rational choice in consumer socio-economic behavior embedding moral and ethical values through the processes of IIE learning in unity of knowledge and its applications to real-world phenomena, the idea of consumer preferences assumes a vastly different meaning. In forming the *maqasid*-choices of TIE, all of the following mainstream economic assumptions are untenable:

(i) Scarcity of resource and thereby of goods in consumption and production.

(ii) Consequently, optimization and steady-state equilibriums and diminishing returns cannot be upheld as objective goals of the consumer.

(iii) The concept of utility function that gives rise to marginal utility, marginal rate of commodity substitution, and indifference curves at the point of optimal utility and steady-state equilibrium with scarcity of household resources are unacceptable in forming pervasively complementary goods. This is the representation of *Tawhidi* unity of knowledge functioning in TIE.

(iv) Price relatives of substitutes cannot be determined by marginal rates of commodity substitution in the case of *continuous* evolutionary learning and consequential reproduction of resources.

(v) Static preferences as datum are abandoned. Instead, dynamic preferences result as the cause and effect of the above-mentioned negations concerning the axiom of rational choice theory of consumer behavior in economics.

Unfortunately, the assumptions of neoclassical and mainstream economics are zealously imitated by the present days' Islamic economists.

The neoclassical assumptions form contradictions to consumption decisions concerning any kind of goods and choices in the real world. Consider the case of selecting any two basic needs (name them as your example) that are recommended by the *shari'ah*. Such basic needs are continuously augmented by the basic-needs technology to produce. Thereby, the continuous and abundant information generation to the consumer is on the basis of *dynamically graduated basic needs* being the good things of life according to the *shari'ah*. Consumer information such as, "An apple a day keeps the doctor away!"; "recycle and reuse!" — form the staying design of TIE.

The topic of life-fulfillment regime of consumption and production was formalized in the previous chapters in terms of the derived nature of *Tawhidi* methodology. This methodology was applied to complementary discursive preferences formed at various levels of the resulting interactive, integrative, and evolutionary learning processes resulting in terms of dynamic preferences. We now extend the earlier formalism by adding in the consequential effects on the type of negations mentioned above respecting (i)–(v).

Formation of dynamic household preferences in TIE (Choudhury, 2011)

Here is how dynamic preferences are formed in the IIE-process-oriented social system. The head of the family does not coerce a household decision on any matter as the "*amir*" and a self-righteous teacher of knowledge, good manners, and attitudes. Instead, he wins his respect by love, affection, and conceding approval of all. This is the idea of the Arabic respectable leader, "*murabbi*". On matters of consumer behavior, the interactive (discursive), integrative (consensual), and evolutionary learning forms the dynamic and co-ordinated decision on qualities, quantities, and choice of goods. The influence of the head of the family remains on galvanizing the members' preferences towards determining basic-needs consumptions. The circular causation relations then imply that organic reinforcing relations of intervariable causality of complementarities are expected to emerge or to be simulated by policy, strategy, technology, and knowledge (*tarbiah*) implications between the variables.

Now, evolutionary learning generating flows of knowledge in terms of unity of knowledge between the good (*maqasid*) choices is denoted by $\theta \in \Omega, S$.

The specified vectors of choice-variables are denoted by

$\mathbf{x_1}(\theta) = \{$wages and income $\mathbf{y}(\theta),$ wealth $\mathbf{w}(\theta),$ quantities $\mathbf{q}(\theta),$ prices $\mathbf{p}(\theta)\}$,

$\mathbf{x_2}(\theta) = \{$quality $\alpha(\theta),$ technologies $\mathbf{T}(\theta)\}$.

Household preference vector of "i" members are denoted by $\{\wp_i(\theta)\}$ including that of head of the household, "$\wp^*(\theta)$". The vector of participatory preferences is denoted by $\wp(\theta) = \{\wp_i(\theta), \wp * (\theta)\}$, $i = 1, 2, 3, \ldots$.

Now, all throughout the various variables in the vectors as shown, the same properties of IIE learning built in the formalism of Expressions (6.1)–(6.6) will operate. Such circular causation relations with induction of the θ-values must be explained. Yet, the explanation need not be by mainstream and neoclassical economic theory, for we question the rational choice theory of consumer behavior throughout the theory and application of TIE. Rather, the rhetoric of socio-economic interrelations can be an alternative to explain (McCloskey, 1985). Observant and conscious understanding of real-world intervariable causality can unravel the explanation of the circular causation results.

Such circular causation results can now be explained in respect of the above-mentioned vectors of sequences of variables in a realist common understanding. The inferences drawn by automaticity of analysis would be contrary to those derived from the mainstream economic theory. First, we formulate the full model of evaluation of wellbeing, subject to the circular causation relations in TIE. Then, in contrast, we will develop the critique and prove the unacceptability of consumer theory based on the theory of rational choice.

Formulation and explanation of a problem of consumer economic theory in TIE

We restate the problem mentioned above as follows:

$\mathbf{x_1}(\theta) = \{$wages and income $\mathbf{y}(\theta)$, wealth $\mathbf{w}(\theta)$, quantities $\mathbf{q}(\theta)$, prices $\mathbf{p}(\theta)\}$,

$\mathbf{x_2}(\theta) = \{$quality $\alpha(\theta)$, technologies $\mathbf{T}(\theta)\}$.

Household preference vector of "i" members $\{\wp_i(\theta)\}$ including that of head of the household "$\wp^*(\theta)$" is denoted by $\wp(\theta) = \{\wp_i(\theta), \wp^*(\theta)\}, i = 1, 2, 3, \ldots$.

According to the *Tawhidi* methodology of unity of knowledge and its underlying analytics, we invoke the simulation problem of evaluating wellbeing subject to circular causation relations. Thus,

1. Circular causation relations in unity of knowledge, endogenous interrelations, and organic intervariable pairing yield

$$y(\theta) = f_y(w, q, p, T, \alpha, \wp)[\theta]. \qquad (6.7)$$

A positive relationship expressed by the estimated coefficients of $w(\theta)$ would mean that as wealth increases the prospect of generating income also increases. An example is of shareholders in a participatory Islamic firm. A negative estimated coefficient could also be possible if, for example, old age wealth out of savings in active young life could be high. Yet, because of retirement, old age will draw down the earnings. In such a case, continued productive life would require activity in industries that are amenable to old age. A simulation of the coefficient is then required in the light of policies and strategies. An example is to implement the policy of non-mandatory retirement. Now, the organic unity of knowledge is expressed by the endogenous circularity between $y(\theta), w(\theta), T(\theta)$. These together would embody the specific policy and strategy consideration.

Likewise, the estimated coefficient of $q(\theta)$ would imply that as consumption levels increase, the increased derived demand for the consumption basket of basic needs comprising necessaries (*dururiyath*), comforts (*hajiyath*), and refinements (*tahsaniyath*) would sustain the levels of earnings from productive activities and spending in the basic needs of life. We note also that, if the resulting dynamics of interrelations are sustained between $(y, q, p, T, \alpha, \wp)[\theta]$ by estimated results, then a complementary set of organic relations is thereby generated between all the variables.

A special explanation is required now for the interrelations concerning $(\alpha, \wp)[\theta]$ with the other variables. Because it is difficult to obtain data for these variables over time-series, therefore, cross-sectional data can be used by respondent groups, regions, and other characteristics. The estimation followed by simulation of all the variables in the series of equations is done by cross-sectional data that can be generated by attending to ordinal values from sample surveys using questionnaires. Increasing quality of consumed commodities measured by ordinal responses in the questionnaires in respect of the requirements of *maqasid as-shari'ah* as, for example, by the upgrading of the *dhururiyath* (necessities), *hajiyath* (comforts as basic needs), and *tahsaniyath* (refinements also as life-fulfillment needs) basket relates positively with spending, quantity, prices, and technology in a sustainable way across diversified levels of development.

Exercise 3

As in the case of explaining the circular causation relations for Expressions (6.7) and (6.8), the reader can complete a similar explanation for Expressions (6.9)–(6.13), keeping in view the social wellbeing objective function given by Expression (6.17).

$$w(\theta) = f_w(y, q, p, T, \alpha, \wp)[\theta]. \tag{6.8}$$

On a circular causality,

$$q(\theta) = f_q(y, w, p, T, \alpha, \wp)[\theta], \tag{6.9}$$

$$p(\theta) = f_p(y, w, q, T, \alpha, \wp)[\theta], \tag{6.10}$$

$$T(\theta) = f_w(y, w, q, p, \alpha, \wp)[\theta], \tag{6.11}$$

$$\alpha(\theta) = f_w(y, w, q, p, T, \wp)[\theta], \tag{6.12}$$

$$\wp(\theta) = f_w(y, w, q, p, \alpha, T)[\theta], \tag{6.13}$$

with

$$\wp_i(\theta) = g_i(\theta, \wp^*(\theta), y, w, q, p, T, \alpha)[\theta], \tag{6.14}$$

$$\wp^*(\theta) = g^*(\theta, \cup_{\text{interaction}} \cap_{\text{integration}} \{\wp_i(\theta)\}, y, w, q, p, T, \alpha)[\theta]), \tag{6.15}$$

$$i = 1, 2, 3, \ldots.$$

The discursive nature of the formation of $\wp^*(\theta)$ is given by its topological form

$$\wp^*(\theta) = A(\theta).[\cup_{\text{interaction}} \cap_{\text{integration}} \{\wp_i(\theta)\}]. \tag{6.16}$$

Expression (6.10) is an explained formula regarding the properties of IIE-learning processes in unity of knowledge concerning household preferences in decision-making and choices of possibilities. It does not have numerical and empirical values. Such IIE-learning preferences are influenced by the consciousness of knowledge and the state of the *shari'ah*-determined variables through their property of pervasive complementarities. These attributes together signify the functioning of unity of knowledge and its induction of the organic intervariables by circular causation. $A(\theta)$ explains the multiplier learning effect on the IIE process produced by household decision-making. Therefore, we can proxy $\wp(\theta)$ by "θ", the linearized though dynamic knowledge parameter.

Now, any of Expressions (6.7)–(6.9) can be interpreted as the wellbeing function. This can be expressed as before in the case of the empirical version of the conceptual wellbeing function, $W(.)$, as,

$$\theta = f_\theta(y, w, q, p, \alpha, T)[\theta], \tag{6.17}$$

$$df_\theta(.)/d\theta = (\partial f_\theta(.)/\partial y).(dy/d\theta) + (\partial f_\theta(.)/\partial w).(dw/d\theta)$$
$$+ (\partial f_\theta(.)/\partial q).(dq/d\theta) + (\partial f_\theta(.)/\partial p).(dp/d\theta)$$
$$+ (\partial f_\theta(.)/\partial \alpha).(d\alpha/d\theta) + (\partial f_\theta(.)/\partial T).(dT/d\theta) > 0, \tag{6.18}$$

identically, over basic-needs stages of participatory development.

After using the implicit function theorem applied to Expressions (6.7)–(6.9), given the properties of continuity and differentiability of the θ-variable, and thereby of its induced variables, Expression (6.17) would then yield the empirical meaning of the positive relationship signifying degrees of complementarities between the circular causal variables. The meaning here is also regarding the endogenous nature of circular causation relations that form intervariable relations according to the epistemology of unity of knowledge.

Contrasting the model of circular causation in TIE to utility maximization in mainstream consumer theory

1. According to the *Tawhidi* methodology of unity of knowledge, the wellbeing function is the criterion signifying degrees of complementarities existing and gained, estimated and simulated, between the selected variables of *maqasid as-shari'ah*. The wellbeing function negates the assumptions underlying the axiom of rational consumer choice. Likewise, the numerical approximate derivation of the wellbeing function by the θ-variable according to unity of knowledge replaces the epistemology of rationalism by the primacy of *Tawhid* as law and its induction of unity of knowledge in the circular causation variables. Now, all the variables being θ-induced, they become endogenously interrelated along the IIE-learning processes over knowledge, space, and time.

2. In the case of rational consumer choice theory, the wellbeing function devolves into the utility function, the axiom of economic

rationality. Then, the assumptions of scarcity of resources, self-interest by methodological individualism, full-information in allocating resources such as income across competing alternatives hold. The consequences of these assumptions are found to set up the so-called mainstream and present days' Islamic economic "objective" criteria as utility maximization under income and resource constraints.

Preferences are pre-determined and static in nature. This enables rational choices to be pre-ordered, as alternative: $A\wp B$; $B\wp C \Rightarrow A\wp C$; $\wp$ symbolizes preference ordering. This postulate of transitivity of rationality preferences is proved to be a rational fallacy, which Sen (1977) refers to as the behavior of "rational fools". Condorcet (1785) noted the emptiness of such preference pre-ordering. Besides, if evolutionary learning is induced via induction by θ-variable, then preferences cannot remain static and pre-ordering is rejected. Thereby, variables like technological change and innovation, resource augmentation, and taste and moral/ethical values are exogenous in the utility function and in its optimizing constraints.

3. Thus, we consider the above-mentioned differences between *Tawhidi* economic approach and the mainstream one within which also is Islamic economics at the present juncture.

We form the Lagrangian,

$$L(\theta) = f(\mathbf{x}(\theta)) - f^*(\mathbf{x}^*(\theta^*)) + \sum_{i=1}^{n} \lambda(\theta)[x_i - f_i(x_j(\theta))],$$

$$dL(\theta)/d\theta = df(x(\theta))/d\theta + \sum_{i=1}^{n}(x_i - f_i(x_j(\theta)).(d\lambda(\theta)) \qquad (6.19)$$

$$+ \sum_{i=1}^{n} \lambda(\theta)[dx_i/d\theta - df_i(x_j)/d\theta] \neq 0.$$

This result is contrary to the constrained maximization problem of the Lagrangian function in neoclassical consumer theory of constrained utility maximization.

Exercise 4

Set up the classical problem of maximization of the household utility function, subject to the budget constraint and show how the circular causation approach in such a household wellbeing simulation problem is contrary to the Lagrangian approach in the case of the mainstream consumer theory of rational economic behavior.

Formation of social preferences and implications

The concept of being "social" implies a complex and interactive aggregation of microorganic preferences, objectives, and goals that are represented by their specific variables. Therefore, in the moral/ethical sense of social preferences, there is a progressive aggregation of these indicators rising from the microeconomic to the macroeconomic levels. This implies that, in the case of the moral and ethical foundations of economics, the true component of the embedded social and economic perspectives corresponding to any economic problem is at the microeconomic level. From the microlevel, appropriate complex aggregations are enacted to form the social behavior and choices. In the Islamic worldview, individual preference and consumer choices are necessarily embedded in a social order via circular causation. This gives rise to circular causality as recursive feedback between the various preferences, wellbeing, and their inherent variables, all of which together experience organic interrelations governed by the epistemology of unity of knowledge according to the *Tawhidi* methodological worldview. In reference to such a complex and interactive aggregation arising from the microeconomic level to the social level, the *Tawhidi* methodological orientation becomes a study in microeconomic foundations of the total social order, while being governed by organic evolutionary learning characterized by the IIE-learning dynamics as this was explained earlier.

Formalism

The microfoundations of social preferences and social choice in the *Tawhidi* methodological context pose a complex accumulative formalism. We take the following steps toward the construction of such social complexity and nonlinear aggregation. The inference to be drawn is that the foundational grassroots representation plays the most important formative basis in Islamic decision making, and the cumulative role of morality/ethicality all through determines the formation of individual, household, and social consumer behaviors.

Individual and household preferences:

This was formalized in earlier chapters and in this chapter as

$$\wp(\theta) = \{\wp_i(\theta), \wp^*(\theta)\}, \quad i = 1, 2, 3, \ldots \qquad (6.20)$$

The discursive nature of the formation of $\wp^*(\theta)$ is given by its topological form

$$\wp^*(\theta) = A(\theta).[\cup_{\text{interaction}} \cap_{\text{integration}} \{\wp_i(\theta)\}], \qquad (6.21)$$

$$\wp(\theta) = f_w(y, w, q, p, \alpha, T)[\theta], \qquad (6.22)$$

with

$$\wp_i(\theta) = g_i(\theta, \wp^*(\theta), y, w, q, p, T, \alpha)[\theta], \qquad (6.23)$$

$$\wp^*(\theta) = g^*(\theta, \cup_{\text{interaction}} \cap_{\text{integration}} \{\wp_i(\theta)\}, y, w, q, p, T, \alpha)[\theta]), \qquad (6.24)$$

$$i = 1, 2, 3, \ldots$$

Exercise 5

Consider the following way of organizing cross-sectional data or data raised from the questionnaire survey. Each of the vectors of variables is θ-induced, although this is not symbolized.

y	w	q	p	T	α	$\wp_i = 1, 2, 3 \ldots$	$\wp^*\wp$	θ

How would household consumer behavior be evaluated in the two cases (1, 2)?

1. Rational choice theory of mainstream economics.
2. *Tawhidi* methodology of unity of knowledge explained by the evaluation of the wellbeing function (*maslaha*) as a microeconomic aggregation of preferences and variables.

3. How is the moral and ethical context explained in case of (2)?
4. How is ethics exogenous in the case of (1)?

Finally, in respect of social choices, wellbeing, and aggregation of ethically induced preferences and consequently its effect on the ethically induced variables, a robust theory of the wellbeing function (*maslaha*) can be formalized. *Maslaha* arises from the study of the purpose and objective of the *shari'ah* called *maqasid as-shari'ah*. This formalism reflects the microeconomic complex aggregation of the variables and preferences involved in forming the corresponding social verities. The inference here is that ethical induction and moral context of all decision-making and their induction by the *maqasid as-shari'ah* choices represented by the corresponding variables as symbols can exist as microlevel realities.

Contrarily, it is impossible to identify an ethical behavior and ethical agent as an institution at the macroeconomic level. It is also impossible to disaggregate from the macroeconomic level to the microeconomic level of economic and social behaviors. That is because, aggregation in mainstream macroeconomics does not mean the lateral aggregation of variables. In macroeconomics, there is no behavioral study, consumer choice issues, and household decision-making to reflect any kind of ethical behavior. Even when governments are studied in respect of decision-making, it becomes a study of microeconomics or microeconomic foundations of macroeconomics as in public choice theory.

In Islamic economics as it presently exists, the *maslaha* function turns out to be of the utilitarian type. This means a lateral addition of additively linear utility functions distributed over individuals and households in the nation as a whole. Even if there are ethical decisions, the utilitarian version of additive utilities imply ethical exogeneity in decision-making.

The following models arise from the above-mentioned Islamic economic way of formalization as these presently exist: the much-misconstrued idea of welfare $(W(\mathbf{U}(\mathbf{x})))$ in mainstream economics, which is now copied zealously by the present cadre of Islamic economists, is formalized as follows. Bold symbols denote vectors:

$$W(\mathbf{U}(\mathbf{x})) = \sum_{i=1}^{n} U_i(\mathbf{x}). \qquad (6.25)$$

This is a utilitarian expression with independently distributed utility functions over society in terms of the basket of goods denoted by quantities, $\mathbf{x} = \{x_1, x_2, x_3, \ldots, x_m\}$. The property of independent distribution of utilities and quantities is reflected in the linear aggregation of utilities. This does not allow for interaction between the utilities and all that otherwise IIE learning employs.

Furthermore, in the case of interdependent utility function, we write

$$U_i = f_i(\mathbf{U}_j(\mathbf{x})), \ i \neq j = 1, 2, 3, \ldots, n \ (\text{say}) \qquad (6.26)$$

If Expression (6.26) holds for the entire domain of utility functions and commodity space, then the postulate of marginal utility and marginal rate of commodity substitution would either hold, or complementarities would exist between all possibilities. In the former of these two cases, the entire neoclassical economic postulates abide in contrast to the postulates of unity of knowledge under *Tawhidi* methodology. In the latter case, neoclassical economic theory is rejected. Islamic economics as science now reverts to the wellbeing analytics of circular causation in the light of *Tawhidi* methodological worldview of unity of knowledge. But in the latter case, the systemic view of IIE-learning processes would be much more extensive and complex than the linear and *ceteris paribus* nature of neoclassical economics. We turn to this imminent complex functional picture of circular causation involving the objective criterion of evaluation of the wellbeing function as technically defined as the *maslaha* function of *maqasid as-shari'ah*.

We note now that none of the variables comprising **U**-functions and $\mathbf{x}(\theta)$ vector of variables remains independent of each other. Thus, the **U**-functions and $\mathbf{x}(\theta)$-variables establish themselves in corresponding relations as follows:

Quantities: 1   2   3. . . . .   n   Final Market
                                                                      Demand, $x_j(\theta)$
                                                                      $= X_j(\theta) - \Sigma_j x_{ji}(\theta)$
$\mathbf{x}(\theta):$ $i = 1, 2, \ldots, m$
goods
Total Quantity $j = 1, 2, \ldots, n$
consumers

$$
\begin{array}{llllll}
X_1(\theta) & x_{11}(\theta) & x_{12}(\theta) & x_{13}(\theta) & x_{1m}(\theta) & x_1 \\
X_2(\theta) & x_{21}(\theta) & x_{22}(\theta) & x_{23}(\theta) & x_{2m}(\theta) & x_2 \\
X_3(\theta) & x_{31}(\theta) & x_{32}(\theta) & x_{33}(\theta) & x_{3m}(\theta) & x_3 \\
\cdot & \cdot & \cdot & \cdot & \cdot & \cdot \\
X_m(\theta) & x_{m1}(\theta) & x_{m2}(\theta) & x_{m3}(\theta) & x_{mm}(\theta) & x_m
\end{array} \tag{6.27}
$$

Total consumption for each good, say for good 1 of m can be expressed as $X_1 = [(\Sigma_{j=2}^{m}.a_{1j}X_j) + x_1(\theta)]/(1 - a_{11})$. Similarly, the equations of material exchange for other consumptions can be written down. The coefficients a_{1j}, a_{11}, and likewise for other equations of material exchange can be simulated. The simulated coefficients convey the meaning of dynamic coefficients model of exchange in the input–output Expression (6.27) (Oxford University Press, 1989). We therefore have a nonlinear dynamic coefficients model of economy-wide consumer goods and preferences, all included in the θ-values that make the model to be of the dynamic coefficients type.

Expression (6.27) in goods consumed by individuals (aggregate households, community, society) corresponds to the following disaggregate wellbeing functions of consumers:

$U_i(\mathbf{x}(\theta))/i$: 1   2   3. . . . .   n   Final Market
                                                                                        Demand, $x_j(\theta)$
                                                                                        $= X_j(\theta) - \Sigma_j x_{ji}(\theta)$
                                                                                        $i = 1, 2, \ldots, n$
consumers
                                                                                        $j = 1, 2, \ldots, m$
goods

Interactive consumer-specific wellbeing from specific goods.

$$
\begin{array}{llllll}
U_1(X_1(\theta)) & U_{11}(x_{11}(\theta)) & U_{12}(x_{12}(\theta)) & U_{13}(x_{13}(\theta)) & U_{1m}(x_{1n}(\theta)) & U_1(x_1(\theta)), \\
U_2(X_2(\theta)) & U_{21}(x_{11}(\theta)) & U_{22}(x_{12}(\theta)) & U_{23}(x_{13}(\theta)) & U_{2m}(x_{2n}(\theta)) & U_2(x_2(\theta)), \\
U_3(X_3(\theta)) & U_{31}(x_{31}(\theta)) & U_{32}(x_{32}(\theta)) & U_{33}(x_{33}(\theta)) & U_{3n}(\mathbf{x}_{3m}(\theta)) & U_3(x_3(\theta)), \\
\cdot & \cdot & \cdot & \cdot & \cdot & \cdot \\
U_m(X_m(\theta)) & U_{m1}(x_{m1}(\theta)) & U_{m2}(x_{m2}(\theta)) & U_{m3}(x_{n3}(\theta)) & U_{mm}(x_{mn}(\theta)) & U_m(x_m(\theta)).
\end{array} \tag{6.28}
$$

An equivalent set of equations like the derived dynamic coefficients equation of consumption of Expression (6.27) can be derived. From the dynamic model, we deduce the equations

$$U_1(X_1(\theta)) = \left[\left(\sum_{j=2}^{m} .b_{1j} U_j(X_j(\theta)) + U(x_1(\theta)) \right) \right] \Big/ (1 - b_{11}) .$$

$$(6.29)$$

Likewise,

$$U_l(X_l(\theta)) = \left[\left(\sum_{k=1}^{m} .b_{kl} U_l(X_l(\theta)) \right) + U(x_l(\theta)) \right] \Big/ (1 - b_{ll}),$$

$$k, l = 1, 2, 3, \ldots, m; k \neq l. \qquad (6.30)$$

One can readily see that the wellbeing function in both its nonlinear and linear forms with the utility functions given in terms of the *maqasid*-choices represented by the variables would be a complex system. Such a property of IIE systems governed by circular causation, best fits into the definition of complex nonlinear systems formalized by Bertuglia and Vaio (2005, p. 269): "The fundamental characteristic of complexity is the fact that, in the study of the evolution of dynamical systems that complexity deals with, the nature of the system in question is usually irrelevant. In the vision proposed by complexity, we can identify forms and evolutive characteristics common to all, or almost all, systems that are made up of numerous elements, between which there are reciprocals, nonlinear interactions and positive feedback mechanisms. These systems, precisely for this reason, are generally called complex systems."

On a simple scale, we can write the wellbeing function as follows:

$$W(\theta) = W(\mathbf{U}(\mathbf{x}(\theta))) = W(\mathbf{x}_{ij}(\theta), \mathbf{x}(\theta); \wp(\theta)).$$

This expression means that evaluation of the wellbeing function in terms of the dynamic coefficients input–output analysis is premised on the formation of choices by preferences under the effect of θ-values. We have explained above that the measurement of the preference function can be subsumed in the evaluation of the θ-values.

Demand functions

Two forms of demand function need to be examined. In usual economic theory, consumer demand is that of each of Robinson Crusoe's and his Man Friday's. These are independent of each other. Thus, no intercausality is shown between the variables to specify how the two consumer demand functions interact. Interaction though is not denied, except that, it is not analytical studied in economic terms.

Next market demand is defined in economic theory as the locus of the sum total of quantities demanded at given prices along the consumer demand curve. Once again, it is noted that intercausality between quantities and prices is not considered analytically. Simply, *ceteris paribus* situation of demand is assumed. The same assumption is made for any other variable in the demand function. The example is of the income variable, which is treated as an exogenous variable to cause shifts in the demand curves of the consumer and the aggregate market demand. In the same way, taste, technology, and ethics as charitable behavior are exogenous variables affecting shifts in the demand curve.

None of these assumptions hold up for the case of evaluating wellbeing, subject to circular causation between the variables. In this case, the price and quantity variables are interrelated endogenously by their interrelationship. We now derive the price vector $(\mathbf{p}(\theta))$ and quantity vector $(\mathbf{q}(\theta))$ relations in multi-markets by the following equations of the entire set of other circular causation equations.

$$p_1(\theta) = f_1(q_1, \ldots, q_n, p_2, p_3, \ldots, p_n, Y, \alpha)[\theta], \tag{6.31}$$

$$\vdots$$

$$p_n(\theta) = f_n(q_1, \ldots, q_n, p_1, \ldots, p_{n-1}, Y, \alpha)[\theta], \tag{6.32}$$

$$q_1(\theta) = f_1(q_2, \ldots, q_n, p_1, p_2, p_3, \ldots, p_n, Y, \alpha)[\theta], \tag{6.33}$$

$$\vdots$$

$$q_n(\theta) = f_n(q_1, q_2, \ldots, q_{n-1}, p_1, p_2, p_3, \ldots, p_n, Y, \alpha)[\theta]. \tag{6.34}$$

The above kinds of multivariate specification of the demand function in its two forms are essential in the case of circular causation relations of endogenous intervariable relationships caused by the *Tawhidi* methodology of unity of knowledge.

Now, preferences can be different among consumers in respect of prices and quantities and the other variables. This is caused by the different effects of θ-variable on the variables. Besides, the random variations in θ-variable will cause no unique positioning of the demand curves. The consumer demand curve is therefore undetermined. Demand remains only a notion of hurt and pain between relative prices for the relative quantities of goods in demand. Since the consumer demand curve remains a notion rather than reality, therefore, the market demand curve is not determinate. It is notional.

Market demand, market supply, and market equilibrium

The market-demand curve in the case of circular causation method of deriving price and quantity equations given a basic-needs regime of consumption and production, as exemplified by the Shatibi basket of *dururiyath, hajiyath,* and *tahsaniyath,* is an *almost* perfectly elastic curve DD as shown in Figure 6.3. The endogenous effect of θ on $\mathbf{p}$ and $\mathbf{q}$ in multi-markets gravitates the demand functions, DD_1, and the many more of these kinds towards the *approximately* perfectly elastic demand curve shown by DD as the θ-induced market demand curve of basic needs. These induced goods are also the *maqasid*-choices. They enter the *maslaha* function, which we evaluate in the light of complementarities between the choices as "possibilities", rather than by substitutes ("alternatives"). Simulation by means of strategies, policies, and knowledge induction are some of the instruments that induce the convergence of D_1D to DD. This kind of specification of the temporary consumer and market demand function implies a change from the marginalist regime of scarcity of resources caused by the absence of endogeneity of knowledge and learning in a complementary regime of approximation to life-fulfilment (basic needs) regime of consumption. The approximation rather than perfection into a fully realized basic-needs regime of consumption is shown by a slightly negatively sloped shape of DD.

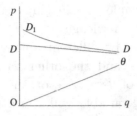

Figure 6.3. Market demand specification by endogenous relationship between $(p(\theta), q(\theta), \theta)$ in the dynamic basic-needs regime of consumption.

The supply function

Construction of the supply function is similarly specified by the method of circular causation model as is the case with the demand specification. In reference to the problem that we formalized above in respect of the market demand function, we will repeat the use of the same variables for the supply function and explain the construction.

Specification of the supply function

$$p_1(\theta) = f_1(q_1, \ldots, q_n, p_2, p_3, \ldots, p_n, Y, \alpha)[\theta], \qquad (6.35)$$

$$\ldots\ldots\ldots\ldots\ldots\ldots\ldots\ldots\ldots$$

$$p_n(\theta) = f_n(q_1, \ldots, q_n, p_1, \ldots, p_{n-1}, Y, \alpha)[\theta]. \qquad (6.36)$$

In the perspective of complementarities signaled by the epistemology of unity of knowledge, which is projected by the circular causation between the variables, the above equations describe the supply functions in multi-market. The degree of complementarities gained between the price, quantity, income, and taste (or technology) variables is a matter of the function of knowledge induction in the supply specification between the variables and by the strategies and policies used to simulate the desired levels of complementarities.

Extensive complementarities between the variables would suggest that the simulated coefficients of Expressions (6.35) and (6.36) would mean: as quantities of any good increases, its own price increases but remains stable along an *approximately perfectly elastic* supply curve. The price of any good increases as the supply prices and quantities of the other goods increase. These results happen because of the *continuous* increase in resources, such as in inputs, technology $(\alpha(\theta))$, revenues $(Y(\theta))$, and stable cost of production in the basic-needs regime of supply specification, i.e. production of goods and services. This in turn meets the demand side of the basic-needs regime of consumption.

Similar relations are confirmed from the side of supply specification of complementarities between any specific supply quantity of a good in relationship with other supply of goods and all with all the prices. The same implication of complementarities and increased resource effect applies as explained above. The *Qur'an* (7:156) declares the blessings and mercy of *Allah* lies on all that is good for this world and the Hereafter: "And decree for us in this world [that which is] good and [also] in the Hereafter; indeed, we have turned back to You." [*Allah*] said, 'My punishment — I afflict with it whom I will, but My mercy encompasses all things. So I will decree it [especially] for those who fear Me and give *zakah* and those who believe in Our verses'.

Specifying supply function in multi-market

$$q_1(\theta) = f_1(q_2, \ldots, q_n, p_1, p_2, p_3, \ldots, p_n, Y, \alpha)[\theta], \qquad (6.37)$$

$$\ldots \ldots \ldots \ldots \ldots \ldots$$

$$q_n(\theta) = f_n(q_1, q_2, \ldots, q_{n-1}, p_1, p_2, p_3, \ldots, p_n, Y, \alpha)[\theta]. \qquad (6.38)$$

The above kind of specification details hold.

Market equilibrium

The important controlling basis of the complementary interrelationships between the *maqasid as-shari'ah* choices specifying the demand and supply functions is the continuously augmenting resource variable induced by the property of θ-variable. Resources include physical and financial inputs, technology, and suchlike inputs that enhance the values for demand and supply. The resource effect on the formation of complementarities changes the nature of market equilibrium into a plethora of non-steady-state evolutionary

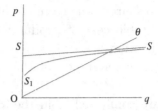

Figure 6.4. Supply function according to the precept of *Tawhidi* unity of knowledge projected in circular causation method of extensive complementarities.

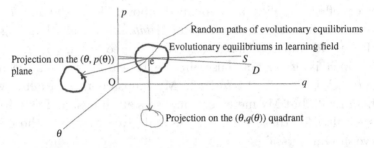

Figure 6.5. Evolutionary market equilibriums as the consequence of circular causation and simulacra of demand and supply with respect to *Tawhidi* precept of unity of knowledge.

equilibriums. The evolutionary processes in the IIE-learning field of equilibriums occur around the "final" equilibrium point, which though cannot be attained. In Islamic terminology, the final yet unattainable equilibrium point is hidden as *"ghayb"* (unseen). The *Qur'an* (6:59) declares in this regard: "With Him are the keys of the unseen (*ghayb*). No one knows them other than Him. He knows what is in land and sea. No leaf falls but He knows it; nor there is not a grain in the darkness (or depths) of the earth nor anything fresh or dry (green or withered), but is (inscribed) in a Record Clear (to those who can read)."

Now, we bring together Figures 6.3 and 6.4 in Figure 6.5 to explain the nature of evolutionary market equilibrium in reference to *Tawhidi* unity of knowledge reflected through circular causation.

The results of the *Tawhidi* methodological worldview of unity of knowledge reflected in the method of circular causation and simulation for complementarities contrast with the mainstream economic theory of market equilibrium. The resulting evolutionary learning world system of intervariable complementarities caused by unity of knowledge between the *maqasid*-choices in the wellbeing (*maslaha*) function contradicts the steady-state market equilibrium concept of mainstream economics. That is because of the assumptions underlying the axiom of rational economic choice. Its core assumption in mainstream economics is that of scarcity of resources.

Abundance versus scarcity in TIE versus mainstream resource concepts

What does scarcity of resources mean in economic theory from which the *Qur'anic* meaning of abundance is distinctly against scarcity? According to the *Qur'an*, abundance as mercy is caused by *Allah's* blessings in all good things. Across the domain of such good things flow his blessings and mercy? The *Qur'an* (31:20) declares: "Do ye not see that *Allah* has subjected/made of benefit to you all things in the heavens and on earth, and has made his bounties flow to you in exceeding measure, (both) seen and unseen? Yet there are among men those who dispute about *Allah*, without knowledge and without guidance, and without a Book to enlighten them!"

The meanings of scarcity and abundance arise from the nature of resources. If resources remain scarce, the logical yet unethical consequence is reflected in the marginal rate of substitution, opportunity cost, competition, and thereby self-interest and methodological individualism. On the other hand, the existence of abundance of resource regeneration is caused by search and discovery of interactive, integrative, and evolutionary knowledge that arise from interaction across diversity of organisms. As we have explained earlier, under the condition of abundance of resources caused by organic unity of knowledge, marginal substitution and opportunity cost do not exist in the resource distribution theory over complementary possibilities of the life-fulfilling regimes of consumption and production — i.e. of demand and supply. Thus, in the *Tawhidi* methodological worldview, there is neither the notion of absolute scarcity nor the relative scarcity conveyed by marginal rate of substitution between alternatives. We have also explained earlier that the limited meaning of complementarity as in neoclassical economics is untenable, because of the concept of continuity of unity of knowledge in *Tawhidi* methodological worldview prevailing over knowledge, space, and time.

Exercise 6

(i) Take the example of land, vegetables, and fruits, all of which are complementary choices of *maqasid as-shari'ah*. The abundance of land is proved by increasing its fertility. The abundance of vegetables and fruits is related to the acceptance of basic-needs regime of development. But in this regime of three resources, the enhancement to fertility and production of land will end.

How then can complementarities be extended to sustain organic relationship between land, vegetables, fruits, and the other complementary factors? Answer by using an example.

(ii) In the life-fulfilling regime of consumption and production, the demand and supply curves tend to converge to establish continuously evolutionary equilibriums.

Re-draw Figure 6.5 to explain this phenomenon. Can the demand and supply curves coincide *perfectly* under the induction of θ-values on the demand and supply sides? Explain.

(iii) In the case of complements and substitutes, for example between tea and milk, the following implications would hold with tea and coffee as substitutes:

(% change in the quantity of tea consumed)/(%change in the price of coffee) > 0, implying tea and coffee are substitutes.

(% change in the quantity of tea consumed)/(%change in the price of coffee) < 0, implying coffee and tea are complements.

How can this happen in the case of extensive complementarities between tea and coffee with θ-effect? Can the assumption of *ceteris paribus* be true in this case?

(iv) Without the relevance of *ceteris paribus*, how could the degree of complementarity be evaluated in the presence of resource augmentation by θ-values? [Use the objective *maslaha* criterion of evaluation of wellbeing subject to circular causation between *maqasid*-choices.]

(v) Explain the extended idea of intervariable complementarities using Expressions (6.31)–(6.34).

Conclusion

Throughout this book, there appears increasing area of critical and formal analyses to prove that the *Tawhidi* epistemological basis of Islamic economics is distinctive and rich in explaining, evaluating, and measuring complex fields of social and economic study inclusively. On the other hand, the assumptions of the axiom of economic rationality and rational choice theory cannot achieve such extended methodological worldview.

The TIE methodology is indeed the most generalized nature of economics and socio-scientific intellection. It dispels the postulates of rational choice, *ceteris paribus*, and partial equilibrium. TIE replaces these with the axiom of abundance arising from the IIE-learning processes by the presence of continuously endogenous intervariable complementarities. Mainstream economic theory does not have the capability to undertake such a knowledge-induced evolutionary learning domain of interdependent study. Contrarily, the emergent field of *Tawhidi* epistemology in the building stages of a new socio-scientific theory with economics as a particularity can universally and uniquely answer the deficiency of mainstream economics and its TIE offshoots. Thereby, in the present age of heterodox economics with new epistemological ways, as of unity of knowledge premised in *Tawhid*, the emergence of the heterodox Islamic economics with its *Tawhidi* epistemology can offer the revolutionary platform of socio-scientific thought, theory, formalism, and applications for all of intellection.

In this chapter, the focus of study has been in the following directions combining with the earlier chapters:

1. TIE contra mainstream consumer theory.
2. TIE contra mainstream theory of the firm.

References

Attia, G. E. (2008). *Towards Realization of the Higher Intents of Islamic Law: A Functional Approach of Maqasid as-Shari'ah*, Herndon, VA: International Institute of Islamic Thought.

Miller, R. E., Polenske, K. R. and Rose, A. Z. (Eds.) (1989). *Frontiers of Input-Output Analysis*, New York, NY: Oxford University Press.

Bertuglia, C. S. and Vaio, F. (2005). "Dynamical systems and the phase space", in *Non-linearity, Chaos & Complexity, the Dynamics of Natural and Social Systems*, Oxford, UK: Oxford University Press, pp. 49–70.

Buchanan, J. M. (1999). "The domain of constitutional economics", in *The Collected Works of James M. Buchanan, The Logical Foundations of Constitutional Liberty*, Indianapolis, IN: Liberty Press, pp. 377–395.

Burstein, M. (1991). "History versus Equilibrium: Joan Robinson and time in economics", in *The Joan Robinson Legacy*, Rima, I. H. (Ed.), Armonk, New York: M. E. Sharpe, Inc., pp. 49–61.

Choudhury, M. A. (2011). "The family as a socioeconomic management system", *International Journal of Management Studies*, 18(1), 99–115.

Condorcet, M. J. A. N. (1785). *Essai sur l'application de l'analyse a la probabilite des decisions rendues a la pluralite des voix*, Paris, France: Imprimerie Royale.

Grandmont, J.-M. (1989). "Temporary equilibrium", in *New Palgrave: General Equilibrium*, Eatwell, J., Milgate, M. and Newman, P. (Eds.), New York, NY: W. W. Norton, pp. 164–185.

Holton, R. L. (1992). *Economy and Society*, London, England: Routledge.

Hull, D. L. (1988). *Science as a Process, an Evolutionary Account of the Social and Conceptual Development of Science*, Chicago, IL: University of Chicago Press.

McCloskey, D. N. (1985). *The Rhetoric of Economics*, Wisconsin, Minnesota: The University of Wisconsin Press, pp. 36–61.

Sen, A. (1977). "Rational fools: A critique of the behavioural foundations of economic theory", *Philosophy and Public Affairs*, 6, 317–44.

Thurow, L. (1983). *Dangerous Currents, the State of Economics*, New York, NY: Random House.

Chapter 7

Dual Theories of the Firm

The general theory of *evaluation* of the objective function of wellbeing (*maslaha*) in the light of the epistemology of unity of knowledge with *maqasid*-choices and using the method of circular causation has been laid down in the previous chapters. The same method and the underlying idea meeting the *Tawhidi* analytical methodology has also been particularized for special problems of economics. Therefore, the building blocks of this theory will not be treated henceforth. What will be accomplished is the *application* of the *Tawhidi* theory of unity of knowledge with the method of evaluation of the wellbeing function subject to circular causation relations.

In the theory of the firm, the contrasting nature of the firm in *Tawhidi* Islamic economics (TIE) and mainstream perspectives need to be understood. The firm uses factors of production, subject to cost of production to produce goods out of the efficient use of resources and the productive use of inputs of production. This is the usual viewpoint of all approaches to the theory of the firm. The difference between the *Tawhidi* methodological approach and its *maqasid as-shari'ah* viewpoint is established by the embedding of θ-values in the organic participatory relationships between all the variables comprising the wellbeing function and the circular causation relations pertinently to the objective of the firm.

The *Tawhidi* analytical methodology and the *maqasid*-viewpoint make the objective criterion not simply of production. Rather, this activity is a subset of the total social picture. The firm then is an institutional entity of this social nexus. Examples of such kinds of firms are firstly, the Islamic firm promoting the consumption and production, and thereby the complementary nature of these activities in a life-fulfilling regime of development in the good things of life (*halal at-tayyabah*). Take another example. This is of the Islamic bank as an Islamic firm. The principle function of the Islamic bank, differently from any other bank, is to mobilize savings into the *maqasid as-shari'ah* directions. This comprises a portfolio of morally and ethically embedded objective directions. The principle of resource mobilization in the *maqasid*-choices involves participatory financial portfolio that must thereby necessarily avoid financial interest (*riba*). *Riba* causes holding back of bank savings against allowing resource mobilization. The complementarities between the good things of life in the evaluation of the *maslaha* function, subject to circular causation between the representative choice variables as the sign of organic evolutionary learning forming inter-variable complementarities stand for the sign of unity of knowledge and its induction of reality in all detail. The evaluation of the wellbeing function, subject to the system of circular causation relations constitutes the actual objective criterion of the Islamic firm. This approach endows the Islamic firm with its institutional, organizational, and factual role in the entire Islamic social economy (Choudhury, 2016).

Now, taking stock of all the details of the method of evaluation of the wellbeing function (*maslaha*), subject to circular causation relations, the formal model of the Islamic firm is written as follows. The following variables are defined.

Q denotes output; K denotes stock of capital; L denotes employment; H denotes human capital; E denotes enterprise; T denotes technology and innovation; R denotes resources such as cost of production and, in the Islamic case, participatory joint financing instruments are used. The last case is one of joint venture in a "pooled fund" of various Islamic financing instruments. This case of pooled financing was explained earlier.

$$\text{Evaluate } \{\theta\} \quad W(Q, K, L, H, E, T, R)[\theta], \tag{7.1}$$

$$\text{subject to} \quad Q = f_1(K, L, H, E, T, R)[\theta], \tag{7.2}$$

$$K = f_2(Q, L, H, E, T, R)[\theta], \tag{7.3}$$

$$L = f_3(Q, K, H, E, T, R)[\theta], \tag{7.4}$$

$$H = f_4(Q, K, L, E, T, R)[\theta], \tag{7.5}$$

$$E = f_5(Q, K, L, H, T, R)[\theta], \tag{7.6}$$

$$T = f_6(Q, K, L, H, E, R)[\theta], \tag{7.7}$$

$$R = f_7(Q, K, L, H, E, T)[\theta], \tag{7.8}$$

$$\theta = F(Q, K, L, H, E, T, R)[\theta]. \tag{7.9}$$

Expression (7.9) is the empirical form of the wellbeing function with θ being assigned ordinal values in terms of the socio-economic variables, as was explained earlier.

In reference to the mainstream economics of production, which is also copied by Islamic economics of the mainstream genre, the resource variable includes more than the cost of production, for the factors of production earn dividends besides factor payments.

In mainstream economics, the cost of production is given by either of the following equations shown by their internal specifications:

$$C = C(Q) = wL + rK. \tag{7.10}$$

Contrarily, the resource equation in the *Tawhidi* analytical concept is given by the full gamut of inputs of production as shown by Expression (7.8). Besides, the payments equation to such inputs of production is given by

$$R(\theta) = (wL + r.K + p_1.H + p_2.E + p_3.T + d.Q)[\theta], \tag{7.11}$$

with "w" being wage rate, "r" being rents, "p_i" being prices of the ith inputs as shown, and "d" being the dividend rate on the production of units of Q. dQ therefore denotes the total dividend on the financing of the production levels.

Expression (7.11) is "similar" to Expression (7.8). Each one of the variables including the price coefficients and "d" is induced by θ-variable. The meaning of this is that, in a life-fulfillment regime of production, consumption and distribution of resources, prices and the variables remain sustainably stable. Such a state of the variables requires organic pairing between the variables along intra-systems and inter-systems of IIE processes. If otherwise, any two of the comparative variables and prices are represented, as an example, by the price relative, (w/r), for matters of incremental choice of the corresponding inputs, then this would mean marginal rate of substitution between those variables. This would be in contrary to the principle of abundance of resources and complementarities between the pairing variables, which is the principal consequence of *Tawhidi* methodological implications.

The production function of the firm is represented by Expression (7.2). All Expressions (7.2)–(7.9) are derived functions of the computational general equilibrium functions of the interactive, integrative, and evolutionary type. The meaning of the wellbeing function (*maslaha*) implies that each of the functional variables is complementary to all other variables. In this regard, one can put an important institutional explanation to the production milieu.

Consider the simple case of Expression (7.2) in the form $Q = f(L, K)[\theta]$. The embedding of both L and K in θ-value implies that there must be an institutional arrangement of cooperation between capital (owners) and workers in determining the *maqasid*-choices. The result then is, as shown earlier, the demand function and the supply function being together near perfectly elastic curves, subject to evolutionary equilibrium all along the continuous organic complementarity between capital and labor demand curves. This would likewise be of the same nature of complementarity and continuity as between variables of the demand and supply functions. Such is the case of participatory financial and organizational instruments in Islam contrary to the effect of the instrument of *riba*.

Exercise 1

(i) Formulate and explain the empirical version of the objective criterion comprising the circular causation relations (7.1)–(7.9) with the following complementary variables: $(Q, K, L, F)[\theta]$.

(ii) Explain the difference but the necessity of having H and θ in any and all of Expressions (7.2)–(7.9).

(iii) Explain the following result derived from Expression (7.5) taken in the following form:

$$\log H = A(\theta) + a_1. \log Q + a_2. \log K + a_3. \log L$$
$$+ a_4. \log E + a_5. \log T + a_6. \log R.$$

Each and every variable and the learning coefficients are θ-induced.

How do you explain $d \log H / d\theta$ with the distinctive meanings for $H(\theta)$ and "θ"?

(iv) What is the difference between the result of (iii) and the marginal productivity idea of mainstream economic theory of the firm? Does this difference in these results change in the intertemporal case along the output expansion path?

(v) How is the idea of increasing returns to wellbeing different from the case of increasing returns to scale of production in the case of mainstream economics? You can work with the case of Expressions (7.2) and (7.9).

Non-viability of marginal productivity theory of wages in TIE

The principle of pervasive complementarity that spans all functions in TIE rejects the relevance of every marginalist formula. In this sense, the marginal productivity theory of wages, rents, and other input payments are not tenable in TIE.

Formally, let us consider the following mainstream formula that is untenable:

$$w = p \cdot \text{Marginal Productivity of}$$

$$L = p \cdot (\partial Q / \partial L) \text{ in perfect competition, and} \quad (7.12)$$

$$w = p \cdot \text{Marginal Revenue Product of } L$$

$$= \text{MR} \times p \cdot \text{MP}_\text{L}$$

$$= p \cdot (\Delta \text{Total Revenue}/\Delta Q) \times (\Delta Q/\Delta L) = \Delta TR/\Delta L$$

$$(7.13)$$

in imperfect competition.

"w" is set by the labor market. No institutional and policy implication is invoked to affect wage setting other than the market. In the basic-needs economic regime, the supply curve of goods and services causes abundance of demand for inputs of production including labor, leaving aside those who cannot work and are therefore not in the active labor force. Temporarily, they may be in the exit and re-entry flux in the potential labor force in the periphery. Consequently, the role of θ-induction in the demand and supply functions of the basic-needs economic regime will cause the supply of production of Q to remain fluctuating around the evolutionary labor market equilibriums. Consequently, MP_L curve remains random and the wage rate undetermined in both the perfect and imperfect markets for goods, services, and factors of production.

Formulas (7.12) and (7.13) being untenable in the case of the sensitive effect of θ-values, the TIE method suggests the multivariate empirical determination of Q, K, L and all prices. This of course does not mean that statistical variations can be avoided. Rather, the random behavior of factor and product markets is accepted as a fact. Thereby, only simulation in the complementary field of multivariates is upheld to be the way to regulate prices by policies, strategies, along with market realities. This proves the case that TIE is always a domain of IIE processes playing out its course in market–institutional conjoint discursive interrelationship. Such is the case also with the implication of circular causation interrelations between the variables of the goods things of life. In case of contrary variables, as of *riba* (i) against trade (rate of gains from trade, π), the wellbeing function given in (7.1) [and thereby, Expression (7.9)], the variable representation for *riba* would be either $(1/i)$ or (π/i).

In Expression (7.11),

$$R(\theta)/d\theta = (d/d\theta)(wL + r \cdot K + p_1 \cdot H + p_2 \cdot E$$
$$+ p_3 \cdot T + d \cdot Q)[\theta],$$

yields

$$w(\overset{>0}{dL/d\theta}) + L(dw/d\theta)$$

$$= \overset{>0}{R(\theta)/d\theta} - (\overset{>0}{d/d\theta})(r \cdot K + \overset{>0}{p_1} \cdot H + p_2 \cdot E + p_3 \cdot T + d \cdot Q)[\theta].$$

$$(7.14)$$

Let

$$\lambda(\theta) = (d/d\theta)(r \cdot K + p_1 \cdot H + p_2 \cdot E + p_3 \cdot T + d \cdot Q)[\theta] > 0. \quad (7.15)$$

Expression (7.14) explains that payments for increases in employment plus increments in wages as bonus paid to the employed labor force are possible as long as the resources increase under the θ-impact of θ-values above the θ-induced positive increases in the payments to all remaining inputs of production.

These consequences can be shown in Figure 7.1.

The region "b" is above the region "a" indicating the possibility of paying wages and bonuses to labor by size and increments as long as the resources of production increases. This is possible under the condition of θ-induced resources being in excess of the positive

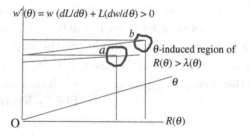

Figure 7.1. The capability of paying wages and wage increments as incentive payment under the impact of knowledge induction to generate increasing returns in resources in the basic-needs economic regime.

changes in the rest of the factor payments as shown. (Mansfield, 1985).

The TIE economics of resources in production

We have pointed out that the theory of pervasive complementarities in light of *Tawhidi* unity of knowledge in the domain of the most extended meaning of *maqasid as-shari'ah* (Choudhury, 2015) depends on the positive augmenting effect of θ-induction of resources. Without this critical case, no possibility of complementarities can be attained. The neoclassical economic theory of marginalism via scarcity of resources as the core property would return lock, stock, and barrels. The possibility of TIE in the face of its methodology of unity of knowledge would drown.

As defined by Expression (7.11), resources of production comprise payments to all factors of payments including the dividend payments. That is because, in the cooperative firm as institution in the Islamic economy with its participatory financing, a factor of production by its entities is a shareholder. The rest of the community in which the firm exists is the stakeholders' social order. This feature of resource formation is signified by the nature of market–institution of the Islamic firm and its growing degree of consciousness that is implied by increasing θ-values.

The nature of θ-induced resources as the total cost of production, is now examined in the contrasting cases of mainstream economics and TIE. In the mainstream theory of cost and production of the firm, the total cost of production remains as the direct cost. Other important cost components such as implicit costs and social costs are not included. Such as, for example, in the control of violence, two kinds of cost escalation may be used. Firstly, in the mainstream economics of the firm, the production of lethal armaments and punishment as control are used. In the TIE, a lesser use of lethal armaments is replaced by the rehabilitation methods to regenerate human resources. Such is presently the case with the Scandinavian approach to its welfare state and rehabilitation policies — an institutional effect (James, 2013).

In Expression (7.10), the θ-induction of cost makes the cost function sensitive to direct cost, indirect implicit cost, and social cost. The sum total of these cost components for the production of Q as social good causes a learning effect on the cost function by way of the IIE-learning processes. The randomness in the total cost component while being caused by statistical observations is also caused in respect of the IIE-learning processes experienced via evolutionary equilibrium changes along the total cost curve. The statistical randomness can be smoothened by certain statistical methods such as by the smoothening of value estimators, and data enveloping analysis (DEA). But there is no method to smoothen the effects of the simulacra of IIE-learning effects that arise from continuous simulations after simulations that arise along the IIE-learning processes, and so on. The nature of evolutionary equilibriums being a consequence of market–institution interaction and discourse around moral/ethical values, such discursive interventions form in the neighborhood of evolutionary equilibrium points consequential to the intensifying learning processes; yet, not reaching the core of the finality because of the inextricable presence of the hidden, the unseen (*ghayb*).

From the above-mentioned nature of intrinsic variations of the total cost function along the IIE-processes, it is obvious that the average variable cost and average fixed cost of production cannot be of the smooth shape, as shown in mainstream theory of the firm. This is because the fixed cost is θ-induced around the continuous plethora of points around its evolutionary learning equilibriums. Consequentially, the shape of the θ-induced fixed cost curve, FC(θ) is not perfectly elastic. Therefore, the average fixed cost curve, AFC(θ) = FC(θ)/$Q(\theta)$, cannot be expected to remain asymptotically smooth along the increasing θ-induced outputs. The simple case of Expression (7.10) now takes the form

$$\mathrm{TC}(\theta) = w(\theta) \cdot L(\theta) + r(\theta) \cdot K(\theta) + \mathrm{FC}(\theta), \qquad (7.16)$$

i.e.

$$\mathrm{TC}(\theta) = \mathrm{AVC}(\theta) + \mathrm{AFC}(\theta) \qquad (7.17)$$

From these expressions, the formula of the average total cost curve is

$$\text{ATC} = \text{TC}(\theta)/Q(\theta) = (\text{ALC} + \text{AKC} + \text{AFC})[\theta], \qquad (7.18)$$

where ALC denotes the average cost in labor use,

$$\{w(\theta) \cdot L(\theta)\}/Q(\theta). \qquad (7.19)$$

Average capital cost is denoted by

$$\text{AKC} = \{r(\theta) \cdot K(\theta)\}/Q(\theta). \qquad (7.20)$$

Between Expressions (7.19) and (7.20), we can write

$$[w(\theta) \cdot L(\theta)]/[r(\theta) \cdot K(\theta)] = \text{wage bill relative to capital cost.}$$
$$(7.21)$$

Since labor and capital are complementary to each other in the TIE domain, therefore, the wage bill and capital cost will be proportionate to each other. This result is opposite to the wage–rental relationship of neoclassical economics. The proportionate relationship is caused by the continuous change in θ-values, thus causing pervasive complementarities between all "possibilities". Such is the case with labor and capital, which otherwise in mainstream economics are substitutes along the production isoquants, even though they are proportionately increasing along the expansion path of output. Yet, every point on the expansion path denotes marginal rate of substitution between factor inputs.

The shape of the average cost curves in TIE

Figure 7.2 shows the shape of the average cost curves on the basis of the above-mentioned explanations. The important points to note now is how the prices of goods are determined, given the price determination method of factor inputs, most importantly labor and capital, as explained above. It is quite clear from the type of learning curve of average cost with continuously increasing θ-values, technological change, and resource augmentation, that no minimum point of the average cost curve can be found. The average cost curve loses its smooth shape in the case of the IIE-learning processes all

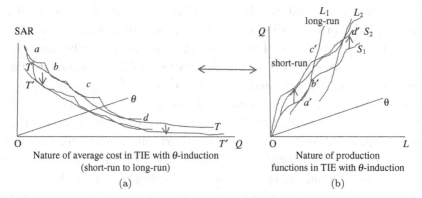

Figure 7.2. Corresponding interrelations between average cost and production function in $(\theta, Q, L, TC)[\theta]$.

along it. Consequently, the price of goods in an equilibrium-perfect competitive goods market cannot be determined by the marginal cost curve. Such a curve does not exist either by construction or by nature of the perfectly competitive markets of goods and services.

The idea of perfectly competitive markets turns out to be a fictive concept. There is none so. TIE proves this fact by its realist arguments based on organic complementarity phenomenon based on the *Tawhidi* methodology. In heterodox mainstream economics too the idea of perfectly competitive markets is rejected by its replacement with the theory of evolutionary economics (Burstein, 1991; Rima, 1986).

Figure 7.2 depicts the case of non-existence of marginalism in the cost and production context of mainstream economics by the IIE properties of evolutionary learning in TIE context. The following symbols are explained: let SAR denote the financial value of average total cost. TT denotes the long-run average cost curve. The long-run adjustment is caused by adaptation to θ-induction. Points "a, b, c, d" denote short-run average curves during the adaptive period of θ-induction. Note that the long-run average curve as a learning curve is shown by uneven curves that are caused by perturbations caused by θ-induction.

On the production side of output corresponding to the average cost of production, we have the cause and effect circularity shown in Figure 7.2(a). The circular causation is explained by the double arrows. The corresponding short-run output curve and the long-run output curve are shown. The variable factor shown is only labor (L); whereas a mathematical formulation will analyze the multivariate case. The short-run production points "a', b', c', d'" correspond recursively with the short run average cost points a, b, c, d, respectively. The domains comprising such points are the IIE-learning points that evolve intra-system with θ-induction (short-run) of the interprocesses in the long run. The important point to note in the shifts shown by the one-directional arrows is that, endogenously caused changes by the circular causation effects of all the interrelating variables in both diminishing average cost of production and the corresponding ascending production levels, reinforce the complementarities between the circular causation relations in these two production and cost regions.

Example

A distinctive example of the above explanations that bring out the unbridgeable contrasts between TIE and mainstream economics is the architecture of the *masjid* (mosque) in the context of the meaning of sustainability. How does the concept of *masjid* play its distinctive role in the architecture of sustainability?

The world is a comprehensive *masjid* with all its values and artefacts of felicity, balance, and extensions of the observations conveying the Signs of *Allah* (*ayath Allah*) (Lings, 1991). These comprise the *Tawhidi* unity of knowledge and its induction in the generality and particularities of consilience in the world system. The world system then assumes its stature as the great and all-comprehensive *ummah*, the world nation of balance and moderation governed by the *Tawhidi* unity principle (Choudhury, 2014).

In the context of such an all-comprehensive meaning of *masjid* in its embedding the world, there are the verses of the *Qur'an* that interactively and organically interconnect the *masjid* with the market (*Qur'an*, 62: 9–11). Now, consider the θ-induction in all these transformations and organic causality of unity of relations.

The bestowed felicity, goodness, and truth lessen the cost of production taken up according to the holistic definition of cost and production as activities within the moral, ethical, and social objectives of the wellbeing (*maslaha*). These attributes are explained by Expressions (7.1)–(7.9) and thereon. The concept of sustainability aptly explained through the function of the world system in the midst of the most-comprehensive meaning of *masjid* involves a greater order than simply the idea of sustainable development and social capital. The greater rewarding moral, ethical, and social values of the *masjid*-world-sustainability interrelationship is the grand example of the consciousness in circular causation and organic complementarities represented by θ-induction of "everything" (Barrow, 1991).

The reader can think of moderation, social cohesion, consciousness in control of crime and punishment costs, rehabilitation as the control of illness, and abundance in the production regime of life-sustaining goods, services, and artefacts for wellbeing. Altogether, these attributes decrease the total costs asymptotically as shown in Figure 7.2(a). The average cost curve learns along the ever-expanding IIE processes of learning in organic unity of knowledge, and all such variables as would be in the sustainability vector. An example of such a vector is given below, namely, $\{Q, K, L, H, E, T, R\}[\theta]$.

Exercise 2

(i) Interpret the idea of fairness as social justice $(J(\theta))$ in regard to complementarity (θ-induction) between labor and capital in the theory of the firm (Choudhury, 1998) using the vector, $\{Q, L, K, J\}[\theta]$.

(ii) If perfect competition is untenable in TIE, how is cost and benefit equalized according to $C(\theta)$ as cost and revenue as benefit, Rev(θ)? Answer by using the idea of resources in TIE as against cost of production in mainstream economics.

(iii) Use the additional variable of financial dividends received by shareholders, $D(\theta) = d(\theta) \cdot Q(\theta)$ to explain how this is at the same time as a financial return and a resource requirement in the theory of cost and production of the firm in TIE.

Irrelevance of the marginal cost, marginal productivity, and returns to scale concepts in TIE

The ideas of all marginals — marginal cost, marginal revenue, and marginal productivity are logically untenable in the TIE methodology. That is because, the continuously learning points along the average cost curve, as in Figure 7.2, caused by evolutionary learning processes and not simply by statistical variations in the data for average cost, do not allow for the marginal cost to exist. Besides, the corresponding total cost curves do not allow a smooth curve structure for the same reason. On the corresponding plane for production curves too, there cannot exist smooth points, as shown by the rough curves. These are noticeable cases for both the short-run and the long-run. More formally, the simple mathematics of marginal formulas would not yield smooth curves to be meaningful in product and input pricing.

For instance,

$$MC = \partial C / \partial Q = [\partial C / \partial \theta] / [\partial Q / \partial \theta], \qquad (7.22)$$

is not measurable around any evolutionary equilibrium point along the θ-induced total cost curve. Thereby, the *ceteris paribus* nature of the resulting cost curve in mainstream economics of the firm does not allow for complementarities between all the variables of the total cost curve, as in the case of Expression (7.11), to uphold. Thereby, also, the circular causation relations are untenable in such a case of a marginalist formula.

The case of the marginal revenue results of mainstream economics of the firm to be untenable was proved before. It is now equally untenable for the marginal productivity curve to be possible. The nature of random fluctuations around the evolutionary learning points apart from simply the statistical variations, establishes circular causation results as implied and explained by the recursive interrelations between Figures 7.2(a) and 7.2(b).

The impossibility of having the marginal cost and marginal productivity curves implies also that the average cost and average productivity curves cannot be used for empirical and strategic inferences. This is because of the random variations of evolutionary learning processes. It is further noted that the idea of marginals is a nicety rather than reality in the midst of multivariate endogenous interrelations. The latter is the case that results from the evaluation of the wellbeing function. This is the *maslaha* function of *maqasid as-shari'ah* as the firm's objective function in a targeted regime of *dynamic* basic-needs regime of development with the effect of consciousness generated in and by the θ-variable. The circular causation relations then must abide along with the *evaluation* of the wellbeing function.

Consequently now, with the irrelevance of the marginal, it is impossible for optimum scale of output and the short-run and long-run curves of marginal cost and productivity curve to be tenable. The only way though that the increasing returns to scale and economies of scope in production must exist in TIE is by the evolutionary learning processes. We can summarize this case by the following formalism:

$$Q = f_1(K, L, H, E, T, R)[\theta], \quad (7.23)$$

yielding

$$dQ/d\theta = (\partial f_1/\partial K) \cdot (dK/d\theta) + (\partial f_1/\partial L) \cdot (dL/d\theta)$$
$$+ (\partial f_1/\partial H) \cdot (dH/d\theta) + (\partial f_1/\partial E) \cdot (dE/d\theta)$$
$$+ (\partial f_1/\partial T) \cdot (dT/d\theta) + (\partial f_1/\partial R) \cdot (dR/d\theta). \quad (7.24)$$

Each of the terms on the right-hand side is positive under the *maslaha* effect of "θ" on the variables. Consequently, $dQ/d\theta > 0$ for all positively learning effect of θ-values intra-system (short-run) and inter-system (long-run). Both of these are continuous phenomena over knowledge, space, and time. Now, no first-order optimal conditions can exist for the mainstream case of maximization of output, and thereby for the attainment of maximum returns to scale, as in the case of perfect competition. Paradoxically too, the firms in imperfect competition also aim at the objective of maximization of profit and output, which though is a fallacy. This fallacy was pointed out in the theory of satisficing behavior of firms formalized by Simon (1987).

The first-order necessary and sufficient conditions of optimal production function of the variables in Expression (7.23) of the mainstream genre like

$$\mathrm{MP}_{L/w} = \mathrm{MP}_{K/r} = \mathrm{MP}_{H/p}1 = \mathrm{MP}_{E/p}2$$

$$= \mathrm{MP}_{T/p}3 = \mathrm{MP}_{R/p}4 = 1/\mathrm{MC} \qquad (7.25)$$

are replaced by the following conditions of IIE-learning process for evaluation (estimation followed by simulation) of the wellbeing function with circular causation relations, of which Expression (7.23) is one.

(Elasticity coefficient of Q in respect of L) $\varepsilon_{QL}/\varepsilon_{QL}$,   (7.26)

= either positive (complementary) or negative, signifying marginalist substitution in the partial sense between K and L in respect of Q. In the latter case, policy, strategy, and consciousness by θ-induction are needed to correct for complementarity or lesser marginalist substitution reducing to complementarities as resources increase continuously under θ-induction.

Exercise 3

(i) Write down and explain the formulas for complementarities contrary to marginal rate of substitution between all the variables of Expression (7.23) according to their various circular causation equations.

(ii) Draw relevant diagrams for the complementary cases along the IIE-learning processes originating from the answer to case (i).

The fallacy of economic efficiency concept in mainstream economics in light of TIE

Economic efficiency is a concept that corresponds with the minimization of total average cost of production and the corresponding maximization of output and profits. Erroneously, the same concept of economic efficiency of a firm is applied to perfect and imperfect competition in terms of their self-same objective criterion of maximization of output and profits. In such a case, the long-run marginal cost curve and the short-run marginal cost curve intersect at a level of price that determines the minimum price and the level of output at which production can continue. At price levels below this level, efficient production ceases.

The fallacy arising from this phenomenon is that no explanation and process of policy, strategy, and technological change that become important to evade the point of firm's operational closure can be endogenously explained, except by means of exogenous impact of such forces. Learning by discourse, manifest in field of evolutionary equilibrium points of the short-run and the long-run remain absent in the firm's closure or restarting points of decision-making. Such alternative possibilities were indeed studied by Schumpeter (Cantner *et al.*, 2000) to explain his theory of creative destruction and rejuvenation.

In the end, therefore, the mainstream neoclassical theory of the firm yields a static theory of economic efficiency and its corresponding theories of maximization, steady-state equilibrium, and exogenous effects. The dynamic concept of efficiency remains impossible in such neoclassical theory of economic efficiency. It is impossible to carry a sequence of economic efficiency points along the time-trend to represent dynamic efficiency concept (Choudhury and Hoque, 2004). Finally, it is equally impossible to use an optimal control model to explain economic efficiency in the case of endogenously learning field of knowledge-induced participatory economic behavior (Choudhury and Korvin, 2002). The TIE model yields its genre of evaluation of wellbeing function with desired and evaluated variables for complementarities, subject to the circular causation relations. The variables and coefficients of such a model of intervariable relations are all θ-induced.

Figure 7.3 explains the impossibility of endogenously determining the price and quantity adjustment between the short-run and long-run in the neoclassical economic theory of the firm. Note that the presence of θ-axis to define coordinates of $(\theta, p, Q)[\theta]$ causes non-Cartesian transformation all over the economic space. Such a space

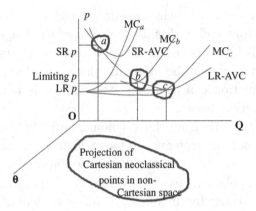

Figure 7.3. Rejecting the postulates of imperfect competition of mainstream economics by TIE.

encompasses diffusion of perturbation points of evolutionary learning such as around points a, b, c, and the like. Each such point would then be formed and regenerated by coordinates of $\{\theta, p, Q\}[\theta]$.

In neoclassical analysis, the gap between the short-run and the long-run in the case of imperfect competition is marked by the change from point "a" to point "b". Then, compared to the firm in perfect competition as the most efficient firm, the gap in price, output, and profit are shown between the points "b" and "c". The adjustment between these gaps "b"–"c" would change the nature of the firm in imperfect competition to perfect competition. This is an undesired case for a firm in imperfect competition to raise above normal profits.

Contrarily, an evolutionary learning firm in TIE would interrelate the points $(\theta, p, Q)[\theta]_a$, $(\theta, p, Q)[\theta]_b$, $(\theta, p, Q)[\theta]_c$ and many more of these kinds all over the non-Cartesian generalization, so as to revert to the objective of evaluation of wellbeing (*maslaha*), subject to intervariable circular causation relations. The formulation is as before, but now introducing time $(t(\theta))$ to mark evolutionary processes of intra-system and inter-systemic adjustments as follows:

$$\text{Evaluate } \{\theta\} \; W(\theta, p, Q, t)[\theta], \tag{7.27}$$

$$\text{subject to } p(\theta) = f_1(\theta, Q(\theta), t(\theta)), \tag{7.28}$$

$$Q(\theta) = f_2((\theta, p(\theta)), t(\theta))). \tag{7.29}$$

Empirical θ-function as measured wellbeing (*maslaha*) is given by

$$\theta = F(\theta, p, Q, t)[\theta].$$

Fallacies of mainstream economic theory in its first-order conditions of maximization objective functions

One of many fallacies of mainstream economic theory is to premise both perfect competition and imperfect competition on the same set of objectives. That is, to maximize the profit function subject to the axiom of economic rationality, although it is obvious that the household on the side of consumer theory and the firm on the side of production theory would lose its possibility to acquire full information in the case of imperfect competition. In this section, we provide the case of incompleteness of information in the combined problem of the following type. Next, we will present the TIE methodology to the same problem and bring out the contrasting analytical results (Samuelson, 1970).

$$\text{Max. } Q = F(x_1, x_2, x_3, \ldots, x_n), \tag{7.30}$$

subject to the derived demand function for inputs of the following type:

$$x_i = f_i(\mathbf{x}_j), \ i = 1, 2, 3, \ldots, n. \tag{7.31}$$

Here some of the variables would be necessarily exogenous according to neoclassical economic theory. Examples of such variables are technological choice and innovation, population, and resource augmentation. These factors are injected from outside the production system to cause shifts. But there does not exist a system of endogenous variables like (Q, K, L) to cause changes. For instance, the choice of the (K/L)-ratio is internal to the firm as institution. In empirical work, a representative value is selected by observing the statistical trend in the (K/L)-ratios to come up with a target value. This ratio is not an input of production. Hence, technological change $T = (K/L)$ must be used along with endogenous variables in the production function. But T cannot be determined conversely by the market determined output of production. All this means that the following functions would be untenable: $T = f(Q)$; $Q = g(T)$. There must be additional endogenous variables to form meaningful functions as $Q = h(K, L, T)$.

Furthermore, we can use the constraints on the demand side of output by consumers in a general equilibrium theory of production in mainstream economics. We formalize as follows:

$$U_k = U_k(\mathbf{Q, x, l, T}). \tag{7.32}$$

Bold letters denote vectors. "l" denotes leisure off work or usage of input ($\mathbf{x}$).

The combined production and consumption problem are stated as follows:

$$\text{Max.} \quad Q_s = F_s(\mathbf{x, l, T}), s \text{ is a system of produced outputs,} \tag{7.33}$$

$$s = 1, 2, \ldots, S,$$

$$\text{subject to} \quad x_i = f_i(\mathbf{x}_j, l, \mathbf{T}), \quad i = 1, 2, 3, \ldots, n, \tag{7.34}$$

$$U_k = U_k(\mathbf{Q, x, l, T}), \quad k = 1, 2, \ldots, m. \tag{7.35}$$

A detailed classical maximization of the above system of functions is by the Lagrangian (L) as follows:

$$L = \text{Max}[F_s(\mathbf{x}, l, \mathbf{T}) + \lambda_1(x_i - f_i(\mathbf{x}_j, l, \mathbf{T}))$$
$$+ \lambda_2(U_k - U_k(\mathbf{Q, x}, l, \mathbf{T}))], \tag{7.36}$$

$$\partial L/\partial x_i = \partial Q/\partial x_i + \lambda_1(1 - \partial f_i/\partial x_i) - \lambda_2(\partial U_k/\partial x_i) = 0, \tag{7.37}$$

$$\partial L/\partial x_k = \partial Q/\partial x_k + \lambda_1(1 - \partial f_i/\partial x_k) - \lambda_2(\partial U_k/\partial x_k) = 0, \tag{7.38}$$

$$\partial L/\partial \lambda_1 = x_i - f_i(\mathbf{x}_j, l, \ \mathbf{T}) = 0, \tag{7.39}$$

$$\partial L/\partial \lambda_2 = U_k - U_k(\mathbf{Q, x}, l, \mathbf{T}) = 0, \tag{7.40}$$

$$s = 1, 2, \ldots, S; \ i = 1, 2, 3, \ldots, n; \ k = 1, 2, \ldots, m.$$

Consider, for example, Equation (7.41) as

$$\partial Q/\partial x_i = \lambda_2(\partial U_k/\partial x_i) - \lambda_1(1 - \partial f_i/\partial x_i),$$

$$\partial Q/\partial x_k = \lambda_2(\partial U_k/\partial x_k) - \lambda_1(1 - \partial f_i/\partial x_k). \tag{7.41}$$

When solved for λ_1 and λ_2, we obtain an expression that depends critically on the marginal rate of substitution between x_i and x_k, for all values of $i = 1, 2, \ldots, n$ number of productions; and k number of consumers. Besides, the values of **T** cannot be solved for as an independent vector of variables. The l-variables are substitutes with **x**-variables according to the income and substitution effects on final choices of consumers (Pindyck and Rubinfeld, 2001).

The meaning of the above results is that a solution to the Lagrangian depends on the postulate of marginal rate of substitution. That is, in the case of work and leisure, the meaning of leisure is unproductive activity in things like self-help, community involvement,informal teaching and learning that do not carry direct pecuniary benefits. The results also convey that some variables must necessarily remain exogenous (like **T**) in determining the solutions for λ_1 and λ_2. Only in recent times, Romer (1986) has published on the theory of new growth, which is also known as the endogenous growth theory. But there is no such contribution presently in microeconomics of the firm's production function.

Perfect and imperfect competition in partial and general equilibriums of mainstream economics critiqued by TIE

Equations (7.30)–(7.40) explain the general equilibrium analysis. While we can treat this case only mathematically, the diagrammatic explanation needs to devolve into a partial equilibrium case. The assumption of *ceteris paribus* of endogenous variables and the exogenous effects of other variables can now be explained by Figure 7.4(a) in the case of perfect competition and by Figure 7.4(b) in the case of imperfect competition.

In perfect competition, scarce resource allocation takes place between goods (x_1, x_2) along the expansion path that is driven by

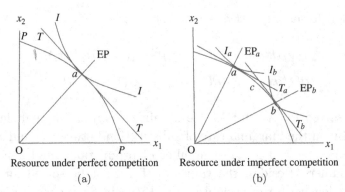

Figure 7.4. Resource allocations in partial equilibrium under perfect and imperfect competitions.

the exogenous effect of technology. The point "a" as the meeting point of the smooth production possibility curve PP and the smooth consumer indifference curve II on the resource line curve (income line) TT, denotes the general equilibrium case of perfect competition. All these cases are shown in Figure 7.4(a).

In imperfect competition, the market is independently segmented between private goods (x_1) and public goods (x_2) along their expansion paths EP_b and EP_a, respectively. The allocations are still again described by the same kinds of production possibility frontiers and the indifference curves. This is the fallacy of mainstream economics in describing the objective function of the two kinds of goods in production and consumption, respectively. In both cases, the objective function is based on output maximization, profit maximization, and utility maximization. The substitution between "a" and "b" in terms of consumer goods and simultaneously producer goods is the case of the market resource allocations being divided independently between private goods and public goods. This is the case of imperfect competition.

The fallacy here is that, in such marginalist substitution, there are transaction costs both by ways and policies that are not implicated. If these were put into effect, then either of the points "a" and "b" would be perturbation points. The effect would be widespread all over the production possibility surface and the consumer indifference curve. The mainstream economic theory of marginal rate of substitution is annulled. Relative prices of the goods do not have determinate role in setting market price relatives or putting policy directions and resource allocations in a specific way by means of marginalist study. Finally, the point "c" is supposed to be the linear combination of the points "a" and "b". This point shares in the problems of perturbations and non-smooth production possibility surface and the consumer indifference curve under the impact of policies, strategies, and technological change. The smooth surfaces cannot hold.

Fallacy in the pricing theory of the firm in imperfect competition

In Figure 7.5(a), the meeting points like "a" is where the first-order conditions of profit and output maximization hold: $p = $ MC along the long-run MC curve, average revenue curve, and MR curve, all coincide at the minimum of the U-shaped average cost curve. At this point as well, $\mathrm{MP}_L/w = \mathrm{MP}_K/r = 1/\mathrm{MC}$, on a limited case of productive inputs in perfectly competitive factor and goods markets. Consequently, $w = \mathrm{MC.MP}_L = p.\mathrm{MP}_L$; $r = \mathrm{MC.MP}_K = p.\mathrm{MP}_K$. Problems of mainstream economic theory regarding all these issues were examined above.

In imperfectly competitive market for goods and productive inputs like "a', b', c'" in Figure 7.5(b), mainstream economics gives the following formula between the demand elasticity (ε) and MR. Thereby, the AR curve as the demand curve under imperfect competition for all kinds of firms in imperfect competition is also an elastic curve with all possible values of elasticity coefficients in the interval $(0, \infty)$ from lower end to upper end progressively. Note now, $\mathrm{MR} = p(1 - 1/\varepsilon)$. The fallacy of such niceties of the theory of the firm arises around the perturbed point "a" in Figure 7.5(b). Around this point, no specific values of AR, therefore ε-values, and thereby values of MR can be read. The marginal measures fail to be determinate. The pricing and output (MR $=$ MC) relations of imperfect competition are annulled. No market values of profit-maximization, policy effects, technological change, and similar

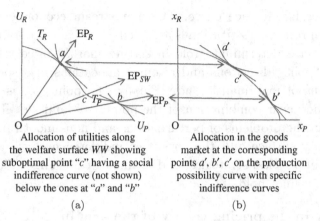

Figure 7.5. Fallacy in the allocation of scarce resources in the welfare concept between the poor and the rich.

exogenous effects can be read by using the formulas of the theory of imperfect competition.

Exercise 4

(i) Consider the allocation of land as resource to grow life suste-nance. But, in mainstream economics, land is seen to be scarce in supply; whereas demand for land is perfectly elastic if land is seen as a right of all to own (Sattar, 2015). The market equilibrium for the mainstream economic idea of land rights is limited to a scarce quantity at a certain price fixed for quantity of land. Under these conditions, can any global governance allocate an increased quantity of land to Palestinians to relieve them of their present refugee status under Israeli rule? How does mainstream theory of the firm explain land allocation in this case?

(ii) What can be the role of discourse as an endogenous force to attain fairness in the Israeli usurpation of Palestinian lands?

(iii) Extend the above land problem to the case of allocation of space. Can you write on the global governance of air-space problem of East–West détente caused by the mainstream kind of pricing of space use between competing countries?

Irrelevant concept of value in mainstream economics of consumer and production theory

In mainstream economics, the concept of value arising from the side of consumer theory is marginal utility $(MU(x))$ of consumption of a certain *ceteris paribus* quantity of good (x). This is a market-oriented concept. By the fact that there is no endogenous relationship between ethics and x, therefore, there cannot be any continuously differentiable utility gained from such ethical induction. Consequently, every $MU(x)$ is in respect of market goods. Thereby, the price of the good, which represents the $MU(x)$ is assumed to be a market price. This is the case of perfectly competitive market exchange.

In the case of imperfect competition, as for the case of public goods, the fallacy of mainstream economics is that the same deductive formulas of marginal utility and marginal productivity are used. Now, $MR = MC = p.(1 - 1/\varepsilon)$, as explained in respect of Figure 7.4(b), also conveys the meaning of ethical independence in the determination of price as value in imperfect competition. Now, the demand curve of the firm's output is given by $AR = (1/2).MR$. Along this demand curve, the values of price elasticity of demand $\varepsilon(p, Q)$ are computed.

Mainstream economic theory is thereby totally independent of any ethical context. Only a *ceteris paribus* concept of intervariable relations of the market-determined types holds. The consequences of such a narrow concept of the theory of value, output, and price are far reaching in limiting the study of policy-making, behavioral and technological endogenous effects, and the like.

Welfare consequences of the market theory of consumption and production

The independence of the utility function and the firm's production function in a combined general equilibrium case formalized by the system of Equations (7.33)–(7.40) implies that the welfare function so studied remains simply a market-centered criterion. There is no ethical embedding in the *welfare* function in neoclassical economics as there is in the wellbeing function (*maslaha*) in TIE.

The extended form of the general equilibrium model of welfare including consumer utilities and production functions takes the form

$$\text{Max } W(\mathbf{x}) = W(U_1(\mathbf{x}), U_2(\mathbf{x}), \ldots, U_n(\mathbf{x})) \qquad (7.42)$$

for n-number of consumers competing for a vector $\mathbf{x}$ of m-number of goods, subject to the system of Equations (7.33)–(7.35). Figure 7.5 explains the nature of ethically independent correspondence of relations between the welfare function, its component utility functions, and the commodity space, all taken up in pure market venue.

Consider the utilities of the poor $(U_p(\mathbf{x}))$ and the rich $(U_R(\mathbf{x}))$. Both P and R consume the same produced quantities of goods of the $\mathbf{x}$-vector. In a market venue, they compete for these goods by their scarce resources T_p of the poor; and T_R of the rich. Similar labels explain the goods quadrant. While the points a and thereby a', b and thereby b' are efficient and optimal points of perfect competition; the point c is a suboptimal and inefficient point. "c" is driven from its inefficient allocation point to the surfaces of Figures 7.6(a) and 7.6(b) by exogenously imposed policies, strategies, technological change, and the like. Yet, the second-order conditions of such reconstructed optimal points cannot reach the desired optimal and efficient surfaces. The theorem in this regard is that, if the first-order conditions of profit maximization are not attained, then there is no need to utilize second-order conditions to improve the market failure to restore efficiency (Henderson and Quandt, 1971).

The case of monopoly, monopolistic competition, and oligopoly with mainstream fallacies

Disintegrating monopoly in TIE

The case of any kind of monopoly is untenable if social discourse and intervariable complementary relations are promoted. In the case of natural monopoly, the non-substitutable nature of the good can be completely altered by allowing for participation via technology, and product and risk diversifications, and transformation of the economic behavioral patterns of consumption and production into dynamic life-sustaining goods and services (basic needs).

In the case of regulated monopoly, the fair return to the monopolist could be used to generate sharing of cost, risk and production, and technology to bring about stable prices and increased production through the employment of resources in constructive reformation of the production structure. Dominant firm case and industry concentration could then be made to share diversified production, as would be the case of supply outlets in MSEs and microenterprises. These are all signs of transformation into a life-fulfilling dynamic basic-needs regime of development in TIE. On the other hand, sustainability of the dynamic basic-needs regimes of development would necessarily be characterized by the rise of SMEs and microenterprises. Thereby, the regime of large monopoly firms will be automatically restricted by endogenous effects in industrial development. The intercausality between consumption and production activities in a dynamic basic-needs regime of constructive transformation for intercausal functioning in ethicality is actualized by the complementary relations between increases in information flow that comes about by the discursive medium of partners, stakeholders, and policy-makers.

Diminishing monopolistic competition in TIE

Discursive experience that embed policies, strategies, technology, and growing ethical consciousness in consumers and producer behaviors through interaction would cause monopoly to be transformed into the state of monopolistic competition as a mid-way transformation. But if such a transformation is considered to be continuous under the flow of information and consciousness, then all the variables would have to be taken as endogenously related. Thereby, the various critiques of marginalism and *ceteris paribus* nature of exogeneity of variables would be upheld to re-establish the fallacies of the monopolistic transformation by the underlying analytical problems encountered, as mentioned above.

The neoclassical explanation of price adjustment as information increases out of chiselling behavior of representative firms in monopolistic competition conveys the overall static pictures of AR, MR, MC, price, and output determination over the long run. This is a fallacy in explaining the transformation from the short-run to the long-run and much more so, when continuity and endogeneity are invoked. Monopolistic competition theory has no analytical grounds in such cases to explain the real case of continuously endogenous θ-induced change.

Oligopolistic competition in TIE

Oligopoly as a production and differentiated price-output decision-making industrial arrangement with number of member firms in it beings less than that in monopolistic competition survives because of its closed membership. Such a structure needs to be sustained by abidance of institutionally decided collusive rules of setting prices and output levels. Yet, it is found as an example that, in the case of Oman (Petroleum Development Oman, https://en.wikipedia.org/wiki/Petroleum_Development_Oman), t openness to oil production and pricing has helped industrial development in the country through enhanced production, technological change, and economic diversification launched by the Petroleum Development Oman (PDO) activities.

Over-reliance on oligopoly production, pricing, and internal decision-making has been found to artificially protect the monopoly character of oil in the world market in the absence of substitutes of oil. The implication is that oil-dependence in such a scenario of development continues on. On the other hand, oil to non-oil diversification is urgently needed to relieve dependence on oil in every aspect of economic and social development. But such a transformation ought not to come out of the neoclassical economic idea of marginal substitution of oil and non-oil productions. Rather, the transformation is to be brought about by a continuous change in pricing, production, and technological change, as information increases via open-ended institutional and inter-country discussions.

The kinked point on the demand curve of oligopolistic pricing and production would then dissolve into a continuously changing decision-making point. The end point of such transformation is again towards the *dynamic* life-sustaining regime of development. It has its objective criterion of wellbeing as defined earlier, quite different from the concept of welfare in mainstream economics, which was critically examined above.

Addressing dynamic market shares and industrial structure: Return to TIE methodology

What then is the realist picture of consumption and production in economic terms? The central points are to restore continuity in the pervasively intervariable endogenous relations. This comprises establishing intervariable relations by means of their organic causality arising from pervasive complementarities. This signifies unity of knowledge as the abiding characteristic of TIE in terms of its methodology. It was amply explained in this and other chapters that the central episteme of unity of knowledge dispels the mainstream economic axiom of economic rationality totally. Within the resulting reformulation, the derived postulate of marginalism, optimization, and steady-state equilibrium are *logically* rejected.

With the above summary critique of mainstream economics and keeping the methodological nature of TIE in view, the mainstream economic idea of imperfect competition is replaced by the continuous process of IIE learning to simulate socially a marginalist or dialectical system of competition into a pervasively partnered complementarity (pairing). These attributes and the imminent circular causation for evaluating social wellbeing in its equivalent conceptual and empirical forms comprise the computational general equilibrium model of consumption and production with moral/ethical social embedding. Equations (7.1)–(7.9) form an exemplary system. The system can be enlarged as the variables and their numbers of observations increase. The price, output, resource, cost, and technological results are empirically determinable now.

The implications of intra-systemic and inter-systemic evaluation are brought into play to obtain empirical and policy, strategic, and technological implications of the θ-induced effects. The entire system with their "estimated" results followed by "simulated" coefficients is thus made up of dynamic conditions of *maslaha* (wellbeing). This implicates a progressively evolutionary transformation of the truly

Islamic economic and social order into a life-sustaining, basic-needs regime of consciousness towards development by the attributes of IIE-process-oriented preference functions and production menus.

The example of such aggregate preferences is

$$\wp(\theta) = \cup_{\text{interaction}} \cap_{\text{integration}} \{\wp_C, \wp_P\}[\theta], \qquad (7.43)$$

where C denotes consumer choices. P denotes production choices.

$$d\wp/d\theta \geq 0. \qquad (7.44)$$

Expressions (7.43) and (7.44) mean that *maqasid as-shari'ah* choices intensify as consciousness of *Tawhidi* unity of knowledge deepens. This too is a fully inclusive discursive undertaking, shown by $\cup_{\text{interaction}} \cap_{\text{integration}}$ in Expression (7.43) by way of market–institution organic interrelations in the context of IIE-process-oriented learning.

Special case of oligopolistic generalization in determining prices and outputs with discursive effects, endogenous technology, and resources

In respect to the kinked demand curve for the oligopoly good and at which point the collusive price and output are determined by market–institutional interactive realities in the TIE case in reference to the variables as example $\{\theta, Q_i, p_i, T_i, R_i\}[\theta]$, the price and output equations for each of the participatory members (i) are as follows:

$$p_i = f_{1i}(\theta_i, Q_i, T_i, R_i)[\theta], \qquad (7.45)$$

$$Q_i = f_{2i}(\theta_i, p_i, T_i, R_i)[\theta]. \qquad (7.46)$$

The wellbeing function beyond the pricing and output mechanisms is evaluated by

$$\theta_i = F(Q_i, p_i, T_i, R_i)[\theta_i]. \qquad (7.47)$$

In these equations, we assign the following sets of meanings to the variables: $\{\theta_i\}$-values denote the individual participatory member's (i) perception of his assessment of depth of unity of knowledge, represented by personalized ordinal value in respect of socio-economic variables. From the interaction and integration between the partners, there arises a convergence of θ-values for all the participants.

That is

$$\theta = \cup_{\text{interaction}} \cap_{\text{integration}} \{\theta_i\}. \tag{7.48}$$

In the same way, any of the variables $x_i \in \{Q_i, p_i, T_i, R_i)[\theta_i]\}$ aggregate to

$$x = \cup_{\text{interaction}} \cap_{\text{integration}} \{x_i\}. \tag{7.49}$$

The personalized variable of technological change denotes that which is used by the specific partners such as between Saudi Arabia, Indonesia, and Nigeria at different levels of oil production as members of OPEC.

Now, the forms of evaluative equations emergent from (7.40)–(7.42) are

$$p = f_1(\theta, Q, T, R)[\theta], \tag{7.50}$$

$$Q = f_2(\theta, p, T, R)[\theta], \tag{7.51}$$

$$\theta = F(Q, p, T, R)[\theta]. \tag{7.52}$$

Expressions (7.48)–(7.49) as the aggregative preference formulas are not quantifiable, being simply conceptual for explanation. Their equivalents in the forms of (7.50)–(7.52) can be empirically evaluated. The price and output variables for the oligopoly resulting from collusion are determined in the TIE by an extensive vector of variables that enter the market–institutional interactive determinants of choices. All such variables are most critically influenced by the evolutionary learning θ-variable as consciousness based on the attainment of complementarities between the *maqasid*-choices in the light of *Tawhidi* unity of knowledge.

The kinked-colluded form of demand function in mainstream microeconomics is now a function of a plethora of similar possibilities in the region of IIE processes in continuity of expanding vector of possibilities. While the above formalism is specified for the oligopoly, the same approach is valid for the monopolistic competition based on the attributes that were mentioned earlier in this section.

Even so, the various price and output adjustment from economic surplus to normal profit condition would not be the case in TIE. That is because, the surplus, little or more, must always exist to be distributed as participatory Islamic dividends. The chiselling behavior of monopolistic competition does not exist because of its logical non-existence in the face of *maqasid as-shari'ah*. The *Tawhidi* methodology of unity of knowledge that is embedded in the IIE processes and that characterizes the dynamics of Expressions (7.48) and (7.49). These dynamics play their critical transformative role in the IIE processes towards the life-fulfilling regime of development.

As it was mentioned before, the TIE methodology can revert to the disintegrated situation when the episteme of unity of knowledge weakens and its induction of the variables becomes weak and results into variables and entities of the differentiated type. In such a case, the evaluation of the wellbeing function subject to circular causation will show deepening degrees of marginalism by the negative values of the coefficients of the intervariable causality in the circular causation system. Besides, the focus on *maqasid as-shari'ah* for making consumption, production, and social choices will dissipate into oblivion. Marginalism will thereby arise. Reversion to mainstream economics will occur. Thus, the TIE methodology with its method of circular causation can answer both the case of learning dynamics in unity of knowledge and the differentiated system of marginalism, where considerations of morality, ethicality, and endogenous intervariable relations do not exist and are taken exogenously.

TIE cannot arise from the marginalist mainstream economics. That is, *Tawhidi* methodological worldview of TIE cannot arise from the neoclassical or any mainstream approach. That is because, the absence of the endogenous nature of morality/ethics and sociality, as in the case of the *Tawhidi* precept of unity of knowledge, would not allow for the rise of consciousness that characterizes the analytical dynamics in TIE. In this kind of dichotomy between materiality and morality/ethics, sociality mainstream economics invokes the nature of dichotomy between *a priori* reasoning and *a posteriori* reasoning; between deductive and inductive reasoning; and between *noumena* and phenomena. These topics were studied earlier in this book. Such is the perennial nature of all of occidental science. It was pointed out by Husserl (1965). (Particularly note his comment on the perceived absence of ethical roots in occidental scientific inquiry).

No such dichotomy can logically exist under the axiom of *Tawhidi* unity of knowledge and its induction of the generality and particulars of diverse world systems. A specific case of such particulars is economics, finance, science, and society. Thus, the divine law (ontology) is intercausally embedded with the mind–matter world system and the evolutionary small "closures" of IIE-learning processes and the eventual "Closure" of the Hereafter. The world system embodies the possibility of knowledge i.e. the epistemology. The small closures via IIE processes and the eventual large Closure of the Hereafter establish the socio-scientific meaning of the *Tawhidi* methodological worldview.

On such a unity of knowledge between ontology and epistemology writes Neville Spencer (2000): "However, for any theory that we have about what knowledge is, we must have a presupposition about what the world is like. That is, we must assume that the world exists in such a way that it makes our theory of knowledge possible. There is no escaping having a theory of ontology, it is only a question of whether or not it is consciously acknowledged and studied or whether it is left as an implicit presupposition of one's theory of epistemology."

Exercise 5

(i) The nickel production project has decided to form an oligopoly of 10 firms to collude on price and output setting. What kind of market and institutional interaction would establish the nickel oligopoly as both a social oligopoly meeting and its objective of collusion and social wellbeing? Select appropriate variables, and set up the system of relations for explaining the market–institutional causality for the oligopoly to realize its integrated objectives.

(ii) In the process of its dissolution under the impact of competition policy, what would be the final status of the social oligopoly?

Explain the process of such re-organization of the oligopoly to address the life-fulfillment regime of development in TIE.

(iii) Construct a participatory relational model between a dominant firm and medium and small enterprises (SMEs) in regard to product sharing and joint pricing decision. How can such a social transformation of production be realized by market and institutional functions?

(iv) Illustrate by suitable diagrams the price and output relations in an ethically induced TIE environment for a dominant firm that starts off with the following schedule:

monopoly pricing, monopoly output, monopoly profit, regulated monopoly condition, predatory pricing mechanism.

The concept of value in TIE

From our study of the concept of value in regard to the mainstream and the ethical perspectives, it is clear that such markets come to have transactions in private goods and public goods that function independently of each other in their own separate markets. In the case of TIE, there is no such good as a purely private good or a purely public good, for these are not independent of each other. An example is of oil drilling in offshore Newfoundland in Canada. The government would like to have participation of private firms. It would not risk public tax dollars by doing the venture all alone for the sake of national enrichment.

Throughout this book we have represented the morally/ethically embedded knowledge-induced material variables by increasing degrees of consciousness. Such knowledge-induced variables in the light of unity of knowledge denoted by $\mathbf{x}(\theta)$ are uniformly social goods, irrespectively of being privately or publicly consumed, produced, and owned. There is no independence of relationship between private goods, so as to turn them into social goods — or strongly still as ethical goods. The social good is thereby a common good with consciousness of unity of participation by complementarities defining the organic intercausal relationships between the consumers and producers at all levels of these activities. In this sense, TIE becomes an ethico-economic particularity in the study of generalized computational equilibrium as an evolutionary system within the expanded domain of the world system.

Now, consider the concept of value of social good in the following example: consider a group of companies and researchers (e.g. producers and consumers) who together make a discovery that is not substitutable (but not complementary) or scarcely substitutable. Mainstream economic theory would characterize such a production group as monopoly and oligopoly, respectively. Any possible dissolution from such production types to more social types will make them representative of monopolistic competition. Thus, the social cleavages of imperfect competition remain. The conditions of a differentiated economic system located apart in the social milieu establish the attributes of self-interest, absolute private property rights, bounded economic rationality, and the like.

The question then is this: differently from the pricing theory of the firm in imperfect competition for goods without or with scarce limits of commodity substitution or factor substitution as in the labor market, how would *maqasid as-shari'ah* recommend such pricing and output generation? What otherwise would be the resulting price and output levels endogenously determined in TIE?

The central characteristic to note in this case is the role of consciousness and the market–institution interface that promotes such consciousness through active realization of *Tawhidi* unity of knowledge in relation to *maqasid*-choices. The momentum in this direction of moral reconstruction of market–institution interrelationship and the goal of sustainability within the life-fulfillment regime of participatory development will incite such policies, strategies, and education. The implementation of such endogenously relational forces will generate the way to attain social choices (Vanek, 1971; Streeten, 1981; Korten, 1995). Examples of such policies, strategies, and development regimes center on participatory development and its production and consumption designs. This is the nature of consumption and production that characterizes the Shatibi-menu of necessaries (*dururiyath*), comforts (*hajiyath*), and refinements (*tahsaniyath*), altogether belonging to the life-fulfilling regime of participatory development.

The rare metal discovery we have referred to above must enter its social goods portfolio in TIE market–institutional interfaced arrangement. Its price and output setting is determined in the following way: We recall Expressions (7.48) and (7.49) for the particular case of interactively integrating private and public goods in the context of forming social preference embedding these attributes in social goods. Thereafter, Equations (7.50)–(7.52) show the partial equilibrium case of the more generalized system that can be formulated to yield price, output, and social wellbeing in terms of the consumption and production of social goods.

The social value formed in TIE with respect to the above problem is given by the evaluated (estimated and simulated) value of the wellbeing function, conceptually explained by $W(\theta)$ and log-linearized to θ-function in terms of the variables $\mathbf{x}(\theta)$ for quantitative viability. The value added by the vector of variables is given by $d\theta = \Sigma_s(\partial W(\mathbf{x}(\theta))/\partial x_s).dx_s$.

Exercise 6

(i) Set up a theory of social value in TIE by taking all variables in their logarithmic form. Thereby, explain the meanings of the coefficients as elasticity in the circular causation equations and the total wellbeing function that can be firstly estimated and secondly simulated to attain better levels of complementarities between the variables. Why would there be increasing returns to scale in value added if $\Sigma_s \text{coeff}_s > 1$?

(ii) The *Qur'anic* model of life-fulfilling participatory development is of the ecological type centered on agricultural abundance, gardens, and fauna and foliage. Such a regime of development is contrasted with the marginalist model, where some alternatives survive at the expense of others such as the contest between labor and capital along any given production possibility surface. See *Qur'an* (14: 24–27).

How does this verse invoke the permanence of increasing returns to value added between complementary variables in their organic interrelations between consumption, production, and knowledge induction?

(iii) Explain the meaning of sustainability of value added in the IIE-process model over knowledge, space, and time dimensions; i.e. intra-system and inter-systems with material and moral valuations.

Conclusion

Like the earlier chapters, this chapter along the generalized way of integrating the consumption and production activities of consumer theory and the pricing theory of the firm has proved that the *Tawhidi* epistemic methodology and its applications through methodical formalism are completely opposite between TIE and mainstream economics. Critical realism does not see the practicality of mainstream postulates in real life. On the other hand, the methodology and imminent formal methods of TIE are complex and extensive in nature. For this reason there are two approaches to solving economic and social problems of TIE. Firstly, there is the discursive approach. According to this approach, the market–institutional relational perspectives of generality in TIE are settled discursively in the venue of market realities, policy, strategy, technology, and consultation. According to the empirical approach, the TIE methodology and its imminent formalism call for the generalized model of *evaluating* wellbeing (*maslaha*), subject to the system of circular causation equations based on diversely selected *maqasid*-choices represented by their specific variables for investigating different problems at hand. Thus, out of the generalized formulation of the objective problem in TIE, there arises the specific problems of consumption and production in their ethical embedding according to the *Tawhidi* principle of unity of knowledge. This is made functional through the analytical method involving *maqasid*-choices.

Mainstream epistemology and its cultural background of material acquisition, economic rationality, and self-interest born out of competition for scarce resources over competing alternatives paint a picture of an acquisitive society. Thereby, the contorted reality is either of optimization and steady-state equilibrium which is not of the real world (Shackle, 1971), or it is dialectics based on perpetual conflict. The consequential *ceteris paribus* nature of the socio-scientific problems generates an unrealistic approach to solving the economic problems.

TIE is perpetually premised on the episteme of *Tawhidi* unity of knowledge. This is explained by *continuous* and *extensive* complementarities through organic intervariable relations. The consequential analytical absence of endogenous nature of the variables negates marginalism everywhere in TIE. Thus, all the formulas of marginalist pricing and production are rejected in TIE and are contrarily upheld in mainstream economics. Thus, the contrast between TIE and mainstream economic theory continues everywhere and in everything of economic analytics and beyond.

In Islamic economics as well, the emergence of the essentially *Tawhidi* methodological way of formalizing ethico-economic theory in particular and the generalized socio-scientific worldview, shows deepening of this field into the clutches of mainstream economics. Thus, existing Islamic economics is found to be deeply embroiled in mainstream economic theory. Thereby, no revolutionary contribution to socio-scientific thought in general and Islamic economics and finance in particular has evolved out of the existing methodological orientation that is contrary to the essential one of TIE. It is now necessary to leave such enslaved situation of Islamic economics and examine the *Qur'an* and the *sunnah* for the much-needed revolutionary epistemological light that the intellectual world and its practitioners so badly need.

In this chapter, the following areas of TIE should be focused upon by the teacher for the students:

TIE contra mainstream consumer theory.
TIE contra mainstream theory of the firm.
TIE contra mainstream imperfect competition.
TIE contra mainstream general equilibrium theory.

References

Barrow, J. D. (1991). "Laws", in s *Theories of Everything, the Quest for Ultimate Explanation*, Oxford, England: Oxford University Press, pp. 12–30.

Burstein, M. (1991). "History versus Equilibrium: Joan Robinson and time in economics", in *The Joan Robinson Legacy*, Rima, I. H. (Ed.), Armonk, New York: M.E. Sharpe, Inc., pp. 49–61.

Choudhury, M. A. (1998). *Reforming the Muslim World*, London, England: Kegan Paul International.

Choudhury, M. A. (2014). *The Islamic Epistemological Worldview and Empirical Study of Socioeconomic Integration in the Ummah*, Kuala Lumpur: International Islamic University of Malaysia Press.

Choudhury, M. A. (2015). "Res extensa et res cogitans de *maqasid as-shari'ah*", *International Journal of Law and Management*, 57(3), 662–693.

Choudhury, M. A. (2016). *God Conscious Organization and the Islamic Social Economy*, London, England: Routledge.

Choudhury, M. A. and Hoque, M. Z. (2004). *An Advanced Exposition of Islamic Economics and Finance*, New York: Edwin Mellen Press.

Choudhury, M. A. and Korvin, G. (2002). "Simulation versus optimization in knowledge-induced fields", *Kybernetes: International Journal of Systems and Cybernetics*, 31(1), 44–60.

Cantner, U. Luc Gaffard, J. and Nesta, L. (Eds.) (2009). *Schumpeterian Perspectives on Innovation, Competition, and Growth*, New York: Springer Verlag.

Henderson, J. M. and Quandt, R. E. (1958). *Microeconomic Theory, A Mathematical Approach*, New York: McGraw-Hill Book Co.

Husserl, E. (1965). *Phenomenology and the Crisis of Philosophy*, Translated by Lauer, Q., New York: Harper & Row Publishers.

James, E. (2013). "The Norwegian prison where inmates are treated like people", *The Guardian*.

Korten, D. C. (1995). *When Corporations Rule the World*, London, England: Earthscan.

Lings, M. (1991). *Symbol & Archetype, A Study of the Meaning of Existence*, Cambridge, England: Quinta Essentia.

Mansfield, E. (1985). *Microeconomics*, New York: W.W. Norton.

Petroleum Development Oman, Internet Version, https://en.wikipedia.org/wiki/Petroleum_Development_Oman.

Rima, I. H. (Ed.), (1986). *The Joan Robinson Legacy*, Armonk, New York: M. E. Sharpe, Inc.

Romer, P. M. (1986). "Increasing returns and long-run growth", *Journal of Political Economy*, 94, 1002–37.

Pindyck, R. S. and Rubinfeld, D. L. (2001). "The degree of economies of scope", in *Microeconomics*, 5th edn., Upper Saddle River, New Jersey: Prentice-Hall Inc., p. 231.

Samuelson, P. A. (1970). *Foundations of Economic Analysis*, New York: Atheneum.

Sattar, N. (2015). "Land rights in Islam", *Dawn Daily Newspaper*.

Shackle, G. L. S., 1971, *Epistemics & Economics*, Cambridge, England: Cambridge University Press.

Simon, H. (1987). "Decision making and organizational design", in Pugh, D.S. (Ed.), *Organizational Theory*, Hammondsworth, Middlesex, England: Penguin Books, pp. 202–223.

Spencer, N. (2000). "On the significance of distinguishing ontology and epistemology", http://www.ethicalpolitics.org/seminars/neville.htm.

Streeten, P. (1981). "From growth to basic needs", in *Development Perspectives*, Streeten, P. (Ed.), New York: St. Martin's Press.

Vanek, J. (1971). "The participatory economy in a theory of social evolution", in *The Participatory Economics: An Evolutionary Hypothesis and a Strategy for Development*, Ithaca, NY: Cornell University Press, pp. 51–89.

Chapter 8

Macroeconomic Theory in Mainstream and *Tawhidi* Islamic Economic (TIE) Perspectives

Nature of macroeconomic analysis

At the first insight of understanding, the field of macroeconomics is seen as the study of the increasing stabilization in the coterminous relationship between price, output, money, and employment for the economic system that is seen to remain in perpetual disequilibrium, little or more. Consequently, the functioning of an economy, in other words, the inquiry as to how the economy works, is rendered to the empirical visage of interactive functioning of the critical variables at the economy-wide level. In such a case, aggregation is necessary. Yet, it is the intricacies faced in the problem of aggregation that pose one of the outstanding irresolutions of the question on how the economy works.

But the nature of macroeconomics as an interactive system study of aggregate economic variables taken in terms of mathematical modeling, invokes a deeply epistemological issue (Lawson and Pesaran, 1989). Keynesian project in this project was centered on the issue of harmonizing certain human behavior within the representation of the emergent models, such as marginal propensity to consume and marginal propensity to save. That is how the epistemological outlook of economic rationality was induced by the

Keynesian macroeconomic approach to the harmonization of human behavioral. This was a nicety of reasoning, not the critical realist nature of reasoning, for Keynes' *Treatise on Probability* (O'Donnell, 1989) was unable to fathom a way out of the legion of subjective probabilities in which economic problems and human behavior remain immersed. Consequently, to resolve this problem, Keynes had to take recourse to the simplifying assumptions of economic rationality. That is, he reduced human behavior into one unique and uniform standard based on economic rationality.

Thus, in the core of his reasoning, Keynes was a thoroughbred neoclassical economic thinker. The difference between the neoclassical economic school and the Keynesian school was essentially in the nature and at the level of aggregate analysis in the latter. Yet, by the formalism of independence of the macroeconomic aggregation from any trace of its microeconomic premises, Keynesian aggregation, and thereby macroeconomics remained a field of study totally different and independent of microeconomic theory. In recent times, despite the emergent theory of microeconomic foundations of macroeconomics (Phelps, 1970), such efforts have remained explorations in rational expectations and social choice theory and public choice theory (Lucas, 1975; Arrow, 1951), all of which are aspects of neoclassical economic theory. Hence, the entire field of economics, comprising microeconomics, macroeconomics, and microeconomic foundations of macroeconomics, is found to be premised on the epistemology of the economic behavioral axiom of rationality.

Besides, the cultural root of the axioms of macroeconomics, as of other aspects of economic reasoning, was inherent in the building blocks. For instance, Keynes' theory of low level liquidity trap is an example in this regard. Keynes abhorred interest rate for a prosperous economy. Yet, he held on to a low-level interest rate that allows for high mobilization of financial resources to establish the fullest expansion of the real output of the economy, and thereby established full employment of productive resources. Thus, although Keynes would have liked to see an economy function at a zero rate of interest, his economic analysis could not uphold such a situation. Such a case of approving of interest rate has been in the cultural heritage of all of Occidentalism. Thomas Aquinas abhorred the existence of interest rate but accepted a "market rate of interest" in economic dealings (Schumpeter, 1968). This idea came to overshadow the Austrian economic thinking despite its leaning on Thomism.

The place of ethics in economic activities was strong in Keynes' thought. Yet, ethics as a social force lost its functional relevance because of several factors of a decisively analytical nature. Firstly, ethics is part of human behavior. It is therefore capable of inclusion in the microeconomics of preference formation. As it was pointed out in the previous chapters, the resulting knowledge-induced conscious preferences also carry on their endogenous effects on the selection of goods and services, such that ethical effects are intercausally related with socio-economic variables. The symbolization of such intercausal relations between knowledge and choices was shown to be $\mathbf{x}(\theta)$ and its functional transforms. Macroeconomic theory of aggregate variables disjoint from microeconomics cannot unravel the ethical preferences and choices.

Also, ethical choices if possible at the macroeconomic level are thought of being *exogenously* included in government austerity measures and direction of spending into social functions. Examples are generating full-employment level of real output, combining fiscal policy and monetary policy to create real economic expansion towards full-employment level of output, attaining price stabilization out of the attenuating balancing role of spending, increase in total productivity, and employment of productive factors. Yet, when it comes to enact the fiscal and monetary policies to realize the social goals and economic stabilization, such underlying policies are exogenously implemented by public actions. Policies, technological change, and ethics are introduced discontinuously as exogenous factors. Thereby, the continuity and endogenous sustainability of consciousness are annulled. This is a case similar to that of neoclassical economics wherein ethics is exogenously transmitted to shift the production possibility curve along the expansion path of output and employment of factors. When the endogenous nature of policies, strategies, technology, and ethics wither away in sustained economic expansion, then the effect of the resulting exogenous factors distort price level. The consequential distortionary effects are felt in the principal macroeconomic goals such as price stabilization, economic growth, employment, international competitiveness, and attainment of equitable distribution of resources.

Keynes wanted to make economics as a handmaiden of ethics. His encounter with Moore was the basis of this academic trend. Yet, Keynes being a rationalist could not agree with the metaphysical approach to ethics of Moore (1903). What resulted from such a partitioned view of ethical reality is similar to the divided view between *a priori* and *a posteriori* reasoning in the model of heteronomy presented by Kant. Consequently, there remains the dichotomy between the deductive reasoning of mainstream microeconomics and macroeconomics, and equally also between the *noumenon* and the phenomenon aspects of reasoning. Scientific reasoning under heteronomy as the central perspective of rationalism became the way of thinking on economic matters and social functions between the fields of microeconomics and macroeconomics. These problems of occidental thinking on socio-scientific matters were discussed earlier as methodological problems.

Macroeconomics has thus a wide sway of scope in it. Yet, its methodological orientation turns out to be inept in addressing the pressing expectations of economic epistemology today. That is regarding bringing together ethics and economic theory as a comprehensive study of socio-scientific consciousness. The dichotomy between microeconomics and macroeconomics is the continuing representation of the occidental way of thinking regarding all scientific fields. This is seen in quantum mechanics of the small scale of physical phenomena and relativity physics of the large scale of physical phenomena. The same characteristic is also found in the divide between economics and politics that barred the rise of political economy (Staniland, 1985). Likewise, it is true of the small-scale psyche projected by the field of psychology and the large-scale characterization of social phenomena in sociology, and so on. The demand for a new epistemological orientation to a methodology that integrates ethics and economics by the endogenous dynamics of socio-scientific consciousness is the march of the future (Heisenberg and Anshen, 1958; Nicolau, 1995).

Despite the shortcomings of Keynes in developing a pure theory of ethical dynamics embedded in his aggregate analysis, thus leaving the Keynesian econometric system with exogenous policy, technological, and other external variables, Keynes may be considered as an epistemological thinker in the field of economics, ethics, and society. He wrote wonderfully as follows (Keynes, 1963, p. 368): "The strenuous purposeful money-makers may carry all of us along with them into the lap of economic abundance. But it will be those peoples, who can keep alive, and cultivate into a fuller perfection, the art of life itself and do not sell themselves for the means of life, who will be able to enjoy the abundance when it comes." The project of endogenously embedding economic variables at the microeconomic level and its aggregation to the economy-wide level (macroeconomics) remains in an analytical void. It calls for fresh epistemological inquiry in socio-scientific discipline in general, and in economic theory in particular.

General flows of goods and services according to macroeconomics with ethical valuation

The general flow of goods and services (GFGS) is a logically accepted accounting measure of the value of spending and gross domestic product economy-wide. The GFGS is not a valuation measure for either the firm or industry-specific level of the flows of goods and services. GFGS does not represent the valuation of the so-called non-economic effects, as of morality, ethics, and consumer and producer consciousness. This book has contended in analytical ways that there cannot be a separate home for economics fortified in itself alone. Keynes, and later on Myrdal (social causation), and today the ontological heterodox school of new economic theory intellectualize economics to be deeply embedded in moral, ethical, and social phenomenology. Such is also the analytical approach of this book to correctly reflect the Islamic valuation of wellbeing (*maslaha*) as part and parcel of the *Tawhidi* Islamic economics (TIE) as science.

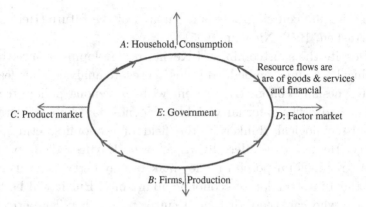

Figure 8.1. Economics independence of relations caused by exogenous policy shifts.
Notes: Denote one-directional exogenous effects; ↔ denote untenable endogenous relations.

Exogenous effects in the GFGS

Figure 8.1 points out the effect of variations in policies and consumption and spending behavior caused on and by the income multiplier effect (Schiller and Wall, 2012). Yet, such a shift is not caused by endogenous effects that convey learning and consciousness in behavioral patterns. Yet, Keynes wanted to see such patterns to be built into economic theory. But, as pointed out above, he devolved into rational economic behavior to resolve the endless problem that he faced in respect of subjective probability and expectations in his macroeconomic reasoning. Consequently, there is no reason to construct continuously evolutionary linked loops of GFGS as otherwise shown in Figure 8.1 as separated loops.

Consequently, none of the economic activities in any of the economic sectors can be truly continuous in nature in respect of the endogenous nature of socially embedded effects. Take an example here. An increase in income via the income multiplier effect takes place firstly by government expenditure along with other spending. Yet, government expenditure represents fiscal policy that exogenously affects the increase in income. Secondly, the increase in income multiplier is also positively affected by the increasing

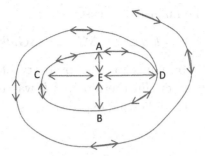

Figure 8.2. Continuously endogenous GFGS with respect to the complementary effect between all variables by the θ-induction.

marginal propensity to spend and the decrease in the marginal propensity to save within a given GFGS. Such household propensities are affected by the assumption of resource scarcity. The assumption poses the continued problem of scarcity of resources. Now, all the postulates of economic rationality reappear in rational economic analysis. Economic analysis thus fails to acquire the realist basis of formalism and analysis on the wider aspects. The possibility of dynamic effects caused by the property of diversification by continuity of complementarities is negated. Consequently, dynamic effects influencing household behavior does not exist in the traditional form of the GFGS as shown in Figure 8.1. Consequently, the example here proves that the dynamic effects on the increase in income multiplier enter an exogenous cycle of relations, denying interrelations between endogenous variables.

The circular causation problem of exogenous property of macroeconomic variables in the GFGS is explained by means of Figure 8.2. Its formal ramification is the following:

$$Y = C + I + G. \tag{8.1}$$

G is an exogenous economic variable and thereby not continuous, unless the government has an endogenous function, such as "a government by discussion", participatory democracy, and discursive institution–market interaction. In this regard, we can refer to Amartya Sen's keynote lecture for Institute for New Economic Thinking (Sen, 2012).

Therefore, in the mainstream case,

$$d\Delta Y = k.d\Delta G + \Delta G.dk = \Delta G.dk, \qquad (8.2)$$

in the sense of discontinuity by the property of exogeneity of G representing fiscal policy. Furthermore, if k was to be endogenous, this would result in the following expression:

$$dk = ds_p/(1 - s_p)^2, \qquad (8.3)$$

is true only if the marginal propensity to spend is to be continuous with either time or behavior. According to the rational economic assumptions, there is no variation in the presumed behavioral propensities. Besides, if the marginal propensity to spend (thereby marginal propensity to save) was continuous with respect to time, then this would imply that government policies and household behavior is continuously changing. Neither of these cases is true in respect of applying exogeneity assumption of government actions and the behavioral convergence to rationality. When changes in spending occur due to changes in income, then a smoothly predictive behavior to changes in income is required. Interactive learning behavior and changes in predictive elements continuously will not ascertain smooth predictive values to marginal and average propensity to spend, and thus to marginal and average propensity to save.

An example of such a case is one that is universally encountered. As gross domestic income increases (Y), households and business spending (S_p) in the market place are replaced by government spending in outstanding liabilities. Thereby, the shape of dS_p/dY remains indeterminate.

Endogenous effects of morality and ethicality in GFGS according to TIE

Morality and ethicality are attributes that are always embedded in complementary (participatory) forms of intercausal relations between variables and their social representations. Hence, every such relationship is endogenous between the social representations and the variables that symbolize them. In such a case, the implications of Figure 8.1 fail to explain the economic and social reality.

Now, the GFGS conveys not simply an accounting way of valuation of the economy-wide flows of goods and services. Rather, each of the goods and services in real, monetary, and financial terms that flow are ethically endogenized. That is, the **x**-variables of mainstream economics are replaced by $\mathbf{x}(\theta)$. These are defined in the extended field of events that happen in knowledge, space, and time horizon. Yet, time is simply a follower of the recording state of the event after the event is caused to occur by the will of *Allah* in knowledge, in space and time. Such ontology of the law of *Allah* — *Tawhid*, causes all things to happen in the causality i.e. $(\Omega, S) \ni \theta \to (\mathbf{x}(\theta), t(\theta)) \to (\theta, \mathbf{x}(\theta), t(\theta))$.[1] Such an endogenous transformation invokes consciousness in the choice of the good things of life. The meaning of this is to explain the social and economic universe in the intercausal way of complementarities between all "possibilities", replacing competing "alternatives" (substitutes) of all of mainstream economics and social system.

The formal explanation of the above kind of difference in valuation of the GFGS in the social economy is as follows.

All variables are embedded in consciousness as we represent them by the vector of extended domains as knowledge increases, spreads, and endogenizes across diversely complementary systems. Thus, we denote any of such variable by $\mathbf{x}(\theta)$. Included in this vector are variables like government spending as fiscal policy, monetary policy, all other policies, technology and innovation effects and the ethicality of consciousness, and thus continuity by way of intercausal relations. All such variables are endogenous.

Thus,

$$(d/d\theta)(dY(\theta)/d\theta) = d^2Y/d\theta^2 = (d/d\theta)[(d/d\theta)[k(\theta) \cdot S_p(\theta)]]$$
$$= (d/d\theta)[k(\theta) \cdot dS_p(\theta)/d\theta + S_p(\theta) \cdot dk(\theta)/d\theta]$$

---

[1] *Qur'an* (14:32-34): "It is *Allah* who created the heavens and the earth and sent down rain from the sky and produced thereby some fruits as provision for you and subjected for you the ships to sail through the sea by His command and subjected for you the rivers." (14:32).

"And He subjected for you the sun and the moon, continuous [in orbit], and subjected for you the night and the day." (14:33).

$$> 0 \qquad > 0 \qquad\qquad > 0$$
$$= (dS_p/d\theta) \cdot (dk(\theta)/d\theta) + k(\theta) \cdot (d^2 S_p(\theta)/d\theta^2)$$
$$> 0 \qquad\qquad > 0$$
$$+ S_p(\theta) \cdot d^2 k(\theta)/d\theta^2 + (dk(\theta)/d\theta) \cdot (S_p(\theta)) > 0.^2 \qquad (8.4)$$

Regarding the explosive nature of the income multiplier on spending in the good things of life, see Choudhury (1999). Keynes, despite his problem of exogenous effect of discontinuous policy, technology, and similar variables, promoted the activity of spending in productive things. He, though, wrote regarding the good things of life as well.

Figure 8.2 can be explained by means of the interconnectivity of various parts of Figure 8.1. The schematic diagram would be like the following one. The symbols are defined as in Figure 8.1. The double arrows explain the pervasively endogenous effects at all parts of the GFGS including the nature of its evolution.

The income multiplier in the ethico-economic valuation process of GFGS according to TIE

From the above explanation of the difference, yet need for an ethically induced valuation process in the GFGS, it is clear that a great gap of such valuation is missed out from simply an accounting approach to valuation in the GFGS. By upholding the importance of the extended scope of valuation, we now define the spending function as

$$S_p = S_p(Y, k)[\theta]. \qquad (8.5)$$

The symbols have been defined throughout this work.

---

[2]The *Qur'an* (2:261) declares regarding the wellbeing effect of spending in the good things of life in many verses. An example of a verse is this: "The parable of those who spend their substance in the way of Allah is that of a grain of corn: it groweth seven ears, and each ear Hath a hundred grains. *Allah* giveth manifold increase to whom He pleaseth: And *Allah* careth for all and He knoweth all things."

In the system of endogenous relations between the variables, $\{Sp, Y, k\}[\theta]$, we derive the relation

$$Y = Y(S_p, k), \text{ with } k = k(S_p, Y)[\theta]. \tag{8.6}$$

From Expression (8.6), we obtain

$$dY/d\theta = (\partial Y/\partial S_p) \cdot (dS_p/d\theta) + (\partial Y/\partial k) \cdot (dk/d\theta). \tag{8.7}$$

Expression (8.7) yields

$$(\partial Y/\partial S_p) = [dY/d\theta - (\partial Y/\partial k) \cdot (dk/d\theta)]/(dS_p/d\theta)$$
$$= dY/dS_p - (\partial Y/\partial k).(dk/dS_p),$$

yielding

$$dY/dS_p = (\partial Y/\partial S_p) + (\partial Y/\partial k) \cdot (dk/dS_p). \tag{8.8}$$

Expression (8.8) implies that the total positive effect of S_p on Y is higher than the marginal propensity to spend, $(\partial Y/\partial S_p)$, by the positive amount, $(\partial Y/\partial k) \cdot (dk/dS_p)$. This is the same as noting that the marginal propensity to consume is less than the total contribution of the change in spending as a ratio to the change in gross domestic product of mainstream economics by the amount $(\partial Y/\partial k) \cdot (dk/dS_p)$. This amount can be interpreted as the change in gross domestic product per unit of change in the multiplier "k", applied to the quantity, dk/dS_p. This quantity in turn denotes the change in the multiplier "k" per unit of the change in spending "S_p".

The conclusion to be drawn from the above analysis is that the role of ethical and social values in the valuation of GFGS plays a significant role to increase the role of the income multiplier by the total effect of spending in the good things of life (*maqasid as-shari'ah*), not simply in the productive things (earlier criticism of cost-benefit mechanism). We will soon find out how such a result affects the general equilibrium system in ethico-economics with focus on the pervasively evolutionary nature of intervariable organic complementarities in TIE and its income generating capability.

Critical issues of consumption, savings, and investment functions

The important point to understand is that between the activities of consumption, savings, and investment, there is not merely an accounting interrelationship. More critically, the ethical consciousness in the social order introduces a complex system of intercausal organic effects that must be noted in the various model specifications that finally lead up to the evolutionary generalized system model of economy-wide thinking.

In the Keynesian macroeconomic modeling, the interconnection between the above-mentioned aggregate variables is via gross domestic output and prices that make up for real output, which in turn affects other macroeconomic variables. Contrarily, in the ethically induced modeling of macroeconomic activities, the ultimate basis is the premise of θ-variable that induces output, prices, and all other variables. The resulting circular causation between the different variables is shown by Figure 8.3. The double arrows again show the circular causation between learning, and the knowledge, space, and time dimensions of the affected variables, and evolutionary learning occurring in continuums. The focus being on the cause and effect of θ-induction, the ultimate objective of the morally/ethically induced ethico-economic system is the wellbeing function. It is studied both conceptually and empirically. All the tenets of analytical methods

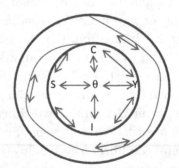

Figure 8.3. Intercausal evolution by the foundational effect of moral/ethical values on ethico-economic variables.

are used, though on contextual relevance to the nature of the morally/ethically induced ethico-economic system.

The question first to be addressed is whether $\{C, S, I, Y\}$ can all be complementary with each other? The meaning of savings needs to be understood to prove the complementarity of savings with consumption and investment. Savings that are held up in banks as bank savings form withdrawals, not injection into the economy (Ventelou, 2005). Thus, bank savings cannot form positive complementarity with spending in the nature of consumption, investment, and also with the endogenous nature of government spending as would be the case with participatory governments — Amartya Sen's "government by discussion" mentioned earlier.

For instance, the following equations would be untenable in Keynesian macroeconomics, but are meaningful in the endogenous nature of ethically induced economic system in the intervariable relational sense:

$$C(Y, \theta) = a_0 + a_1 \cdot S(Y, \theta) + a_2 \cdot I(\theta, Y) + a_3 \cdot G(\theta, Y). \qquad (8.9)$$

In mainstream economics, $C + S + G = C + I + G = Y$, with $S = I$ in all states of equilibrium of the macroeconomics systems, underemployment, and full employment states. But in the states of disequilibrium with $S < I$, savings are increased by the build-up of bondholding. The savings gap is closed up partly by market function and partly by policy effects. If $S > I$, the resulting lower rate of interest will increase investment, and thereby absorb the excess amount of savings. As the macroeconomy is found to be always in certain states of disequilibrium, including underemployment equilibrium, therefore, it is permanently alternating between $S > I$ (recessionary), $S < I$ (inflationary), $S = I$ denoting temporary equilibrium from the underemployment states to the full-employment state. All these economic states imply that resources remain scarce in full-mobilization to attain the desired, though not maximum, level of income multiplier effect. The presence of interest inherent in the macroeconomic system in mainstream economics does not allow sustainable full-employment levels of the real output to be attained. Price stability is lost, as is also pointed out by the monetarists against the Keynesian defense of fiscal expansion for

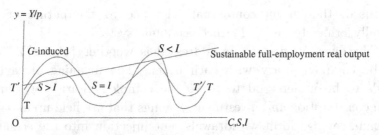

Figure 8.4. Perpetual disequilibrium of the macroeconomy in the absence of intervariable coterminous endogenous relations.

productive expansion, though with exogenous effect of $G(\cdot)$ as autonomous economic variable (Blaug, 1993). Figure 8.4 displays the perpetual disequilibrium of the economy in the absence of continuous prevalence of sustainability.

Ironically, inter-temporal bank savings for stabilizing a growing sustainable economy forever fails. We can prove this fact here. In the end, the intervariable relationship cannot be explained by Equation (8.9) in Keynesian consumption function. Yet, this failure is because of the impossibility of Keynesian general equilibrium system to get over the underlying assumption of resource scarcity, and to retain the interest rate as the key-player in economic adjustment. These two underlying conditions are the foundational problems of the Keynesian argument and functioning. Therefore, for Equation (8.9) to be meaningful, the structure and assumptions of the economy must be contrary to the above cases. This will reflect in the permanence of resource regeneration, causing phasing out of interest rate continuously across all economic and social functions. The result would then be to cause increasing complementarities among the endogenous relations between $\{Y/p, C, S, I, G\}$ and their positive transformation. An example of such positive effects is of the morally/ethically induced total valuation by the total valuation effect of the income multiplier.

Exercise 1

In the world over today, the menace of absolute poverty is a serious problem that must be reduced by means of social consciousness and

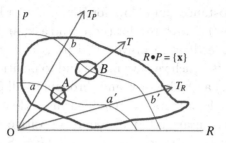

Figure 8.5. The impossibility of attaining complementarities between the possibilities of life in mainstream ethico-economic explanations — Keynes and Rawls.

economic activities and programs. Keynes' grand idea of economics as a handmaiden of ethics failed because of his economic model being incapable to be consciously inclusive of ethics as endogenous realization.

If each country was under the incidence of government fiscal policy, while resources remained scarce globally, what would be the effectiveness of global flow of resources on poverty alleviation? How can the underlying problem be changed with the endogenous consciousness of moral and ethical values in fiscal strategy?

Take the example of a two-country world, Rich and Poor (Singer and Ansari, 1988). In Figure 8.5, scarcity will drive countries to think of a specific way of addressing the problem of the wellbeing competition between social justice (P) and economic growth (R). The mainstream optimal point of scarce allocation of resources in global governance and resource flows will be determined within the scatter of points shown by A, B, etc. (Rawls, 1971). The complementarities between $\{y, C, S, I\}$ will evolve along the resource allocation path OT. If policy-induced points like a, b, etc. were selected, then the paths OT_R, OT_P will explain the complementarities between independently competing resource allocations between the competing "alternatives". The ethical endogeneity of consciousness for interrelating the Rich and the Poor is lost.

Yet, true moral and ethical consciousness demands as the *Qur'an* (2:177) says: "It is not righteousness that ye turn your faces Towards East or West; but it is righteousness — to believe in *Allah* and the Last Day, and the Angels, and the Book, and the Messengers; to spend of your substance, out of love for Him, for your kin, for orphans, for the needy, for the wayfarer, for those who ask, and for the ransom of slaves; to be steadfast in prayer, and practice regular charity; to fulfill the contracts which ye have made; and to be firm and patient, in pain (or suffering) and adversity, and throughout all periods of panic. Such are the people of truth, the God fearing." Hence, the extensive nature of complementary relations requires positive interdependence by intercausality between $\mathbf{x}_P = \{y, C, S, I, G = S_p\}$ $[\theta]$ and $\mathbf{x}_R = \{y, C, S, I, G = S_p\}$ $[\theta]$.

In the endogenous ethical sense of interrelations between R and P, a combination of market and institutional interactions and integration with discursive learning will jointly generate the following two coterminous results simultaneously and correspondingly according to the IIE-learning process arising from the methodology of unity of knowledge and the world system.

$$\theta = \cup_{\text{interactions}} \cap_{\text{integration}} \{\wp_R, \wp_P\}, \text{ yielding}$$
$$\mathbf{x} = \cup_{\text{interactions}} \cap_{\text{integration}} \{x_R, x_P\}. \tag{8.10}$$

Such a point of social choice is shown within the open domain encircled by $(R \bullet P)$ in Figure 8.5. Thus, neither the Keynesian ethical concern nor Rawlsian control of the economy to allocate around the $45°$ line from the origin, works out to gain the ethical endogeneity of a conscious ethico-economic transformation by extensive complementarities between the good things of life.

Further extensions of the problems of sustainability of the Keynesian general equilibrium

Along the lines of similar explanations given before, we can prove that in a general equilibrium system of relations of the extensively complementary type, the nature of the interrelations between the critical variables changes into different ones. Thus, the following equations can be explained in the pervasively complementary nature of economic system. Yet, they remain unexplained in mainstream economics.

$$S(Y, \theta) = a_0 + a_1 \cdot C(Y, \theta) + a_2 \cdot I(\theta, Y) + a_3 \cdot G(\theta, Y), \qquad (8.11)$$

$$I(Y, \theta) = a_0 + a_1 \cdot S(Y, \theta) + a_2 \cdot C(\theta, Y) + a_3 \cdot G(\theta, Y), \qquad (8.12)$$

$$G(Y, \theta) = a_0 + a_1 \cdot S(Y, \theta) + a_2 \cdot I(\theta, Y) + a_3 \cdot C(\theta, Y). \qquad (8.13)$$

The question of critical importance is this: how can we formulate and interpret the contrasting general equilibrium systems of relations in mainstream macroeconomics and the ethico-economics of pervasive complementarities? Let us address this question now. The mainstream general equilibrium is well-known, as given in the following.

The general equilibrium treatment of mainstream macroeconomics

Expenditure sector equation

In reference to the standard macroeconomic theory, the so-called Islamic economists introduce the additional variable of price (profits) instead of the rate of interest "i". The *zakah* variable (Z) would also be introduced. The expenditure sector curve is then written in the form

$$Y = a_0 + a_1 \cdot p + a_2 \cdot Z, a_0 > 0, a_1 > 0, a_2 > 0. \qquad (8.14)$$

Monetary sector equation

$$Y = b_0 + b_1 \cdot p + b_2 \cdot Z + b_3 M_s^o, b_0 > 0, b_1 > 0, b_2 > 0, b_3 > 0. \qquad (8.15)$$

For the present-day formulation of the Islamic version of mainstream general equilibrium, the following relations would hold.

The same amount of *zakah* (Z) would hold from either side of fiscal policy and monetary policy in the state of macroeconomic equilibrium in the present understanding of Islamic economy. Thus, for all possible equilibrium points according to the various fiscal and monetary policy effects, the relationship between Y and p will yield the general equilibrium points moving towards full employment across all possible underemployment equilibriums. The equation of

Islamic version of general equilibrium we derive is of the following form:

$$Y = A_0 + A_1 \cdot P + A_2 \cdot M_s^o. \tag{8.16}$$

The signs of the coefficients are not determinate. They would depend on the nature of effects of fiscal and monetary policies, i.e. either on a substitution basis or complementary basis. When contractionary fiscal policy is substituted by expansionary monetary policy, there can be crowding-out effect on income at lower prices. This can result in a stagflationary economic state.

When contractionary monetary policy is substituted by expansionary fiscal policy, there can occur inflationary forms of crowding-out effect on income. When there is complementarity between fiscal policy and monetary policy, both expansionary, then non-inflationary economic growth can be realized. If both policies are contractionary, then non-inflationary economic deceleration can occur and cause the Dutch disease problem on a continued basis.

The lesson to learn from the above formulation of Islamic mainstream economics is that it contributes nothing original to economic reasoning. The economic expansionary effect of easy complementary monetary and fiscal policies is recognized. But the nature of learning type general equilibriums is non-existent, as needs to be explained by the continuously repeated simulation (simulacra) of Equations (8.9)–(8.13).

Generalized system model of evolutionary ethico-economic equilibrium in TIE

We now bring back the essential elements of TIE to characterize the nature of the generalized system model of evolutionary equilibrium. Keynes may have thought about a similar form of equilibrium system when he did not see the economy to adjust according to flexible price pressure affecting wage rates to an equilibrium in labor market. The inflexible wage rate caused by market–institutional interface causes a continuous system of underemployment condition to prevail, although the economy in such a state remains locked in stable (inflexible) prices and low-level liquidity trap at a low level of interest. The problem with the Keynesian system arises at or around the full-employment level of real output at a given price level. The attainment of such an equilibrium state brings about scarcity of resources, competition, and resulting price escalation along the classical version of the supply curve of output. Contrarily, in the case of resource regeneration, technological change, entrepreneurship, and the like, the full-employment equilibrium can continuously shift along the elastic form of the short-run supply curve of real output. Complementarity between all variables including the policy variables cause the evolutionary equilibrium state of full employment to occur. There remains no concept of the long-run full-employment rate at which the economy ceases to be reactive to further policies effects.

The objectives of mainstream macroeconomics are reformed in TIE. In mainstream macroeconomics, the objectives are attaining of non-inflationary economic growth, full-employment level of real output, price competitiveness in the open trading economy, and the goal of distributive equity. In the concept of economic welfare, these goals of macroeconomics combine together to translate into the objective of macroeconomic welfare maximization, given the relationship between the above-mentioned objectives. But in the process of attaining the maximization objective, the growth rate of the economy is assigned (Gordon, 1967). The policy variables are exogenously applied and thus intervariable continuity of causality ends. Finally, under the assumption of scarcity of resources of the physical and financial kinds, the goal of attaining devolves into marginalist substitution between distributive equity and economic efficiency (growth). Thus, we find that Keynes, in his roots of thinking, was a neoclassicist in a macroeconomic garb (Dasgupta, 1987).

The TIE argues that any trace of marginalism and exogeneity of certain variables in macroeconomic models with their resulting mathematical discontinuity altogether must be replaced by pervasive continuity, endogeneity, and resource regeneration in the market–institutional discursive venue. The result of such relationships is extensive complementarities between all the good things of life (*maqasid*-choices) in the midst of interactive, integrative, and evolutionary (IIE) learning processes, both intra-system and inter-systems. These consequences of the realist system of circular causation between the complementary variables or a transformation to such a system, introduces the perspective of unity of knowledge into the wellbeing function. The concept of wellbeing was substantially defined as the *maslaha*-function in terms of the *maqasid*-choices that continuously participate and complement.

The form of the generalized model of evolutionary system learning in aggregative TIE

Exercise 2

Using Equations (8.9)–(8.13) and Figure 8.3 write down the problem of simulation of the objective function of *maslaha*, subject to the circular causation relations between the complementary variables. Explain the various circular causation equations in this *maqasid-as shari'ah maslaha* function.

Keep in view that, in TIE, savings mean resource mobilization into *maqasid*-choices through the participatory forms of financial instruments. Savings in the form of financial flows form mobilized resources into consumption, investment, and government spending that merge with private resources in market–institution interface to share risk and enjoy returns.

See the following section on the contrariness of mainstream conclusion regarding savings and growth of economic output. If the savings function is discarded to be bank savings, then two questions are critical to inquire about. Firstly, we question: what can be the role of interest if at all in the savings function? Secondly: what would be the role of the central bank and commercial banks in TIE? The answers to these questions are interrelated and intertwined.

To investigate the first question, we note the simple reasoning that, if by savings we mean the transfer of liquid wealth into the real economy through the function of banks as an organized institution for this purpose, then such a financial instrument must be used that heightens all kinds of resource mobilization. Contrarily, there must be the avoidance of such instruments that hinder resource mobilization into the real economy, which is governed by ethico-economic possibilities as of *maqasid as-shari'ah*. In mainstream economics, the argument underlying for financial requirement to nurture economic growth is capital accumulation via present abstinence to spend more in the future and with more to save. The financial instrument that renders this function is the rate of interest taken up in its various forms.[3]

On the second question, we will treat it in the section on 100% reserve requirement monetary system fully in Chapter 9, on this topic. We note, though, that the function of banks as bank-saving financial institutions ceases to exist. Islamic banks are defined as the financial intermediary to mobilize savings into productive spending in the light of *maqasid as-shari'ah* choices to increase the wellbeing objective criterion function and to avoid the impermissible *maqasid*-"bads" from the recommended basket. Besides, we also include the objective of Islamic banks in this respect to be development financing institutions to actualize dynamic life-fulfillment regime of participatory development out of the encompassing principle of *Tawhidi* unity of knowledge as the governing episteme of belief, thought, and action.

---

[3]Interest includes all kinds: simple and compound; real and expected; effective and term structure; small and large of any dimensions. In Islam, the following two terms are used to define the complete idea of interest (*riba*). This kind of definition, though, is unnecessary, for there is always a one-to-one interrelationship between financial transactions and the corresponding real transactions. *Riba al-nasiya* is defined as excess in finance in real exchange. *Riba al-fadl* is defined as the corresponding excess in the commodities connected with the excess financial demand or supply by banks. Only the banks including central bank and commercial banks and their financial derivatives, such as bond markets and financial companies, and individuals such as the Kabliwala who notoriously charges usury on loans. In fact, there is no such thing as a simple rate of interest. Every so-called simple rate of interest is the compound result of a large number of term structures of interest rates over any length of time. Time is of the essence for interest rates to realize their full value. Therefore, there is no such concept as usury versus interest rate in the *Qur'anic* meaning of interest and usury taken synonymously. The *Qur'an* (2:278) declares: "O ye who believe! Fear God; and give up what remains of your demand for *riba*, if ye are indeed believers."

The role of central bank is to supervise the mobilization of money through financial intermediaries in sustaining the 100% reserve requirement monetary system. In such a monetary and connected financial system, as the market-friendly institutional interface, the moral/ethical and material use of money is realized in full valuation of the good economy (Choudhury and Hoque, 2006). The function of money and finance to mobilize resources toward sustaining the development of life-fulfillment regime of development, the *maqasid*-way transfers the endogenous function of the circular causation relations exemplified by Equations (8.9)–(8.13) and its further extensions to commercial banks and their associated financial institutions. This is an idea that comes closest to the theory of money found in the Austrian School of Economics (Yeager, 1997).

Resource mobilization through the above ways of circulating the quantity of good money and finance through the real economy of the *maqasid*-vintage and regenerating the quantity of money by doing so is the explanation that is necessary and sufficient in establishing the savings function as follows:

$$S = S(\theta, y, r, C, I, G, P)[\theta], \qquad (8.17)$$

where P denotes the endogenous policy vector such as fiscal and monetary policies.

Equation (8.17) is an extended form of the system of Expressions (8.9)–(8.13) with the objective of simulating the wellbeing function, $W(\theta) \approx \theta$ in the linearized empirical and applied policy-theoretic form. Consequentially, the fullest actualization of ethico-economic value is realized by mobilizing resources and regenerating it under the episteme, $\{\theta\} \in (\Omega, S)$ universally. Thus, the domain of markets encompasses the ultimate playground of the *sunnat-Allah* (divine law) as the beckoner of the Signs of *Allah* (*ayath Allah*) unraveling the good and the bad choices of living experience end to end. *Sunnat Allah* includes *maqasid as-shari'ah* not as the complete law, but as the subset of *Sunnat Allah* at any moment of evolutionary learning explained by the *Tawhidi* worldview.

The following identity forms an accounting measure, not an ethico-economic *relational* one that can explain interrelations in the economy. In the relational order avoiding sheer accounting identity, the full scope of the moral/ethical valuation effect can be explained. For example, take the case of caring, love, and affection that extend total wellbeing relationship beyond simply physical love in marriage. So does the moral/ethical economy realize its heightened level of moral/ethical and material valuation, as was explained earlier.

$$C = (Y - T) - S. \tag{8.18}$$

Now, include with this *zakah* (Z) and write

$$C = (Y - T - Z) - S. \tag{8.19}$$

Equation (8.19) is questionable in TIE, for Z is not interpreted as deduction in disposable income when it gets included in the *maqasid*-spending in TIE. The *Qur'an* declares in this regard.[4] The accounting nature of the identity cannot explain the moral/ethical valuation effect of Z in *maqasid*-spending. Regarding explosive-type income multipliers under the effect of heightened Islamic transformation and endogenous consciousness, see Choudhury and Malik (1992).

Yet, T is a withdrawal, because it forms delayed spending in exigencies that the government faces in its expenditure in development. This may not have any ethical/moral valuation attached to it to be handed over to assuage social difficulties by productive and ethical means. Examples are the ineptness of T in reducing unemployment and poverty as is known to be the case with the welfare trap (Enke, 1963). Thus, the way to include the spending effect of Z in *maqasid*-spending is to use the circular causation relations of intervariable causality, as shown before.

When T exists along with Z, this kind of relation causes resource scarcity and substitution between T and Z, thereby reducing the effectiveness of Z in the moral/ethical economic order. To increase ethico-economic effectiveness, the amount of T is to be reduced while

---

[4] *Qur'an* (2:261): "The parable of those who spend their substance in the way of *Allah* is that of a grain of corn: it grows seven years, and each ear has a hundred grains. *Allah* gives manifold increase to whom He pleases and *Allah* cares for all and He knows all things."

the resource exposure of Z needs to be increased. The consequences of such a situation in the imperfect TIE will be felt. This calls for simulation procedure of wellbeing. Such simulations are represented by the continuous changes in the coefficients of the circular causation relations. This in turn calls for reorganization and endogenous (discursive) policy reconstruction. It is suggested as a matter of policy reorganization and increased valuation effectiveness in TIE that the simulation form of the T, Z relationship should look as. This is desired as a goal, but not necessarily factual in any existing experience in real life.

$$(-) + + + + +$$
$$Z(\theta) = f(T, Y, C, S, I, P)[\theta]. \qquad (8.20)$$

Exercise 3

By your ethico-economic explanation as exemplified above and by taking the source of the *Qur'an*, describe the policy-theoretic and market–institutional relations underlying the following equation in an imperfect state of TIE, but aimed at moral/ethical reconstruction by way of simulation:

$$(-) + + + + +$$
$$I(\theta) = f(T, Y, C, S, Z, P)[\theta]. \qquad (8.21)$$

Figure 8.6 summarizes the kind of circular causation relations between institutions, their activities, and their representative variables as explained by Expressions (8.17), (8.20), and (8.21). Figure 8.6 extends Figure 8.3. Figure 8.7 shows the intervariable effects in respect of Equations (8.20) and (8.21).

Adverse effect of bank-savings on potential real output

It is claimed in mainstream economics, which Islamic economics emulates, that savings are necessary for capital accumulation to finance future economic growth (Ramsey, 1928). This is a fallacy, for even as present savings are accumulated, this requires the incentive of banks to provide via the rate of interest or a similar instrument,

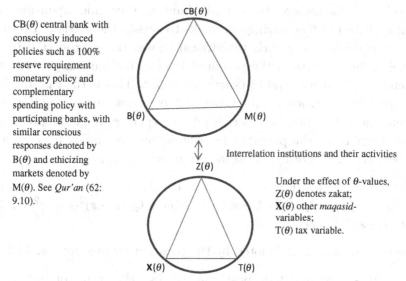

CB(θ) central bank with consciously induced policies such as 100% reserve requirement monetary policy and complementary spending policy with participating banks, with similar conscious responses denoted by B(θ) and ethicizing markets denoted by M(θ). See *Qur'an* (62: 9.10).

Interrelation institutions and their activities

Under the effect of θ-values, Z(θ) denotes zakat; X(θ) other *maqasid*-variables; T(θ) tax variable.

Figure 8.6. Institutions and their activities under the effect of evolutionary θ-values.

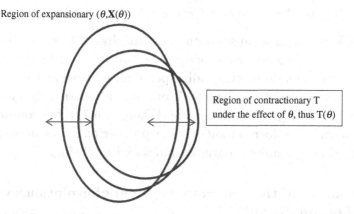

Region of expansionary (θ,X(θ))

Region of contractionary T under the effect of θ, thus T(θ)

Figure 8.7. Positive θ-effects on expansionary region of $(Z(\theta), X(\theta))$ and decreasing region of T under the simulation effect of θ, thus $T(\theta)$.

say bonds and capital market gambles between various risky instruments. The higher such rates are on savings withheld in banks, the more the capital accumulation is in the promise of future economic growth. However, one notes in such a regime of bank-savings *vis-à-vis* economic growth that, all along the economic expansionary path, there must be savings in banks to satisfy the needs of capital accumulation. Every such withdrawal causes the depressed output level to be lower than the potential level of real output or the full factor-employment level of potential output. This is the case of the mainstream macroeconomic theory and its prototype usage in Islamic economics. This fact of a perpetual underperforming economy that can never reach the potential level of output to employ fully all its productive and moral/ethical factors is proved as follows:

Time: $t = 0$ $t = 1$ $t = 2$ $t = n$

Output: Q_0 $Q_1 = Q_0(1 - s)(1 + i)$ $Q_2 = Q_0(1 - s)^2(1 + i)^2$ $Q_n = Q_0(1 - s)^n(1 + i)^n$

Return on savings is denoted by the constant savings rate, s. (8.22)

Resources accumulated post saving by the rate of interest: $Q_0(1 - s)$ $Q_1(1 - s) = Q_0(1 - s)^2(1 + i)$ $Q_n = Q_0(1 - s)^n(1 + i)^n$

Output returns on spending without saving and interest rate: Q_0 $Q'_1 = Q_0(1 + r)$ $Q'_2 = Q_0(1 + r)^2$ $Q'_n = Q_0(1 + r)^n$

Thus, bank savings cause continuous withdrawal from the potential real output. The adverse consequences are followed by depravation in resource mobilization, goodly spending, employment generation, participation instead of competition, and profit-sharing instead of self-aggrandizing profit-mongering. Wherewithal, there comes about the coterminous degradation of trade, prosperity, economic and social stability, sustainability, fairness, and social wellbeing.

The nature of the generalized system of evolutionary equilibrium model

Since the universal model of TIE is one of process formulation in the midst of the IIE learning, therefore there cannot be usage of the idea of static full-employment equilibrium. Endogenous effects of policies (monetary and fiscal), technology, innovation, and ethical consciousness on the scale of extensive participation of the type exemplified in Figures 8.6 and 8.7 will forever shift the evolutionary full-employment points along the expansionary path shown in Figure 8.4. This is also the idea of creative destruction according to Schumpeter (Cantner *et al.*, 2009). Writes: "As shown with the model used by means of numerical simulations, the introduction of the new technology generates an initial fluctuation, which brings about temporary unemployment as well as a temporary fall in productivity. However, this fluctuation very soon dampens down and the economy converges to a new steady-state corresponding to the superior technology, with a higher level of productivity — which allows lower prices and higher real wages — and full employment".

Yet, the TIE phenomenon of dynamic supply curve of output is different from the Schumpeterian case. In Schumpeter's case, the temporary full-employment case comes to a halt and needs to be re-started. Such temporary halting points are characterized by disequilibrium. TIE solves this problem by its logical consequence of continuous evolutionary learning intra-system and inter-system across knowledge, space, and time dimensions.

Thus, we can introduce more variables to any set of circular causation relations of the computational general evolutionary equilibrium model of TIE as partially presented by the system of Equations (8.9)–(8.13) and (8.17)–(8.21). In this respect, we will study the system of interrelations between $(\theta, Z, T_r, y, r/i)[\theta]$. T_r denotes trade in its general meaning of market exchange. "r" denotes the rate of return. "i" denotes interest rate. (r/i) denotes the financial price-relative between real rate of return and the real rate of interest.

The example of generalized system of evolutionary equilibrium model in the vector of variables, $(\theta, Z, T_r, y, r/i)[\theta]$

The *Qur'anic* verse (2:275) declares: "Those who devour usury will not stand except as stand one whom the Evil one by his touch hath driven to madness. That is because they say: 'Trade is like usury', but *Allah* hath permitted trade and forbidden usury. Those who after receiving direction from their Lord, desist, shall be pardoned for the past; their case is for *Allah* (to judge); but those who repeat (the offence) are companions of the Fire: They will abide therein (for ever)." The important issue in the exegesis of this verse in conjunction with the pervasive message of organic pairing of the universe in all its details and particulars is that trade as exchange of resources, and *riba* as withdrawal, create all the increase or obstruction of wellbeing (*maslaha*), respectively. Besides, via the extensive relationship that both trade and *riba* establishes with every opposite kind of thought, activities and artefacts, respectively, trade and *riba* get entangled by their continuously regenerative causality with every other such thing according to their categories.[5]

For instance, take the case of teaching generations after generations of students in the field of trade and *riba*. Whichever way the morality-and-ethics-centered intellectual worldview will tilt, there will be the results of the future generation comprising the minds, the belief, the action, and applications. That is what has happened with the morally and socially corrupting *riba* world at large.

Yet, another subtle example is of *riba* and science as human transaction of the purposeful mind. The actuarial mathematics of annuity calculation depends extensively on interest rate-based accumulation, valuation, and discounting of assets. The closed life table of mortality is used to standardize the risk premiums and returns. Yet, the actuarial approach despite its scientific approach does not institutionally and socially consider the discursive medium of decision-making inherent in random variations of contingencies. It does not account for the epistemic of future versus present pricing of cash flows (annuities).

---

[5]The logical conclusion is this: since exchange is the divine conferment over the entirety of creation from the beginning to the end in every detail and because *riba* obstructs the realization of trade as exchange in its widest send of total valuation, therefore *riba* turns out to be *the root cause* of all evil, misery, disorder, and hardship. The *Qur'an* (2:278-279) declares regarding the universal evil of *riba*: "O ye who believe! Fear *Allah*, and give up what remains of your demand for usury, if ye are indeed believers. If ye do it not, take notice of war from *Allah* and His Messenger: But if ye turn back, ye shall have your capital sums: Deal not unjustly, and ye shall not be dealt with unjustly".

Finally, we have already established abundantly that the inclusion of knowledge-induced variables in the general equilibrium system changes its nature radically by the episteme of the *Tawhidi* unity of knowledge and the ethico-economic world system. Indeed, we note that in the case of the issue of trade and *riba*, reality and the world, hang for meaning and purpose in the contrast between trade and *riba*. Reality commences by the law of *Tawhidi* unity of knowledge, whose instrument of continuous lubrication is knowledge and its relational interrelations with the world system. Likewise, the reality of the *Akhira* is the end of the purposive nature of the Hereafter that is found through human activity of markets and institutions at large. Thereby, the reality of the world system is enveloped by *Tawhid* in the Beginning and *Tawhid* in the End of the completely spanned domain across knowledge, space, and time. This comprises the full moral and physical valuation of the socio-scientific universe of mind and matter. Thus, everything in the universe is a representation of markets and institutions, i.e. of exchange or *riba*. This is true for the social sciences and for the natural sciences: there is the science and technology for the discovery of energy and there is the economic management of such discovery of new sources of energy. Thus, there is the interplay between markets and institutions. This causes the intrinsic need for extension of resources (trade and exchange) and the diversion of resources into competing ends (*riba*). The *Qur'an* is a message of sustainability through market–institution relations. These are induced by the episteme of *Tawhidi* unity of knowledge as consciousness.[6]

Now, returning to the intrinsic circular causation of organic forms of relationships of unity of knowledge between the good things of life while shunning the false things of life, we explore the relational meaning in the vector $(\theta, Z, T_r, y, r/i)[\theta]$ by their circular causation

---

[6]*Qur'an* (2:267): "O ye who believe! Give of the good things which ye have (honourably) earned, and of the fruits of the earth which We have produced for you, and do not even aim at getting anything which is bad, in order that out of it ye may give away something, when ye yourselves would not receive it except with closed eyes. And know that *Allah* is Free of all wants, and worthy of all praise."

relations and the simulation objective of the wellbeing function (*maslaha*). It is essential to understand such a relational meaning by the exegesis of the *Qur'anic* verse mentioned above (*Qur'an*, 2:275).

Exercise 4

Write down and explain the objective of simulating the wellbeing, subject to the circular causation relations between the variables of the vector $(\theta, Z, T_r, y, r/i)[\theta]$.

Of especial attention is the equation

$$
\overset{+}{(r/i)[\theta]} = f(\overset{+}{g(Z)}, \overset{+}{g(T_r)}, \overset{+}{g(y)})[\theta], \tag{8.23}
$$

where $g(\cdot)$'s denote rates of change of the bracketed variables, with $\theta = F(g(Z), g(T_r), g(y), r/i)[\theta]$.

The table of observations as explained earlier will be of the form given in the following box. It is worth mentioning here that concepts, formalism, and empirical observations are recommended methods of the *Qur'an* and the *sunnah*. The *Qur'an* invokes them in reference to the signs of *Allah*. The sunnah invokes them by the authority of the Prophet. The Prophet Muhammad explained the worldly realities in reference to the *Tawhid* and thus *Akhira*.[7] That is why we write the embedding of all variables by the endogeneity of knowledge and consciousness as $\{\mathbf{x}(\theta)\}$.

	1	2	3	4					
Time	(r/i)	$g(Z)$	$g(T_r)$	$g(y)$	θ_1	θ_2	θ_3	θ_4	Avg $\cdot\,\theta$

---

[7]Al-Bukhari, Vol. 8, Book. 76, Number 426: "Narrated 'Abdullah: The Prophet drew a square and then drew a line in the middle of it and let it extend outside the square and then drew several small lines attached to that central line, and said, 'This is the human being, and this, (the square) in his lease of life, encircles him from all sides (or has encircled him), and this (line), which is outside (the square), is his hope, and these small lines are the calamities and troubles (which may befall him), and if one misses him, another will snap (i.e. overtake) him, and if the other misses him, a third will snap (i.e. overtake) him.'"

Draw figures like Figures 8.6 and 8.7 to explain the circular causation relations among variables of the vector $(\theta, Z, T_r, y, r/i)[\theta]$.

The law of *zakah* mandates all proceeds to be raised from the good things of life, the *maqasid*-choices. Some of these were noted earlier. In the form, shape, and objective of wellbeing (*maslaha*) in a life-fulfilling regime of sustainability, $Z(\theta)$ is mobilized in ethical and productive directions that raise the real economy and cause "r" to increase as *riba* "i" is decreased and vice versa. Consequently, (r/i) increases. Likewise, trade "T_r" as market exchange in the life-fulfilling choices increases as the output $(y = Y/p)$ of the real economy of the life-fulfilling kind increases.

None of the coefficients of Relation (8.23) is pre-assigned in signs. Firstly, the straightforward "estimation" is carried out with actual data as would be collected in the box shown. In the case of non-complementary coefficient-signs, the simulation of the wellbeing function subject to the "estimated" circular causation equations will be taken. This would reflect the discursively endogenous effects of the market–institutional (IIE) learning processes on the circular causation relations between the variables. All such gainful benefits of the reduction of *riba* by the organic causality of trade (exchange) in the *maqasid*-goods is summarized by the *Qur'anic* (2: 276) verse: "*Allah* destroys interest and gives increase for charities. And *Allah* does not like every sinning disbeliever."

Exercise 5

Even after keeping the usual goals of macroeconomic study the same as in mainstream economics, namely, non-inflationary economic growth and thus price stability, full-employment, international competitiveness, and distributive justice, how would you model the goal of price stabilization in relation to the other variables? Write down the objective function of the corresponding wellbeing (*maslaha*), subject to the circular causation relations. Thereby, attempt to answer the above question in Exercise 4.

Conclusion

The principal characteristic of TIE is the moral and ethical valuation of the economy-wide economic and social activities. In modeling such total valuation, TIE constructs a generalized system model of evolutionary equilibriums that endogenously unifies the moral/ethical values into the economic functions. This methodological approach arises from the *Tawhidi* episteme of unity of knowledge and its induction of the generality and particulars of the world system, of which economics and society are specific cases. Such an endogenously embedded approach to economy-wide aggregation is necessary to realize the objective of attaining wellbeing (*maslaha*), the ethical *maqasid*-choices, and dispelling the contrary goods and services from the choices. The resulting simulated choices that arise form the result and cause of unification between morality/ethics and economic variables was unsuccessful in Keynes' approach to macroeconomics and his formulation of the general equilibrium model.

Thus, Keynes' macroeconomic theory and all of mainstream macroeconomics ever since suffered of the dichotomy between ethics as an exogenous category and partially endogenous economic variables. On the other hand, microeconomics does not treat the topic of endogeneity of preferences and ethical values. Besides, there is no mechanism known to fully formalize the microeconomic aggregation principle into macroeconomics. This is despite the attempts carried out by rational expectations theory and public choice theory.

The problem of ethical endogeneity and fully endogenous system of circular causation variables is the continuing problem of all of western scientific thought. Earlier, we discussed as the problem of heteronomy between the *a priori* and *a posteriori* ways of reasoning. That is the same as the demarcation between deductive and inductive ways of reasoning. As long as this problem abides in socio-scientific reasoning, the possibility of unifying morality/ethics with physical reality including economic variables remains distanced. The generalized system of evolutionary equilibrium model of simulating the wellbeing objective criterion subject to the system of circular causation relations between all variables that are universally endogenous is a formal consequence of the episteme of unity of knowledge in TIE.

Mainstream macroeconomics like microeconomics neither can stand for the methodology nor for the formalism and explanations of TIE. It is pity that such deficient systems of formal reasoning continue to be ineptly used today in Islamic economics.

The results that arise are most misleading for facts of TIE. Take the example of interest rate setting as in the case of Exercise 4. In mainstream economics, interest rate is seen to be exogenously set by the central bank's prime rate that governs the commercial bank rates. In the process of transformation of an imperfect Islamic economics into the *riba*-free economy, the relationship between the central bank, commercial bank, and the market process as institutions and the corresponding endogenous relationship with the other variables are all endogenous in nature. This was explained with the help of Figures 8.6 and 8.7. The policy-theoretic inferences derived from these disparate approaches to the study of the role of interest in ethico-economic reconstruction are vastly opposite. The exogenous nature of interest rate determines the exogenous nature of fiscal and monetary policies. Interest rate is therefore seen as a financial policy instrument. On the other hand, in TIE during its process of ethical reconstruction, interest rate exists as a diminishing financial instrument that disappears as the policy variable increasingly becomes endogenous and unified in nature. Interest rate in a transforming TIE towards a deepening ethical state causes its reduction out of the intercausal relationship with the rate of return. This is shown by the variations in (r/i) as is explained in Exercise 4.

Consequently, the Islamic economic theory and applications cannot be derived from or by the use of mainstream economics. This is true both on methodological grounds and by way of inferences and formal applications. One can conclude from all this on the premise of the *Qur'anic* verses (5:16–18):

"O People of the Book! There hath come to you our Apostle, revealing to you much that ye used to hide in the Book, and passing over much (that is now unnecessary):

There hath come to you from God a (new) light and perspicuous Book, — Wherewith God guides all who seek His good pleasure to ways of peace and safety, and leads them out of darkness, by His Will, unto the light, — guides them to a Path that is Straight."

In this chapter, the teacher can focus on the following topics for students:

TIE contra mainstream generation of outputs and macroeconomic variables.

Maqasid as-shari'ah, Islamicization, and *Tawhidi* Islamic economic science.

References

Arrow, K. J. (1951). *Social Choice and Individual Values*, New York: John Wiley & Sons. Blaug, methodology.

Blaug, M. (1993), *The Methodology of Economics*, Cambridge, UK: Cambridge University Press.

Cantner, U. Luc Gaffard, J. and Nesta, L. (Eds.) (2009). *Schumpeterian Perspectives on Innovation, Competition, and Growth*, New York: Springer.

Choudhury M. A. (1999). *Comparative Economic Perspectives: Occidental and Islamic Perspectives*, Norwell, MA: Kluwer Academic.

Choudhury, M. A. and Hoque, M. Z. (2006). "Chapter 8, micro-money and real economic relationship in the 100 per cent reserve requirement monetary system", in *An Advanced Exposition of Islamic Economics and Finance*, Lewiston, NY: The Edwin Melen Press.

Choudhury, M. A. and Malik. U. A. (1992). "The essence of the Islamic political economy", in *The Foundations of Islamic Political Economy*, Chapter 1, London, England: Macmillan and New York: St. Martin's.

Dasgupta, A. K. (1987). "Marginalist challenge", in *Epochs of Economic Theory*, Oxford, UK: Basil Blackwell, pp. 74–98.

Enke, S. (1963). "Population and growth: A general theorem", *Quarterly Journal of Economics*, 77(1), 202–212.

Gordon, R. A. (1967). *Goals of Full-Employment*, New York, USA: John Wiley & Sons.

Heisenberg, W. and Anshen, R. N. (1958). *Physics and Philosophy*, New York: Harper & Brothers Publishers.

Keynes, J. M. ([1930], 1963). "Economic possibilities for our grandchildren", in *John Maynard Keynes Essays in Persuasion*, New York: W.W. Norton, pp. 358–373.

Lawson, T. and Pesaran, H. (1989). "Methodological issues in Keynes' economics: An introduction", in *Keynes' Economics, Methodological Issues*, London, England: Routledge, p. 1.

Lucas, R. E. Jr. (1975), "An equilibrium model of the business cycle", *Journal of Political Economy*, 83, 1113–1144.

Moore, G. E. (1903). *Principia Ethica*, Cambridge, England: Cambridge University Press.

Nicolau, E. (1995). "Cybernetics: The bridge between divided knowledge and interdisciplinarity", *Kybernetes: International Journal of Systems and Cybernetics*, 24(7), 21–25.

O'Donnell, R. M. (1989). "Types of probabilities and their measurement", "Epistemology", in *Keynes: Philosophy, Economics & Politics*, London, England: Macmillan Press Ltd., pp. 50–66, pp. 81–105.

Phelps, E. S. (Ed.) (1970). *Microeconomic Foundations of Employment and Inflation Theory*, New York: W. W. Norton.

Ramsey, F. P. (1928). "A mathematical theory of savings", *Economic Journal*, 38(152), 543–550.

Rawls, J. (1971). *A Theory of Justice*, Cambridge, Massachusetts: Harvard University Press.

Schiller, B. H., Hill, C. and Wall, S. (2012). *The Macroeconomy Today*, 13th Edn., New York: McGraw-Hill Education.

Schumpeter, J. S. (1968). "The scholastic doctors and the philosophers of natural law", in *History of Economic Analysis*, New York: Oxford University Press.

Sen, A. (2012). *Paradigm Lost Conference in Berlin*, https://www.youtube.com/watch?v=OBw5fJkjXiM.

Singer, H. W. and Ansari, J. A. (1988). *Rich Nations and Poor Nations*, London, England: Unwin Hyman.

Staniland, M. (1985). "The fall and rise of political economy", in *What is Political Economy? A Study of Social Theory and Underdevelopment*, New Haven, CT: Yale University Press, pp. 10–35.

Ventelou, B. (2005). "Economic thought on the eve of the General Theory", in *Millennial Keynes*, Chapter 2, Armonk, New York: M. E. Sharpe.

Yeager, L. B. (1997), *The Fluttering Veil, Essays on Monetary Disequilibrium*, Indianapolis, IN: The Liberty Press.

Chapter 9

Monetary, Financial, and Real Economy Issues in TIE in Comparative Perspectives[1]

The following prologue is the starting premise of this chapter:

> "The strenuous purposeful money makers may carry all of us along with them into the lap of economic abundance. But it will be those peoples, who can keep alive, and cultivate into a fuller perfection, the art of life itself and do not sell themselves for the means of life, who will be able to enjoy the abundance when it comes."

Keynes (1963, p. 368)

Such are the messages of moral highness and wisdom picked up in this chapter. The fundamental point here is to establish the fact that the only way of phasing out interest rate from Islamic transactions is to understand and implement the formalism of the inverse relationship that permanently exists between trade in the good things of life and the rate of interest as the impediment to the free flow of resources into such tradable activities. The central bank, the commercial banks, and financial intermediaries as practitioners must understand this organic relational concept of intellection

---

[1]This chapter is a substantively rewritten and expanded version of the paper by Choudhury and Sofyan (2012).

in relation to money and the real economy. The monetary system and the real economy with the financial instruments in between would thus be shown to formalize the intellection paradigm — which indeed is a truly scientific revolution. The result is replacement of the fractional reserve requirement monetary system (RRMS) by the 100% RRMS backed by the gold standard. Likewise, the organic relationships of such a monetary arrangement including its monetary policy and transmission mechanism would structurally change the nature of markets and its institutional relations and individual preferences. The result at the end will be a phased-down interest rate regime changing into a trade-related one by the rise of the tradable relationships that are generated. The foundational methodology that enters this kind of organically relational worldview with the episteme of unity of knowledge (the *Tawhidi* law in Islam) provides the functional ontology of the socially and morally constructed money, production, and real economy circular causation relations. It models the legitimacy of trade as the resource mobilization instrument, while rejecting interest as the permanent impediment of resource mobilization.

Objective

Our objective in this chapter is to explain the necessary and sufficient conditions of economic and social bliss that are reached by the endogenous interaction between money, finance, and the real economy.

The idea of endogenous relations is conveyed by the systemic interrelations between entities and variables of the socio-economic problem under study. These internal dynamics generate causality and learning by interaction. The concept is similar to what Krugman (1989) termed as "self-governing equilibrium" resulting in self-organized behavior. The social and economic changes occur simultaneously with the phasing down of interest rates. This kind of total change is also tantamount to the pursuit of endogenous interrelationships between the central bank, the commercial banks, and the market economy exchanging in the good things of life (*hallal at-tayyabah* in the *Qur'an*) according to *maqasid as-shari'ah*.

The explanation of these kinds of changes is carried out in reference to the same fundamental *Tawhidi* model of unity of knowledge, upon which the *Tawhidi* methodological worldview governing "everything" permanently and indispensably stands.

Zero rate of interest: A necessary but not sufficient instrument for TIE

The experience with the now diminishing *mudarabah* (profit-sharing) and *musharaka* (equity participation) forms of financing proves that these instruments are replaced by secondary financial instruments, all of which are subject to *shari'ah* concerns (Choudhury, 2008a). Likewise, despite earnest efforts to promote Islamic financing and profitability in the face of interest-free financing of projects and investments, Islamic banks in Malaysia could not herald even a distinct prospect for the wellbeing of the *ummah* in the field of Islamic networked flow of resources and organization of institutions for resource sharing (trade). This assertion is borne out by the fact that Islamic banks and development planning in Malaysia never accounted for a clear direction of Islamic financing towards ameliorating either her own broader Islamic global picture or the momentum of trade, development, and related policy instrumentation for the Muslim block.

The current lure with *sukuk*, bonds that revolve around the principal financing instruments of *mudarabah* and *musharakah*, and the market of sale of *musharakah*-linked bonds in real assets to the private sector to finance mega-projects have ended up in deep *shari'ah* concerns (Usmani, n.d; Parker, 2012). *Sukuk* financing problems arise from the sale of debt with interest to private outlets. The *sukuk* holders can then proportion this equity instrument between the government and private businesses through public shareholding. Consequently, the debt coverage in such projects passes on the debt as an intergenerational burden to debtor companies.

An alternative would be for such companies to engage in debt-equity swaps (Krugman, 1989; Blackwell and Nocera, 1989; Choudhury, 1989). Debt-equity swaps involve large investors to retire the debt or a part of it for an indebted country by paying it out in these proportions, i.e. investing to buy the debt. In exchange, the debt-ameliorated country treats such an investment as an equity swap for the debt-retired. Debt-equity swaps can be managed effectively in the case of equity-participation (*musharakah*). The debt overhang and the allowance for financing debt in the private sector is thus at best extended over time, rather than being a comprehensive financing mode that can be instituted for phasing out the interest rate regime caused by debt overhang. The goal of financing interest-bearing, debt-ridden projects by interest-free financing instruments therefore does not cure the interest-rate enigma. Thereby, the true impact of financing by Islamic participatory instruments is not attained, even when the interest-free goal is targeted to reach a given level of acceptance. Yet, in the name of interest-free financing as the focus of Islamic finance, Islamic banks, and finance companies, Muslim governments and large businesses and projects are raising the flag of *sukuk* (Gassner, 2008; *Business Islamica*, 2008).

Capitalization of income flows and the rate of interest

The notion of a low interest rate or phased-down interest rate in economic and financial arrangements has prevailed in the literature. But the concept of how the rate of interest emerges in the economy and how it can be phased out from this system, has not matured either in the mainstream literature and practice or within the theory and practice of Islamic economics and finance. The latter area remains inextricably submerged in mainstream academic thinking relating to money, finance, interest rate, and the real economy relations.

The position of Islamic economics and finance in respect of capitalization of assets with interest-free instruments

Islamic economic and finance gurus have adopted a time value of money discounting approach in asset valuation. They thus failed to understand the interest-rate implications of the discounting approach. The result in asset valuation is that, a future market, which remains undetermined, would be capitalized at a rate either lesser or greater than the expected rate of return on the stream of future income flows. Especially, in such a case of discount-rate indeterminacy, microenterprises have difficulty in tying up commitment to a mark-up that determines the investors' and shareholders' dividends and profits. Microenterprises bear the burden of the excessive cost of capital. The problem arises when large shareholders aim at discounting their risk by taking a larger share of the profits in joint venture. This leaves smaller residual shares and dividends for the small borrowers and participants in Islamic funds. Microenterprises thus find it costly to refinance their assets by means of the lower share of total profits of joint ventures. The same result can swing in favor of microenterprises at the expense of shareholders when an under-valuation of the intergenerational flow of projected returns takes place. In such a case, the question is this: can the investor be risk-averse and divert potential investments into risk-free alternatives, such as short-term trade using the *murabahah* (mark-up) financing instrument? None of these alternatives comes to the benefit of socio-economic development of the community and beyond of the *ummah*.

Indeed, a prevalent problem of Islamic banks is either a lack of investments or an oversubscription of shareholders' capital. These results are reflected in the variable, "financing/deposit ratio", which is found to move away on either side from the expected value of unity (Choudhury, 2009) in Islamic banks. Islamic banks in Indonesia show such financing problems in their annual reports (Bank Muamalat, 2007; Bank Mandiri, 2006). Consequently, although interest-free financing has been promoted by Islamic banks, yet the method towards realizing this goal has not been well defined in terms of investment, liquidity problem, asset valuation, and socio-economic development of the *ummah*. Besides, it was pointed out above that secondary financing instruments have been used in place of the principal Islamic financing instruments to legitimate in favor of operations in interest-free financing. Yet, there are looming *shari'ah* problems relating to interest rates in these secondary financing instruments. Two of these problems are as follows: The first one is the absence of the idea of "pooled funds" made by combining individual types of financing modes. The *shari'ah* gurus have not looked into this possibility. We have referred to this kind of participatory portfolio earlier in this book. The second one is the difference of the often-used jargon of "*shari'ah*-compliance" differently from the great purpose and objective of the *shari'ah*, known as the *maqasid as-shari'ah* (Choudhury, 2009).

Both of these approaches in asset valuation and financing run into the same kinds of methodological problems. These problems in turn generate ineffective socio-economic development effects.

The money, finance, and real economy (MFRE) relationships in an interest-free regime of socio-economic change

Islamic economists argue on behalf of establishing an interest-free regime of socio-economic change by retaining the existing fractional monetary reserve system, despite introducing the compelling need for delivering social justice (Chapra, 1985). The arguments, prescriptions, and implementation of such an approach through interest-free targeting are untenable. We explain this problem here in terms of a general system of comprehensive socio-economic transformation.

It was explained in the previous chapter that, if interest-based financing is inverted by the rise of trade-based instruments in the Islamic case, then there is a decreasing need and incentive for holding savings in banks and capital markets. Consequently, Islamic banks become outlets of mobilizing savings *continuously* into spending in the good and productive things of life. This process, which is *continuous*, generates participatory dynamics between spending possibilities (relations) and between their entities. The entities are symbolized by their representative factors denoting socio-economic variables and financing instrumental variables, as formalized in Chapter 8. These variables define the relations and represent the agencies (e.g. agents, institutions, markets, etc., underlying the relations and their constituent variables). Indeed, the Islamic world system, within which are studied the complementary relations between money, finance, and the real economy, is fully participatory in nature

(Choudhury *et al.*, 2008). The result then is to interactively integrate the three domains — MFRE in participatory ways, so that they learn continuously by circular causation between them.

How can an Islamic capital market arise from the circular causation relations of complementarities between money, finance, and the real economy? The transformation into the complementary linkages remains hampered by the blockage in the flow of resources in the mere presence of the catchword "*shari'ah*-compliance" idea. A better possibility for realizing the impact of interest-free financing in the real economy is to establish the wide range of linkages that MFRE interrelations generate and are sustained.

Therefore, to base all transactions on interest-free instruments in the Islamic economic and financial system is only *a necessary condition* of Islamizing the financing and banking system. By itself, the abolition of interest financing is *not a sufficient condition* in establishing the alternative of trade and participatory development in the Islamic *ummah*. It is therefore necessary to combine the interest-free transformation as a process that is linked with a simultaneous change in monetary policies and money–finance–real economy relations. Such relations are generated between the central bank, the commercial bank, and the real economy by circular causation. The resulting new economic arrangement based on complementary circular causation between variables and their representative agents would cause the emergence of unified and synergetic interrelationships between the monetary system, financial instrumentation, and the real economy. We now turn to a formalism of the underlying dynamics in such a case.

The circular causation between the central bank, commercial banks, and the real economy in the midst of MFRE relations

Consider the case of continuous regeneration and flow of all forms of resource that remain interconnected by causality. The emergent circular connections explain the circular-causation relations between the various entities. Most importantly, in this kind of circular-causation relations, there occur the simultaneously complementary and participatory linkages between the central bank, the commercial banks (Islamic banks and other banks), and the resulting complementarities in the real economy between the good things of life, as ordained by the *maqasid as-shari'ah*. Such unifying relationships bring out the nature of monetary policy and the complementary money, finance, and market relational transformation in TIE. There is no equivalent explanation for such participatory relations in Islamic economics as we know it.

TIE is essentially based on free-market orientation. But at the same time, it is guided by knowledge induction and appropriate *shari'ah* instruments and policies to realize resource mobilization into the good things of life. In this respect, the central bank generates a supply of money as required by the market-oriented projects in which commercial banks become partners with the market-determined projects. Contrarily, the central bank avoids maintaining the supply of money to banks in excess reserve. This would otherwise cause multiple credit creation backed by promissory notes. Also, the intent of the underlying Islamic monetary policy is to attain a stable and productive macroeconomic state of the general (circular) flows of goods and services in physical and monetary terms and with total moral/ethical valuation as explained in Chapter 8.

Thus, in the Islamic case, the concept of money supply is replaced by the concept of "quantity of *micro-money*" pursuing the needs of specific projects that are based on the tenets of *maqasid as-shari'ah*. The concepts of demand and supply of money are untenable. These concepts are now replaced by that of "quantity of *micro-money that is specific* to approved projects". In other words, such projects are financed by the full quantum of a given quantity of circulation of micromoney in specific projects, as needed. An example of such project-specific quantity of micromoney is given by the real bills (Green, 1989). Real bills can be endogenously generated by commercial banks under the authority of the central bank (Green, 1989). Now, there would be an automatic equilibrium circulation of currency through the commercial banks entering the real economy. This kind of an evolutionary equilibrium process of money, finance, and real resource linkage must however be governed by appropriate central bank regulations on sustaining a stable and growing economy in the absence of *riba* and in the presence of trade as exchange according to choices under *maqasid as-shari'ah*.

Case 1 of monetary mobilization: Perfect 100% RRMS

We note in the TIE context of micromoney that there is no excess creation of money by the central bank when an automatic equilibrium process is maintained between the monetary flows generated by resource linkages between the commercial banks and the real economy. The commercial banks under the authority of central bank guidance can generate the real bills (micromoney) for the increased resource mobilization as needed. Alternatively, it is possible that central banks create the extra quantity of money needed to finance a growing real economy. The cost underlying this additional flow of a quantity of money will be recovered from bank seigniorage. This is revenue raised by the central bank to cover the cost of producing a quantity of money by gold-backing. The cost will be collected from the borrowing commercial banks that themselves earn participatory returns from the yields of the real economy funding of projects, also from market exchange in approved goods and services. The central bank and commercial bank interrelationship abides. The quantity of money required to finance additional projects in the real economy arises from the increased demand for goods and services that result in project development.

Now, on the one side, there is the quantity of goods and services in demand. On the other side, this demand in the real economy is satisfied by monetary injection that is carried over by financial instruments including currency in circulation. This injection of money equals a quantity of currency in circulation. The carrier of this circularly regenerated monetary stock through the real economy in response to the demand for regenerated resources, comprise the bundle of trade-related instruments. Trade and commerce thereby replace interest-based businesses of all kinds. The principal meaning and objective of the quantity of money now becomes the need for currency to finance productive *maqasid* projects in response to the increased demand for the corresponding kinds of goods and services connected with such approved projects in the light of the *shari'ah*. An effective transmission of money through financial instruments would thus take place to finance the real economy of goods, services, and projects in the light of *maqasid as- shari'ah.*

The result thus is contrary to bank savings. We mean by bank savings the part of the earned and national income that is withheld by banks to serve interest-bearing and speculative portfolio over time. Now, just as trade increases, the flow of resource into the real economy is enhanced. The quantity of micromoney increases in pursuit of such a real demand for goods and services connected with projects. The diversion of income into bank savings to earn interest rate is diminished. This kind of internal adjustment in the financing medium brings out the logical and formal basis of trade, thus positively affecting resource mobilization through the market-oriented real economic transformation with linkage to monetary flows through financing instruments. The consequence of this kind of circular flow dynamics is a continuous liquidation of savings at every moment of time in the life of the economy by its mobilization into approved spending outlets in a market economy that remains conscious of *maqasid as-shari'ah*. The emphasis on such an ethicizing market economy transformation is not the way of present days' Islamic economics. The latter study promotes excessive government and institutional governance that defies endogenous ethical market transformation.

Case 2: Imperfect 100% RRMS with excess demand by commercial bank

However, when the total financing cannot be met by the available bank deposits by households, wherein savings = resource mobilization continuously generated, the banks call for additional financing from shareholders and depositors. The expansion of a quantity of money by the central bank can be loaned out to the commercial banks to finance projects. In such a case, the (financing/deposit)-ratio exceeds unity. The principal shareholder/stakeholder of the Islamic banks, in the sense of the lender of last resort, is the central bank. Besides, other principal shareholders' share-capital can be secured in the central bank for the benefit of lending to commercial banks in the situation of excess demand for funds to finance approved projects.

Case 3: Lower demand for financing the real sector

There is yet another type of monetary flow between the commercial banks and the central bank. When the demand for money to finance projects declines due to lower market demand, the "excess reserve" in commercial banks is liquidated. The resulting amount of unmobilized financial resources cannot remain in the commercial banks. The commercial banks are not allowed to hold this saving as excess reserve, for fear of causing multiple credit creation, and thereby cause all the ills this carries. Excess reserves held in commercial banks will otherwise negate the above-mentioned dynamics of trade-over saving in regenerating resources and the quantity of micromoney to meet the real demand for goods, services, and projects. The unutilized savings must thus be deposited fully as "reserve" with the central bank. Such transfer of central bank reserve forms inventory of unmobilized monetary stock. Such reserve is now held with the central bank. They will form Islamic instruments once again when they are mobilized through the commercial banks upon demand. The fund remains with the central bank until it is called back by the commercial banks to finance subsequent rounds of enhanced demand in the real economy.

The central bank holds none of the statutory reserve. This though is the ideal case of 100% utilization of commercial bank micromoney (real bills) in the real economy in pursuit of approved possibilities. Say, an initial amount from the central bank to the market via commercial banks is the case where the investment demand in the real economy is high and the commercial banks fall short of this amount to finance all projects. Consequently, the (financing/deposit)-ratio exceeds unity.

Case 4: Resource leakages from the banking system under fractional reserve requirement

We next examine the possibility of resource leakage from the banking system. The important issue here is to note that the quantity of money exists in circularity between the demand of the real sector, the availability of loanable funds by the banks, and the additional requirements from the central bank.

In the last case, certain amounts of funds could fail to meet the requirements of the real economy, thus causing leakages from the desired MFRE interrelationship. Indeed, the usual case of resource mobilization must accept leakages through the commercial banks in the real economy linkages with financial instruments carrying money.

Consequently, the resulting contraction of yields in the real economy allows for say, $900 resource mobilization out of $1,000 with the banks. This would then cause $100 to remain as savings in the commercial banks to yield interest income on idle financial resources when fractional reserves return is allowed. Thereby, the inter-bank flows of such savings in speculative assets will trigger multiple credit creation and an accumulating amount of interest cost on debt capital.

To avoid such a situation when the resources are not fully mobilized into the real economy, the commercial banks hand over the $100 unutilized financial resource to the central bank for safe-keeping. *This amount becomes the 100% potential reserve of the commercial bank in a monetary arrangement with the central bank.* Note here that this definition of the 100% RRMS with the gold standard (explained in the following), is quite different from the 100% reserve requirement monetary idea explained in the literature (Rist, 1940; Friedman, 1968).

The commercial bank would use this "saved" resource at a later date on the basis of its legitimate claim based on credit-worthiness due to increased possibility in financing diversified projects. At the time of such a future release of funds from the central bank, the 100% reserve converts to money in circulation in the form of a quantity of currency as money.

The central bank is entrusted with the protection of the value of the under-utilized resources through the commercial banks. This exchange-value protection cannot be done by paper and promissory notes or by any such *numeraire* whose long-term stability is in question. The choice is gold as the required stable monetary *numeraire*. The long-term stability of gold has been proven historically (Choudhury and Hoque, 2004). Thus, a stock of gold (denoted by G) is stored by the central bank to stabilize the value of the central bank reserve, which subsequently becomes the currency in circulation.

It can be proved that the value of gold, which protects the marginal amount of money by a corresponding marginal amount of gold stock simultaneously, protects the entire currency as money in circulation in the real economy. Thus, only effective pricing in the real economy values the currency value per unit of gold-backing of temporarily unmobilized commercial bank reserve held with the central bank as 100% RRMS.

Central bank functions in 100% RRMS

The conclusion now is astounding. A small amount of gold is needed to protect the entire stock of currency in circulation. The regulatory condition though is this: the central bank must regulate the stable price of gold over the long run. Stability of gold price can be maintained by regulating the stock of gold in the economy/society. The Islamic state has the duty of moral suasion to attain such a goal of moderation on holding gold as precious metal.

The same kind of regulation is extended to the mixed precious bi-metals, gold and silver. In the 100% RRMS, the role of the central bank in monetary management is reduced to policy-making and regulation for supervising a sustainable market economy in approved goods, services, and projects. This situation would involve supervising the management of a stable and growing economy in concert with the participation of commercial banks as the principal medium for mobilizing money and finance between banks, the financial sector, and the real economy.

The power of creating money by the central bank is reduced to managing a stock of gold to maintain the value of money as currency in circulation (see Money Matters http://www.themoneymasters. com/mra.htm). This function too is inversely related with the velocity and volume of the circularly mobilized money and finance through the real economy.

Gaining from the extensively participatory nature of the 100% RRMS and the real economy, the central bank also engages in a *continuous* activity of knowledge sharing with the central bank and the agents representing the real economy. This generates an overarching "learning process" toward determining the general system relations involving the central bank, the commercial banks, and the real economy. Thereby, technical analysis, the resulting information sharing, and development of such learnt policies and endogenous learning experiences become the principal attributes in central bank function in the MFRE interrelationships with 100% RRMS.

All functions conventionally endowed on the central bank cease to have effect. Undue governance as by government, central bank, and monetary policies is replaced by the participatory decision-making analytical forums of discourse and conscious-invoking. The conventional functions including those promoted in present days' Islamic economics on the other hand are money supply and monetary regulation, interest rate and exchange-rate setting by regulating the monetary reserve of the countries' balance of payments. All these targets are converted into endogenous causality in the 100% RRMS of TIE. Inflation targeting too is left to market adjustment in the midst of the features of 100% RRMS with the protection of exchange value by the gold standard and the micromonetary perspective of project financing.

The *Laissez-faire* concept of money and medium of exchange in the literature: Micromoney

Our delineation of a predominantly commercial banking role in resource mobilization in the real economy with the central bank being a lender of last resort and an overseer of the currency value in market exchange in terms of a quantity of gold-backing, has strong precedence in the literature (Saving, 1977; Klein, 1975; Tullock, 1976; Tobin, 1963). Hayek thought about such a kind of private monetary system in which private banks will play the role of money in circulation (Hayek, 1976). In this case, private money would all be valued on the basis of a given standard, such as gold, but they would compete with each other. In other words, competing quantities of money would be held by private institutions, especially banks, and this would be like holding money in terms of financial and other assets.

Yeager (1997, pp. 412–413) writes in regard to privately supplied money: "Commercial banks would supply such funds. The central bank's authority in such a monetary system would be minimal." This is his prescription of monetary reform, which Yeager expands upon the work of Black, Fama, and Hall (BFH) (Yeager, 1983): "Government would be banished from any role in the monetary system other than that of defining a unit of account or *numeraire*. We envisage a unit defined by a bundle of goods and services comprehensive enough for the general level of prices quoted in it to be practically steady. Merely by conducting its own accounting and transactions in the Unit — we tentatively so name it, with a capital U — the government would give private parties a strong incentive to adopt the same Unit."

Yeager (1997, p. 413) continues: "No longer would the size of the *numeraire*, one Unit, be determined by the supply and demand for any medium of exchange. The Unit would be defined by goods and services having supplies and demands of an almost entirely *non-monetary* character."

The praxis of the Islamic approach to trade and interest relationship

Our arguments establish the fact that interest-rate eradication in the Islamic economy cannot be enforced by exogenous imposition of policies and restrictive measures. If it is so, as is presently practiced by Islamic venues, the replacement of the interest rate will not be sustained without simultaneously charting the constructive change that the trade and financing instruments must generate between money, finance, and the real economy. Presently, there is no such attempt by Islamic banks and Muslim countries in their Islamicization experiment. Consequently, the programme of Islamicization of the financial sector has not proceeded to the extent of contributing to the rise of the *ummah* endowed by its own capital markets, inter-communal international trade dynamics, coordinated markets, and socio-economic development programmes along the direction of life-fulfillment regimes. This is the continued import of idea from our earlier mentioned ones. That is, merely a construal of interest-free financing modes does not form an adequate benchmark of the *shari'ah*. Islamicization is not an adequate approach in such a partial view of Islamic change. The *ummah* view, in which MFRE interrelationships play the crucial role of structural change and monetary reform must emanate from the general system objective based on the epistemology of systemic unity of knowledge.

We have argued and explained that the Islamic programme to phase out interest rate and replace them with trade instruments must be carried out within a generalized evolutionary equilibrium system of circular causal relations between money, finance, and the real economy. This would simultaneously involve pervasively complementary interrelations between the central bank, the commercial banks, and the functioning of the 100% reserve requirements monetary system with the gold standard. Such pervasively complementary relations generate organic relations in reference to the epistemology of systemic unity of knowledge.

Thus, the question arises: can the central principle of pervasive complementarities be derived from any other epistemological premise other than the *Qur'anic* foundations? We note here the empirical and policy directional role played by the principle of pervasive complementarities in explaining the epistemology of unity of knowledge by using the constructed functional ontology of that unity in diverse problems of the world system. In this chapter, we have narrowed down such a treatment to the topic of MFRE participatory unity of relations.

The answer to the above question is in the negative. The dividing line between Islam and all other comparative socio-scientific systems is the ultimate quintessence of epistemological reference to the oneness of God, *Tawhid* as belief and as law, or equivalently, the principle of unity as law in respect of organic relationals between the *maqasid*-goods. This worldview projects the episteme of unity of knowledge in relation to the world-system. In all other socio-scientific systems, the origin of knowledge is premised on the epistemology of rationalism. Rationalism and its entire constructed system operate on the basis of methodological individualism, conflict, competition and notions of scarcity of resources, and thereby, of substitution between contested entities. The rationalist mind is inextricably rooted in such behavior at the level of the individual, institution, society, and human relations. Such a character remains globally at large in this rationalist world system. Even socio-scientific theories and programmes of rationalist origin stand upon this nature of the world system and "everything" in it (Barrow, 1991; Von Mises, 1976; Choudhury, 2008b).

Extending the arguments to the open economy case

Two cases need to be studied here. The first one is when a regional group together adopts a common currency. Such an arrangement is gaining grounds. It is voiced strongly by Mundell (2000) in respect of his prescription for a one-world currency. Likewise, there is the Euro, the American dollar, and there used to be a growing interest in a common Gulf Cooperation Council (GCC) currency following the inception of a future GCC common market and monetary union. In our case, the example is of an incomplete regional arrangement for the 100% reserve requirements with the gold standard. Such an imperfect 100% RRMS can learn along evolutionary processes into the higher echelons of its realization.

In the latter case, the fractional reserve monetary system is treated as dual with the Islamic banking system. Chapter 10 would be necessary to establish the desired MFRE interrelations. This kind of an incomplete monetary transformation is presently practised by some Islamic financial outlets, notably the Islami Bank Bangladesh and the Islamic Society of North America Housing Co-operative. In general, the phasing out of interest rates in Islamic financial operations is embedded in a general system of simulated interrelations that must be realized with the simultaneous development of the emergent trade versus interest paradigm. Following such a recent development, a return to the 100% RRMS with the gold standard would be extended within the segmented region idea that would adopt this arrangement. The principle of resource mobilization is promoted in regional grouping to establish a complementary and participatory trade and development regime. A regulatory and combining market–institutional interactive learning medium is enhanced by means of active networking between partners and Islamic banks.

A given stock of gold is parceled through the medium of an Islamic bank for settlement of payments. This is a significant global project that can be considered by the Islamic Development Bank. Since the stock of gold required for stabilizing currencies would not be great and would be inversely proportional to the extent and speed of effective resource mobilization, therefore a large stock of gold and its minting cost would be avoided. Besides, the cost of gold minting would be covered by the seigniorage that the central bank would collect from the commercial banks in terms of the cost of production of gold required to protect the currency value with a legitimate mark-up (Black, 1989) of the reserve held. Seigniorage would also be collected by participatory arrangements that would exist in a cooperative agreement to share risk and returns between the central bank and commercial banks, and between the commercial banks and the clientele in the real economy. The latter case is well-known in the profit-loss (*mudarabah*) and equity participation (*musharakah*) arrangements of Islamic banks.

For the participatory sharing of risk and return between the central bank and the commercial banks, the resulting seigniorage arises in the case of partial resource mobilization by the commercial banks. Now, the commercial banks share the services that the central bank renders by paying for these services in terms of the cost of procuring gold stock by the central bank plus a service charge on the commercial banks. The commercial banks can roll over this cost to their clientele in the real economy by way of service charges. This shows that both service charges and interest rates are inversely related to productivity and product and risk diversifications. These positive changes are causally related to resource mobilization through commercial banks.

The principal cost that would exist is caused by leakages. This is where the full productivity of the use of money and finance in the real economy fails — always, partially, but increasingly so in the interest-bearing system. In order to reduce such leakages and share in the full realization of profitability and cost reduction, Islamic banks benefit from the joint consequences of risk and product diversifications. These conditions always exist effectively in a joint pursuit of resource mobilization, which is exemplified by the Islamic economic and financial system in TIE.

The paradigm of the participatory, thus endogenous relations between the central bank, commercial banks (Islamic banks), and the real economy remains unchanged for the open economy, as is the case with the closed domestic economy. In the open economy case, the national central bank, commercial, and real economy relations are further extended by the bank of international settlements of payments in the Islamic-networked monetary arrangement.

Productivity-determined exchange rate in 100% RRMS with the gold standard

The exchange rate (E) is defined on grounds of productivity relations, avoiding the monetary intervention except in exigency of under-mobilization of financial resources. The following formula reflects this:

$$\text{Terms-of-trade,} \quad t = p_X.X/p_M.M, \tag{9.1}$$

where X denotes volume of exports, p_X denotes price export, M denotes volume of imports, and p_M denotes price of imports.

Rewrite Equation (9.1) as

$$E = p_X/p_M = t.(M/X) \text{ is the nominal exchange rate.} \qquad (9.2)$$

Because X and M are both determined by their similar dynamics within the country-specific or region-specific 100% RRMS with the gold standard, therefore, (M/X) assumes a stable value, say "a". Thereby,

$$E = a.t, \qquad (9.3)$$

where E defines the exchange rate. It is shown to have a stable relationship with the terms-of-trade variable.

As free trade expands between partners in the region with full or partial 100% RRMS with the gold standard, as explained above, then M/X tends to 1. Hence, trade liberalization along with a phase of transformation into a 100% RRMS arrangement within and across the integrating region, result in stability of the exchange rate and the terms-of-trade simultaneously.

It is implied from our continuing formalism in the following section that with greater speed of economic integration, institutional networking of every kind, technological diffusion, factor mobility, and production and risk diversifications in the midst of the 100% RRMS arrangement, Expression (9.3) will cause an upward trend in t, and thereby, in E. The coefficient "a" will be induced by the force of economic integration, which in our case of participatory trade and development is based on learning and endogenous interrelations in the spirit of systemic unity of knowledge.

The functions of money in the 100% RRMS

The issue of resource mobilization in trade versus financial interest implies that increased complementarities in the system are required so as to simulate the wellbeing that is attained from such complementarities over learning processes. The function of money, finance, and Islamic banks is precisely to attain this wellbeing objective that yields the total valuation of the ethical economy.

So, what are the functions of monetary aggregate in such a system?

Money is not a store of value in TIE

Is money a *store of value*? The value of money arises from the real economy in terms of *maqasid*-approved exchange of goods, services, and project financing. The absence of the property of a store of value in money means that there is no productive value in money as such. Rather, the stability of currency value in international exchange is attained by means of the gold standard in the way as we have explained for the 100% RRMS in MFRE circular causation relations.

Money is indeed a unit of value in exchange in TIE

Is money a *unit* of exchange? Yes, this is true, for money in 100% RRMS determines the true relationship between the unit value of money and the price of goods and services in exchange. Currency is equivalent to money in circulation in this system. This amount of money that remains in circulation is supported by the gold standard in order to be stable in international exchange value, forming this sound money as currency (Von Mises, 1981).

Indeed, the Prophet Muhammad informally denominated various values to monetary units called *danaq* and *mithqal* in terms of physical units of basic needs (Allouche, 1994). The importance of denominations of weights and measures appears in the *Qur'an* (83:1): "Woe to the defaulters in weights and measures, those who take full measure when they take from men and who give less when they measure out to them or weigh to them."

Money is not necessarily a medium of exchange in TIE

Is money a *medium* of exchange? This property of money is true only in the static case of exchange. In the intertemporal case of resource mobilization, it is difficult to ascertain the state of demand and supply of goods and services at future time-periods. It is also difficult to ascertain the risk-contingencies that exist at future points of time. Also, consumer preferences, systemic risk, and costs of future flows of goods and services, and financial demand in projects are based on subjective factors and are thus undeterminable. Consequently, it is impossible to ascertain the value of goods and services in exchange, and thereby, the value of money that would back up such a real economic value. Therefore, money does not have any market of its own, which otherwise would result in interest rate as the price of money and financial instruments. Islamic money being micromoney and specific to projects that need to be financed, the quantity of money (currency) in circulation in the economy is determined by full quantum flows into projects. This requires such projects to exist to match up its market value with the quantity of micromoney that is mobilized by financial instruments. We write the equation of the quantity of micromoney as follows in this case between micromoney and project-specific financing:

$$M * V = P * y, \text{ or } M = (P * y)/V. \tag{9.4}$$

When $V = 1$ or 100% circulation (full micromoney mobilization through banks), then

$$M = P * y. \tag{9.5}$$

Expression (9.4) means that the value of a stock of micromoney equals the total spending value in terms of the prices and quantities of approved goods and services in exchange pertaining to specific projects (activities).

Note that "y" denotes real output. Thus, an alternative definition of money is the value of GDP, which in turn represents the value of all spending (expenditures). But all these implications are specified in respect of projects, rather than by the economy as a whole. We therefore, interpret that a quantity of money, M, is driven fully into financing a project(s). This is the meaning of full quantum financing of projects by micromoney.

Hence, $V \cong 1$. This is equivalent to the consequence of 100% RRMS in which any saved (unmobilized) money as currency is totally surrendered to the central bank. Otherwise, the micromoney as currency would be totally mobilized as resource to fit into projects in the real economy.

We can write Equation (9.5) in the light of the project-specific condition of micromoney transmission (M^*) through commercial banks as

$$M^* = \sum_i M_i = \sum P_i.y_i = P.y \text{ for the economy-wide case.} \quad (9.6)$$

These kinds of project-specific circulation of micromonetary "units" were considered by Yeager (1983) in his *laissez-faire* approach to monetary reform. Yeager's *Unit* of money and Hayek's (1976) *competitive currency units* are weighted against a bundle of goods and services whose prices remain stable by the forces of supply and demand in market exchange against the value of the currencies used as monetary units for denoting exchange value of real goods and services. This kind of currency valuation against the real goods and services in market exchange can be used both in the regional and international sense. On top of this, there is the multiplier affecting real goods and services and thereby money in circulation that carry the total valuation of the transforming moral/ethical real economy.

For example, units of currency can be the Islamic Dinar. The common commodity base for valuation is gold and silver in the 100% RRMS with the gold standard. Yet, the currencies in circulation may not be strictly in terms of these precious metals. Any government-certified way of holding money as a means of settling payments nationally, regionally, and internationally can be protected by the minting of the "residual" stock of gold, G.

In the end: Functions of money

We have debated against the notions of demand and supply of money, and replaced the concept of quantity of micromoney mobilized into projects through the banking sector in complementary relations with the real economy and by appropriate participatory financing instruments. This chapter has also rejected the unquestioned acceptance of the notions of the mainstream functions of money in prevalent Islamic economic ideas. Of these, only the function of unit of exchange as it is actually realized or intertemporally established with market transactions is acceptable.

The function of store of value for money is untenable, for value is jointly claimed by money and market exchange of real *maqasid*-related goods and services as they are temporally realized as payments get settled. The function of money as the medium of exchange is rejected in the absence of well-determined exchange values of goods and services over time.

Von Mises (1981, p. 84) writes in regard to the notion of money as a medium of exchange (slightly edited):

> Its (state) task thus becomes that of determining, in accordance with the intent of the contracting parties, what is to be understood by money in commercial transactions. From the legal point of view, money is not the common medium of exchange, but the common medium of payment of debt settlement.

In TIE, we go a step further by arguing that money is a convention to settle payment contracts at *every* determined moment of clearly realized market exchange in the real economy across the model of interaction, integration, and evolutionary learning. These are the logical properties of TIE.

Conclusion: Inferences on the Islamic alternative regarding global financial crisis

Islamic banks are claimed to have remained safe from the financial crisis that is sweeping the world today. Central banks of most countries have cut down their prime lending rates to near zero to stimulate consumer and investment lending. Yet, the deepening crisis continues. Islamic banks although insulated from the global financial crisis due to their operations that do not involve the stock market and speculative financing, yet have not gained advantage of the situation to contribute to the future of the *ummah*. And thereby to show the path out of the crisis for the rest of the world, except by pointing out the zero-interest agenda and the alternative trade financing instruments.

This chapter argued that reducing the financial interest toward zero is not a new recommendation of any economic system during financial crisis. Spending and innovation require venture capital to be freely mobilized by development-financing instruments through commercial banks. Yet, such a central bank policy is not taking effect toward stabilizing the global financial system.

This chapter points out that simultaneously with the phasing out of interest rate to zero, it is necessary to reconstruct the general system design of the relations between the central bank, the commercial bank, and the real economy. Within such general system reconstruction must be taken up all such circular causation synergies that establish pervasive complementarities between the productive and socially good things of life. We have denied the caption "*shari'ah*-compliant" to these goods. Instead, we have emphasized the much-forgotten substantive term today, *maqasid as-shari'ah*. The *maqasid*-goods meet the demands of the greater purpose of wellbeing that is embedded in the wider field of valuation including moral and ethical values with material ones.

The result would be a panacea for the Muslim and non-Muslim alike — because unethical, unsocial, and thereby, immoral things are equally abhorred by all peoples and cultures. Most fundamentally, underlying this common heritage of mankind upon which to build, renew, or reconstruct old and fallen systems, there is the epistemological shift away from rationalism. Rationalism breeds methodological individualism and the inextricable problem of heteronomy. This is the broken glass of reality breeding entropy. Contrarily, the epistemology of systemic unity of knowledge as the core of unity of the *Tawhidi* law in relation to the unity of the world system, establishes the world system on the foothold of organic participation and thereby cooperation in the good things of life while sorting out the unwanted ones.

Discourse with convergence towards consensus is the goal and the result universally. Discourse leads to new pattern of monetary futures. The global financial crisis requires a change in the monetary arrangements along with fiscal stimulus through reduced interest rates to restore stability. Likewise, the reality of organic unity of relations between the good things of life that sustain a healthy society and economy, mind and material artefacts is the most natural order and scheme of everything. Any system that competes itself and does not participate and complement in the attempt to interconnect amicably within system is bound to fail by the futile objective of specialization and maximization of the acquisitive self. These social predicaments are not realities of systems. They are imposed by the rationality axioms of certain self-interested psyche. That is what we find in the artificial configuration of the mainstream and neoclassical economic science as a specialization which has left out moral, ethical, and social reality in everything. See the following exercise.

Our above-mentioned recommendations can be extended for global institutional reform. In that case, the central banks of member states would be superseded by a regional bank of reconstruction and development. In the case of the Islamic *ummah*, such a global monetary reform can be guided by Islamic Development Bank.

On such an issue, the International Monetary Fund (IMF) (2008) has a standing idea. The IMF, U.S. Treasury Secretary muses on such a direction of monetary reform in the following words (IMF, 2008):

> "This is an important moment for the IMF and its future. The IMF has a critical role to play in the global resolution of the financial crisis. The proposed modernizing reforms will begin the process of making the IMF more representative of the global economy. It is strongly in the U.S. interest that the Fund fulfills these responsibilities in order to retain its relevance and preeminent place in the international monetary system. The need for a strong and effective IMF is all the more pressing in the challenging global economic environment we find ourselves in today." (http://www.treas.gov/press/releases/hp1307.html, U.S. Department of the Treasury, Deputy Assistant Secretary Sobel Remarks on the Global Financial Crisis and the IMF's Response, Dec. 2, 2008).

The above quote signifies the urgency of the time to launch the blueprint of a future reform of the monetary system in conjunction with the outlook of the MFRE unity of organic relations to gain global economic and financial stability. This chapter has pointed out what structure of reasoning and institutional change will be required inside such an alternative form of MFRE interlinked system in the Islamic economic and financial framework.

Exercise 1

1. Draw figures to explain the three kinds of monetary, financial, and real economy relations in 100% RRMS.
2. Now, insert the following values in different loops in the figures to denote financial resource mobilization as in (9.1):

   (i) Full mobilization of $1,000 into the real economy through the commercial banks, and recursive accumulation of savings as capital for remobilization at a rate of 5% through each sequence of savings mobilized as financial resource.

   (ii) Mobilization of $900 out of $1,000 of financial resources into the real economy through the commercial banks at an yield on returning savings of 5% per sequence.

   (iii) Mobilization of financial resource to meet excess demand of $1,500 in the real economy in relation to the creation of additional money by the central bank for commercial banks to meet the excess demand.

3. Set up the objective criterion of wellbeing for simulating the MFRE circular causation relations.
4. How is the total valuation measured by the wellbeing function (*maslaha*)?
5. Draw the figure of systemic interrelationships that we find in an interconnected enterprise with organic linkages to various sectoral parts of the social economy that aims at its total valuation with the good things of life (e.g. stakeholder model of social decision-making). As an example, define total valuation by the wellbeing function as usual as we have defined this concept of *maslaha* throughout this book.

Example

Assume the following information:

1. Savings $(S(\theta))$ are formed in Islamic banks by continuous mobilization of funds and thus extensive *organic pairing,* i.e. *complementarities in the sense of total valuation* $(\{\theta\})$. Say $S(\theta) = S_0(\theta)$ to start with.

2. Let $r(\theta)$ denote rate of return from the total valuation ($\{\theta\}$).
3. R_i denotes resources in the real economy across total valuation $E(\theta) = \{\theta, \mathbf{X}(\theta), t(\theta)\}$.
4. Rounds of inter-causality around the system interconnecting money (central bank), finance (Islamic banks), and the real economy ($\mathbf{X}(\theta)$) depend upon knowledge regeneration over time ($t(\theta)$). Let $\mathbf{X}(\theta)$ include $S(\theta)$.
5. Thus, MFRE activities are regenerated over $E(\theta) = \{\theta, \mathbf{X}(\theta), t(\theta)\}$.

Consider the following cases of interrelations between central bank, Islamic banks, and real economy, i.e. between money, finance, and the real economy (MFRE) in the case of 100% RRMS:

1. Full mobilization of S_0 through financing (i.e. finance/deposit ratio = 1). This is the ideal case of 100% RRMS with the Islamic banks holding all the savings as reserve for continuous mobilization into the real economy. That is, excess reserve = 100%. The central bank does not hold any reserve. That is, statutory reserve = 0%.

$S_0(\theta_0, X_0, t_0)$.

In the second round of resource mobilization, $S_1 = S_0(1 + r_1)$; all variables are θ-induced in rounds of total valuation. The assumption here is that all of savings when mobilized generates activities that increases at least by the rate "r".
The nth round of such regenerating of MFRE causes total resources allocation $= S_0 \Pi_{i=1}^n (1 + r_i)$.
The financial statements are as follows:
Central bank statutory reserve = 0; Islamic bank excess reserve = 100%; resource in the real economy $= S_i, i = 1, 2, \ldots, n$; and yield equals $S_0 \Pi_{i=1}^n (1 + r_i)$.
2. Excess demand for mobilization, resource $R_i > S_i, i = 1, 2, \ldots, n$. Same conditions hold relating to $E(\theta) = \{\theta, \mathbf{X}(\theta), t(\theta)\}$. This is the case of (i.e. finance/deposit ratio > 1).
Now, the central bank creates the excess demand of money worth of $(R_i - S_i)$ to Islamic banks to finance required projects in the

real economy to earn "r". The condition for 100% RRMS is once again completed with the central bank as the lender of last resort. The value of "r" as profit-sharing rate is then shared between the central bank (r_c), Islamic banks (r_b), and the agents in the real economy (r_e). Note that the yield increases with the wider valuation meaning of "θ" to include all forms of increasing returns to scale continuously over the events $E(\theta)$. The resources are regenerated in rounds of $E(\theta)$ and distributed by the respective shares. The central bank claim of $(R_i - S_i)$ is completed by the Islamic banks. The agents of the real economy participate in making up for this principal of excess demand for resources in the real economy.

The financial statements are as follows:

Central bank statutory reserve $= 0$; Islamic bank excess reserve $= 100\%$, with $S_0 < R_0$; resource in the real economy $= S_i$, $i = 1, 2, \ldots, n$ are generated as follows: $R_i^* \Pi_{i=1}^n (1 + r_{ei})$. "$r_{ei}$" denotes profit-sharing rate for the real economy in the ith round of real economic activity corresponding to circular causation by $\{\theta_i\}$-values explaining total valuation.

3. Excess demand for mobilization, resource $S_i > R_i, i = 1, 2, \ldots, n$. Same conditions hold relating to $E(\theta) = \{\theta, \mathbf{X}(\theta), t(\theta)\}$. This is the case of (finance/deposit ratio < 1).

In this case, the excess savings over resource used for *maqasid*-spending (emphasized by "θ" values are $(S_i - R_i), i = 1, 2, \ldots, n$. This quantity of financing is deposited by Islamic banks with the central bank in order to avoid multiple credit creation on excess reserves. The 100% RRMS is still satisfied at a lower level of *maqasid*-spending, causing lower level of economic activity, but still subjected to total valuation. For this reason, the prospect of returning back to improved economic levels remains to fill up the gap, $(S_i - R_i), i = 1, 2, \ldots, n$ over $E(\theta)$.

The central bank creates a small amount of gold (G) to shore the quantity of financing $(S_i - R_i), i = 1, 2, \ldots, n$ over $E(\theta)$. We note that $[G/(S_i - R_i)]^* R_i$ is the amount of gold that needs to be circularity to shore the unit amount of money that is held with the central bank and the same unit gold for protecting R_i of resources in circulation. Now, $[G/(S_i - R_i)]^* R_i = G/(S_i/R_i - 1)$, $i = 1, 2, \ldots, n$. This quantity decreases as S_i/R_i decreases until the states (1) and (2) are established. In this case, the quantity of seigniorage decreases and r_b and r_e yield increased yields with the continuity of "θ" effect across $E(\theta)$.

The financing conditions now are as follows: central bank statutory reserve $= (S_i - R_i)$; Islamic bank excess reserve $= 100\%$, with $S_0 > R_0$; resource in the real economy $= R_i, i = 1, 2, \ldots, n$ are generated as follows: $R_i'^* \Pi_{i=1}^n (1 + r_{ei}')$ — seigniorage for creating G of gold in the central bank. "r_{ei}" denotes profit-sharing rate for the real economy in the ith round of real economic activity corresponding to circular causation by $\{\theta_i\}$-values explaining total valuation.

4. The combination of the above three cases can happen particularly in times of financial volatility. In that case, the sum-total of the yields from the money (central bank), finance (Islamic banks), and real economy — the MFRE model is the following: $S_0 \Pi_{i=1}^n (1 + r_i) + R_i^* \Pi_{i=1}^n (1 + r_{ei}) + R_i'^* \Pi_{i=1}^n (1 + r_{ei}')$ — seigniorage over all possible states of $E(\theta)$.

In the case of an average constant rate of return "r_i", as may be approximated across $E(\theta)$, we obtain $(S_0 + R_i + R_i')\Pi_{i=1}^n (1 + r_i)$.

The above construction of the resource flow through the MFRE model in 100% RRMS is shown in Figure 9.1.

Exercise 2

(1) Discuss the MFRE-modeled system for the four cases mentioned in the example given above for a segmented market that is divided in assets between the real rate of return and real interest rate. See also Choudhury (2015).

(2) Neither the central bank nor the Islamic banks have any authority to create money at a price except charge seigniorage for the minting of gold that the central bank uses to shore the value of currency that stays with the central bank and also protect the residual financial resources that circulate in the real economy. Therefore, money in Islam is simply a resource. See also Haines

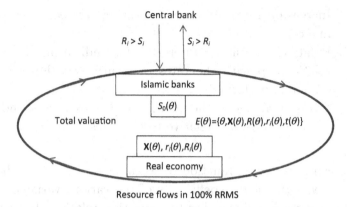

Figure 9.1. The MFRE inter-flow of resource signifying $E(\theta)$-activity in 100% RRMS in TIE.

(1987) on Maritain. Its quantity and value depend directly on the amount of spending (Sp) that is in demand and supply in the real economy across the *maqasid* forms of $E(\theta)$. In such a case, discuss the equation

$$M(\theta) = \text{Sp}(\theta) = M(X, p, r, t)[\theta].$$

(3) Because money circulates across events $E(\theta)$ in the real economy, it causes wellbeing by organic linkages with the good things of life (*hallal at-tayyabah* of *maqasid as-shari'ah*). Explain this fact by writing down the model of simulating wellbeing in money and the variables shown in (2), subject to the system of circular causation relations.

(4) Derive the meaning of your formulation and explanation in question (3) in respect of the following verses of the *Qur'an* (18:19) relating money ($M(\theta)$) to resource (silver coins) and the good things of life (best food): "Now send ye then one of you with that money of yours to the town: Let him find out which is the best food (to be had) and bring some to you, that (ye may) satisfy your hunger therewith".

(5) Consider the following illustrative values that represent:[2]

---

[2]Enumeration, numeracy, narratives, and exemplification in conveying the singularity of the divine message of *Tawhid* is a central method of the *Qur'an*

(i) Increasing rates of return indicating real economy performance.

(ii) Relatively declining interest rates indicating the inverse relationship with the rates of return and thus with real economic performance.

(iii) Rates of change in the quantity of money corresponding to the rates of return relative to the rates of interest.

Write down a wellbeing function between these variables indicating the expected signs of the coefficients of the various variables in the wellbeing function and the circular causation relations between the variables.

Draw the expected trends of the above-mentioned variables.

Explain this expected system of relations with the selected signs of the coefficients.

Can you suggest an endogenous policy related with the total valuation concept of $E(\theta)$ that could be undertaken in the economy as a whole to attain the kind of reformation that you are suggesting?

t:	1	2	3	4	5	6	7	8	9	10
"r":	2	4	8	8	8	9	9	10	10	8
"i":	10	9	8	7	7	6	6	5	5	7
M:										

$$M = M(r/i, R, \mathrm{Sp}, \mathbf{X})[\theta]$$

(74:30): "Over it are Nineteen". To borrow from Yusuf Ali' exegesis, the term "Nineteen" conveys the 19 faculties of man that enable him to excel if properly cultivated, or if abused cause man's perdition (*Qur'an* (95:4–6)). As an extension of this exegesis, this author includes in "Nineteen" the human faculties of numeracy, enumeration, narratives, exemplification, precision, measurement, formalism, observation, configuration, identification of events, reckoning of the measurement of time, measurement of such time and events, predictive capacity, organic conjugation, capacity to decipher truth against falsehood, minute details of excellence, the civil ways of precise discourse, identification of specific signs of *Allah*, the identification of the systems of the universal order like the cosmological order and the seven heavens (*buruj*), the discovery of world systems (*a'lameen*), and the like in multiples of 19.

References

Allouche, A. (1994). "Currency [Islamic currency]", in *Mamluk Economics, A Study and Translation of Al-Maqrizi's Ighathah*, Salt Lake City, UT: University of Utah Press.

Bank Mandiri (2006). *Bank Mandiri Annual Report 2006*, Jakarta, Indonesia.

Bank Muamalat (2007). *Annual Report 2007*, Jakarta, Indonesia.

Barrow, J. D. (1991). *Theories of Everything, the Quest for Ultimate Explanation.* Oxford, England: Oxford University Press.

Black, S. (1989). "Seigniorage", in *New Palgrave: Money*, Eatwell, J., Milgate, M. and Newman, P. (Eds.), New York: W.W. Norton, pp. 314–315.

Blackwell, M. and Nocera, S. (1989). "Debt-equity swaps", In *Analytical issues in debt*, Frenkel, J. A., Dooley, M. P. and Wickhman, P. (Eds.), Washington, D.C: International Monetary Fund, pp. 311–345.

Business Islamica. (March 2008). Gulf mega-*sukuk* issues a rich man's club, pp. 18–19.

Chapra, M. U. (1985). *Towards a Just Monetary System*, Leicester, UK: The Islamic Foundation.

Choudhury, M. A. (1989). "Privatisation of the Islamic dinar as an instrument for the development of an Islamic capital market", in *Islamic Economic Co-operation*, London, England: Macmillan, pp. 272–294.

Choudhury, M. A. (2008a). "Islamic economics and finance — A fiasco", in *The Middle East Business and Economic Review*, 20(1), 38–51.

Choudhury, M. A. (2008b). "Islam versus liberalism: Contrasting epistemological inquiries", *International Journal of Social Economics*, 35(4), 239–268.

Choudhury, M. A. (2008–2009). "Islamic asset valuation by using a terminal-value overlapping generation model", Funded Internal Research Project, College of Economics and Political Science. Sultan Qaboos University. This publication now appeared as a chapter in A part appeared in Choudhury, M. A. (2011). "Overlapping generation model for Islamic asset valuation: A phenomenological application", in *Islamic Economics and Finance: An Epistemological Inquiry*, Chapter 8, Bingley, UK: Emerald.

Choudhury, M. A. (2015). "Monetary and fiscal (spending) complementarities to attain socioeconomic sustainability", *ACRN Journal of Finance and Risk Perspectives Special Issue of Social and Sustainable Finance*, 4(3), 63–80.

Choudhury, M. A. and Hoque, M. Z. (2004). "Micro-money and real economic relationships in the 100 per cent reserve requirement and the gold standard", in *An Advanced Exposition of Islamic Economics and Finance*, Lewiston, New York: The Edwin Mellen Press, pp. 199–220.

Friedman, M. (1968). "Real and pseudo gold standards", in *Dollars and Deficits*, Englewood Cliffs, NJ: Prentice-Hall, pp. 247–65.

Gassner, M. S. (2008). "Revisiting Islamic bonds, are 85% of *sukuk haram*?", *Business Islamica*, 22–23.

Green, R. (1989). "Real bills doctrine", in *New Palgrave: Money*, Eatwell, J., Milgate, M. and Newman, P. (Eds.), New York: W. W. Norton, pp. 310–313.

Haines, W. W. (1987). "A society without money: Reflections on Jacques Maritain", *International Journal of Social Economics*, 14: 3/4/5, 97–104.

Hayek, F. (1976). *Choice in Currency (Occasional Paper 48)*, London, England: Institute of Economic Affairs.

International Monetary Fund (IMF) (2008). Retrieved from http://www.treas.gov/press/releases/hp1307.html.

Keynes, J. M. (1963). "Economic possibilities for our grandchildren", in *Essays in Persuasion*, New York: W. W. Norton, p. 368.

Krugman, P. R. (1989). "Market-based debt-reduction schemes", in *Analytical issues in debt*, Frenkel, J. A., Dooley, M. P. and Wickhman, P. (Eds.), Washington, D.C: International Monetary Fund, pp. 258–278.

Money Matters. Retrieved from http://www.themoneymasters.com/mra.html.

Mundell, R. A. (2000, November 8). *Presentation at the Economic Forum on "One World, One Currency: Destination or Delusion?"* Washington D.C: International Monetary Fund.

Parker, M. (2012, January 3). "Comments on al-Amine, M. al-Bashir's global Sukuk and Islamic securitization market", Arab News.

Rist, C. (1940). *History of Monetary and Credit Theory from John Law to the Present Day*, London, UK: Allen Unwin.

Saving, T. R. (1977). "A theory of the money supply with competitive banking", *Journal of Monetary Economics*, 3, 289–303.

Tobin, J. (1963). "Commercial banks as creators of 'money'", in *Banking and Monetary Studies*, Carson, D. (Eds.), Homewood, ILL: Irwin, pp. 408–419.

Tullock, G. (1976). "Competing moneys", *Journal of Money, Credit and Banking*, 7.

Usmani, M. T. (n.d). Usmani Sukuk applications.pdf, Retrieved from http://www.failaka.com/downloads/.

Von Mises, L. (1976). *The Ultimate Foundation of Economic Science*, Kansas City, Kansas: Sheed Andrews & McMeel.

Von Mises, L. (1981). "The return to sound money", in *The theory of money and credit*, Chapter 23, Indianapolis, IN: Liberty Fund.

Yeager, L. B. (1983). "Stable money and free-market currencies", *CATO Journal*, 305—326.

Yeager, L. B. (1997). *The Fluttering Veil*, Indianapolis, IN: Liberty Fund.

Chapter 10

Conclusion: What Have We Learnt? *Quo Vadis?*

The objective of this book is to expose the thoughtful student and the awakened Islamic scholar to the *Tawhidi* methodological worldview of TIE

This book began with the objective of the search and discovery of the epistemic methodology of Islamic scientific thought in general. The particularity of this generalized domain is the field of economics and society. This search and discovery was accomplished in the premise of the ultimate truth of unity of being and becoming. The underlying methodology for formalizing and applying this episteme of unity of knowledge could not be found in any other area of intellection but the monotheistic consilience to explain everything. This encompasses the conclusively universal explanation of the nature of truth versus falsehood, i.e. oneness versus dichotomous differentiation, discursive holism to embrace collective resolution versus methodological individualism, and wherewithal formalize the organic interrelationship between all the good things of life as determined by the law of oneness versus rationalistic speculations on goodness.

The nature of Islamic socio-scientific order in its universal entirety is inextricably premised on the monotheistic consilience of unity of knowledge in "everything". This methodology is conclusively contrary to the epistemology of rationalism. Rationalism neither has the methodology to reach out for the ultimate consilience of unity of knowledge, nor does it give due attention to the theme of *Tawhidi* epistemic unity of knowledge and its induction and explanation of the generality and particularity of the world system. This problem of heteronomy is the obstruction inside all of reality. Any episteme that does not decipher it and remove it from intellection does not attain the sure reality of the socio-scientific order.[1]

Neither occidental scientific intellection nor its imitation by present days' study of Islamic economics has been able to unravel the theory of consilience that remains intrinsic in sure reality. The nature and discovery of this final truth and the beginning of science and reality though does not mean the unraveling of any arbitrary new reality. Contrarily, it is to explain what reality truly is always, everywhere, and in everything, i.e. over the entirety of knowledge, space, and time.

This book has accomplished the epistemic and logical basis of *Tawhidi* oneness as dynamic organic unity of relations that spreads its wings as the invincible law. *Tawhid* as *Qur'anic* monotheism is reality that is ingrained in belief and in the order of reality. It is also the methodology of how formally and in applicative ways of discovering the nature of that everlasting consilience of being and becoming. *Tawhid as law*, thereby, spans "everything", and it constructs upon this understanding the incessant evolutionary processes of knowing oneness through the discursive intellectual process. Indeed, the *Qur'an* (81:26–29) declares in respect of the finality, power, and logical basis of explanation the phrase — *Quo vadis*, "Then wither go ye? 'Verily this is no less than a Message to (all) the Worlds: (With profit) to whoever among ye wills to go straight: But ye shall not will except as *Allah* wills, — the Cherisher of the Worlds.'"

The guidance of this book arising from the *Qur'an* is to know how the socio-scientific universality needs to be learnt, formalized, and applied with great constructive inferences. These goals taken

---

[1] *Qur'an* (69:1–3): "The Sure Reality! What is the Sure Reality? And what will make thee realise what the Sure Reality is?"

ensemble, *TIE* up the good in participatory and complementary relations. The manifestation comprises complementary wholeness. Such is the tying up of the particular case of the emergent *Tawhidi* Islamic economics (TIE). In a substantively analytical form of the nature and essence of evolutionary learning in TIE, we have the resemblance of mathematical "knot theory": The evolutionary loops stretch out like elastic from one to the next evolutionary phase of the learning universe and so on across knowledge, space, and time dimensions until the Hereafter.[2]

Teaching and learning the nature of *Tawhid* as law of oneness ingrained in and unraveled by the signs of *Allah* in the order and scheme of reality is therefore neither too difficult nor too easy for the reflective mind. The demand of evolutionary learning to fathom the universe of *Tawhidi* organic oneness is to keep up advancing from the beginning to the end. That is, the Islamic methodological worldview into which the students and the academia must be introduced to launch understanding of the ultimate originality and end of being and becoming. This book has kept this foundational methodology of evolutionary learning in view, while it introduced its originality in terms of the epistemology of *Tawhid* and carried it through in details over sufficiently many economic topics in comparative critical perspectives. The end is not near.

The universe is the science of the signs of *Allah* in generalized manifestation of *Tawhid*

The endless evolutionary "mathematical knots" as continuous loops of evolutionary learning in the knowledge, space, and time dimensions

---

[2]C. Rovelli, "Knot Theory and Space-Time", in *1993 Yearbook of Science and the Future*, Chicago, ILL: Encyclopaedia Britannica, Inc., defines a mathematical knot as follows: "One starts with a loop — a closed smooth curve — in space. The loop must never intersect itself. Then two closed loops represent the same knot if one of them can be deformed continuously into the other without ever introducing self-intersections. Equivalently, one may think of space as superstretchable rubber; two closed loops represent the same knot if one can stretch, bend, and shrink the space until one curve takes the position of the other.... A knot is a link formed by a single loop".

explain the universality of mind–matter interplay in the nexus that appears and enlarges. Such nexus forms the conceptual and manifest signs of *Allah* in the order and scheme of everything. Within such vastly comprehensible complexity, TIE becomes the study of the economic universe that applies in specificity *Tawhid* as the law of monotheistic oneness in organic intercausality of being and becoming.

Indeed, the *Qur'anic* design of the universe is a fecund ecological completeness. Within such a domain, all things exchange by discourse, complements, and participation to form their organic unity of being.[3] The signs of *Allah* are reflective of the cause and effect

---

[3]We have pointed out in Chapter 3 that the *Qur'an* explains the complete order of creation as the domain of exchange. Such exchange is not only in respect of the material artefacts. In fact, wherever there is the concept of everlasting learning equilibriums and not steady-state terminal equilibrium, there is the reality of balance and exchange. Equally as well there is the contrariety to these principles as in the case of disequilibrium of exchange caused by the choices of the forbidden things in the concept of total valuation. Consider the following verse of the *Qur'an* (24:38) in respect of the rewards as exchange in heaven: "That *Allah* may reward them [according to] the best of what they did and increase them from His bounty. And *Allah* gives provision to whom He wills without account."

One finds similar place of universal importance given to trade in the sayings of the Prophet Muhammad. As for example there is this: Hadith no: 385, Narrated: Abu Said Al-Khudri, "Allah's Apostle said, 'Do not sell gold for gold unless equivalent in weight, and do not sell less amount for greater amount or vice versa; and do not sell silver for silver unless equivalent in weight, and do not sell less amount for greater amount or vice versa and do not sell gold or silver that is not present at the moment of exchange for gold or silver that is present.'"

Here is another saying of the Prophet Muhammad (hadith): Hadith no: 511, Narrated: Abu Said Al-Khudri Once Bilal brought Barni (i.e. a kind of dates) to the Prophet (SAW) and the Prophet (SAW) asked him, "From where have you brought these?" Bilal replied, "I had some inferior type of dates and exchanged two *Sas* of it for one Sa of Barni dates in order to give it to the Prophet (SAW) to eat". Thereupon the Prophet (SAW) said, "Beware! Beware! This is definitely *riba* (usury)! This is definitely *riba* (usury)! Don't do so, but if you want to buy (a superior kind of dates) sell the inferior dates for money and then buy the superior kind of dates with that money".

There is also the message of the central role of exchange as reward between *Allah* and his beloved ones in heaven: The Messenger said, "When the inhabitants of Paradise enter Paradise, *Allah* will say to them, 'Do you want Me to give you anything more?' They will reply, 'Have You not made our faces bright? Have You

of such organic explanation of the evolutionary learning universe of *Tawhidi* unity of knowledge and its induction of everything. These elements can be the good ones or the oppositely false ones. Yet, they are uniformly explained and analyzed by the self-same method that arises from the methodology of *Tawhidi* unity of knowledge. This book has developed this perspective of analytical universality in a thoroughly methodical way, while also being critically comparative of mainstream economic reasoning and its blind imitation by the so-called Islamic economics today.

Thus, the coterminous problems of economics and society taken together, and along with the diversity of specific ones centering on the objective criterion of wellbeing as substantively defined in this book, form the totality of the *Qur'anic* world system. As an example, even in the distant cosmology of the universe, there abides the economic meaning, when we interpret economic science as we have done in this book, as the holistic socio-scientific study centering on the objective of the multi-dimensional concept of wellbeing (*maslaha*). That is how the *maqasid as-shari'ah* is extendible to study problems that extend beyond the narrow domain of commercial matters (*muamalat*) (Choudhury, 2015).

This book has shown the design of the learning universe reflected in the world system not to be dissociated from the *Tawhidi* law. If it were so, then contrary to the *Qur'anic* worldview of unity, the world system would express the belief: "Give unto God what is God's; and unto Caesar what is Caesar's". That would be contrary to Islamic belief. In this regard, Pickthall (2005, p. 22) comments:

> "Islam is a worldly religion which considers first the worldly affairs of humanity, then the Hereafter that is an eternal continuation of the worldly life. It is difficult to believe that man can be saved in the Hereafter without being saved in this world. To be saved in the Hereafter without being saved in this world is simply unthinkable. The sensible approach is to follow the way shown to us by Prophet Muhammad. When his wife, Aishah was asked by a Companion

---

not brought us into Paradise and moved us from Hell?' *Allah* will then remove the Veil and they will feel that they have not been awarded anything dearer to them than looking at their Lord."

about the Prophet's daily conduct, Aishah replied that the conduct of the Prophet was the *Qur'an*, which is the guidance from God and for which Muhammad was given authority by God to interpret. That is why his conduct was the most exemplary expression of human conduct."

Economic science is a particular characterization of *Tawhid* as the law of consilience

The *Qur'anic* verses point to the extension of the economic and social phenomena from the earth to the heavens according to the same law of *Tawhid*. In this regard, we note the *Qur'anic* verse (14:24–27):

"Seest thou not how *Allah* sets forth a parable? — A goodly word like a goodly tree, whose root is firmly fixed, and its branches (reach) to the heavens, — of its Lord. So *Allah* sets forth parables for men, in order that they may receive admonition."

"It brings forth its fruit at all times, by the leave of its Lord. So *Allah* sets forth parables for men, in order that they may receive admonition."

"And the parable of an evil Word is that of an evil tree: It is torn up by the root from the surface of the earth: it has no stability."

"*Allah* will establish in strength those who believe, with the word that stands firm, in this world and in the Hereafter; but Allah will leave, to stray, those who do wrong: *Allah* doeth what He willeth."

The semblance of the tree of knowledge by its fecundity and its opposite as the dying tree can be interpreted by the moral productivity of resource abundance and its contrariness. In this book, we have treated the topic of continuity of resource regeneration as a central issue of rejecting the postulates of mainstream economics. Knowledge makes the difference along the tree of abundance and its contrariety in resource scarcity along the dying tree. The latter comprises the central issue of the mainstream economics contrary to the first attribute that characterizes resource abundance in TIE. The *Qur'an* thus extends the economic and social scenario by inducing the episteme of unity of knowledge in it as the life-sustaining possibility and *vice-a-versa*. This book has extensively studied such a *Qur'anic* explanation of knowledge induction and its opposite in the economic and social picture, which spans the universe.

Economics and science are therefore not separated in the eyes of the *Tawhidi* methodological worldview. We have therefore developed the scientific version of TIE without for a moment leaving out the pervasive relevance of the *Tawhidi* episteme of unity of knowledge inducing all things in both generality and details. The extension of economics and society in the broadened meaning of complementarities between these disciplines is not simply restricted to the effect of technology and innovation that economics quantifies to make policy prescriptions. Rather on the methodological scale of understanding, we have invoked formalism and applications that remain universal between economics and science so that these disciplines can intermingle to be intercausal and organically tied. This book has implicated the meaning of the science of the signs of *Allah* in this sense of its universality. Economics is the intermingling field that remains universal when embedded with science and multi-disciplines in this sense of knowledge induction.

This book has established the facts that, for the universality of a specific scientific worldview to overarch all the socio-scientific disciplines, two foundational premises must be satisfied. These are firstly that, the conceptual and formal arguments must self-reference by means of the methodology and methods that are used. Secondly, the method of addressing the objective criterion of the problem must be unique in all domains both by generality and particulars. Such a comprehensive model must be applicable both in the domains of truth and falsehood to establish the inherent objective. In the *Tawhidi* methodological worldview, we have established this unique and universal groundwork to lie on the objective criterion of simulation of the wellbeing function (*maslaha*), subject to the system of circular causation relations between the representative variables of *maqasid*-choices. The truth and the false domains of investigation produce their own opposite results. This work has profusely established this case with many examples, exercises, and comparative critiques.

According to the *Qur'an*, the universe of the known, the knowable, and the unknown, the unknowable comprise an extended economic venue

The universality of *Tawhidi* worldview is across all of the existence encompassing mind, matter, and the extensive domain of the unseen that may not be fathomed. But despite this hidden quality of the core of things resting on *Tawhidi* unity of knowledge, the unseen has its own effect in reality, though it is never known by a reverse causality from the material world system to the unseen domain (*ghayb*). Such exogenous one-directional influence of *ghayb* on materiality is essential in impressing unity of knowledge in everything. The obvious example of such exogeneity is of *Tawhid* in relation to the world system. *Tawhid* establishes the nature of the world system in both truth and falsehood. But the world system cannot attain the completeness of the supercardinal domain of *Tawhid*. The evolutionary learning of the world system as the interactive, integrative, and evolutionary (IIE)-learning processes intra-system and inter-system, as the characterization of *Tawhidi* methodology of learning in this book, develops consciousness of the *Tawhidi* law into higher planes of knowledge. It simultaneously unravels the details of the world system in greater depth. This book has derived such a process characterization from the *Qur'an* as the starting point of the ensuing circular causation of unity of knowledge and of its opposites that lie in falsehood.

Both of these realities, truth and falsehood, are essential to know well in order to guide reality into the directions of moral/ethical social reconstruction. In this regard, this book has explained that the well-established knowledge of trade and *riba* are necessary to understand the inverse nature of intercausal relations between them, and thereby, the nature of their inverse dynamics and the underlying cultures and institutionalism. Such analytical understanding can lead the *ummah* to its moral/ethical reconstruction, away from *riba* and into an increasingly integrated and sustainable social economy.

The entire *Qur'an* is simply the endless study of *Tawhid* comprising its belief, and its influence on the organization of the generality and particularity of the world system encompassing mind, matter, the seen and discoverable, and the unseen and unfathomable. This book has been a study of the *Qur'anic* reconstructive methodology along such ultimate epistemic foundations of organic unity.

Here is one such foundational characterization of the dynamics of *Tawhid* derived from the *Qur'an*. It reflects the IIE-learning processes underlying the *Tawhidi* episteme of unity of knowledge and its induction of unity in the world-system.

"See they not how *Allah* Originates creation, then Repeats it: truly that Is easy for *Allah*." (*Qur'an* 29:19).

Say: "Travel through the earth And see how *Allah* did Originate creation; so will *Allah* produce a later creation: For *Allah* has power Over all things." (*Qur'an* 29:20).

"Not on earth nor in heaven Will ye be able (fleeing) To frustrate (His Plan), Nor have ye, besides *Allah*, Any protector or helper." (*Qur'an* 29:22).

↕

↕

↕

The re-origination process as of evolutionary learning is in the design of *Tawhid* (*Allah*). It reflects the design of divine law.

Continuity of the divine characterization of the evolutionary learning reality. This characterization is unraveled in the small experiences of life and is established in the final "Closure" of the Great Event, the Hereafter. Thus, *Tawhid*, the world system, and *Akhira* all together establish the sure reality. This comprises the socio-scientific methodology of *Tawhidi* phenomenology.

The *Tawhidi* Law is the overwhelming truth as the core of everything. Thus, the entire world system of mind and matter including centrally the Islamic world must turn to the *Tawhidi* centricity and nowhere else. Besides *Tawhid* there is no other ontological source to guide to and explain the sure reality.

The double arrows establish the confirmation of the conscious truth of *Tawhid* and the world system. This book has emphasized that the critical nature of *Tawhidi* methodology is continuous in knowledge, space, and time dimensions. Such is the socio-scientific study in which economics shares its spreading across the design of the universe according to the *Tawhidi* episteme of organic unity of knowledge. Such a spread is referred to in this book as *continuity* across *continuums*.

Socio-scientific thought is disabled in the absence of *Tawhidi* episteme of unity of knowledge

While the world of learning is always in search of a new episteme to ascertain socio-scientific reality, Islamic economists and scientists today must realize that they are faced with the challenge to host the *Tawhidi* methodology at the heart of this endless field of inquiry (Iqbal, 2012).[4] Failing to undertake this great task is to both deny truth that remains embedded in reality, and to fail in offering a substantially revolutionary methodological worldview to the world of learning at large so as to abide for all times. This book has presented this challenge to the young and reflective minds at this juncture of the world of learning. There is no religious and ritualistic

---

[4] Allama Mohammad Iqbal wrote (reprinted 1958): "The not-yet of man does mean pursuit and may mean failure; the 'not-yet' of God means unfailing realization of the infinite creative possibilities of His being which retains its wholeness throughout the entire process:

> In the endless self-repeating
> For evermore flows the Same,
> Myriad arches springing, meeting,
> Hold at rest the mighty frame.
> Streams from all things love of living,
> Grandest star and humblest cold
> All the straining, all the striving
> Is eternal peace in God
> (Goethe)."

partitioning in this study. According to the *Qur'an,* there is the over-whelmingly great intellectual undertaking with the abiding truth in it for all.[5]

Now, when we realize that the *Qur'an* has bestowed the entire universe to mankind as a field of socio-scientific inquiry of the signs of *Allah,* then the question to be faced squarely is how the study of science and economics has been engulfed in the error of heteronomy? This book has explained this gigantic problem in which the Muslims today have immersed themselves. TIE is the revolu-tionary new outlook of the sure reality in a garb of methodology of unity of knowledge. TIE is conceptual, applied, and explains the real issues of collective market–institutional interrelations, and the interdisciplinary moral/ethical embedding.

In this sense of its socio-scientific inclusion, TIE represents the totality of conscious transactions according to the good things of life (*hallal at-tayyabah, maqasid as-shari'ah*). TIE is also based conceptually and in applied and inferential ways on the analytics of the wellbeing criterion (*maslaha*) linked with *maqasid*-choices. TIE is also based on the avoidance of the choices that are opposed to or are not recommended by *maqasid as-shari'ah.* In all such determinations, TIE undertakes the *Qur'anic* discursive approach (*shura*) to differentiate between truth and falsehood, good and evil (*Qur'an,* 3:104): "Let there arise out of you a group of people inviting to all that is good (Islam), enjoining *al-ma'roof* (i.e. Islamic monotheism and all that Islam recommends) and forbidding *al-munkar* (polytheism and disbelief and all that Islam has forbid-den). And it is they who are the successful".

In the universal socio-scientific transactional understanding of TIE, the answer is now offered to those who ask: Why is it necessary to invoke the *Tawhidi* epistemology to establish the field of TIE as the only true way to understand the sure reality? Why is it that without this foundational methodological worldview there cannot be and there has not been any such field of authenticity as Islamic economics as it stands today?

---

[5] *Qur'an* (38:87): "It (the *Qur'an*) is indeed a message to the worlds."

These questions can be answered by firstly understanding the exegesis of the *Qur'anic* verses. Secondly, we examine the analytical truth of these *Qur'anic* verses. We apply the exegeses to the great watershed of TIE in the meaning of the universal socio-scientific transactions. Why is the present days' idea of Islamic economics untenable in the light of the *Qur'anic* verses? How do these verses address the validity of TIE above all others?

The *Qur'anic* verse we consider is the following one with its exegeses made by Choudhury (2003):

"Such is *Allah,* your Lord, the Creator of all things, there is no god but He: Then how ye are deluded away from the Truth!" (40:62).

Delusion is to be away from the singular truth of *Tawhid* in belief, thought, and action. There is no other sure reality than *Tawhid* because of its central theme of unity of knowledge and the absoluteness of knowledge with *Allah* and in His law that differentiates the good things from the bad things of life. This cardinal law is reflected in the universe by the signs of *Allah.* When man has been given the revelation through the prophet then it must be considered for its truth in "everything". This does not mean compulsion of belief. It means the credibility of this singular ground of truth that is premised on the epistemic unity of being and becoming. Thus, we find Hawking's words in regard to the failure and challenge of science to recognize this foundational objective of unity of science. Or else, this concept is distorted to give it simply the meaning in physicalism without God in it as the divine One, and His law as the law of epistemic unity in explaining everything. Thus, Muslims in particular and the world of learning in all ought to build upon the *Tawhidi* methodological worldview. There is no excuse.

The *Qur'an* denies the place of truth to the rationalists and their speculative philosophy. Thus, *Tawhid* stands single, universal, and unique by its episteme of unity of knowledge and the world system against the doctrine of rationalism. The *Qur'an* (51:10–11) says in this regard: "Woe to the falsehood-mongers, — Those who (flounder) heedless in a flood of confusion."

Hawking (1988, pp. 10–11) writes by his own emphasis on the need for unity of science:

"The eventual goal of science is to provide a single theory that describes the whole universe. However, the approach most scientists actually follow is to separate the problem into two parts. First, there are the laws that will tell us how the universe changes with time..... Second, there is the question of the initial state of the universe. Some people feel that science should be concerned with only the first part; they regard the question of the initial situation as a matter for metaphysics or religion. They would say that God, being omnipotent, could have started the universe off any way he wanted. That may be so, but in that case he also could have made it develop in a completely arbitrary way. Yet it appears that he chose to make it evolve in a very regular way according to certain laws. It therefore seems equally reasonable to suppose that there are also laws governing the initial state."

The problems of science are steeply buried in rationalism along with its ultimate premise on human claim of supremacy of reason above God. Economics reflects this over-weaning problem of self and individualism (O'Donnell, 1989; Buchanan, 1999) as does science by its heteronomy. Thereby, the extension of science of the signs of *Allah* in which TIE, not mainstream economics or Islamic economics as of today, resides as the great beacon of universality, has been laid aside. This book has brought out many of the errors in economic reasoning in the face of TIE.

Islamic economists today by immersing themselves into occidental epistemology of socio-scientific thought and application have imbibed heart and soul in the inherent episteme that characterizes rationalism and its heteronomy. Such ideas have contradicted the *Qur'anic* challenge to the world of belief, thought, conduct, inference, and application. There can be no hope for man at the end of this kind of rationalist muddle. This is the meaning of "floundering in floods of confusion" in the above verse.

On the contrary to rationalism, the *Qur'an* (24:35) declares: "*Allah* is the Light of the heavens and the earth. The example of His Light is like a niche within which is a lamp, the lamp is within a glass, the glass as if it were a pearly [white] star lit from [the oil of] a blessed olive tree, neither of the east nor of the west, whose oil would almost glow even if untouched by fire. Light upon light. *Allah* guides to His light whom He wills. And *Allah* presents examples for the people, and *Allah* is knowing of all things."

The *Qur'an* (24:40) continues on explaining the nature of rationalist inclinations: "Or (the Unbelievers' state) is like the depths of darkness in a vast deep ocean, overwhelmed with billow topped by billow, topped by (dark) clouds: depths of darkness, one above another: if a man stretches out his hands, he can hardly see it! For any to whom *Allah* gives not light, there is no light!"

The contrast of the ultimate truth of *Tawhid* in the sure reality against rationalism of the non-*Tawhidi* world system continues on in these two uncompromising opposites. The challenge of all of socio-scientific projects is to believe, discover, formalize, and apply the *Tawhidi* methodology as a carrier of the divine light against the darkness of the rationalist and heteronomous world system in entirety. One cannot discover truth out of darkness. Yet, one can decipher falsehood and explain it in contrariness to truth by the divine law, which is complete and governs over the domains of truth and falsehood to establish the distinction between them in every sphere of experience.

Such a rise of consciousness in intellection as also in belief is the duty of Islamic scholarship to boldly and clearly unravel in the highest frontiers of knowledge. Indeed, *Allah* and the *Qur'an* (*Tawhid*) form the ultimate absoluteness of knowledge. The *Qur'an* (96:1–5) declares in this regard: "Read, in the name of your Lord Who created; created man from a clot of blood. Read! Your Lord is endlessly generous, Who taught by the pen, taught man what he did not know." Not to be able to present this declaration in the best of ways is to hide truth and to be ignorant. By such intellectual negligence, the Muslim had failed.

The exhortation of the *Qur'an* (2:42) on the indispensable belief and practice of *Tawhid* is this: "And cover not *Truth* with *falsehood*, nor conceal the *Truth* when ye know (what it is)."

While the universe that *Allah* has bestowed for the benefit of mankind is the playground for experiencing the blessings out of the functional nature of consciousness of *Tawhid* in the order and scheme of things, *Tawhid* by itself remains complete and fecund. The *Tawhidi* worldview does not need to be mixed with the rationalist origin of non-*Tawhidi* episteme. In the above verse, the *Qur'an* asks for restraint from mixing up truth with falsehood. This is the same act as mixing up monotheistic oneness with rationalism in belief and intellection.

The foundational ontology is based on the domain of methodology — *Tawhid* versus rationalism. On the other hand, the diversity of methods and formalism that arises in compliance with the *Tawhidi* methodology is an acceptable venue of action. However, not all methods comply with the *Tawhidi* methodology. This book has shown that all the postulates of mainstream microeconomics and macroeconomics are contrary to TIE. Thereby, the method of maximization objective of neoclassical economics in microeconomics and its prototype in macroeconomics and all different fields of science and economics are contrary to the *Tawhidi* methodological worldview of the IIE-process-oriented learning methods. TIE cannot accept methods that depart away from the *Tawhidi* axiomatic reality. Yet, all fields of criticism must be studied deeply well. This book had thus been comparatively critical in nature to nurture the young and the thoughtful minds.

Teach and application: How is TIE different from existing "Islamic" economics?

The field of TIE is multi-disciplinary in nature. Its study goes through stages of teaching and comprehension that are no different from the way that thoughtful and useful subjects are taught and studied for the good of the learning world academia. Even though students and scholars will begin from soft launching pads of the study of TIE, the field will prepare them into critical investigation at the advanced levels of multi-disciplinarity. These approaches entail the following directions and none of them is isolated from the rest. Without this holistic study, TIE will not be understood and will fail to be beneficial to the world of learning, for students, scholars, and progeny.

1. The methodology of *Tawhid* (TIE) must be strictly in accordance with the *Qur'an* and the *sunnah* while treating human contributions in this area to be subject to critical discourse (*shura* and *ijtihad*). While *fiqh* as jurisprudential interpretation is to be treated as a necessary way of understanding the law, rules, and circumstances, the practice of the *fiqhi* approach must be in continuous reference to the *Qur'an* and the *sunnah* along with the discursive venue of *shura* and *ijtihad* in addressing emergent issues and problem of every kind. Exception must be given to matters of *aqidah*, which are practices linked with Islamic belief and practices directly derived from the *Qur'an* and the *sunnah*. In the case of socio-scientific investigations, this approach remains most vivid. But since the socio-scientific universe is the universal world system expression of *Tawhid* as law, therefore, the method of *fiqh al-Qur'an wal-sunnah at-Tawhid* along with discourse remains permanently continuous in generality and particulars. Continuity over the systemic continuums of knowledge, space, and time dimensions is an essential characteristic of the IIE-learning processes in the theory and application of TIE to all issues and problems in generality and particulars.

2. The derived exegeses of the *Qur'an* and the *sunnah* in respect of the *Tawhidi* centerpiece of methodology must be made to yield its relevant formal and explanatory structure. This discovery of the socio-scientific permanence of the *Qur'an* and the *sunnah* must result in a unique and universal formalism of "everything". The method that so emanates can be diverse but, on the basis of critical examination, such methods must comply with the nature of the *Tawhidi* methodology in respect of issues and problems under investigation.

The universal and unique formal method this book has mathematized is simulation of the wellbeing function (*maslaha*), subject to circular causation variables. The methodology along with the derived method extends the legitimate bounds of the *maqasid as-shari'ah* to the entire socio-scientific subtleties. Such a model is equally applicable in investigating the potential of moral/ethical reconstruction out of the temporary imperfections caused by non-*maqasid* variables. Such a model and method can also critically investigate the nature of relations of the non-*Tawhidi* cases.

3. The formal model is always of a system and cybernetic type because of the organic nature of *Tawhidi* methodology of unity of knowledge and its induction of the diversity of issues and problems. These may be of the purely *maqasid*-type, purely non-*maqasid* type, or a mix of these. The end goal is interpretation of the existing state of the intervariable relations and the inferences so derived for moral/ethical reconstruction in accordance with the *Tawhidi* worldview.

   The analytical properties of the formal model and its extensions must be studied in the most rigorous of ways. Such an approach will bring out the truly socio-scientific nature of analytical *Tawhidi* nature of TIE, while purifying the imminent socio-scientific inquiry from pseudo-science or polemics.

4. The *Tawhidi* methodology and the formal and explanatory methods, the analytical design, knowledge of the comprehensive mathematical properties, and the institutional discursive practices along with knowledge of the real-world phenomena must be combined together in methodical and applied approaches. These will take the form of empirical models and/or institutional discourse models determined on the basis of the nature of TIE methodology and analytics. But at the same time, there is no need to tally the explanation of TIE concept, formalism, and empirical results with mainstream economic interpretations. We have thus followed the approach that McCloskey (1985) has suggested in regard to using a common sense realistic explanation of results as opposed to the stylized conceptual entrapping of mainstream economic theory. Almost all the time, such theories have proved erroneous and unpredicted. The neoclassical economic theory has no empirical bearing.

5. There is good reason to exemplify all TIE conceptual points with real-life examples. The chapters of this book have followed such a direction. There are several exercises and examples that bring

out the contrast of TIE with mainstream economic theory and applications.

It is highly recommended for students and teachers for purposes of relevantly referring to *Qur'anic* verses for their exegeses on various topics of TIE being studied, to bring and use the *Qur'an* in class lectures. It is necessary for teachers of TIE to master this field of economic heterodoxy even as they are teaching. There are also many concepts mentioned for both mainstream economics and TIE that are not elaborated upon. The teacher of TIE would be required to explain such concepts and details to students. In every case, the use of diagrams, examples, and exercises, several of which are given in this text, should be used by the teacher. PowerPoints can be prepared from this text as a separate tool for presentation to students. This text covers rigorous materials for a six credits course.

One of the tests of versatility of TIE is its application to the study of non-*Tawhidi* mainstream methodological problems from the critical viewpoint. This is how TIE assumes its growing universality and uniqueness. No wonder, this has been proven in the case of a wide coverage of issues and problems of modern nature, in the critical light of *Tawhidi* methodology and its derived methods. Yet, the *Tawhidi* methodology and its derived methods remain of a different category.

This book has examined a number of such issues and problems contrasting TIE with the mainstream economic approach. Many more problems and issues can be inquired that bring out the distinctive nature of TIE and the *Tawhidi* methodology and its derived analytical and discursive methods.

The comprehensive example that we will finally wind up with is the TIE orientation to complement the issues of poverty alleviation with human resource development, microenterprise development, and sustainable development. Over this is the understanding of justice as balance (*al-wasatiyyah*). In mainstream economic approaches to the above issues, the argument made is that governments ought to lead the way to spend to alleviate poverty. It is also argued that human capital development ought to be the way toward the goal of poverty alleviation via productive employment. The goal of sustainable development focuses on the study of intergenerational conservation of environment, avoidance of waste, and reformation of consumption habits. Population growth is seen to be a menace to sustainable development and to the good standards of life. The idea of sustainability as the role of complementarities as balance between the good things of life and the overarching organic interrelationships between the good things of life is subjected to humanistic decisions. Humanism too is a form of ethical rationalism.

For instance, government spending to avert poverty is not the way to raise moral and ethical consciousness in concert with individual, institutions, and society by extended participatory development (Bordo, 1998). There is theoretical impossibility in moving an interior "starvation point" to the production possibility surface by policy measures, as has been theorized by Amartya Sen (Sen, 1986). Human capital theory is a neoclassical concept. It focuses on the labor market efficiency out of the mainstream concept of efficiency and productivity. Yet, the intergeneration effect of human capital theory can result in utter inequality (Bowles and Gintis, 1975). The concept of social justice in the frame of social welfare function poised between social justice and economic efficiency is a competition and conflict model based on resource scarcity. So-called "Islamic" economics has absorbed such mainstream errors by avoiding the *Tawhidi* epistemic worldview.

Exercise 1

Make a critical assessment by using the *Tawhidi* methodological worldview in TIE of the following outcry being raised in western circles on the issue of "*Man and Machine*" for use in warfare, such as by future robotic and today's drone warfare technology. The western citizenry and its academic mindset are promoting the use of robots in war machinery to replace soldiers on the ground to carry out the function of belligerence. The arguments the proponents make are that fewer soldiers would be lost in battle. More destruction at least cost will be inflicted on the enemy. Thus, it will be conducive to win an efficient warfare. The proponents call such a robotic approach to war as being moral and ethical.

How would you raise a critique on the theme of *"Humanity and Machine"* in the light of the *Tawhidi* methodological worldview of TIE regarding the occidental mindset of warfare efficiency, social cost evaluation, and the consequential objective of optimization of the war output?

Final Thoughts

This book has argued against such a futile moral and ethical concept that cannot be embedded in the ethico-economic theory. This book has argued against every such concept of mainstream economic theory. Instead, the idea of sustainability was translated in terms of the balance (*al-wasatiyyah*) of sustainability by way of extensive complementarities reflecting the *Tawhidi* unity of knowledge induced in and between the *maqasid*-choices in the wellbeing function (*maslaha*).

It is noteworthy to understand the following approach suggested by the World Bank (2000, p. 6) in poverty alleviation by means of factors of extensive complementarities:

> "The choice and implementation of public actions that are responsive to the needs of poor people depend on the interaction of political, social, and other institutional processes. Access to market opportunities and to public sector services is often strongly influenced by state and social institutions, which must be responsive and accountable to poor people. Achieving access, responsibility, and accountability is intrinsically political and requires active collaboration among poor people, the middle class, and other groups in society. Active collaboration can be greatly facilitated by changes in governance that make public administration, legal institutions, and public service delivery more efficient and accountable to all citizens — and by strengthening the participation of poor people in political processes and local decision-making. Also important is removing the social and institutional barriers that result from distinctions of gender, ethnicity, and social status. Sound and responsive institutions are not only important to benefit the poor but also fundamental to the overall growth."

Example 1: Failure of studying social justice in mainstream economics and the alternative in TIE

Here is another example concerning the concept of justice in the Qur'an that points out the economic and scientific relevance in such a study of social justice. Muslims have not been able to offer a *theory of justice* out of the *Qur'an*. What has been done is a personal thought regarding certain *attributes of justice* (Kamali, 2002). Yet, personally felt enumeration and discussion of attributes are polemics. They cannot convey the true universal picture. For the universal *theory of justice*, it is necessary to derive it from the precept of *Tawhidi* worldview arising from the *Qur'an* regarding a *theory of justice*. Bayrakli (1992) writes regarding Al-Farabi's understanding of justice in the *Qur'an* as balance. And in the vastness of knowledge, space, and time, the precept of balance (*al-wasatiyyah*) spans the heavens and the earth in the divine law. Thus, if life-fulfilling regime of development that has been studied in the book is the direction to contain the *maslaha*-complementarities for poverty alleviation, then there ought to be the organic balance of intercausal relations between poverty alleviation and the other factors of *muamalat* and the cosmo-logical issues to sustain such regimes of participatory development *res extensa* and *res cogitans*. A theory of justice according to the *Tawhidi* worldview must therefore arise from the intercausal relationships between *Tawhid, al-wasatiyyah,* and *maqasid as-shari'ah* according to the principle of balance (*mizan*) in the *Qur'an*. This book has treated such a holistic organically linked approach to the *maslaha* of *zakat*, trade by exchange, and inversion of *riba* in the economy-wide context.

The call to Islamic thinkers

The Islamic thinkers and students must dispel mainstream socio-scientific rationalist errors of heteronomy that abound in it. They must rise to seriously intellectualize the *Tawhidi* methodological worldview as in the economic science of TIE. This is the way to render the revolutionary originality of the new way of thinking and constructing the moral and ethical reality inside socio-scientific order, with science and economics progressing the entire way. It is not too late for this challenge. All it needs is the will, organization of thought, and bold conduct of *Qur'anic* intellection and its application in "everything" across the world of learning.

Shall we then rhyme together with conviction?

The long day wanes: the slow moon climbs: the deep
Moans round with many voices. Come, my friends,
'T is not too late to seek a newer world.
Push off, and sitting well in order smite
The sounding furrows; for my purpose holds
To sail beyond the sunset, and the baths
Of all the western stars, until I die.

Alfred Lord Tennyson, *Ulysses*

References

Bayrakli, B. (1992). "The concept of justice (*Adl*) in the philosophy of Al-Farabi", *Hamdard Islamicus*, V(3).

Bordo, O. F. (Ed.) (1998). *People's Participation, Challenges Ahead*, New York: Apex Press.

Bowles, S. and Gintis, H. (1975). "The problem with human capital theory — A Marxian critique", *American Economic Review*, 65(2), 74–82.

Buchanan, J. M. (1999). "The domain of constitutional economics", in *The Logical Foundations of Constitutional Liberty*, Indianapolis, IN: Liberty Fund.

Choudhury, M. A. (2003). *Explaining the Qur'an, A Socio-Scientific Inquiry*, 2 Volumes, Lewiston, MA: Edwin Mellen Press.

Choudhury, M. A. (2015). "*Res extensa et res cogitans de maqasid as-shari'ah*", *International Journal of Law and Management*, 57(6), 662–693.

Hawking, S. W. (1988). *A Brief History of Time, From the Big Bang to Black Holes*, New York: Bantam Books, Inc.

Iqbal, M. (1958). *The Reconstruction of Religious Thought in Islam*, Lahore, Pakistan: Ashraf Printing Press.

Iqbal, M. (Ed.). (2012). *Studies in the Islam and Science Nexus Volume I*, London, England: Ashgate.

Kamali, H. (2002). *Freedom, Equality, and Justice in Islam*, London, England: Islamic Texts Society.

McCloskey, D. N. (1985), *The Rhetoric of Economics*, Wisconsin, Minnesota: The University of Wisconsin Press.

O'Donnell, R. M. (1989). *Keynes: Philosophy, Economics and Politics*, London, England: Macmillan Press Ltd.

Pickthall, M. M. (2005), *The Quran Translated, Message for Humanity*, Washington D.C: International Committee for the Support of the Final Prophet.

Sen, A. (1986). "Exchange entitlement", in *Poverty and Famines, An Essay on Entitlement and Deprivation*, Oxford, England: Clarendon Press, pp. 167–73.

World Bank (2000). *World Development Report 2000–2001*. New York: Oxford University Press.

Index

Printed in the United States
By Bookmasters